Professional
SharePoint® 2007 Web Content Management Development

Professional
SharePoint® 2007 Web Content Management Development
Building Publishing Sites with Office SharePoint Server 2007

Andrew Connell

WILEY

Wiley Publishing, Inc.

Professional SharePoint® 2007 Web Content Management Development: Building Publishing Sites with Office SharePoint Server 2007

Published by
Wiley Publishing, Inc.
10475 Crosspoint Boulevard
Indianapolis, IN 46256
www.wiley.com

Published simultaneously in Canada

ISBN: 978-0-470-22475-5

Manufactured in the United States of America

10 9 8 7 6 5 4 3 2 1

Library of Congress Cataloging-in-Publication Data:

Connell, Andrew, 1976-
 Professional SharePoint 2007 Web content management development : building publishing sites with Office SharePoint server 2007 / Andrew Connell.
   p. cm.
   Includes index.
   ISBN 978-0-470-22475-5 (paper/website)
    1. Web site development—Computer programs.   2. Web sites—Management.
 3. Database management.   4. Microsoft Office SharePoint server.   I. Title.
 TK5105.8885.M54C66 2008   006.7'8—dc22
                                                        2008016811

About the Author

Andrew Connell has a background in content management solutions and Web development that spans back to his time as a student at the University of Florida in the late 1990s managing class sites. He has consistently focused on the challenges facing businesses to maintain a current and dynamic online presence without having to rely constantly on Web developers or have a proficiency in Web technologies.

In 2005 and 2006 he was designated a Microsoft Most Valuable Professional (MVP) for Microsoft Content Management Server for his contributions to the MCMS community. When the functionality of MCMS was merged into the SharePoint platform, he became a MOSS MVP (2007 and 2008). Andrew has contributed to numerous MCMS and SharePoint books over the years.

He has spoken on the subject of MOSS 2007 development and WCM at various events and national conferences such as TechEd, SharePoint Connections, VSLive, Office Developer Conference, and the Microsoft SharePoint Conference.

Technology is not only Andrew's job, but also a personal passion: He thrives on expanding his technical knowledge. When not in front of his computer, he enjoys football, golf, the beach, and spending time with his family. He lives in Jacksonville, Florida, with his wife, Meredith, his son, Steven, and their two dogs. You can always find Andrew online at his SharePoint development and WCM-focused blog at `www.andrewconnell.com/blog`.

About the Technical Editors

The technical editing of this book was performed by quite a few industry experts, all of whom served a pivotal role in ensuring that the content and code samples in this book are factually correct:

❑ J. Dan Attis (`www.devcow.com/blogs/jdattis`), Microsoft MVP for Windows SharePoint Services, has been heavily involved in the local developer community in the Atlanta, Georgia area for nine years. He has been known to spend many nights and weekends working to promote SharePoint in the community as a development platform. He is a stickler for details and an ideal choice for editing the book.

❑ Jason Conway (`http://weblogs.asp.net/jasonconway`) is a senior application developer and team lead for Ascentium, with over a decade of experience delivering custom solutions in a large range of markets and industries. He now applies that experience to designing and developing solutions for corporate intranets and extranets using SharePoint 2007.

❑ Stefan Gordon (`www.stefangordon.com`) is a software architect with Ascentium, an avid blogger, and a dedicated SharePoint evangelist.

❑ Cale Hoopes (`http://calehoopes.blogspot.com`) is a mountaineer, application developer with Ascentium, SharePoint enthusiast, musician, gamer, and beloved husband.

❑ Jared Lasater is an application developer with Ascentium. He has been working with SharePoint 2007 since Beta 2 and has developed a wide range of enterprise solutions for clients, including intranets, extranets, and collaboration and publishing portals.

About the Technical Editors

- ❑ George Olson is a developer in the portals and collaboration practice at Ascentium and is an expert in designing and developing custom SharePoint workflows as part of large enterprise solutions.

- ❑ Michael Panciroli is a solutions architect with Ascentium who successfully delivered the first Technology Adoption Program (TAP) project for Office SharePoint Server. He architects custom enterprise solutions with SharePoint to deliver corporate intranets and partner extranets in the health care, automotive, and online retail verticals.

- ❑ Brendon Schwartz (http://blogs.sharepointguys.com/brendon) is a principal consultant in Atlanta, Georgia, specializing in SharePoint 2007. A Microsoft MVP for Microsoft Office SharePoint Server, Brendon is also a co-author of *Professional SharePoint 2007 Development* (Wiley, 2007), author of several magazine articles, a conference speaker, and co-founder of the Atlanta .NET Regular Guys, which is hosted at DevCow (www.devcow.com).

- ❑ Clint Simon (www.ascentium.com/blog/sp) is a technology lead with Ascentium who draws on his vast experience with SharePoint to create innovative development and platform tools for SharePoint; his advancements extend and enhance SharePoint as a custom application development platform.

- ❑ Patrick Tisseghem (www.u2u.info/Blogs/Patrick) is a managing partner at U2U, a SharePoint training company in Belgium. Patrick is also a Microsoft MVP for Windows SharePoint Services and author of *Inside Microsoft Office SharePoint Server 2007* (Microsoft Press, 2007).

- ❑ Roxana Tzau has many years of experience as a Web developer and helped build one of the largest corporate intranet portals within Microsoft using SharePoint Server 2007 with Ascentium. She continues to develop solutions for enterprise corporate intranets by extending the SharePoint platform.

- ❑ Thomas Wyrick is a Senior Software Engineer at the Ascentium Corporation and has had part in delivering enterprise class solutions on the Microsoft platform.

Credits

Acquisitions Editor
Katie Mohr

Development Editor
Kenyon Brown

Technical Editors
J. Dan Attis
Jason Conway
Stefan Gordon
Cale Hoopes
Jared Lasater
George Olson
Michael Panciroli
Brendon Schwartz
Clint Simon
Patrick Tisseghem
Roxana Tzau
Thomas Wyrick

Production Editor
William A. Barton

Copy Editor
Luann Rouff

Editorial Manager
Mary Beth Wakefield

Production Manager
Tim Tate

Vice President and Executive Group Publisher
Richard Swadley

Vice President and Executive Publisher
Joseph B. Wikert

Project Coordinator, Cover
Lynsey Stanford

Proofreader
Jennifer Larsen, Word One

Indexer
Robert Swanson

Acknowledgments

No project of this size can come be completed in a vacuum. I asked some of my trusted associates to contribute to the book by writing a few of the chapters. First and foremost, I want to thank Spencer Harbar (www.harbar.net), MVP for Office SharePoint Server, a good friend who I met in the days of Microsoft Content Management Server 2002. Spencer was instrumental in developing the structure and approach of this book, acting as a sounding board for various decision points in the process. He also contributed Chapter 3, "Overview of Office SharePoint Server 2007 and Web Content Management," and Chapter 17, "Content Deployment." Bob German (http://blogs.msdn.com/bobgerman) contributed Chapter 1, "Embarking on Web Content Management Projects," and Chapter 16, "Implementing Sites with Multiple Languages and Devices." Matt McDermott (http://blogs.catapultsystems.com/matthew), MVP for Office SharePoint Server, contributed Chapter 13, "Search," and John Holliday (www.johnholliday.net), MVP for Office SharePoint Server, contributed Chapter 5, "Minimal Publishing Site Definition."

I also want to thank those at Microsoft who provided support, as well as those who assisted in answering some of the technical questions: Arpan Shah, Ryan Duguid, Lawrence Liu, Jim Masson, George Perantatos, and Tyler Butler.

No technical book is complete without a solid review to ensure that the code compiles and the text in the chapters is factually correct. Many members of Ascentium were instrumental in reviewing the book. Ascentium is an interactive marketing and technology consultancy that delivers solutions ranging from interactive marketing, customer relationship management, business intelligence, portals, and collaboration to application and product development and infrastructure management. A special thanks to Jason Conway, who coordinated the review efforts of Stefan Gordon, Cale Hoops, Jared Lasater, George Olson, Michael Panciroli, Clint Simon, Roxana Tzau, and Thomas Wyrick. I'd also like to thank my fellow SharePoint MVPs Patrick Tisseghem and especially Dan Attis and Brendon Schwartz, who reviewed a handful of chapters in a very short amount of time.

I would like to thank everyone at Wiley Publishing who helped me get this book to you. Like all projects of this magnitude, the original plans were thrown out the window a few times when unexpected turns presented themselves. Katie Mohr, Jim Minatel, and Kenyon Brown made this a fun and rewarding experience.

In addition, I'd like to thank all of my former students who spent a week with me attending my Office SharePoint Server 2007 Web Content Management class for developers (www.andrewconnell.com/go/299), and those who left comments on my blog (www.andrewconnell.com/blog). All of you were instrumental in helping with the development of the presentation of topics covered in this book and I greatly appreciate the dialog we have shared.

Finally, I'd like to thank those in the MVP SharePoint community for the energetic, passionate, challenging, and at times insane discussions that we share on a private distribution list. I cannot express how privileged I feel to be among some of the best and brightest minds in the SharePoint field. Hats off to April Spence, Melissa Travers, and Lawrence Liu at Microsoft for all they have done to help build, facilitate, and bring this community together.

Contents

Contents

Contents

Contents

Contents

Contents

Foreword

The importance of Web technology has increased tremendously over the last few years. People rely on the Internet to find and research information, interact with applications, connect with people, and make purchases. In a world where storage is becoming cheaper and broadband access is becoming increasingly ubiquitous, companies both small and large are competing for the attention of an entire generation that has grown up with applications such as MSN, Facebook, and YouTube. The ability of a corporation to deliver a compelling Web experience is not just important, but essential to stay alive. If your content is not relevant, then you'll lose your business to your competitors with a simple Internet search.

For more than a decade, many software vendors have addressed the Web content management (WCM) need with specialized, vertical software. I remember when Microsoft acquired NCompass Labs in 2001 for its WCM technology and released subsequent versions of Microsoft Content Management Server (MCMS). In fact, that's when I first met Andrew, when he was working closely with MCMS 2002 and developing cutting-edge applications. While MCMS met the needs for WCM, the consistent feedback from customers was that Web content management was a misnomer. It's not "Web content" management; it's content management for Web applications. This means it's important for a technology to really take a look at the entire life cycle of all content that eventually makes its way to the Web — intranet, extranet, or Internet site.

We listened and made the decision to merge the MCMS and SharePoint teams to deliver on the vision of a single platform for managing enterprise content. In late 2006, we released Microsoft Office SharePoint Server (MOSS) 2007, which not only provides rich out-of-the-box WCM capabilities, but also provides a platform for end-to-end enterprise content management. With its rich set of APIs and extension points, it can be extended in many ways to meet very specific customer needs. Of course, as Stan Lee, creator of Spider-Man, appropriately stated, "With great power comes great responsibility" — it's important to understand when and how to extend the platform.

In this book, Andrew has done an excellent job of stepping through all the different ways you can extend and customize MOSS to meet your specific WCM needs. His in-depth experience and knowledge really shine as he covers topics from development methodology and content deployment to tips and tricks. That makes *Professional SharePoint 2007 Web Content Management Development* a must-have book not only for every SharePoint developer interested in WCM, but also for *all* SharePoint developers.

Arpan Shah
Director, SharePoint Technical Product Management
Microsoft Corporation
`http://blogs.msdn.com/arpans`

Introduction

In late 2003 I joined a Fortune 500 in Jacksonville, Florida, as your typical .NET developer, focusing mostly on ASP.NET. I was immediately assigned the role of technical lead on the new corporate Internet site that would be implemented using Microsoft Content Management Server (MCMS) 2002. Up to that point I had worked with many homegrown content management systems in previous jobs. I quickly latched on and really enjoyed the flexibility of MCMS. Once that project was launched, I moved into the role of technical lead for our new corporate intranet site, which was to be implemented using SharePoint Portal Server 2003. We quickly had a need for both content management and collaboration, and merged the two products together to create a very impressive implementation for our customer base.

I find it amusing that at the same time we were doing this, the wheels were in motion at Microsoft to take the best concepts and capabilities from MCMS and implement them on the SharePoint platform, resulting in Office SharePoint Server's (MOSS) Web Content Management (WCM) capabilities. After watching the void for a good book on MOSS WCM development topics sit unfilled, and after many people at conferences and community events asked me, "Where is your WCM book?", I decided to do something about it, which resulted in what you are holding in your hands. I am incredibly proud of both this book and those who were involved in the project.

One approach I took in this book was not to dwell on the more common minutia of creating projects in Visual Studio, or the huge topics of core Windows SharePoint Services (WSS) 3.0 development or SharePoint administration. These topics warrant their own books, and throughout this book you will find recommended resources for these topics. This book does cover some subjects that have their roots in WSS, but they are presented within the context of a Publishing site.

Finally, this book approaches every topic of implementation from the perspective of SharePoint customization and SharePoint development. While one implementation may seem to be better than the other, I take no position on either, as my goal is to simply educate readers about the advantages and disadvantages of each. These concepts are defined in Chapter 2, "Windows SharePoint Services 3.0 Development Primer."

Who This Book Is For

This book is for SharePoint developers working with Publishing sites — sites that leverage MOSS 2007 WCM capabilities. It does not cover administrative topics in any great detail, only where absolutely necessary. For the most part, no two chapters are dependent upon each other, so each chapter can be used as a reference independently of the others. Readers need not have any development experience with SharePoint, but they should have some experience with and a working knowledge of ASP.NET 2.0 development practices and topics. Of course, it is beneficial if the reader does have at least a working knowledge of what SharePoint is all about.

How This Book Is Structured

This book covers MOSS 2007 WCM Publishing sites. You will find some chapters that seem to cover general WSS 3.0 topics, but everything is treated in the context of a Publishing site. While the chapters are arranged in a logical order, it is not necessary to read the book from cover to cover in a linear fashion. The following is a brief description of each chapter:

❑ Chapter 1, "Embarking on Web Content Management Projects" — This chapter explains what this book is all about, who the target audience is, and who will benefit most from the book. It also details what the reader needs in terms of a local development environment in order to implement the solutions. In addition, each of the subsequent chapters is explained very briefly to provide an overview and clarify how each chapter fits in.

❑ Chapter 2, "Windows SharePoint Services 3.0 Development Primer" — This chapter covers the fundamentals of WSS, including definitions of terms such as farm, Web application, site collection, site, list, and document library, and the general architecture of WSS. Some basic object model techniques are demonstrated in this chapter.

❑ Chapter 3, "Overview of Office SharePoint Server 2007 and Web Content Management" — This chapter briefly explains each of the various components that make up MOSS. In addition, while the book is development-focused, the "ABCs" of content-centric Internet sites is covered.

❑ Chapter 4, "SharePoint Features and the Solution Framework" — Both new to WSS 3.0, the SharePoint Feature and solution frameworks are covered in great detail in this chapter, as well as a process for automatically creating WSS solution packages on every project build.

❑ Chapter 5, "Minimal Publishing Site Definition" — Many users create new WCM sites by using the Publishing Portal template. Unfortunately, this adds quite a bit of unnecessary content to the site. This chapter picks apart the Publishing Portal template and Publishing Features and demonstrates how to create a minimal Publishing Portal template.

❑ Chapter 6, "Site Columns, Content Types, and Lists" — Three core components to every WSS 3.0 site — site columns, content types, and lists — are covered in this chapter.

❑ Chapter 7, "Master Pages and Page Layouts" — This chapter covers everything you need to know about creating, editing, and leveraging master pages and page layouts within Publishing sites.

❑ Chapter 8, "Navigation" — While WSS 3.0's navigation is founded on the ASP.NET 2.0 navigation provider framework, there are a few SharePoint-specific topics, which are covered in this chapter.

❑ Chapter 9, "Accessibility" — If it's not already, accessibility is becoming an increasingly important topic with regard to Web sites. This chapter explains the different levels of accessibility and discusses some techniques and tools developers can leverage to create sites for users with disabilities.

❑ Chapter 10, "Field Types and Field Controls" — Although it's a WSS 3.0 concept, field types and field controls are covered in this chapter in the context of a Publishing site. This includes creating custom field types with custom values types and controls, as well as custom field controls that leverage existing field types.

❑ Chapter 11, "Web Parts" — This chapter covers creating custom Web Parts and some advanced topics related to custom Web Part development, such as Editor Parts, customizing the Verbs menu, and leveraging asynchronous programming techniques. This chapter also covers the three Publishing-specific Web Parts and some advanced customization and styling options of the Content Query Web Part.

❑ Chapter 12, "Leveraging Workflow" — The Windows Workflow Foundation, part of the .NET Framework 3.0, is fully leveraged by WSS 3.0 and MOSS 2007. This chapter explains how to create custom workflows using Visual Studio and leveraging InfoPath Web-rendered forms.

❑ Chapter 13, "Search" — Every content-centric site needs a robust search offering. This chapter explains the different components of MOSS search, as well as many customization opportunities such as modifying the search results.

❑ Chapter 14, "Authoring Experience Extensibility" — While the authoring experience in Publishing sites is quite robust, at times developers need to extend this offering for specific content owner requirements. This chapter covers this, including customizing the Page Editing Toolbar and the Rich Text Editor HTML field control.

❑ Chapter 15, "Authentication and Authorization" — This chapter covers everything you need to know about the ASP.NET 2.0 authentication provider model SharePoint fully leverages.

❑ Chapter 16, "Implementing Sites with Multiple Languages and Devices" — This chapter covers the topic of maintaining sites that need to offer their content in multiple languages, as well as developing custom Web Parts that are multilingual aware.

❑ Chapter 17, "Content Deployment" — A common request for larger content-centric Web sites is to have an internal authoring environment for content and then push the changed content out to a destination site, either in an organization's DMZ or at a co-location facility. This chapter describes the content deployment capability in MOSS designed to handle such business requirements.

❑ Chapter 18, "Offline Authoring with Document Converters" — While MOSS 2007 Publishing sites offer a very robust Web-based content authoring experience, SharePoint provides a way to author content offline using tools such as Microsoft Word or InfoPath. This chapter explains what you need to know about configuring the document converter infrastructure and creating custom document converters.

❑ Chapter 19, "Performance Tips, Tricks, and Traps" — Internet-facing content-centric sites built on the SharePoint platform need to be designed and developed with performance in mind. This chapter provides numerous guidelines and tips that developers can leverage to create the most performant sites.

❑ Chapter 20, "Incorporating ASP.NET 2.0 Applications" — SharePoint (both WSS 3.0 and MOSS 2007) is not an end-to-end solution but an application platform. While it provides a significant amount of functionality out of the box, developers can leverage this platform in building custom applications. This chapter discusses some techniques that can be used for such tasks.

What You Need to Use This Book

To get the most out of this book, readers should have a SharePoint development environment in which they can work through the chapters. Active Directory is not required. This book was written and tested using Windows Server 2003 R2 Standard Edition with Service Pack 2, Office SharePoint Server 2007 with Service Pack 1, and Visual Studio 2008.

Embarking on Web Content Management Projects

Ever since the advent of the World Wide Web in the early 1990s, there has been a focus on publishing information. Indeed, the very first Web sites were set up by scientists at CERN, the European Organization for Nuclear Research, so physicists around the world could publish information in a consistently accessible way. Since then, the Web has moved to more than publishing; this started with transactional Web sites, and led to collaboration, social networking, and aggregation-focused sites, to name a few, and all of these are addressed by Microsoft Office SharePoint Server (MOSS) 2007, if not by this book.

Even as the technology has evolved, the need for Web publishing remains pervasive. For example, transactional Web sites publish catalogs and terms of sale; collaboration and social networking sites publish usage guides and ground rules. Therefore, Web publishing remains a core function of any public, extranet or intranet Web site, even if it is more than just "brochureware."

Take a moment to consider this book, which is the product of a modern and technically advanced publishing company. In addition to the authors, there are many other contributors to this book. Someone selected the topic as part of the publisher's catalog and developed the title and "brand" for the book; other people designed the cover and page layout; editors checked for quality and consistency, and still other people typeset and printed the book.

Publishing a Web site is no different: People in specialized roles each want to control particular aspects of the final product. However, unlike a book, the Web site is being constantly updated, and people associated with the site want the freedom necessary to change their aspects of the site without affecting one another. For example, an author may want to add a new page, an editor may want to reorganize several pages, and a branding manager may want to change the colors and logo of all pages, all at the same time. The final "product" — a connected set of Web pages — needs to reflect the input of each of these contributors at any given point in time.

This is the problem solved by Web Content Management (WCM). A WCM system organizes the content and design from all of the site's contributors, allows for versioning, editing, and moderation, and stitches it all together for the end user.

Consider a typical Web page. The banner, color scheme, and general look and feel are part of the branding of the site. Some sort of navigation is probably visible, revealing the organization of the site. In addition to the site navigation, there may be listings of content such as a "front page" list of articles or other topics. These are another form of navigation, one which cuts across the formal structure of the site to highlight contextually relevant content. Authored content — that is, content written by an author and possibly run through an editorial process — may appear in one or more sections of the page, along with images that may require acquisition and approval. Syndicated content, such as news feeds and advertisements, might also appear. Down at the bottom, in the fine print, there may be a legal notice or other disclaimer. Within a typical organization that has a Web site, different people will want to manage each of these aspects of the same Web page, all while the site is up and serving customers.

In the bad old days, the approach to managing a Web site was to edit Web pages and associated files on the file system of each Web server. This approach is simple enough at first, but makes it very hard to modify things such as branding, navigation, or legal disclaimers that appear repeatedly on many Web pages. Moreover, if the authored content is stored in the same files as branding, navigation, and other page features, in the course of editing a paragraph an author could accidentally modify the wrong thing and break the page entirely. This led to the role of Webmaster, a person to whom all Web site content and other changes are fed, and who knows the intricacies of HTML and CSS and any other page programming. The Webmaster's job quickly became a tedious one — copying, pasting, and reformatting content submitted via e-mail and in documents. As the single gatekeeper for all aspects of a Web site, Webmasters often were seen as bottlenecks by contributors whose changes had to wait at the end of the queue.

As a WCM system, MOSS 2007 provides flexibility and independent control over all these aspects of a Web page. The Webmaster bottleneck is largely eliminated by giving control over the many aspects of a site directly to business users, information architects, developers, and designers. Instead of endlessly copying and pasting content, Webmasters can focus on system administration, site design, and development, enabling them to have a much greater impact than ever before.

The Web Content Management Experience

To better understand the use cases for WCM, this section will follow a couple of typical users through their interaction with the system. At first the focus is on authors and editors who produce the authored content on the site. Then the focus shifts to the role of designers and developers, who have a very different kind of interaction with the site.

Authors and Editors

The scenario opens with a product marketing manager who is about to launch a new product and wants to add some information about it to her company's Web site. Rather than having to ask someone to do this for her, she can simply edit the Web site directly, as shown in Figure 1-1. She navigates to the Web site (possibly using a special, internal URL that allows the necessary authentication) and adds a few pages. She enters the product information based on her knowledge as product manager, and is able to format the text as she likes, as long as she stays within company style guidelines. Next, she posts some product images to the site's image library and uses them in the pages as well. She sets each page's start date to the product launch date, which is a couple of weeks in the future, and submits the pages for approval.

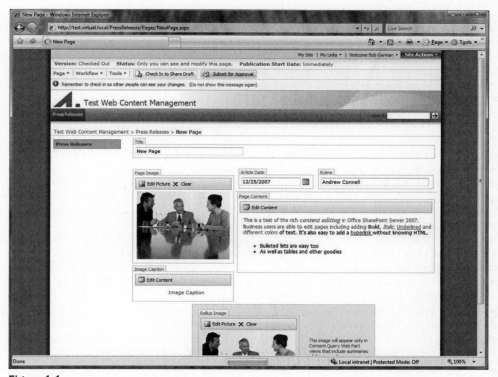

Figure 1-1

Next, an editor gets an e-mail notifying him that there are new Web pages awaiting approval. He clicks a URL in the e-mail and is led to the pages the product manager just created. He makes a few minor changes and approves the pages. The author is then notified that the pages have been approved, and she checks them over one more time to ensure that they look right. However, only she, the editor, and a few other privileged users can see the pages; the general public will get to see them when the product is launched.

On the product launch day, the marketing manager is busy at a big press event, but knows that her new Web pages went live at 8:00 A.M. that morning, and that she has carefully reviewed them in her own Web browser. Furthermore, the pages will automatically appear in the site navigation and on summary pages at the moment the pages go live.

Designers and Developers

The new product was so successful that the company has decided to expand, and has just merged with one of their best partners. The merger will result in a new company, with a new brand. A complete overhaul of the Web site is in order. All the existing Web site content is still relevant — it just needs a new look and branding.

The marketing manager hires a Web design firm to help them create their new site. An information architect draws up a series of wire-frame diagrams showing the new page layouts, while a graphics designer starts working on a look for the new site in the form of mock-ups, which are really just image files showing what the site will look like. Ultimately, the marketing manager agrees to an approach, and chooses one of the mock-ups and a set of wire frames for the new site.

Because the designer's mock-up is just an image file, the next step is to translate it into HTML with Cascading Style Sheets (CSS) and a bunch of smaller image files that will make up each kind of page on the site, resulting in an HTML mock-up. So far, the steps for the new MOSS site branding resemble those that would be used in any Web site.

Next, a SharePoint developer takes the HTML mock-up and merges it with a SharePoint blank *master page* she downloaded from the Microsoft Web site. This provides the basis for all the newly branded Web pages, with placeholders for all the SharePoint functionality to show through. She packages the master page, CSS, and supporting image files into a SharePoint *solution package* and checks it into the source control system.

Meanwhile, the information architect wants to change the page layouts to match the new wire-frame diagrams. To do this, she creates (or modifies existing) MOSS *page layouts,* which define where *fields* should appear on each type of page. For example, she might specify that all product pages should have a title at the top, followed by the model number and list price, and that the main body of the page will have a large floating image on the right. A developer translates this into a page layout, which contains an HTML fragment with the structure of the page. The HTML fragment includes *field controls,* which alternately render or allow editing of the content. The properties of each field control define what text formatting and CSS styles are permitted in each field.

The master page and page layouts could be developed using SharePoint Designer 2007 directly on the production servers (so they would be treated as part of the site content), or they could be developed using Visual Studio and included in a solution package. The fundamental difference between these approaches is that a Visual Studio solution package is installed on the file system of each of the SharePoint Web servers in a farm, whereas SharePoint Designer modifies the SharePoint content database. SharePoint Designer can *customize* SharePoint pages, which means that at runtime, the customized page from the database is substituted for any original page that may have been on the Web servers (or the customized page may only exist in the database, with no file-system-based counterpart at all). Because content is not subject to the same release cycle as code, this often means that SharePoint Designer customizations — which are really content changes, as they are in the content database — are put directly into production, whereas SharePoint solution packages can go through a regular software development life cycle, including controlled releases through a formal testing process. The latter is the recommended approach. Keep in mind that SharePoint Designer is still useful as a developer tool, enabling developers to start with customized pages on a development server, and then migrate the markup into Visual Studio; it is also useful to allow business users to customize their sites directly.

In the scenario, it is determined that the new branding on the site is core functionality and that it should be subject to a controlled release cycle. The SharePoint solution package is part of a Visual Studio solution stored in a source control system, and installed on servers in development, quality assurance (QA)/staging, and ultimately production. In this case, the package deploys the master page, page layouts, and dependent files to every Web server in the farm. Once the new master page is enabled, the new branding appears on all the site's Web pages. The new page layouts also take effect, even on existing pages if they used the same layout name and set of fields (or *content type*).

After thorough testing, development releases the new solution package to a system administrator who installs it on the production SharePoint farm and switches the site to use the new master page. Immediately, the new look and feel takes effect, even on existing pages. In other words, a new site was not really needed after all — the infrastructure and existing content were all reused. Only the branding and layout were changed, without affecting other aspects of the Web site.

Developers can go much further in customizing and extending the WCM system, using solution packages that are listed in the following table:

Extension	Description	Example of Use	Chapter
Custom site definitions	A set of XML-based instructions for creating a new site with specific settings and initial content. Note that in MOSS, a *site* refers to a container in a larger *site collection*, not what users consider to be a whole "Web site."	A starting point for a specific class of site, such as a product information site, a job posting site, a business partner site, etc.	5
Custom site columns, content types, and lists	A set of XML-based instructions for creating new site columns (to store specific kinds of information), content types (groups of columns to use in a list or library), including when a site is created or a Feature is activated	For a product information site, a site column could be created for each product attribute to be displayed, and a new "product page" content type would be created with these and some of the built-in columns.	6
Master pages and page layouts	As described above, master pages provide the branding and overall page structure, and page layouts define the position of field controls on the page.	For a product information site, there might be a master page with the overall branding, and a page layout defining how the product page's columns should be displayed.	7

Table continued on following page

Extension	Description	Example of Use	Chapter
Custom navigation	A new and different way to render site navigation, or custom links added to the navigation across many pages or sites	A new MOSS WCM site is being set up alongside an existing site that is not going to be changed; navigation for the old site needs to be stitched into the MOSS site to make a consistent user experience.	8
Custom field types and field controls	A custom field type is a new data type, which may inherit one of the existing types, and can be used in site columns. A field control is an ASP.NET Web control that renders and allows editing of a particular field type.	Fields requiring custom storage and/or rendering might lead to a custom field type, such as a page rating or a compound part number. Field controls are used for custom and out-of-the-box field types whenever any special rendering or editing is required. For example, a complex field might be stored as XML, edited using a grid control, and rendered using an XSLT style sheet.	10
Custom Web Parts	An ASP.NET Web control that renders external or internal site content	Display external information such as a weather report or stock feed; display lists of items or search-driven results.	11
Custom workflow and forms	A workflow definition for managing content and content-related work, with forms to capture information from end users	A more complex approval workflow than is built into MOSS, with special business rules or exceptions.	12
Custom Authoring Console	Additional menu options or formatting capabilities when editing Web pages	A simple option is added to perform common formatting, content insertion, or other tasks on the page.	14

Designing and Planning a Successful WCM Solution

Anyone who has tried to find their way around a new city knows that the experience varies considerably between a planned city, such as most of New York or Washington, DC, versus an unplanned city such as London or Boston. A planned city has some kind of logical organization or grid layout that makes navigation much easier, whereas an unplanned city may seem like a twisting maze of confusing passages, presenting quite a challenge for newcomers. A Web site is no different, and a little planning and forethought will go a long way in terms of site usability and control.

Information architecture is the emerging field of designing the structure of shared information environments, such as Web sites, to improve usability and facilitate the finding of information. Professional information architects often have a background in library science or cognitive psychology; and depending on the scope of a project, it may be desirable to enlist such a specialist to lead the effort. On smaller projects, or projects for which the basic structure is well understood, the information architecture may be created by the analysts and design team, with input from developers, users, and other stakeholders.

It is important to remember that *every WCM solution has an information architecture*, whether it is designed to be compelling and intuitive or left to evolve randomly.

MOSS comes loaded with a very simple information architecture and visual design that is set up when a Publishing site is created. The out-of-the-box Publishing site definition offers a choice of about half a dozen master pages, basic layouts for welcome and article pages, and a simple navigation structure with a home page and a child site for press releases. This is great for getting a quick start, and indeed some of the default settings may prove useful. However, it is worth at least considering each aspect of the WCM solution and deciding which of the defaults to keep and which to augment or replace.

The sections that follow describe the major areas to consider, along with general best practices and ideas about how to get started.

Use Case Scenarios

As with any system, the first step is to identify the site's target users and determine the major use cases for the site — for example, "a reseller looks up product specifications," "a patient looks up side-effects of a prescription drug," or "a recruiter posts a new job opening." Answering this question should produce an idea of who the users are, their degree of expertise, and what it is that they want to do. Don't forget to include internal as well as external users, such as content contributors and editors. Prioritize the uses cases and make them the basis for the decisions that follow.

Site Structure and Navigation

Navigation begins with the overall site structure or a site map, and this is a good place to start the information architecture. SharePoint sites are always part of a *site collection*, which has a single parent or *top-level site*. The top-level site can have any number of child sites, grandchildren, and so on, and each site will have one or more *pages* in a *page library*. The site structure is therefore based on pages (the leaf nodes, which are viewable by end users) and sites (the containers, each of which has at least one default page to display). This is illustrated in Figure 1-2.

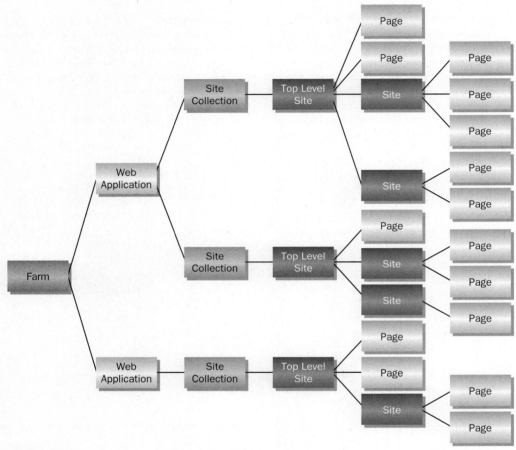

Figure 1-2

Begin with the logical site structure or site map. The site map is generally determined based on weighing a number of considerations, including the following:

❑   **What is the most logical browsing structure for end users?** This is certainly the most important consideration, but not an end-all, as other forms of navigation can short-circuit the site's structure, such as the Content Query Web Part (these are discussed in general later in this section and in greater detail in Chapter 11, "Web Parts").

❑   **What permissions will be set on the sites?** By default, SharePoint sites inherit their permissions from their parent site, so grouping sites with the same permissions (who can author, edit, etc.) under a common parent simplifies managing the permissions.

❑ **What is the look and feel of the sites?** By default, SharePoint sites inherit their master page settings and Cascading Style Sheets from their parent site, so grouping sites with the same look and feel under a common parent simplifies configuration and provides a more consistent browsing experience.

❑ **What information might need to be queried within the sites?** This refers not to search queries, which can span site collections and even external content, but to the Content Query Web Part and similar Web Parts developers create using the SPQuery object in the Windows SharePoint Services (WSS) object model. These queries are more like database queries that retrieve items based on their location, type, and property values, as long as they are within the same site collection. For example, a content query might locate Web pages on a particular topic, events in a particular location, or tasks assigned to a particular user. Content queries can be set to scan a site and all its descendents, so if the content to be queried is grouped within the same site hierarchy, the queries are easier to set up and maintain.

Site Collection Boundaries

In many cases, the entire site structure can be contained in a single site collection, and indeed this is convenient because the built-in navigation is based on the sites and pages within the collection. In addition, content queries, content types, storage quotas, and numerous other SharePoint capabilities are scoped at a site collection, so there is a tendency to design large site collections to make them work over a large set of content. However, sometimes it makes sense to break the solution down into multiple site collections. The primary reasons are as follows:

❑ A site collection is always stored in a single SharePoint content database, although a content database can contain many site collections. If the site collection becomes too large — this includes all the content, such as documents, images, and videos, along with the Web pages — then the database can become unwieldy and hard to back up and restore in a timely manner. Therefore, many SharePoint administrators limit site collections to 50–200GB, and place large site collections in their own, dedicated content database.

❑ SharePoint's built-in groups (for permissions) are scoped at the site-collection level, so if separate sets of groups are desired for administrative control, separate site collections will be necessary.

❑ Some SharePoint Features are scoped at the site collection level, and if these Features are desired in some areas but not others, then the areas need to be in different site collections. For example, the WCM capabilities are controlled by a site collection Feature called "Office SharePoint Server Publishing Infrastructure," so team collaboration sites that don't need WCM Features could be kept in a separate site collection.

❑ Anonymous access is scoped at the site collection level, so if part of a Web site is to be open to anonymous users, whereas another part forces a login, these sections should be in separate site collections.

SharePoint makes it very easy to reorganize sites within a site collection, but not so easy to move them to a new site collection, so it is worth thinking through the site collection boundaries up front. A common pitfall is to build a solution with one giant site collection and then find out months or years later that the database has become too large to restore from backup within the service-level agreement, or that very expensive backup solutions are needed to handle it. If a site will contain large items such as videos, then consider putting them in separate site collection(s) and linking to them to divide the storage.

Navigation and Page Listings

The built-in navigation is based on the site hierarchy and the pages within each site in a site collection. Two views of the navigation are shown: *global navigation* (by default at the top of the page, the global navigation starts at the top-level site, or wherever the inheritance is broken) and *current navigation* (by default on the left of the page, the current navigation starts at the current site). It is easy to add arbitrary links to the navigation, or to hide sites and pages that should not be displayed. The navigation system can be fully customized; for details see Chapter 8, "Navigation."

Two other types of "navigation," which are really just ways of listing links to relevant pages, are also provided out of the box (OOTB):

❑ **Summary Link fields** — These manage a list of hyperlinks as content, and provide navigation to related pages, both within and beyond the WCM solution. These hyperlinks become part of the "authored content" and are thus subject to the normal page approval workflow.

❑ **Content Query Web Parts** — These dynamically query a site collection for content matching key criteria, such as "press releases issued this year" or "events in Oklahoma." They provide links to cross-sections of site content based on the query settings, and have the advantage that they are updated automatically as new content is added.

Combined with the built-in navigation, these features enable placement of relevant links. In general, try to logically group links, and keep in mind that people tend to stop reading after the first four or five links in a list. In addition, they will only click a few levels deep, so this can limit the practical size of the site map. If the site map becomes unwieldy, consider breaking the solution down into multiple Web sites or *Web applications,* each with its own URL, and enable users to begin by selecting an appropriate starting point (e.g., sales information versus support). The same SharePoint farm can host these applications and provide a common search infrastructure that spans them all, so choose a structure that is logical from a usability and maintenance point of view.

Page Layouts and Content Types

Just as navigation planning begins with the site map, the page layout planning begins with page wireframes. A *wireframe* is simply a sketch indicating how information will be laid out on each type of page. This includes *welcome* pages (as they are called in the MOSS-provided templates), which are intended to provide summary information on a site or section of a site, and *detail* pages ("article" detail pages are in the MOSS-provided templates).

In general, for each type of page identified in the wireframes, there is a single page layout. The page layout consists of an HTML fragment that defines the layout itself (often this is an HTML table). Places for content are inserted as needed within the HTML, and can include any combination of the following:

❑ **Field controls** — Each field control displays a piece of content that is stored in a field of each page that uses the page layout. The content in these fields is approved and versioned along with the rest of the page. Field controls are provided for HTML content (and text), images, and summary links; and as shown in Chapter 10, "Field Types and Field Controls," it is easy to create your own for other types of information. Field controls are the most common way to present content in a MOSS WCM site.

❑ **Web Part zones** — Web Part zones enable authors and editors to place Web Parts on the page. This is very useful for adding functionality, such as Content Queries, RSS feeds, or KPI lists. However, note that Web Parts are part of the ASP.NET 2.0 infrastructure, and therefore are not aware of the MOSS publishing system.

A common confusion arises because Web Part zones store the Web Part placements and metadata in a separate Web Part store, not in fields of the page. As a result, changes to Web Parts within a zone are subject to approval along with the page, *but not to versioning*. Therefore, the expected approval behavior will work fine, but if a page is rolled back to a previous version, the Web Part zones won't be affected. For this reason, Web Parts are best used to add functionality, rather than pure content to a page. For example, the Content Editor Web Part might seem to be the same as a Rich HTML field control but it is not, because the Web Part's content is not versioned along with the page.

❑ **Web Parts and ASP.NET controls** — Web Parts and other ASP.NET controls can be embedded directly in the page layout. As such, they cannot be edited on the individual page instances; this can be quite useful to ensure that certain information is always displayed in a certain way.

Page layouts are closely related to the use of content types. A *content type* is simply a set of columns and policy settings that define some kind of content, be it a catalog page, a contract document, or a calendar event. Content types can share columns — for example, an article page, a press release page, and a product description page might all contain an Author column, and by mapping them all to the same Author site column, MOSS realizes that they are the same information when performing queries, constructing views of content, and so on.

The fields available for use in a page layout depend on its underlying content type. It is entirely possible to have multiple page layouts for a single content type; for example, the built-in MOSS page layouts include three layouts (`ArticleLeft.aspx`, `ArticleRight.aspx` and `ArticleLinks.aspx`), which are all layouts of the same content type ("article page"). This enables the page layout to be changed independently of the content — for example, an article page could be changed from `ArticleLeft.aspx` to `ArticleRight.aspx` in order to move its image to the right of the main text on the page.

It is useful to group the page layouts from your wireframe into content types, and to identify the site columns that will make up the fields of each page layout. If multiple page layouts can share a content type, this will provide more flexibility later. Keep in mind that some page layouts may not expose all the fields in the content type. Moreover, it's possible to put field controls inside an Edit Mode Panel control to make them appear only when the page is edited. This can be useful to capture metadata that will be shown in summaries (via the Content Query Web Part) without showing it on the detail page.

For planning purposes, understanding these distinctions and sketching out the wireframes should be sufficient; for details about how to implement page layouts, see Chapter 7, "Master Pages and Page Layouts."

Supporting Content: Images, Attachments and Reusable Content

MOSS field controls will place much of the page content directly in fields of the page, but there will inevitably be other content that needs to be managed outside of the page. For example, the image field control does not store an image but a link to an image that is stored elsewhere. Likewise, a Web author may want to include attachment links to downloadable documents, but where do the documents themselves reside?

The natural answer is to store this supporting content right in MOSS, where it will be easily accessible, subject to the same business rules and permissions, and backed up in the same content database. The image field control looks for image libraries named Images in the current and top-level site of the site collection, and these libraries are convenient places to store images. Policy and permissions can be set on these libraries to allow only selected people to add images and to require an approval before they are available. This can be very useful in enforcing site policy and avoiding the problem of authors who might upload unlicensed images for use on the site.

Part of the information architecture includes providing places to store images and other supporting content, such as documents, on the site. In general, it is a good idea to store assets at the root of the hierarchy in which they will be used. For example, general company images might be stored on the top-level site for use throughout all the child sites, and images relating to a particular product line might be stored on that product's site, which has all the related sites underneath it.

Reusable content is a MOSS feature for managing snippets of content, such as legal disclaimers and trademark declarations, which must appear on many or all pages. These snippets are kept in a special list, aptly named Reusable Content, in the top-level site. Authors can insert the reusable content on their pages, and rather than copy the content into the page, a reference to the content is stored and replaced with the snippet at runtime. This enables the reusable content to be changed in one place for every page in which it is used. Planning this up front is a good idea, before the site contains thousands of copy-and-paste snippets (each of which would have to be updated individually).

Site Definitions

With a site navigation structure, wireframes for the page layouts, and a plan to store supporting content, turn to the containers that will hold the pages and other content. These are MOSS sites, and if the Publishing site definitions that come with MOSS provide everything you need, then no additional work is required here.

However, it may be desirable to allow users to create a site that has certain lists, content, or features already set up. This is most common in collaboration scenarios, but it sometimes is useful in publishing scenarios as well. For example, a product site might contain a specific set of pre-defined pages ready to fill with content, an image library for product pictures, and a special workflow associated with the page library.

To automate this, it's possible to create a new site definition, which tells MOSS how to create the new product sites. For planning purposes, determine what site definitions will be needed and what they need to do.

For details on implementation, see Chapter 5, "Minimal Publishing Site Definition."

Note that WSS has a similar concept called *site templates*, which can be created by simply clicking Save Site as Template on the Site Settings page. This link is not available for Publishing sites, and it would not be a good idea to use it if it were because site templates, like customized pages, live in the content database and cannot easily be staged and tested in a software release cycle. Instead, it is better to create a new site definition in Visual Studio and use your normal release cycle to test and deploy it.

Roles and Permissions

Another planning activity is designing the security settings for your WCM solution. MOSS provides a number of authentication options; for details see Chapter 15, "Authentication and Authorization." It is also possible to manage the content on one physical infrastructure and deploy it to a separate hosting environment; this is detailed in Chapter 17, "Content Deployment." However, it is authorization that is of the greatest concern to the information architecture, as it is directly related to content.

MOSS provides just two levels of groups, *SharePoint groups* and *permission levels,* as shown in Figure 1-3.

> *Just to be clear, in previous versions of SharePoint, groups were called "cross-site groups" and permission levels were called "site groups."*

In addition, an ASP.NET role provider can add additional levels of grouping stored outside of SharePoint; out of the box, MOSS supports Active Directory (AD) groups in this manner, so with no code or extra effort, developers can use AD groups freely in MOSS. Here, the term "role provider group" is used to highlight the fact that it can be any external directory or other data source that has an ASP.NET role provider.

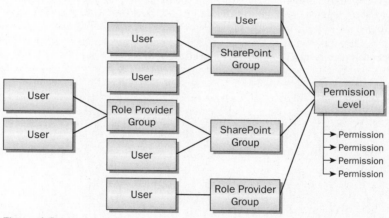

Figure 1-3

Permission levels are stored at the site level, though by default they are inherited from the parent site. Out of the box, a Publishing site has eight permission levels: Full Control, Design, Manage Hierarchy, Approve, Contribute, Read, Restricted Read, and Limited Access. Each of these has a set of fine-grained permissions associated with it, such as permission to view, add, edit, or delete items; the ability to add pages and child sites, and so on.

Permission levels grant their granular permissions on a site to a specific set of users, SharePoint groups and role provider groups. Within a site, the permission levels for these users and groups will apply to all the lists, libraries, folders, and items in the site, unless explicit permission levels are assigned to an object. For example, the user Joe may have Restricted Read access to the site, but Full Control over a particular folder of documents, and no access at all to a specific security Web page.

It is possible to create custom permission levels, or to edit the granular permissions of the OOTB ones, except for Full Control and Limited Access. Full Control always allows complete access to the site, and Limited Access allows no direct access to site content at all, but is intended to allow users to traverse the site in order to access items within it that they have explicit permission to see. For example, a user might have access only to one page of a site, but still need access to style sheets and other supporting site infrastructure in order to view it; in that case, the user would need Limited Access permission on the site and Restricted Read access to the page.

The other groups within MOSS are SharePoint groups, which are more traditional groupings. SharePoint groups cannot be nested, but can contain external role provider groups. Note that SharePoint groups are stored at the site-collection level; this makes the same groups available in all sites in the site collection. This can be good or bad; it is convenient to have groups that apply across many sites, but sometimes it would be nice to have a second level of grouping (other than permission levels) within a site.

More details about permissions and groups can be found in the WSS documentation at www.andrewconnell.com/go/200.

The task then is to design the setup of permission levels, SharePoint groups, and role provider groups and how they will apply to the content in the site map. Think of the permission levels as roles — going back to the use cases, who are the actors, and what roles will they take on with respect to the various sites and content in the system? Those roles will end up reflecting the permission levels. The OOTB levels may be fine, but walk through them and see whether they make sense.

In general, it is better to grant permissions to SharePoint or role provider groups, rather than to individual users, as it is a lot easier to edit a group membership when you have organizational changes than it is to remember all the permissions that need to be set. The built-in SharePoint groups are also role oriented, but these are roles that extend throughout the site collection. This is a good approach, but a large site will probably need to have more explicit groups, such as Marketing Page Approvers or Product Site Authors, to easily manage different permissions in various parts of the site collection.

If you are using AD (or another role provider) and have the authority to create groups there, then groups can be nested as much as desired. This can be used, for example, to manage organizational groups — for example, if all the design engineers are already in a Design Engineers AD group, and these are the same people who can approve specification changes, then the existing Design Engineers AD group can be placed into a Specification Approvers SharePoint group.

A common pitfall is developing a solution in an environment where everybody has full control, only to later discover in system testing that it does not work in production, where more restrictive permissions are in place. Planning the permissions up front and making them part of unit testing is much less painful in the long run!

User Profiles and Targeting

If users are authenticated, then MOSS can do more than just set permissions for them. MOSS also contains a user profile system to store information about users, and a targeting system to automatically select relevant content based on the user's profile.

User profiles can be configured in the shared service provider (SSP) to have whatever properties are of interest. The usual approach is to populate the profile database by periodically importing data from the directory service and to allow users to modify their profiles in their *My Sites*, although profiles can also be created and updated programmatically.

SharePoint *audiences* select users based on rules about their user profiles — for example, users whose country is equal to Australia, whose list of interests includes the word "boating" or who are members of the Top Partners group in AD. Content, including Web pages, can be targeted to specific audiences by placing a list of audiences in the Target Audiences field. The Content Query Web Part can be set to respect these audience settings, so users are presented only with content that matches the query *and* the user's audiences. Note that audience targeting is different from security; users can still get to content via navigation, search, or an explicit URL, even if they are not in the target audience. Rather than security, targeting is intended to highlight content of interest to users.

Search Strategy

Site users expect to be able to both search for content and navigate to it, and fortunately MOSS has a great built-in search engine to accommodate their needs. MOSS search is a huge topic that is beyond the scope of this book, but it is worth pointing out some of the possibilities.

In addition to indexing MOSS content, the MOSS search engine can index external file shares, Microsoft Exchange public folders, and Lotus Notes databases. It can also crawl any Web site, which can be useful when there are related sites that are not in MOSS.

Here are some strategies for optimizing MOSS search in a WCM solution:

❑ **Branding** — Naturally, the search pages inherit the master page and Cascading Style Sheets (CSS) along with the rest of the site. Further customizations are easy, but the search user interface is comprised of Web Parts that can be reconfigured and rearranged to meet your needs.

❑ **Search scopes** — A *search scope* is basically a set of partial queries called *scope rules* that narrow down a user's search. Users normally see scopes in a drop-down list next to the search box, or as tabs on the results page. For example, a News search might show only news stories matching the user's query, and the scope rule behind it could select the news based on Web address, content source, or other properties.

When planning a search scope that is not based on the location of the content, the scope needs to be based on a property of some kind. One of the built-in properties is `contentclass`, which contains the name of the content type; therefore, if there is a content type for press releases, then making a Press Releases search scope would be easy.

In other cases, it may be necessary to include a property in the page content type, visible only at editing time, that puts pages into the scope. For example, if a random cross-section of pages contains medical information, and Medical search scope is planned, placing the word Medical in a hidden field would enable these pages to be selected in a search scope.

Search scopes can be set up in the SSP administration site.

❑ **Authoritative pages** — Search relevancy can be adjusted by specifying authoritative pages in the search catalog. Pages can be designated as most, second, or third most authoritative, and their relevancy is adjusted upwards; pages can also be designated as non-authoritative and their relevancy is demoted. This can be useful when areas of a site contain information that needs to be highlighted (authored information, for example) or pushed to the bottom (such as old or less popular content). Note that an authoritative page also affects the pages to which it links: For example, a product summary page that links to all products could be marked as authoritative to raise the relevancy of all the product pages, as well as the summary. Authoritative pages can be set up in the SSP administration site.

❑ **Keywords/best bets** — Pages can be designated as *best bets* and associated with keywords. When the keyword is included in a search query, any related best bets will show up in their own section of the search results page. Keywords can be set up as best bets in the top-level site settings of each site collection.

A best practice is to monitor the Search Usage reports (in the SSP administration sites) and look at the Search Results report called Queries with Zero Results. Guess what? There is a frustrated user behind every one of those queries! These are candidates for keywords and best bets.

Traditional Web sites place metadata in META tags, but this isn't necessary for the MOSS search engine to pick up the metadata when crawling MOSS content; it can query the metadata directly. However, it may be desirable to include META tags in order to allow external search engines to crawl a WCM solution. This can be accomplished by incorporating a custom control or Web Part in the master page, which emits the desired META tags based on the page content (some of which may be hidden from site visitors by placing it within an Edit Mode Panel so they only appear when the page is being edited). An example of such a control, called `MetaTagsGenerator`, is available on CodePlex at `www.andrewconnell.com/go/201`.

Summary

WCM removes bottlenecks in the process of Web publishing by enabling business users to directly author and edit content independently of one another and of site designers. Similarly, site designers can work independently of the content creators, and can update existing content with new branding and other visual changes.

WCM can also improve the quality and consistency of a Web site by providing a structure, but only if the solution has the structure implemented as part of the design. Here is a checklist of planning activities:

❑ Use case scenarios defining both internal and external actors and how they will use the site

❑ Overall site map showing the site structure, including the placement of site collections if there is more than one

❑ Image, and eventually HTML mock-ups, of the visual design

❑ Wireframe representations of desired page layouts, mapped to documented content types that will define the fields used to store the data

❑ A list of required custom features for development based on the wireframe representations and visual design

❑ Defined locations for supporting content such as images and attached documents

❑ A structure for SharePoint groups and permission levels, perhaps color coded to sites on the site map

Remember that your Web site will have information architecture, just as every city has a street map. Whether yours will be easy or confusing depends on the planning and thought that goes into the solution. Keep in mind that the real point of Web publishing is not the cool technology, but the content itself. Organizing the content in the most helpful way possible will do more for a site's success than any other factor, and a well designed WCM site will make that easy.

The following two resources are useful for designing usable Web sites:

❑ Improving Web Site Usability and Appeal: www.andrewconnell.com/go/202

❑ Step-by-Step Usability Guide: www.andrewconnell.com/go/203

2

Windows SharePoint Server 3.0 Development Primer

Before digging into Microsoft Office SharePoint Server 2007 (MOSS) Web Content Management (WCM) development topics, developers must have a firm understanding of Windows SharePoint Services 3.0 (WSS). Of course, it is not possible to fully cover the subject of WSS development in a single chapter. It is a very large and far-reaching topic, as it is the foundation for everything in the SharePoint product stack. This chapter touches on some of the more important and relevant topics in WSS that are relevant to the WCM/Publishing topics covered in this book.

> For in-depth development and architecture coverage of Windows SharePoint Services 3.0, see Inside Microsoft Windows SharePoint Services 3.0 by Ted Pattison and Dan Larson (Microsoft Press, 2007).

SharePoint Architecture

In WSS 2.0, SharePoint was integrated into ASP.NET 1.1 via an ISAPI filter (see Figure 2-1). This ISAPI filter was needed because ASP.NET 1.1 had no mechanism that enabled applications to reroute how the source of a file was retrieved: ASP.NET 1.1 always assumed the files lived on the file system. This ISAPI filter presented many challenges in WSS 2.0, specifically in the areas of performance and extensibility. It was not easy to do things such as add custom HTTP handlers or modules, leverage custom user controls (ASCXs), or plug custom code into the ASP.NET page life cycle, changing the execution process.

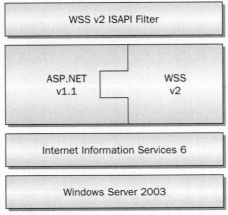

WSS v2 ISAPI Filter

ASP.NET v1.1	WSS v2

Internet Information Services 6

Windows Server 2003

Figure 2-1

Thankfully, Microsoft dramatically changed the fundamental architecture of WSS 3.0 from the previous release (WSS 2.0). This is largely due to the fact that the ASP.NET 2.0 team added functionality and certain hooks that enable third-party developers to customize the ASP.NET 2.0 infrastructure. The most significant addition to ASP.NET 2.0 is the *virtual path provider,* which abstracts the location of the requested files from ASP.NET. ASP.NET 2.0 utilizes a built-in virtual path provider that retrieves files from the file system by default, but the virtual path provider enables developers to plug in custom providers to customize the source of the requested files.

> *For more information on the virtual path provider, refer to the official documentation on MSDN* (www.andrewconnell.com/go/204) *and the Microsoft Knowledge Base article #910441* (www.andrewconnell.com/go/205) *for an example.*

By adding the virtual path provider, the SharePoint team was able to completely implement WSS 3.0 using a custom HTTP application, modules, and handlers; and route all requests for a SharePoint site through ASP.NET 2.0. The SharePoint team created a custom virtual path provider, `Microsoft.SharePoint.ApplicationRuntime.SPVirtualPathProvider`, that supports SharePoint's concept of page customization, covered later in the chapter. This allowed Microsoft to discard the ISAPI filter and the approach of integrating WSS 2.0 with ASP.NET 1.1.

However, ASP.NET 2.0 is not the only part of the .NET Framework that SharePoint relies upon. The other main component is Windows Workflow Foundation (WF), one of the four components in addition to the .NET 2.0 Framework included in the .NET 3.0 Framework (the others being Windows Communication Foundation, Windows Presentation Foundation, and Windows CardSpace).

Due to the architectural changes and improvements to the ASP.NET 2.0 platform, the SharePoint team was able to build WSS 3.0 on top of the existing .NET Framework stack, as shown in Figure 2-2.

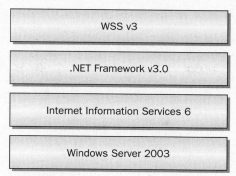

Figure 2-2

This new architecture also enables SharePoint to fully leverage and benefit from everything that ASP.NET 2.0 has to offer, such as page output caching, user controls, server controls, and custom HTTP handlers and modules.

Some of the ASP.NET 2.0 features that SharePoint leverages are covered in more detail later in the book, such as master pages (see Chapter 7), the navigation provider model (see Chapter 8), Web Parts (see Chapter 11), workflow (see Chapter 12) and the authentication provider model (see Chapter 15).

SharePoint on the File System and in Internet Information Services

When installing SharePoint, all the application files are installed into a directory nested deep within the Program Files path: `c:\Program Files\Common Files\Microsoft Shared\web server extensions\12`. Throughout this book, this folder is referred to as the "SharePoint 12 folder" or `[..]\12\`. The SharePoint 12 folder contains everything necessary to run MOSS and WSS, including Features (covered in Chapter 4), images, Cascading Style Sheets (CSS), Web services, and all assemblies containing the compiled logic necessary for SharePoint to execute. Most of the custom code solutions are deployed to a folder nested somewhere in SharePoint's `12` folder structure.

One thing that is not kept in this path is the root directory for each new Web application, or Web site, created in Internet Information Services (IIS). By default, these are created in `c:\Inetpub\wwwroot\wss\VirtualDirectories\[site's host header][site's port number]`. Web applications are used as the HTTP entry point to a SharePoint site and define certain aspects that are shared across all SharePoint sites hosted within the Web application, such as HTTP handlers and modules, authentication configuration, and a list of which controls have been registered with SharePoint's safe mode page parser. Opening a SharePoint extended Web application in IIS exposes four virtual directories created by SharePoint: _vti_bin, _controltemplates, _layouts, and _wpresources. Each virtual directory has a specific use within a SharePoint Web application and is shared across all sites hosted within that Web application:

❑   **_vti_bin** — This exposes SharePoint Web services and assemblies to SharePoint and non-SharePoint applications alike; this virtual directory points to the path `c:\Program Files\Common Files\Microsoft Shared\web server extensions\12\ISAPI`.

❑ **_controltemplates** — This points to a shared folder within the SharePoint 12 directory structure that only contains ASP.NET 2.0 user controls; this virtual directory points to the path `c:\Program Files\Common Files\Microsoft Shared\web server extensions\ 12\TEMPLATE\CONTROLTEMPLATES`.

❑ **_layouts** — This points to a shared folder within the SharePoint 12 directory structure containing application pages, covered later in this chapter; this virtual directory points to the path `c:\Program Files\Common Files\Microsoft Shared\web server extensions\ 12\TEMPLATE\LAYOUTS`.

❑ **_wpresources** — This points to a shared folder that contains resources used by Web Parts deployed globally to the server; this virtual directory points to the path `c:\Program Files\ Common Files\Microsoft Shared\web server extensions\wpresources`.

SharePoint Site Topology

The topology and structure of a WSS site, as well as the site collection in which the site lives, is very important to WCM developers. To best understand it, it is easiest to look at the topology of a WSS site and site collection from the top-down approach. As shown in Figure 2-3, the entry point for all SharePoint sites is the Web application. The previous section explained how a Web application is just another name for an IIS Web site and the folder structure that makes up the Web application.

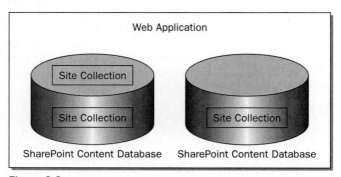

Figure 2-3

Web applications host SharePoint site collections. Web applications can also contain more than one site collection. Recall that a site collection is an administrative and management construct within SharePoint. Many capabilities are scoped within a specific site collection and do not cross to other site collections, such as the scope of a search query created using the Content Query Web Part in a WCM site (the Content Query Web Part is covered in detail in Chapter 11).

Developers can use the `Microsoft.SharePoint.Administration.SPWebApplication` class to obtain a reference to an existing SharePoint extended Web application to perform administrative tasks such as setting the number of days the "New!" icon appears next to new list items and documents:

```
SPWebApplication webApp = SPWebApplication.Lookup(new Uri("http://wss"));
webApp.DaysToShowNewIndicator = 7;
webApp.Update();
```

While site collections are hosted by Web applications, they are stored within SharePoint content databases — another name for a SharePoint-specific Microsoft SQL Server database. Administrators can add multiple content databases to a Web application, but a site collection can only live within exactly one content database. This highlights the fact that administrators need to plan the structure of a site collection because the larger the site collection, the larger the SQL Server database. As a result, when a site collection becomes extremely large, the site has to be taken offline while the database is backed up. Although you shouldn't fret too much over the size of a site collection in the early stages of a project, as sites can be moved from one site collection to another using custom code and working with the SharePoint API, spend some time planning for the site collection's growth. Administrators can leverage quotas to control how much a site collection can grow in terms of storage space. These quotas can be defined when a site collection is created or on existing site collections.

As previously stated, site collections are used for both administrative and management purposes. However, at their core, SharePoint site collections simply contain SharePoint sites. When a new site collection is created, the user is immediately directed to enter information such as the display name, the description, and the owner of the site. This site is called the *top-level* or *root* site within the site collection. Each site collection can have one top-level site, with as many subsites as desired. Each site contains lists and libraries that are the fundamental and lowest-level storage constructs within SharePoint . . . similar to SQL Server database tables. Like records within a database table, SharePoint lists and libraries contain list items and documents. A new feature of WSS 3.0 is that SharePoint lists can also contain folders (previously, in WSS 2.0, only document libraries supported folders).

Chapter 6, "Site Columns, Content Types, and Lists," takes a detailed look at SharePoint lists and libraries.

Developers can use the `Microsoft.SharePoint.SPSite` class to obtain a reference to an existing site collection, and `Microsoft.SharePoint.SPWeb` to obtain a reference to a site within a site collection. The following code demonstrates obtaining a reference to a site collection and determining how many lists the top-level site contains:

```
SPSite siteCollection = new SPSite("http://wss");
SPWeb topLevelSite = siteCollection.RootWeb;
Console.Out.WriteLine("Total lists in the top-level site: "
+topLevelSite.Lists.Count.ToString());
```

In addition, developers can also use the classes `Microsoft.SharePoint.SPList` and `Microsoft.SharePoint.SPDocumentLibrary` to interact with lists and libraries via the SharePoint API.

When a new site is created, an administrator is prompted to select a site template, including when prompted to create the top-level site after creating a site collection. Site templates are used to define an initial starting point for the SharePoint site. Templates can include things such as list templates, as well as instances of those list templates (covered in Chapter 6), Web Parts (covered in Chapter 11), default content, and Features that are activated by default (covered in Chapter 4), among other things. However, administrators can also elect to start from the equivalent of a clean slate by creating a site based on the Blank Site template, which only adds the absolute minimum components necessary for a site to function, such as the site template, list template, and Web Part libraries.

Each of these different elements within the site topology is used within Publishing sites. Chapter 3 covers in greater depth how the various site topology objects — specifically, `SPSite`, `SPWeb`, `SPList`, and `SPListItem` — are leveraged within Publishing sites.

SharePoint Administration

SharePoint includes various interfaces that enable administrators to manage a SharePoint implementation, both for SharePoint farm administrators and SharePoint site administrators. There are essentially four different administration interfaces within a SharePoint environment: Central Administration, Site Settings, List Settings, and STSADM.EXE.

Keep one thing in mind with respect to administration: While the browser-based and command-line administration experience provides a significant amount of administrative capability, everything is implemented using the SharePoint API. Thus, the SharePoint API can do everything the browser-based or command-line interface can do, as well as many other things.

Central Administration

When an administrator installs SharePoint for the first time and creates a new farm, the installer automatically creates a special WSS 3.0 site called Central Administration (see Figure 2-4). This site is primarily used by farm administrators to manage all the servers in the SharePoint server farm, as well as the SharePoint services on those servers. Central Administration is also used to manage and create new Web applications, which creates new IIS Web sites automatically extended with the necessary things for SharePoint to function, manage, and create new site collections, manage the SharePoint farm's *solution store* (covered in Chapter 4), manage the security and authentication configuration for Web applications, and configure farm settings such as e-mail settings, anti-virus settings, and diagnostic logging.

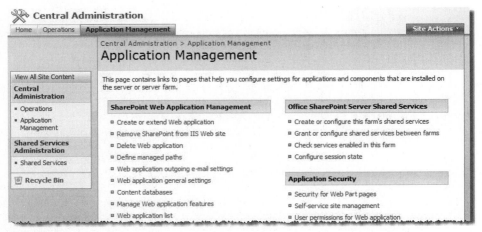

Figure 2-4

Site Settings

One thing notably missing from the Central Administration site is the capability to manage the settings of specific site collections and sites within the SharePoint farm. This is by design, in order to accomplish SharePoint's goal of empowering end users. Users can be assigned as the owners of site collections, with the authority to administer the site, but not granted rights to the Central Administration site.

With this separation of responsibility, each site contains an administrative capability accessible via a special page named Site Settings. The Site Settings page is accessible from the Site Actions menu or by entering the URL http://[site URL]/_layouts/settings.aspx. It is from this page that site owners can manage the security of a site, create new lists and libraries, customize the site's navigation, manage the site columns and content types, and activate/deactivate site-scoped Features. The top-level site within a site collection contains an additional column of links to administer the entire site collection, including things such as activating/deactivating site-collection-scoped Features, search settings, recycle bin settings, and site collection usage reports (see Figure 2-5).

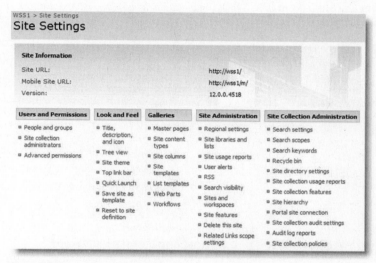

Figure 2-5

List Settings

Aside from the Site Settings administration page, a site contains a page that enables those with appropriate rights to edit the settings of a list. While on a list view, the List Information page, shown in Figure 2-6, is accessible from the Settings toolbar menu. It enables users to manage the list's title, description, navigation, version settings, audience targeting settings, views, and permissions. Users can also manage the list's columns, as well as its content types.

As previously mentioned, WSS 3.0 is built on top of the .NET 3.0 Framework and fully leverages Windows Workflow Foundation. From the List Settings page, users can also configure the workflow settings, such as associating workflow templates previously deployed to the site collection with the list, and configure their startup options, such as automatically when new list items are created or updated, or manually. Users can also remove workflows or keep new workflows from being started on an association-by-association basis, from the Workflow Settings page accessible from the List Settings page.

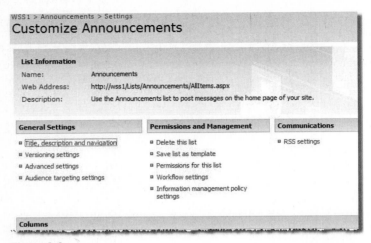

Figure 2-6

STSADM.EXE

STSADM.EXE is a command-line utility used for the administration of SharePoint sites and servers. Every WSS 3.0 install includes STSADM.EXE, which can be found in the following directory: `c:\Program Files\Common Files\Microsoft Shared\web server extensions\12\bin\`. STSADM.EXE is based on the premise of operations. Administrators specify an operation to perform, followed by a series of required or optional switches. For example, the following command lists all the InfoPath form templates that have been deployed to the SharePoint farm's Form Template library within Central Administration:

```
stsadm.exe -o enumformtemplates
```

To retrieve a list of all the operations available, either execute STSADM.EXE using no parameters or with the single –help parameter. Get operation-specific help and syntax by specifying –help and the name of the operation, such as the following:

```
stsadm.exe -help enumformtemplates
```

As a SharePoint developer, it is beneficial to become very familiar with STSADM.EXE, as it provides additional functionality not included (and sometimes not possible) through Central Administration or Site Settings. Some of these exclusive STSADM.EXE operations include activating/deactivating hidden Features, and adding or upgrading WSS solution packages to the SharePoint farm's solution store.

> STSADM.EXE *is also extensible, enabling developers to add custom operations to the list of available operations. Once a custom operation has been deployed, it will show up in the list of available operations. For more information on extending* STSADM.EXE, *refer to the WSS 3.0 online help on MSDN:* www.andrewconnell.com/go/206.

WSS 3.0 and ASP.NET 2.0 Development

Because Microsoft changed the architecture approach of SharePoint by building on top of ASP.NET 2.0, SharePoint development is very much like ASP.NET 2.0 development. Nearly everything available within ASP.NET 2.0 is available within a SharePoint environment. Aside from the similarities, SharePoint also adds some additional development opportunities above and beyond what is at the disposal of a standard ASP.NET 2.0 site. However, SharePoint is a separate product from ASP.NET 2.0, so there are some differences.

Like ASP.NET 2.0

This chapter previously explained how SharePoint — specifically, WSS 3.0 — is now built on top of ASP.NET 2.0 and is implemented using a custom HTTP application, handlers, and modules. This new approach enables all native ASP.NET 2.0 concepts to bleed through for use within SharePoint. The following few sections touch on some of the similarities between standard ASP.NET 2.0 development and SharePoint-specific development.

Master Pages

SharePoint heavily leverages ASP.NET 2.0 master pages. All SharePoint sites are based on the same initial master page called `default.master` found in the `[..]\12\TEMPLATE\GLOBAL` directory. This master page contains many content placeholders required in most master pages leveraged within SharePoint. It also contains an instance of a special SharePoint implementation of the ASP.NET 2.0 Web Part Manager control, which acts as the hub for the Web Part framework on all customizable pages and imports the SharePoint-specific CSS files required to implement the SharePoint user experience (such as the Web Part zones and Site Actions menu).

Developers are not limited to this single master page. Just like a typical ASP.NET 2.0 Web site, developers can customize the provided master page or create custom master pages for use within SharePoint. For more information, refer to Chapter 7, "Master Pages and Page Layouts," which covers the creation and customization of new master pages in depth.

One minor difference is the utilization of master pages within an ASP.NET 2.0 Web site versus a SharePoint site. In SharePoint, the master page is specified at the site level, and generally all pages within that site leverage the selected master page; whereas in ASP.NET 2.0, developers configure which master page is utilized on a content-page by content-page basis.

Navigation Provider Model

In ASP.NET 2.0, Microsoft introduced the navigation provider model, which dramatically simplifies creating custom navigation components, as well as plugging custom or third-party components into ASP.NET 2.0 Web sites. Unlike its previous version, WSS 3.0 navigation is much easier to customize because it is fully leverages the ASP.NET 2.0 navigation provider model. Microsoft includes some custom navigation controls that can only be used within SharePoint sites, but it is incredibly easy to replace these controls with a commercial or custom navigation rendering component if the need arises. Refer to Chapter 8 for an in-depth discussion on customizing and working with navigation within a SharePoint — and, specifically, a MOSS Publishing — site.

Membership Provider Model

Another addition to the .NET Framework was the inclusion of the membership provider model within ASP.NET 2.0 Web sites. This abstracts the authentication mechanism and plumbing from an ASP.NET 2.0 application, simplifying development and configuration. It also makes it much easier to add new authentication mechanisms to an existing application.

WSS 2.0 was, for the most part, restricted to Active Directory authentication. While it was possible to hook into other authentication mechanisms such as a generic LDAP provider, enabling it required a lot of work and it was problematic. Thanks to WSS 3.0's ability to leverage everything ASP.NET 2.0 has to offer, a SharePoint site can now fully utilize the membership provider model and authenticate against a virtually unlimited number of identity stores. Moreover, SharePoint provides an additional capability that enables multiple entry points into a single site collection via different URLs, each configured with a different authentication mechanism, such as Active Directory, forms-based authentication, or LDAP. Chapter 15, "Authentication and Authorization," deals with SharePoint's implementation of the membership provider model and configuring authentication providers.

Server Controls and User Controls

ASP.NET 2.0 server controls are elements that encapsulate logic, functionality, and a user interface. Developers can build custom ASP.NET 2.0 server controls for use within Web sites or they can leverage one of the many included controls. User controls, commonly referred to as *ASCX files,* are server controls that enable developers to describe the behavior and user interface of a server control declaratively. Some examples of server controls include `<asp:TextBox />` and `<asp:DataGrid />`.

Like ASP.NET 2.0, SharePoint ships with many server and user controls, and developers are free to build custom server and user controls for use within SharePoint applications. In fact, many of the user interface components developers build in SharePoint are server controls such as Web Parts and field controls. One difference from leveraging server and user controls within SharePoint compared to ASP.NET 2.0 is that SharePoint runs in a lower level of trust (covered in the sections "Code Access Security" and "Safe Mode Parser" later in this chapter), so assemblies need to be flagged as "safe" for execution within a SharePoint site.

Web Parts

WSS 2.0 introduced the Web Part framework, and until ASP.NET 2.0 was released, the only way to leverage Web Parts was within a SharePoint site. However, with the release of ASP.NET 2.0, Microsoft added the Web Part framework (albeit the implementation was a bit different from WSS 2.0) to non-SharePoint sites. When the SharePoint team made the decision to change the fundamental architecture of WSS 3.0 to be built on top of ASP.NET 2.0, it also elected to rewire the SharePoint platform to leverage the ASP.NET 2.0 Web Part framework implementation as the recommended Web Part development approach.

In addition, the older SharePoint-specific Web Part class and associated classes were redeveloped for backward compatibility so that WSS 2.0 Web Parts would continue to function within WSS 3.0. Regardless, the recommended approach for Web Part development within WSS 3.0 is now to build ASP.NET 2.0 Web Parts, rather than SharePoint-specific Web Parts. Chapter 11, "Web Parts," takes an in-depth look at creating custom Web Parts.

Unlike ASP.NET 2.0

Although WSS 3.0 is built on top of the .NET Framework 3.0, with many striking similarities between ASP.NET 2.0 and SharePoint development, there are some unique differences between the two platforms. The following sections outline a few of the more visible and glaring differences where the development experience diverges.

Development Tools and Experience

ASP.NET 2.0 developers typically build sites using Microsoft Visual Studio. Visual Studio provides multiple deployment methods, hosts a slimmed-down version of IIS (to reduce the surface area of security-related attacks and compromises), and includes a rich designer interface that enables developers to drag and drop controls onto the design surface when constructing new master pages, content pages, and user controls.

Unfortunately, this rich design-time interface is generally not available within Visual Studio when developing SharePoint assets. Instead, Microsoft encourages developers to use a new tool introduced in the 2007 Office System called Office SharePoint Designer 2007. This tool is the successor to FrontPage 2003. Developers can use this tool to create new master pages and content pages visually with a rich WYSIWYG design-time interface. However, this approach to development also has associated baggage that developers should be aware of (see the section "Customization versus Development" later in this chapter).

User controls are even more negatively affected by this, as SharePoint Designer does not provide a development experience for these types of ASP.NET 2.0 assets.

Even with these limitations, developers are not without options. Visual Studio can still be used to develop master pages, content pages, page layouts (within the context of MOSS Publishing sites) and user controls, although development must be done in the HTML or Code view, rather than the Design view, and there is no live debugging experience: Components must be deployed and implemented within a SharePoint site in order to be tested and debugged.

Code-Behind Files

Building off the previous section on the development tools and experience, SharePoint developers' use of code-behind files within master pages, content pages, page layouts (within the context of MOSS Publishing sites), and user controls differs from that within a pure ASP.NET 2.0 Web site. ASP.NET 2.0 developers can easily code-behind files to the aforementioned types of files: When in Design mode, right-click the design surface and select View Code. Visual Studio handles the wiring up of the user interface file (i.e., master, ASPX, or ASCX) and the code-behind class, and provides a nice expansion experience within the Solution Explorer tool window.

Unfortunately, Visual Studio has no such integration within SharePoint. This does not mean that it isn't possible to have code-behind files within SharePoint files — this is a common misunderstanding for those who are new to the SharePoint platform. Instead, developers simply need to wire the two files together manually. The code-behind files containing classes inheriting from `System.Web.UI.Page` (in the case of a content page) are compiled into assemblies using something like the Class Library project template within Visual Studio. A developer would then wire up the two files by adding an `Inherits` attribute to the `Page` (or `Master` or `Control`) directive in the source of the user interface file. The `Inherits` attribute contains the five-part name of the class, which includes the full class, or type, the name of the object containing the server-side logic for the type (e.g., `namespace.typename`), the assembly containing the type, culture, and version, and the public key token of the signed assembly.

For example, consider the following class compiled into the assembly `SharepointWebSite.dll`:

```
using System;
namespace WROX {
  public class SomePage : System.Web.UI.Page {
    protected void OnLoad(object sender, EventArgs e){
      Response.Write(DateTime.Today.ToString());
    }
  }
}
```

The ASPX file that is wired up to the code-behind containing the type for this page would contain a `Page` directive like the following:

```
<%@ Page Language="C#" Inherits="WROX.SomePage, SharePointWebSite, Culture=Neutral,
Version=1.0.0.0, PublicKeyToken=[ ... ]" %>
```

Code Access Security

Code access security (CAS), included with the .NET Framework, enables developers and administrators to grant specific permissions and rights to managed code. Another type of security most people are familiar with is user-based security, whereby code assumes the rights and permissions that the current user has been assigned. Using CAS effectively enables administrators to restrict what managed code is allowed to do, limiting the surface area of attack and vulnerability on a system.

While not a SharePoint-specific topic by any means, many ASP.NET 2.0 developers are immune from dealing with CAS in Web projects, as most sites run fully trusted by default. Some developers may be familiar with running in what is referred to as *medium trust*, as that is what many shared hosting providers are now using to exert more control over their assets hosting many Web sites for multiple customers on the same hardware.

By default, new SharePoint Web applications are configured to run within a very low and restricted level of trust called *WSS_Minimal*. For example, some things are not possible out-of-the-box (OOTB), such as consuming a Web service that exists outside the current domain or connecting to a SQL Server database. In order to perform these types of tasks, you must do one of the following:

❑   Create a custom CAS policy that assigns the necessary permissions to the assembly(s) containing the managed code attempting to perform such an action.

❑   Change the SharePoint Web application CAS policy from WSS_Minimal to WSS_Medium or Full (which is the least secure and most pervasive). This affects all assemblies within the Web application, not just the specific assembly needing elevated permissions.

❑   Deploy the assembly containing the managed code attempting to perform such an action to the server's GAC, thus granting the assembly full trust and making it globally available on the server.

Safe Mode Parser

While ASP.NET 2.0 sites generally live on the file system, SharePoint sites are virtualized within a content database. These virtualized files exist in one of two states: customized or uncustomized. This topic is covered in greater detail in the section "Uncustomized versus Customized Files" later in the chapter. For now, understand that customized files are those for which the source lives within the content database. SharePoint Designer enables developers and information workers to create and customize files in existing SharePoint sites. This is not an issue within ASP.NET 2.0 sites because end users cannot easily open ASPX pages within a production site and randomly change the source of the files. However, users with appropriate permissions can do this within SharePoint, so Microsoft needed to add a control capability that enables administrators to restrict what end users can and cannot do.

For instance, consider an information worker within an organization who picked up a C# book for beginners. The last thing that site owners — and, more important, administrators — want to allow is for this person to add some custom inline code using the `<script runat="server">` tag within an existing site. If this were permitted, then there would be no way to control what managed code was being executed within an environment, thus greatly increasing the attack surface area.

To address this, the SharePoint team included a safe mode parser in ASP.NET. All customized pages are routed through the safe more parser that prohibits inline code within customized files. In addition, the safe mode parser disallows adding controls to pages that have not been flagged as safe.

Types of Pages

While SharePoint is built on top of ASP.NET 2.0, it has a unique concept of two types of pages: *site pages* and *application pages*. Both types of pages have unique characteristics and exist in every SharePoint site. As a SharePoint developer, you should have a strong grasp of the two, where they are used, and what can and cannot be done with each.

Site Pages

Site pages are those types of pages that support customization or personalization, and thus can be themed and host Web Parts. These are the most common types of pages end users see in a SharePoint site. These are also the types of pages that developers and designers can modify and edit within SharePoint Designer, because they are virtualized within the site's logical architecture and live within the site collection's content database either as customized or uncustomized pages.

As far as security goes, site pages should never contain inline script. While inline script will compile and execute just fine when a page is uncustomized, after the page becomes customized it is passed through SharePoint's safe mode parser, which will throw a runtime exception if the page contains inline script. A site page may or may not become customized, but the mere fact that it is possible should be reason enough to avoid using inline script.

Note also that site pages typically use whichever master page their parent site has been configured to use.

Application Pages

All application pages live within the `_layouts` virtual directory that exists within each SharePoint site. Applications pages, unlike site pages, cannot be customized or personalized, as these files do not live within a site's content database. This explains why the `_layouts` virtual directory is not seen within SharePoint Designer. All applications pages are shared and are available across all SharePoint sites living on the same server. However, each page may hide some links via security trimming, as each page runs within the context of a specific site.

Unlike site pages, all application pages leverage the same master page, `application.master`. Because they all use the same master page, this means that all applications across all sites on a server have the same user interface. SharePoint *themes* are the only supported customization technique for implementing a different look and feel on application pages across different SharePoint sites on the same server. Themes provide a way for developers and designers to customize the look and feel of a SharePoint site using CSS and images.

A common example of an application page is the Site Settings page that exists for all sites. As a developer, when creating custom application pages (described in Chapter 14, "Authoring Experience Extensibility," which covers extending the OOTB authoring experience), the custom pages should inherit from `Microsoft.SharePoint.WebControls.LayoutsPageBase`.

Uncustomized Versus Customized Files

So far, this chapter has alluded to the customization of uncustomized files a few times. Now it is time for a deeper explanation of the topic, as it is a recurring point of discussion throughout this book. SharePoint developers should be intimately familiar with the difference between these two file types. Unfortunately, most developers don't realize there is actually a difference, or the implications of that difference, until they have progressed quite far into their project. Although a project is not stuck with the approach originally taken, moving from one implementation to the other can become quite a daunting and time-intensive task.

When a new SharePoint site is provisioned, either when it is created as the top-level site within a new site collection or as a subsite within an existing site collection, most files start off in an uncustomized state. This means that while the file lives within the logical structure of a SharePoint site and is seen from within SharePoint Designer (and thus, is in the content database), the entry in the content database simply points to the file it is based off of on the file system. This file is sometimes referred to as a *template file* or *file definition* because by itself it is not very usable. However, when creating a new file based on it within a SharePoint site, also referred to as *provisioning* the file, the file now acts as the source to the one within the content database. The file remains in an uncustomized state as long as its source is not modified using SharePoint Designer. Operations such as adding Web Parts using the browser interface do not affect the customization state of the page.

There are a few different ways in which a file can become customized. The most common way to customize a file is to open it in SharePoint Designer, make any changes, and then save the file. When someone saves a file in SharePoint Designer, the source of the updated file is saved to the content database. Subsequent requests for the file result in the `SPVirtualPathProvider` (SharePoint's custom virtual path provider) retrieving the source of the file from the content database, rather than the file system. Once a file is customized, users with appropriate rights can undo the customization and perform what is referred to in the browser and SharePoint Designer user experience as "reset to site definition." This deletes the customized version of the file and causes the file to be served from the file system again.

Another type of customized file is one that starts initially as customized, rather than being provisioned from a template on the file system. This can be done by creating a new file in SharePoint Designer and saving it to a site, creating a new page within the site's browser interface or through the SharePoint API, as shown in Listing 2-1. These types of pages cannot be reverted back to a site definition or the underlying template file, because they were never based off one.

Listing 2-1: Creating a customized page in a SharePoint site using the SharePoint API

```csharp
using System;
using System.IO;
using Microsoft.SharePoint;

namespace Listing2_a {
  class Program {
    static void Main (string[] args) {

      using (SPSite siteCollection = new SPSite("http://wss")) {
        using (SPWeb site = siteCollection.RootWeb) {
          MemoryStream fileStream = new MemoryStream();
          StreamWriter fileWriter = new StreamWriter(fileStream);

          // write the source of the page (include meta:progid so SharePoint
Designer understands this file
          fileWriter.WriteLine("<%@ Page
MasterPageFile=\"~masterurl/default.master\"
meta:progid=\"SharePoint.WebPartPage.Document\" %>");
          fileWriter.WriteLine("<asp:Content runat=\"server\"
ContentPlaceHolderID=\"PlaceHolderMain\">");
          fileWriter.WriteLine("<h1>WROX</h1>");
          fileWriter.WriteLine("</asp:Content>");
          fileWriter.Flush();

          // save the file to SharePoint
          site.Files.Add("ApiGeneratedPage.aspx", fileStream);

          // cleanup
          fileWriter.Close();
          fileWriter.Dispose();
          fileStream.Close();
          fileStream.Dispose();
        } // SPWeb using statement
      } // SPSite using statement

    } // method "Main"
  }
}
```

Developers can programmatically check whether a file is customized or uncustomized using the `Microsoft.SharePoint.SPFile.SPCustomizedPageStatus` property and reset the file back to an uncustomized state using the `Microsoft.SharePoint.SPFile.RevertContentStream()` method. Listing 2-2 demonstrates the use of this property and method.

Listing 2-2: Checking the customization status of a file, removing any customization, and reverting it back to the template file

```
using System;
using Microsoft.SharePoint;

namespace Listing2_b {
  class Program {
    static void Main (string[] args) {

      using (SPSite siteCollection = new SPSite("http://wss")) {
        using (SPWeb site = siteCollection.RootWeb) {

          SPFile file = site.GetFile("default.aspx");

          // if file is customized, revert to underlying template file
          if (file.CustomizedPageStatus == SPCustomizedPageStatus.Customized)
            file.RevertContentStream();

        } // SPWeb using statement
      } // SPSite using statement

    } // method "Main"
  }
}
```

What bearing does the customization status of a file have on a Publishing site? Consider SharePoint site customization compared to development.

Customization versus Development

With an understanding of what it means when a file within a SharePoint site is uncustomized or customized, let's take a look at how that affects the development of a SharePoint site — specifically, a Publishing site. Whereas many traditional SharePoint sites are used primarily for collaboration and are inward facing (only company employees see and use them), publicly facing sites, which are what Publishing sites are primarily intended to be used for, typically are created within a controlled development environment, within which files are moved around for internal testing, quality assurance and user acceptance testing, and staging, before being put into production.

SharePoint Customization

As previously covered, when files are customized, they exist within the SharePoint site's content database. While some may have originally been based on an underlying template, the source of the customized file still lives within the database. Files living within the database present a challenge in promoting them through the different environments. How can this occur within a site comprised simply of customized files? While not impossible, it is a bit tedious to achieve. Consider the following options:

❑ One option would be to simply recreate the files in each environment manually, obviously a less than ideal approach.

❑ Another option would be to backup the content database from the development environment and restore it into production. This method is not recommended. It may be acceptable when a site is first launched, but it is not very viable over time, as future updates would overwrite published content on the production site.

❑ The development team could also leverage the Publishing site capability of content deployment, which packages entire site collections (or, optionally, sites within a site collection) for deployment to a destination server that is either connected or disconnected. Similar to the previous option, using content deployment in this manner is only an option for the initial rollout of a site because it is designed for deployment to a read-only destination server. Errors could (and likely would) potentially occur if the destination site has changed since the last content deployment job, which is almost guaranteed to be the case because content will likely have been added or updated on the destination site. Chapter 17 provides a detailed look at content deployment.

❑ A fourth option is to write custom code or scripts that would automate the deployment of files within the development environment to the target environment. While a viable option, this produces custom code that must be maintained and well written to handle any exceptions that might arise.

The customization approach of creating a Publishing site has associated baggage. Many of these points are mitigated when developers make UI changes to files directly to the production environment using tools such as SharePoint Designer. However, many larger organizations do not allow developers and designers write access to a production environment.

SharePoint Development

Another approach to developing Publishing sites, or any SharePoint site for that matter, is to avoid customizing any files and strive to have as many files as possible (if not all) exist within a Publishing site in an uncustomized state. This approach involves working at a much lower level, the file system level, compared to site customization done directly at the site level.

In order to keep files within a SharePoint site uncustomized, they must be created as physical files on the file system. The challenge here is that developers have no rich preview experience of the changes, which SharePoint Designer provides. After files have been created, how are they added to the SharePoint sites? The answer lies within the SharePoint Feature framework. One of the schemas provided in Feature element's manifest files is the `<Module>` and its associated `<File>` element. Using this schema, developers can provision files into SharePoint based off file templates that exist within the Feature.

This approach has added benefits that some developers may already be wondering about. One of the most significant benefits is that it works well with those development teams that have a prescribed process for all projects. This process is generally known as a Software Development Lifecycle (SDL), which involves tasks such as real testing, and, more important, incorporating everything into some sort of a source control management (SCM) system such as Microsoft's Visual Studio Team Foundation Server or the open-source SubVersion solution. When customizing files with SharePoint Designer in a

Publishing site, developers are required to check files in and out, and publish and approve changes to files. Each of these steps permits users to specify comments on each check-in and approval. However, this is not true source control; this is version control.

Source control includes things such as atomic commits of multiple files as a single action, branching multiple lines of parallel development, and tagging/labeling/naming to indicate that the main line of development (commonly referred to as the *trunk*) has reached a certain milestone (usually a release). Unfortunately, SCM solutions do not integrate well with SharePoint without a lot of custom development. However, in a site created using the SharePoint development approach, the files live on the file system, which is exactly what virtually all SCM solutions understand and support.

Another thing to understand is that SharePoint development doesn't only apply to files such as master pages and ASPX files. It also applies to SharePoint-specific topics such as site columns, content types, list templates, and workflows. Each of the topics covered in this book addresses the issue of SharePoint site customization versus development. This provides developers with all the information necessary to evaluate both approaches.

Please keep one thing in mind: While this book presents both approaches (customization and development), it neither passes judgment on either approach nor concludes that one approach is better or worse than the other. The goal is simply to educate SharePoint developers regarding all aspects of site customization versus site development. One approach may be more familiar and preferred to some developers, while the other approach is favored by others. The approach selected depends on the scope of the project as well as the development team and process.

Introducing the Microsoft.SharePoint Namespace

Thankfully, Microsoft shipped a very extensive and robust API that enables developers to write custom code solutions to add, extend, and change functionality, as well as manage SharePoint. Keep in mind that the SharePoint API is the only supported way to access data within SharePoint. Never go directly to the SQL Server databases to make changes or select data — always use the SharePoint API. In addition, the SharePoint API is how the provided tools and interfaces interact with SharePoint, including the browser-based interface, the included Web services, and the command-line utility STSADM.EXE. Not only did Microsoft use the SharePoint API that ships with WSS 3.0 and MOSS 2007 for all the included administration interfaces, but there are additional things that the admin interfaces do not expose that developers can implement using the SharePoint API.

The core of the SharePoint API is the Microsoft.SharePoint namespace, which is found in the Microsoft.SharePoint.dll assembly located in [..]\12\ISAPI. All developer projects created in Visual Studio need to contain a reference to this assembly, as all other SharePoint assemblies are dependent upon the core Microsoft.SharePoint.dll assembly.

This chapter has already touched on some of the more important and common classes within the Microsoft.SharePoint namespace, such as SPSite for site collections and SPWeb for SharePoint sites. Additional classes found in the root of the Microsoft.SharePoint namespace include SPList for lists, SPListItem for items within lists, SPDocumentLibrary for documents within document libraries,

`SPQuery` for creating queries using Collaborative Markup Language (CAML), as well as `SPGroup` and `SPUser` for SharePoint groups and users, respectively.

Debugging in WSS 3.0

One of the biggest differences between ASP.NET 2.0 development and SharePoint development is the debugging experience. When developing an ASP.NET 2.0 application, Visual Studio dramatically simplifies the debugging experience. Intuitive and straightforward, developers need only press the F5 key to automatically build the project and attach the debugger to the process hosting the ASP.NET 2.0 application. Unfortunately, the default experience in Visual Studio is not the same when developing SharePoint applications.

Visual Studio contains no special hooks into a SharePoint site. Thus, pressing F5 will result in an error because the application must be running within the process hosting the SharePoint application (the IIS application pool). The only time this isn't the case is when developing console or Windows Forms applications because they run within their own process.

So, how do developers debug assemblies designed to run within a SharePoint process, such as those containing Web Parts, custom field types and controls, event receivers, and workflows? The answer is to manually attach the debugger to the process hosting the application pool configured with the Web application that contains the target SharePoint site. The difference between this process and F5 debugging is that the developer has to perform the steps of attaching the debugger to the process manually; whereas with traditional ASP.NET 2.0 applications, pressing F5 performs the steps for the developer automatically, similar to a macro.

To manually attach the debugger, first build and deploy the custom assembly that will be debugged. Next, within Visual Studio, select Debug, and then Attach to Process. In the Attach to Process dialog, select the `w3wp.exe` process that is hosting the application pool and the Web application hosting the target SharePoint site that contains the assembly to be debugged and click Attach.

If multiple `w3wp.exe` processes are running, the developer can attach to all of them. Use the identity the application pool is running as in the User Name column or enter the following command at the command line to view a list of all the running `w3wp.exe` processes, their respective process IDs (PIDs), and the name of the application pool they are hosting (use the PID to find the process to attach to):

```
cscript.exe %windir%\system32\iisapp.vbs
```

Debugging assemblies deployed to the Global Assembly Cache (GAC) is a bit more challenging and requires some additional work. Before attaching the debugger to the application pool process, the debugger symbols (`*.PDB` files) must be copied to a specific directory. To find the directory, select Start ⇨ Run and enter the following:

```
%systemroot%\Assembly\GAC
```

Next, open the directory with the same name of the assembly that contains the code to be debugged and then select the subdirectory that is named in the following format: `[AssemblyVersion]__[AssemblyPublicKeyToken]`. Copy the debugger symbols into that directory. Now the debugger can be manually attached to the appropriate `w3wp.exe` process.

Summary

This chapter provided a high-level overview of WSS 3.0 from the perspective of a developer. One of the most important points to take away from this chapter is the difference between uncustomized and customized files, as well as SharePoint customization compared to SharePoint development. This chapter also compared common ASP.NET 2.0 development topics to SharePoint development topics. Although this chapter provided only an overview of WSS 3.0, as it is a very large topic that warrants a book of its own, developers creating MOSS Publishing sites must have a good grasp of the fundamental concepts covered in this chapter, as they are pervasive throughout the complete SharePoint product stack, including Publishing sites.

Overview of Web Content Management in Microsoft Office SharePoint Server 2007

The previous chapter explained how core Windows SharePoint Services (WSS) concepts embrace and extend ASP.NET to provide the platform foundation upon which Office SharePoint Server (MOSS) solutions, including Web Content Management (WCM), are built. This chapter explores the additional functionality offered by MOSS, including aspects that are critical to a successful WCM implementation.

Before looking at MOSS itself it is worth briefly considering the Microsoft precursors to MOSS WCM, the lessons learned, which were applied to this release, the rationale for building WCM on the SharePoint platform, and the considerable opportunities offered by such rich integration.

This chapter begins by looking at the different features and editions of MOSS and then drills down into WCM-specific features. The WCM experience is demonstrated from the perspective of both the author and the end user. Also covered are the ABCs of publishing. In addition, the Shared Services Provider (SSP), a critical element of any Publishing site, is described. Finally, the chapter concludes with a brief tour of the `Microsoft.SharePoint.Publishing` namespace, covering the fundamental objects with examples of common uses within Publishing sites.

Web Content Management on the Microsoft Platform

Prior to MOSS, Microsoft had separate, distinct offerings for WCM, portal content aggregation, and search. The WCM offering came in the form of Content Management Server 2002 (MCMS). MCMS provided traditional WCM functionality such as a templated page model, in-context content authoring, and dynamic runtime compilation. MCMS provided a .NET-accessible Publishing API and ASP.NET integration, which enabled developers to build solutions on this framework. While certainly a successful product in its own right, the architecture of MCMS was very different from SharePoint and often constrained solutions development. Many organizations felt they had to choose between the previous versions of SharePoint and MCMS when embarking on a Web site project, and many chose to implement both with loose integration between them. Possibly the most common example of such integration was that of a WSS document library being used for document collaboration and versioning "inside the firewall," with the result made accessible via the public Web site hosted on MCMS. Unfortunately, there were core architectural differences between SharePoint and MCMS.

For example, MCMS did not embrace Internet Information Server 6.0's (IIS) worker process isolation mode and did not expose its security API to developers. Various SharePoint integration scenarios were provided for by an add-on connector ("Spark"), but it was clear that this bolt-on to bridge the architecture gap would not scale to meet growing customer demand for deep and rich SharePoint integration.

Very much a toolkit with a blank canvas, MCMS provided a rich framework but at the same time required a significant amount of repetitive custom code to achieve core WCM functionality such as site navigation and content aggregation. While MCMS Service Pack 2 provided some support for ASP.NET 2.0 enhancements such as master pages, navigation, and authentication providers, it was not uncommon for such standard elements to be reimplemented for each individual Web site project. Freeing MCMS developers from these costly, routine, and ineffective tasks was a main goal moving forward.

Key functional elements missing from MCMS, such as an integrated search capability, flexible authentication mechanisms, and security APIs, also increased development time, cost, and support of solutions.

Each of the these issues, along with a long list of common customer pain points, drove Microsoft to consider leveraging SharePoint as the underlying platform of its next WCM offering. Following several months of assessment, it was decided to build the next generation of MCMS upon the WSS 3.0 platform as part of MOSS 2007.

Microsoft Office SharePoint Server

MOSS 2007 builds on the WSS 3.0 platform to offer six additional broad areas of functionality. As shown in Figure 3-1, WSS provides the center circle of platform services and the collaboration slice. The additional portal, search, content management, business forms, and business intelligence slices are provided by MOSS.

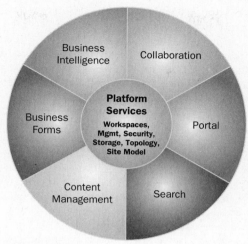

Figure 3-1

MOSS is available in three flavors, or SKUs. MOSS Standard Edition includes collaboration, portal, search, and content management. MOSS Enterprise Edition adds business forms and business intelligence. In addition, there is a MOSS for Internet Sites Edition, which featurewise is identical to Enterprise but is licensed for the hosting of applications deployed to the Internet.

> *More information on MOSS licensing and which edition is appropriate can be found at* www.andrewconnell.com/go/207 *and* www.andrewconnell.com/go/208.

In brief, the key feature areas of MOSS include the following:

❏ **Collaboration** — Document libraries/tasks/calendars, blogs, wikis, e-mail integration, project management "lite," Office Outlook 2007 integration, offline documents, and lists.

❏ **Portal** — Enterprise portal template, site directory, my sites, social networking, and privacy control.

❏ **Search** — Enterprise scalability, contextual relevance, rich people and business data search.

❏ **Content Management** — Integrated document management, records management, WCM with policies and workflow.

❏ **Business Forms** — Rich and Web-forms-based front ends, line of business (LOB) actions, pluggable single sign-on (SSO).

❏ **Business Intelligence** — Server-based Office Excel 2007 spreadsheets and data visualization, report center, BI Web Parts, key performance indicators (KPIs)/dashboards.

Building WCM on top of WSS as part of MOSS means that the WCM feature set is concentrated on its core functionality, rather than infrastructure plumbing such as check in/check out, storage, security, backup/restore, and so on. In addition, WCM can take advantage of advances in the WSS platform, such as pluggable authentication and workflow. As a result of being freed from this infrastructure plumbing,

WCM has also delivered advanced functionality such as variations, which enable content to be published to multilingual sites for translation.

Overall, MOSS provides an incredible breadth of functionality across popular business scenarios. WCM is simply one part of the content management feature set. The Collaboration Portal site template, primarily intended for an enterprise or departmental portal "within the firewall," utilizes key WCM features such as page layouts, field controls, document libraries, the page editing toolbar, versioning, and workflow. In other words, WCM brings to MOSS some fundamental core features that greatly enhance solutions within the portal space. Other examples of features brought to MOSS by WCM include content deployment and advanced caching. By taking this approach, Microsoft has been able to leverage WCM features to enable rich portal scenarios.

At its core, a Publishing site is just another SharePoint site, and as such it can integrate with the other features with little or no code. Integrating a search capability previously required the purchase of an additional product and significant custom integration code. With MOSS, a Publishing site essentially has an extremely powerful and scalable search capability for free. Other examples include the capability to richly target content to groups of users based upon profile information by leveraging audiences. MOSS is also capable of integrating with external LOB data through the Business Data Catalog (BDC). Due to the rich ASP.NET extensibility capabilities in MOSS, it is also possible to integrate with external systems such as Microsoft Commerce Server, which is used to provide rich end-to-end WCM, including common Internet scenarios such as e-commerce. This capability is one of the core assets of a MOSS-based WCM solution, providing an extremely broad canvas for building integration solutions while reducing significantly the amount of custom code required to do so.

The ABCs of Web Content Management

MOSS follows a traditional approach to the management of Web content by removing the IT bottleneck, enabling content authors and owners to take control of the contribution, approval, and publishing of content. MOSS provides a pipeline that is capable of managing complex interactions among contributors, enforcing business rules, applying branding and content reuse, and aggregation. Microsoft refers to this process as the ABCs of WCM, which neatly encapsulates the core WCM feature set in MOSS.

Authoring

Authoring is the process of content authors contributing content to a Publishing site. MOSS offers a DHTML-based authoring environment that provides an in-context view of a Web page, including field controls, where different types of content can be provided. These field controls include support for rich HTML editing, images, attachments, and metadata. Even though the author can see and edit the metadata while in Edit mode, the metadata is not displayed to the end user. In addition, the Web browser interface includes a Page Editing Toolbar that enables users to perform common operations such as check in or check out, spell check, and workflow management. Field controls are covered in depth in Chapter 10. The Page Editing Toolbar is covered in depth in Chapter 14.

Reusable content provides the capability to store HTML content snippets for reuse across a site collection. Examples of reusable content include copyright notices, legal disclaimers, and unmanaged hyperlinks.

An alternative to the Web browser–based environment, MOSS allows content authoring from rich clients such as Office Word 2007 and Office InfoPath 2007. This enables content authors to stay within their familiar Office clients while still interacting with MOSS. Rich client authoring is covered in depth in Chapter 14.

In addition, MOSS provides the capability to author content offline via the use of *document converters*, which enable format translation from, for example, a Microsoft Word 2007 document (`*.docx`) to HTML. Document converters are covered in depth in Chapter 18.

MOSS also provides a number of Web Parts, which are also useful within Publishing sites. One example is the Content Query Web Part, which supports content aggregation or "roll-up" within a site collection. The Content Query Web Part can be customized extensively to display various types of data. Web Parts are covered in depth in Chapter 11.

Branding

Branding is the process of applying a consistent look and feel to a Publishing site, including navigation and common content. A fundamental principle of WCM systems is the delivery of a lot of content using only a few templates. MOSS leverages WSS's support for ASP.NET master pages and combines them with page layouts at runtime to assemble the HTML output.

The master page is responsible for providing a common look and feel, including the placement of navigational elements. A page layout can be thought of as a content template that controls how specific types of content are displayed. Master pages and page layouts are developed in a rich editor such as Office SharePoint Designer 2007 or Visual Studio, which provides rich client Web editing. When content authors create a new page, they select an available page layout and then enter the content using a Web browser. This enables content authors to focus on the content, without worrying about styling, layout, or any shared common elements. Master pages and page layouts are covered in depth in Chapter 7.

Controlled Publishing

Controlled publishing is the process of managing the content life cycle. Contributed content in MOSS is simply items in a SharePoint list or document library. Each of these items can therefore utilize features that control the life cycle of content. Examples include check in and check out, versioning, moderation, and workflows.

MOSS provides approval and review workflows that can be configured to meet the vast majority of WCM content approval scenarios. If this pre-fab workflow does not suit the project's needs, custom workflows can be created. Workflow tasks appear within a configured task list within the site. Workflow is covered in depth in Chapter 12.

Contributed hyperlinks to other SharePoint content are managed hyperlinks within MOSS. Should content be moved, all hyperlinks to it are automatically updated within other content or common elements such as navigational controls. Navigation can also be manually configured or tweaked within Site Settings to change the order of items or to include links external to MOSS within the main navigation.

Content scheduling provides the capability to configure content to "go live" and expire at specified dates and times. MOSS also offers a site management tool that provides a 10,000' view, or holistic view, of a site collection. This enables content to be bulk edited or moved around within the hierarchy.

Content deployment provides a capability to control the release into a production environment from a staging environment. This is most often useful in a classic deployment scenario in which there are separate authoring and read-only production environments. Content deployment is covered in depth in Chapter 17.

Variations also play a role within controlled publishing, providing a framework for multiple versions of the same content. Common examples here include multiple branding, multiple languages, or multiple devices. In the case of multiple languages, the framework provides support for content exclusion or a different page layout per variation. Workflows and variations can be combined to fire off human- or software-based translation. Variations are covered in depth in Chapter 16.

Publishing Sites

At its core, a MOSS Publishing site is simply a SharePoint site that has had the Publishing Features activated. The Publishing Features are scoped at the site collection level; and when these Features are provisioned, a number of pre-defined elements such as the Pages list are added to the site. Once these features are enabled, it is possible to create new Publishing pages within the site for the purposes of WCM. MOSS provides a Publishing site template geared toward WCM scenarios, such as the Publishing Portal, as a starting point for exploring the WCM capability. The Publishing Portal includes a home page, a News section with some sample content, and pointers to common configuration steps necessary in a WCM scenario. Figure 3-2 shows the Publishing Portal in Presentation mode, the view experienced by read-only site visitors.

Figure 3-2

The same page in Edit mode as experienced by content authors is shown in Figure 3-3.

Figure 3-3

Figure 3-4 shows the Web design view of a page layout within Office SharePoint Designer 2007.

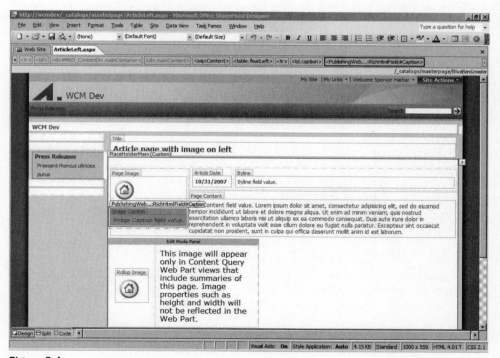

Figure 3-4

The following table provides a brief overview of each key element within a Publishing site:

Element	Description
Publishing Page	An item stored within the Pages List that contains the page content and metadata.
Publishing Site	A WSS site with the Publishing Features activated.
Content Type	The definition of the page's content and metadata. Think of this as the definition of a page template.
Master Page	An ASP.NET master page, including various SharePoint and WCM-specific controls.
Page Layout	An ASP.NET page, including field controls and Web Parts, that provides the template for content pages.
Field Controls	Provides a design time and author time experience for the content elements of a page.
Master Page Gallery	Stores master pages and page layouts.
Image Library	Stores images for the site in a managed fashion.
Documents Library	Stores documents and other resources for the site in a managed fashion.

When a MOSS Publishing page is requested, the page layout associated with that page is looked up and retrieved. In turn, the associated master page is retrieved along with the content of each field control. The resultant composite of these elements is then assembled as HTML and returned to the end user.

Site Collections

As described in the previous chapter, site collections are the core content, security, and administration boundary in WSS. Site collection design and their possible partitioning is a key design decision in Publishing site projects. Many common tasks, such as applying a master page or functionality such as variations and the Content Query Web Part, cannot be used across site collections. In addition, common administrative functions such as caching configuration are applied at the site collection level, so it makes sense for each Publishing site to reside within a single site collection. Conceptually, a single Web site equals a single site collection. This is a key decision in the planning of a Publishing site. Generally, a single site collection should be used unless there are specific requirements for multiple site collections and the overhead of doing so is well understood.

Shared Services Providers

Every MOSS deployment, even if it is a single server deployment, must include at least one shared service provider (SSP). While complete coverage of SSPs is beyond this book's scope, it is critical to understand the role played by this required component.

For more information on shared services providers, please see Beginning SharePoint 2007 Administration *(Wrox, 2007) and* Office SharePoint Server 2007 Administrators Companion *(Microsoft Press, 2007).*

An SSP is itself a SharePoint Web application, primarily for administration purposes, alongside a non-SharePoint IIS virtual Web site called "Office Server," which hosts SSP-related Web services. In addition, there are several Microsoft SQL Server databases for configuration and data storage.

The SSP provides application services and data, which are shared by one or more SharePoint Web applications. These services and data are those which by nature are central and for which it does not make sense to deploy them individually on each Web application. Examples of such application services include search and indexing, user profiles, audiences, and session state.

Microsoft.SharePoint.Publishing Namespace

Before diving into building WCM solutions, it is good to have a broad view of the key Publishing APIs provided by the `Microsoft.SharePoint.Publishing` namespace.

The `Microsoft.SharePoint.Publishing` namespace provides the cores classes and can be thought of as the infrastructure plumbing for working within Publishing sites. Commonly used classes within this namespace are described in the following table:

Class	Description
`Microsoft.SharePoint.Publishing.PublishingSite`	Provides access to Publishing Features on a `SPSite` object.
`Microsoft.SharePoint.Publishing.PublishingWeb`	Provides access to Publishing Features on a `SPWeb` object — e.g., accessing the pages collection, accessing other objects in the hierarchy, or executing queries directly.
`Microsoft.SharePoint.Publishing.PublishingPage`	Provides access to Publishing Features on a `SPListItem` object. A page is an extended `SPList` object.

The code in Listing 3-1 demonstrates how to enumerate a list of sites in the current site collection within a Web control.

Listing 3-1: Enumerating Publishing sites

```
using System;
using System.ComponentModel;
using System.Web;
using System.Web.UI;
using System.Web.UI.WebControls;
using Microsoft.SharePoint;
using Microsoft.SharePoint.Publishing;

namespace EnumerateSites {
  public class EnumerateSitesInSiteCollection : WebControl {

    protected void ListWebs (PublishingWeb pubWeb, HtmlTextWriter output) {
        output.Write(string.Format("<A href=\"{0}\">{1}</A>", pubWeb.Url,
pubWeb.Title));
        foreach (PublishingWeb childPubWeb in pubWeb.GetPublishingWebs()) {
          ListWebs(childPubWeb, output);
        }
    }

    protected override void RenderContents (HtmlTextWriter output) {
        using (SPSite site = SPContext.Current.Site) {
          output.Write("<H1>Sites in Site Collection</H1><BR>");
          foreach (SPWeb site in site.AllWebs) {
            if (PublishingWeb.IsPublishingWeb(site)) {
              PublishingWeb publishingWeb = PublishingWeb.GetPublishingWeb(site);
              ListWebs(publishingWeb, output);
            }
          }
        }
    }
  }
}
```

The code in Listing 3-2 demonstrates how to create a new Publishing site.

Listing 3-2: Creating Publishing sites

```
using (SPWeb web = SPControl.GetContextWeb(Context)) {
  PublishingWeb pubWeb = PublishingWeb.GetPublishingWeb(web);
  PublishingWeb newWeb = pubWeb.GetPublishingWebs().Add("SiteName");
  newWeb.Title = "Display Name";
  newWeb.Description = "Description of Site";
  newWeb.Update();
}
```

Listing 3-3 demonstrates how to create a new Publishing page.

Listing 3-3: Creating Publishing pages

```
using (SPWeb web = SPControl.GetContextWeb(HttpContext.Current)) {
  PublishingWeb pubWeb = PublishingWeb.GetPublishingWeb(web);
  PageLayout layout = null;
  SPContentTypeId contentType = new SPContentTypeId();
  PageLayout[] layouts = pubWeb.GetAvailablePageLayouts(contentType);
  if (layouts != null && layouts.Length > 0) {
    layout = layouts[0];
    PublishingPage newPage;
    newPage = pubWeb.GetPublishingPages().Add("SiteName", layout);
    newPage.Description = "Description of site";
    newPage.ListItem["Page Content"] = " Sample Content Here";
    newPage.Update();
  }
}
```

The code in Listing 3-4 demonstrates how to set page properties and publish a page.

Listing 3-4: Setting properties and publishing pages

```
publishingPage = PublishingPage.GetPublishingPage(listItem);
if (publishingPage.ListItem.File.CheckOutStatus == SPFile.SPCheckOutStatus.None) {
  publishingPage.CheckOut();
}

publishingPage.Title = "Title";
publishingPage.Description = "Description";
publishingPage.Update();

publishingPage.CheckIn("Comments");
SPFile pageFile = publishingPage.ListItem.File;
pageFile.Publish(checkInComment);
pageFile.Approve(checkInComment);
```

Summary

This chapter has covered the core elements of WCM in MOSS, including the rationale and benefits of building upon the WSS platform. As a part of MOSS, WCM solutions are capable of leveraging powerful integration with other elements, such as search and the Business Data Catalog. In addition, WCM brings to MOSS portals powerful Web content features and capabilities. MOSS WCM provides the core capabilities, authoring, branding, and controlled publishing upon which Publishing sites can be developed.

SharePoint Features and the Solution Framework

4

In the second generation of SharePoint, Windows SharePoint Services 2.0 (WSS), Microsoft provided many different opportunities for developers to customize sites as well as augment sites using custom code. These various points of integration provided developers with many opportunities, but seasoned SharePoint developers became familiar with a few pain points with the second generation of SharePoint. These included issues such as promoting code reuse, incorporating new functionality or changes in existing sites, empowering site owners to add/ remove this functionally without developer involvement, and deploying (as well as updating) custom code and files.

Thankfully, in the latest SharePoint release, WSS 3.0, Microsoft addresses these issues in two ways: Features and solutions. Features facilitate much more code reuse and provide developers with an easy way to not only introduce new and updated components and functionality into existing SharePoint sites, but also to empower site owners and administrators to implement it without developer involvement. The solution framework provides developers and administrators with a way to easily deploy custom code and files throughout a SharePoint implementation, including a SharePoint farm containing multiple servers such as load-balanced Web front-end (WFE) servers. This chapter explores the details of the Feature and solution frameworks, and provides some guidance on how to best create Features and WSS solution packages.

Overview of SharePoint Features

Microsoft introduced the concept of Features in WSS 3.0 to address numerous challenges presented in the previous version, as well as to provide additional functionality. The previous version of SharePoint, WSS 2.0, did not provide an easy way to define a site element such as a list template one time and reference it from multiple site templates. Instead, the list template definition had to be copied to each and every site template where it was used. This does not adhere to good code reuse practices and increases the possibility of the same template getting out of sync.

Another challenge with WSS 2.0 was adding new elements or functionality to sites already created. WSS 2.0 did not offer an easy way to incorporate new functionality into existing sites; developers were forced to craft a custom process such as a script that would add a new list template to each individual site in WSS 2.0.

The cases presented here are just two examples illustrating why Microsoft added the Feature framework to WSS 3.0. In addition to addressing WSS 2.0 challenges, Microsoft also added capabilities to the Feature framework to deploy certain custom code solutions such as event receivers, document converters, and custom workflow templates. This chapter covers the basics of SharePoint Features, although it does not include an exhaustive analysis of all the things Features can do because Features are everywhere in SharePoint and are covered throughout the book. For example, the deployment of custom workflow templates created using Visual Studio is performed using Features. The same is true for provisioning instances of file templates on the file system such as master pages and page layouts. Therefore, each chapter in the book covers a specific capability of SharePoint Features as necessary.

Once a Feature has been created, it then needs to be activated. The activation of a Feature is dependent upon the defined scope of the Feature (Feature scope is covered later in the chapter). When a Feature is activated, SharePoint performs the work defined within the Feature. This activation and deactivation of a Feature provides developers and site administrators with the capability to toggle functionality on or off with ease via the browser interface.

Anatomy of a Feature

All SharePoint Features live in a special folder within the SharePoint 12 folder — specifically, in `[..]\12\TEMPLATE\FEATURES`. The `FEATURES` folder contains folders for each Feature that has been deployed to the server. After a clean Office SharePoint Server (MOSS) 2007 installation, the `FEATURES` folder will contain more than 130 folders, each signifying a Feature that is part of the out-of-the-box (OOTB) MOSS 2007 installation. This is where developers create and/or deploy custom Features.

To create a new Feature, create a new folder in the `FEATURES` folder such as `MyFirstFeature`. Every Feature must have a definition file containing all the information that SharePoint needs to know about the Feature. This definition file is simply an XML file that is given the name `feature.xml`. The Feature definition file contains information such as a unique identifier for the Feature, a title, a description, and the scope and visibility of the Feature. The following Collaborative Application Markup Language (CAML) contains what is quite possibly the simplest Feature definition, with the minimal information:

```xml
<?xml version="1.0" encoding="utf-8"?>
<Feature xmlns="http://schemas.microsoft.com/sharepoint/"
         Id="32DECDEF-C37C-4AC3-BA65-D49639668E7C"
         Title="My First Feature"
         Description="The simplest Feature ever."
         Hidden="FALSE"
         Scope="Web">
</Feature>
```

Once the definition has been created and saved into a new folder within the `FEATURES` folder, SharePoint must then be made aware of the Feature. This is done by installing the Feature using `STSADM.EXE` and the `installfeature` operation:

```
stsadm.exe -o installfeature -name MyFirstFeature
```

After SharePoint is made aware of the Feature, it can then be activated. In the case of `MyFirstFeature`, activation can occur at the site level as defined by the scope of the Feature (`Scope=Web`). To activate `MyFirstFeature`, browse to any SharePoint site and select Site Actions ⇨ Site Settings and then select Site Features under the Site Administration section to load the Site Features administration page. The Feature should appear in the list as the title defined in the `feature.xml` file, My First Feature, with an Activate button to the right. Click the Activate button to activate the Feature. Because this simple Feature does not do anything important, nothing happens when the page refreshes from the postback. Notice, though, that the page indicates that the Feature is now active, and the button has changed to Deactivate.

As demonstrated, the `MyFirstFeature` Feature does not do anything upon activation. In order for a Feature to do something, it must contain one of two things: element manifests and/or a Feature receiver. Before taking a look at element manifests and Feature receivers, it is important to understand the concept of Feature scope.

Feature Scope

A very important aspect of Features is the concept of Feature scope. A Feature's scope enables developers to quantify how broad the effects of activating the Feature are. If a Feature is scoped at the site level, then the activation affects only the SharePoint site it is activated within. However, if it is scoped at a site collection level, then the activation affects all sites within the site collection.

For example, a project may require adding a new menu item to the Site Actions menu for a particular site. A developer can create a Feature that uses the `<CustomAction>` element type and set the scope to `Web` (SharePoint site). However, if the menu item needs to be visible on all Site Action menus in all sites within the site collection, then the scope can easily be changed to `Site` (site collection). To take it even further, suppose a company wanted to add a menu item to all Site Action menus for all SharePoint sites in the organization that displayed a privacy policy or emergency contact information. This could easily be done with a single Feature with a scope of `Farm`.

> *The scope options for SharePoint site and site collections seems to be a point of confusion for many developers new to the platform. An easy way to remember the difference is to think about the two within the context of the SharePoint API. Remember from Chapter 2 that a SharePoint site is represented by the* `SPWeb` *object, and a site collection is represented by* `SPSite`.

There are four different scope options for Features, listed in the following table:

Scope	Description
Web (SharePoint site)	Applies to a specific SharePoint site.
Site (site collection)	Applies to a SharePoint site collection and all SharePoint sites within the site collection.
WebApplication	Applies to a SharePoint extended Web application, all site collections within the Web application, and all sites within those site collections.
Farm	Applies to a SharePoint farm, all SharePoint extended Web applications, all site collections, and all SharePoint sites within the SharePoint farm.

Element Manifests

Element manifests, another type of XML file found in a Feature's folder, contains CAML that defines site elements. The SharePoint Feature schema contains many different types of site elements. As stated previously, this chapter does not include an exhaustive discussion about each and every component of the Feature schema because all of them are covered in more detail in respective chapters throughout the book. The following table contains a list of all the Feature element types, including the chapter in which a more in-depth discussion can be found, as well as the possible scoping options for each:

Element Type	Chapter	Scope: Web	Scope: Site	Scope: WebApplication	Scope: Farm
Content type and content type bindings	Ch. 6		X		
Custom actions	Ch. 8 and Ch. 14	X	X	X	X
Delegate controls	Ch. 7	X	X	X	X
Document converters	Ch. 18			X	
Event registrations	Ch. 6	X			
Feature site template associations (stapling)	Ch. 4		X	X	X
Field definitions (site columns)	Ch. 6		X		
List templates and instances	Ch. 6	X	X		
Modules	Ch. 7 and Ch. 11	X	X		
Workflow	Ch. 12		X		

Once an element manifest file has been created, it needs to be associated with the Feature. To do this, create a `<ElementManifests>` node that contains `<ElementManifest>` nodes containing a reference to the element manifest files in the Feature. The `<ElementManifests>` node is then added to the `<Feature>` node, as shown in Listing 4-1.

Listing 4-1: Feature definition file

```xml
<?xml version="1.0" encoding="utf-8"?>
<Feature xmlns="http://schemas.microsoft.com/sharepoint/"
        Id="32DECDEF-C37C-4ac3-BA65-D49639668E7C"
        Title="My First Feature"
        Description="The simplest Feature ever."
        Hidden="FALSE"
        Scope="Web">
    <ElementManifests>
      <ElementManifest Location="elements.xml"/>
    </ElementManifests>
</Feature>
```

For more information on the Feature schema, refer to the official documentation on MSDN (www.andrewconnell.com/go/209).

Feature Receivers

The Feature site elements contained in element manifest files provide developers with a significant amount of functionality, but what if they don't meet existing business needs? For example, what if, upon Feature activation, a project requires the creation of a child SharePoint site using a specific site template? Thankfully, Microsoft anticipated such as scenario and added the capability for developers to write event handlers for certain events within an assembly. The following table lists the four events exposed by Features that developers can take advantage of:

Event	Description
FeatureInstalled	Raised after a Feature has been installed
FeatureActivated	Raised after a Feature has been activated
FeatureDeactivating	Raised before a Feature is deactivated
FeatureUninstalling	Raised before a Feature is uninstalled

By using Feature receivers, developers can now achieve endless possibilities in the process of activating or deactivating a Feature. In addition, this provides a vehicle for developers to offer additional functionality to site owners, who can select — on a site-by-site basis or according to the specified scope of the Feature — what they want to add to or remove from their site.

The class that contains the event handlers developers create for Feature events is called a *Feature receiver*. In order to create a Feature receiver, developers must create a new class that inherits from `Microsoft.SharePoint.SPFeatureReceiver` and implements all four events. This class needs to be compiled into a signed assembly (to generate a strong name) and deployed by the assembly to the Global Assembly Cache (GAC). Listing 4-2 contains an example of a Feature receiver that changes the name of the current site with the current timestamp upon activation and sets the original name back upon deactivation using the site's property bag (`SPWeb.Properties`).

Listing 4-2: Using the FeatureActivated Feature receiver event

```
using System;
using Microsoft.SharePoint;

namespace WROX {
  public class MyFirstFeatureReceiver : SPFeatureReceiver {
    public override void FeatureActivated (
                        SPFeatureReceiverProperties properties) {
      SPWeb site = properties.Feature.Parent as SPWeb;

      // save current site's title
      site.Properties["SiteTitle"] = site.Title;
```

(continued)

Listing 4-2 *(continued)*

```
        site.Properties.Update();

        // change the site title
        site.Title = DateTime.Now.ToString();
        site.Update();
    }

    public override void FeatureDeactivating (
                        SPFeatureReceiverProperties properties) {
        SPWeb site = properties.Feature.Parent as SPWeb;

        // reset the site's title
        site.Title = site.Properties["SiteTitle"].ToString();
        site.Update();
    }

    public override void FeatureInstalled (
                        SPFeatureReceiverProperties properties) {
        // do nothing
    }
    public override void FeatureUninstalling (
                        SPFeatureReceiverProperties properties) {
        // do nothing
    }
  }
}
```

Once the assembly containing the Feature receiver has been compiled and deployed to the GAC, the Feature must be configured to call the event handlers in the Feature receiver class. To do this, add two new attributes to the <Feature> node in the feature.xml definition file: ReceiverAssembly, which contains the assembly's strong name (aka its four-part name) and the ReceiverClass, which contains a fully qualified name to the Feature receiver, as shown in Listing 4-3.

Listing 4-3: Feature definition with a Feature receiver

```
<?xml version="1.0" encoding="utf-8"?>
<Feature xmlns="http://schemas.microsoft.com/sharepoint/"
        Id="32DECDEF-C37C-4ac3-BA65-D49639668E7C"
        Title="My First Feature"
        Description="The simplest Feature ever."
        Hidden="FALSE"
        Scope="Web"
        ReceiverAssembly="MyFirstFeature, Version=1.0.0.0, Culture=neutral,
PublicKeyToken=c591e70cfdf9ce4f"
        ReceiverClass="WROX.MyFirstFeatureReceiver">
</Feature>
```

Feature Administration

In addition to Feature scope, developers and administrators should be aware of a few additional administrative aspects to Features. The first involves Feature installation and uninstallation. Features can only be installed by SharePoint administrators who have access to the SharePoint server console. This is because Features can only be installed in one of three ways: using STSADM.EXE, using WSS solution packages (covered later in the chapter), or via the SharePoint API. As previously covered, once the folders and files associated with a Feature have been copied to the necessary locations on the server, the STSADM.EXE operation installfeature is used to install the Feature. Conversely, the STSADM.EXE operation uninstallfeature is used to uninstall an installed Feature.

Unlike the installation and uninstallation of a Feature, activation and deactivation can occur either using STSADM.EXE or using the browser interface. If activating a Feature using STSADM.EXE, use the operation activatefeature:

```
stsadm.exe -o activatefeature -name myfirstfeature -url http://wss1
```

As shown in the preceding command-line operation, activatefeature accepts additional parameters such as -url. These are not always required; it depends on the scope of the Feature. The MyFirstFeature is scoped at the site level (scope=Web), so a specific site must be provided upon activating the Feature. Deactivation works the same way, using the operation deactivatefeature:

```
stsadm.exe -o deactivatefeature -name myfirstfeature -url http://wss1
```

Another capability at the disposal of SharePoint developers and administrators is the visibility of a Feature. Within the Feature definition file, feature.xml, the <Feature Hidden=""> attribute can be used to hide or show a Feature in the browser interface. By default, all Features are visible (Hidden=FALSE). When would a Feature need to be hidden? Consider a Feature that added functionality or a site element to a site collection; its activation state should not be delegated to site owners; instead, SharePoint farm administrators should be the ones required to activate or deactivate this special Feature for a site collection. Activation and deactivation for hidden Features must then be handled using STSADM.EXE exclusively.

> When creating a Feature that contains a Feature receiver performing certain tasks that require special permissions, consider making it a hidden Feature, thereby requiring activation via STSADM.EXE. Why? When a Feature is activated from the browser interface, the code is executed within the context of the configured identity of the application pool hosting the Web application containing the site collection. This identity may not have the necessary permissions, such as writing to the file system. However, when a Feature is activated using STSADM.EXE, the identity of the user performing the command is used, who may have more permissions than the application pool's identity.

Feature Dependencies and Stapling Features

In addition to the activation and deactivation capabilities of Features previously covered, Features can also be configured to activate other Features they are dependent upon. Developers can even create Features that do nothing other than activate other Features — in fact, that is all the PublishingWeb Feature does! Activation dependency is also intelligently handled. For instance, suppose Feature A activates Features X, Y, and Z. In addition, Feature B activates Features Y and Z. If both Features A and B are activated, all three Features (X, Y, and Z) are activated, but if Feature B is then deactivated, SharePoint is intelligent enough to see that Feature Y is also a dependent of Feature A, leaving it activated).

To create a Feature activation dependency, add an `<ActivationDependencies>` node containing one or more `<ActivationDependency>` nodes referencing the ID of the Feature that should be activated. For example, take the `MyFirstFeature` Feature. The Feature definition shown in Listing 4-4 will now tell SharePoint to automatically activate Feature `ContactList` whose ID is 00BFEA71-7E6D-4186-9BA8-C047AC750105.

Listing 4-4: Feature definition file with an activation dependency

```xml
<?xml version="1.0" encoding="utf-8"?>
<Feature xmlns="http://schemas.microsoft.com/sharepoint/"
         Id="32DECDEF-C37C-4ac3-BA65-D49639668E7C"
         Title="My First Feature"
         Description="The simplest Feature ever."
         Hidden="FALSE"
         Scope="Web">
  <ElementManifests>
    <ElementManifest Location="elements.xml"/>
  </ElementManifests>
  <ActivationDependencies>
    <ActivationDependency FeatureId="00BFEA71-7E6D-4186-9BA8-C047AC750105" />
  </ActivationDependencies>
</Feature>
```

Another technique the Feature framework provides is referred to as *Feature stapling*. One of the challenges in WSS 2.0 was adding new functionality to existing site definitions and templates. This was because the official guidance from Microsoft was to never edit an existing site definition or template once sites have been provisioned using it, and that developers should not modify the site definitions provided in the out-of-the-box installations, as future updates (hotfixes and service packs) could overwrite the files. To address this, Microsoft added the capability of Feature stapling.

Feature stapling involves creating a special Feature, known as a *stapling Feature,* that associates a Feature with an existing site template. Once a Feature has been stapled to a site template, any future sites provisioned using the site template will automatically activate the stapled Feature. This enables developers to customize site templates without actually changing the site template itself; instead they can append functionality without touching the source files that make up the site template.

Stapling is achieved using the `<FeatureSiteTemplateAssociation>` site element. This element accepts two attributes: `Id`, the ID of the Feature to be stapled, and `TemplateName`, the ID of the site template. For example, the following CAML contained in a Feature element manifest file would staple the `MyFirstFeature` to all future sites provisioned using the Blank Site site template (`STS#1`), assuming the stapling Feature were activated:

```xml
<?xml version="1.0" encoding="utf-8"?>
<Elements xmlns="http://schemas.microsoft.com/sharepoint/">
  <FeatureSiteTemplateAssociation Id="32DECDEF-C37C-4ac3-BA65-D49639668E7C"
                                  TemplateName="STS#1" />
</Elements>
```

Removing a stapling reference is as easy as deactivating the Feature.

While not required, typically developers give stapling Features the same name as the Feature they are stapling but simply append "Stapling" to the name. For example, the name of the Feature that contains the previous element manifest file would be called `MyFirstFeatureStapling`.

Creating Features Using Visual Studio

While Features can be created loosely by manually creating the folder in the `[..]\12\TEMPLATE\FEATURES` folder and the necessary XML files, this is tedious and it poses challenges trying to keep all the files involved in a single project together. Another approach is to leverage Visual Studio for Feature development.

When using Visual Studio to create projects, use either the VB.NET/C# Class Library (when creating a Feature that contains any compiled code) or the Empty Project template (when the Feature won't contain any compiled code). With a project created, mimic the folder structure under the SharePoint 12 folder in the project. For example, in the case of the `MyFirstFeature` Feature, the project structure would look similar to Figure 4-1.

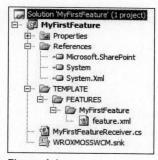

Figure 4-1

In the case of `MyFirstFeature`, a C# Class Library project template was used to create the project and sign it to generate the strong-named assembly. For deployment, files can be manually copied or a custom command-line batch script can be written and added to the Post Build event in the project's Properties window that would add the assembly to the GAC, copy the necessary files to the SharePoint 12 folder, and, optionally, install and activate the Feature.

Does that feel old school? Isn't there a better and more efficient way to package files and custom code up for deployment in SharePoint? Unfortunately, in WSS 2.0 there was no such mechanism, but this is yet another area where Microsoft expended a considerable effort in the latest release of SharePoint: WSS 3.0. The new mechanism for packaging files and custom code for deployment is the WSS solution package framework.

Overview of WSS Solution Packages

Developers writing custom code and creating files for use within a WSS 2.0 site were left with the challenges of deploying their custom code and files to SharePoint servers in homegrown ways. Some developers used the manual deployment of copying files around and making manual edits to the `web.config` file. Others created scripts or installers that did everything for them, but these were tedious to build and did not cleanly integrate with the SharePoint framework — basically, they were simply scripted actions working with the object model and running `STSADM.EXE` batch commands. Deployment of Web Parts in WSS 2.0 was a little better, as it included a tool that helped package up the files for deployment. Called the Web Part Packager, this tool proved to be a bit buggy and Microsoft eventually pulled support for it.

Fortunately, Microsoft expended considerable effort in this area in WSS 3.0 with the addition of the solution framework and WSS solution packages. Think of the solution framework as SharePoint's own installer framework, similar to the Microsoft Installer files (`*.MSI`). The solution framework enables developers to collate custom code and files, among other things, into a single package and add an instruction file to the package telling SharePoint what to do with the files. SharePoint then takes the package and deploys all the changes, outlined in the instruction file, to servers in the farm at a scheduled time. It is even intelligent enough to realize that multiple WFEs exist in the farm, and will deploy necessary code to all of them at the same time.

Anatomy of a WSS Solution Package

A WSS solution package contains two things: all the files required in the deployment and an instruction file telling SharePoint what to do with these files. Everything is packaged together into a Microsoft cabinet file with a file extension of `*.WSP` (for WSS solution package). This package is then added to the SharePoint farm's solution store using `STSADM.EXE`.

What can be included in a WSS solution package? Essentially, four different things can be deployed using WSS solution packages:

❑   **Assemblies** — Many development tasks in SharePoint require custom code to be compiled into assemblies and added to the server. These assemblies can be deployed to a particular SharePoint extended Web application's `\bin` folder or the server's GAC.

❑   **Anything to the SharePoint** `12` **folder** — While there are many options within the WSS solution package schema, most boil down to deploying files to specific places in the SharePoint `12` folder structure. When there is no schema option when a project requires deploying a file somewhere in the SharePoint `12` folder structure, developers can always fall back on the `<RootFiles>` element, which deploys files starting at the `12` folder.

❑   **Custom Code Access Security policies** — CAS policies are typically stored in the `[..]\12\` `CONFIG` folder, but what is special about the WSS solution package deployment method is that developers include what additions to make to a CAS policy and SharePoint adds the changes to a copy of the currently used CAS policy. This automatically updates the SharePoint extended Web application's `web.config` file to contain a registration to the new CAS policy file, and changes the trust level of the Web application all at once.

❑   **Web Part definitions and resources** — Deployment of Web Parts can include many different files. Web Part definition files (`*.webpart`) can be deployed to a site collection's Web Part Gallery (to deploy a Web Part to a specific site collection) or to the `wpcatalog` directory within a Web application's webroot on the file system (to deploy the Web Part to all site collections within a SharePoint extended Web application).

In addition, resource files, such as images, CSS files, JavaScript, and so on can be deployed to the `wpresources` directory within a Web application's webroot on the file system (making them available to all site collections in a SharePoint extended Web application) or to a special `wpresources` directory that all Web applications share, thus deploying the resource files one time on a server. This folder can be found parallel to the SharePoint `12` folder: `c:\Program Files\Common Files\Microsoft Shared\ web server extensions\wpresources`.

Packaging up all the files included in the WSS solution package is covered later in this chapter. For now, focus on the instruction file included in the package SharePoint uses to determine what to do with all the files. This instruction file SharePoint uses is called a *solution manifest*. It is simply an XML file named `manifest.xml` that contains CAML and is added to the root of the solution.

The `manifest.xml` file contains some metadata about the solution for SharePoint, such as a unique ID (GUID), whether the solution should be deployed to WFEs or application servers, and whether the World Wide Web Publishing Services should be recycled upon completion of the deployment (required for some things such as the deployment of custom field types). The minimal CAML required in a `manifest.xml` file is shown in Listing 4-5. It provides SharePoint with just enough information it needs about the solution, but it will not do anything.

Listing 4-5: WSS solution manifest.xml file

```xml
<?xml version="1.0" encoding="utf-8" ?>
<Solution xmlns="http://schemas.microsoft.com/sharepoint/"
          SolutionId="AEF06666-1351-4E9D-A151-63032C94E2D6"
          DeploymentServerType="WebFrontEnd"
          ResetWebServer="FALSE">
</Solution>
```

The next step is to add instructions telling SharePoint what to do with the files included in the solution. Using the `MyFirstFeature` that was created previously in this chapter, two things need to be deployed: the Feature itself and the assembly containing the Feature receiver. First add the assembly. Remember that the assembly needs to be added to the server's GAC. This is done using the `<Assemblies>` element, part of the WSS solution package schema, as shown in Listing 4-6.

Listing 4-6: WSS solution manfiest.xml file deploying an assembly

```xml
<?xml version="1.0" encoding="utf-8" ?>
<Solution xmlns="http://schemas.microsoft.com/sharepoint/"
          SolutionId="AEF06666-1351-4E9D-A151-63032C94E2D6"
          DeploymentServerType="WebFrontEnd"
          ResetWebServer="FALSE">
  <Assemblies>
    <Assembly DeploymentTarget="GlobalAssemblyCache"
          Location="MyFirstFeature.dll" />
  </Assemblies>
</Solution>
```

Note that the assembly's deployment location is the server's GAC. The location of the assembly is the relative path to the file within the package. Again, the process of packaging all the files up into a `*.WSP` file is covered later in the chapter. In addition, if the assembly contains something that requires an entry to the `<SafeControls>` collection in the targeted Web application's `web.config` file, developers can use the `<SafeControls>` element as a child node to the `<Assembly>` node in the `manifest.xml` file. SharePoint automatically adds the `<SafeControl>` entry to `web.config` when deploying the package.

Next, the Feature needs to be deployed. To do that, use the `<FeatureManifests>` element and other components of the WSS solution package schema, as shown in Listing 4-7.

Listing 4-7: WSS solution manifest.xml file deploying a Feature

```xml
<?xml version="1.0" encoding="utf-8" ?>
<Solution xmlns="http://schemas.microsoft.com/sharepoint/"
          SolutionId="AEF06666-1351-4E9D-A151-63032C94E2D6"
          DeploymentServerType="WebFrontEnd"
          ResetWebServer="FALSE">
  <Assemblies>
    <Assembly DeploymentTarget="GlobalAssemblyCache"
              Location="MyFirstFeature.dll" />
  </Assemblies>
  <FeatureManifests>
    <FeatureManifest Location="MyFirstFeature\feature.xml" />
  </FeatureManifests>
</Solution>
```

Recall from the discussion about installation and activation of Features that in order for a Feature to be available for activation, it must first be installed. Thankfully, SharePoint handles installation of the Feature when it deploys it. Another aspect of Features with respect to WSS solution packages requires some explanation. The `MyFirstFeature` Feature contained a reference to an element manifest file. Notice how this file is not listed in the `manifest.xml` file. This is because SharePoint looks at the Feature definition to determine what files are required by the Feature and automatically includes them in the deployment.

However, element manifest files are not the only kind of file found in a Feature. Other types of files include master pages, page layouts, images, and so on (this is very common in the provisioning of files, as covered in Chapter 7). The WSS solution framework will not see these files referenced from element manifest files; therefore, these files are not deployed. So how do they get deployed? One option is to use the `<TemplateFiles>` element, part of the WSS solution package schema, to deploy the files, but a much cleaner approach is to register the files within the Feature's definition file using the `<ElementFile>` element, part of the Feature schema. For example, suppose the `MyFirstFeature` provisioned a new image to a SharePoint site using the `<Module>` element in an element manifest file. In order to register the image, you add an `<ElementFile>` element to the `feature.xml` definition file, as shown in Listing 4-8.

Listing 4-8: Feature definition leveraging the ElementFile element

```xml
<?xml version="1.0" encoding="utf-8"?>
<Feature xmlns="http://schemas.microsoft.com/sharepoint/"
         Id="32DECDEF-C37C-4ac3-BA65-D49639668E7C"
         Title="My First Feature"
         Description="The simplest Feature ever."
         Hidden="FALSE"
         Scope="Web"
         ReceiverAssembly="MyFirstFeature, Version=1.0.0.0, Culture=neutral,
PublicKeyToken=c591e70cfdf9ce4f"
         ReceiverClass="WROX.MyFirstFeatureReceiver">
    <ElementManifests>
```

```
        <ElementManifest Location="elements.xml"/>
        <ElementFile Location="image.gif" />
    </ElementManifests>
    <ActivationDependencies>
      <ActivationDependency FeatureId="00BFEA71-7E6D-4186-9BA8-C047AC750105" />
    </ActivationDependencies>
  </Feature>
```

Solution Deployment

Once the package has been added to the solution store, it can then be scheduled for immediate or future deployment. If the package contains files or changes to a specific SharePoint site (such as adding an entry to the <SafeControls> section of web.config), the administrator is prompted to select which SharePoint extended Web application the solution should be deployed to (or all Web applications can be selected). This enables SharePoint to know which web.config file to update.

If, at some point in the future, the files need to be updated, an administrator can use the STSADM.EXE operation upgradesolution. This re-adds the solution to the solution store, overwriting the previous one after first backing it up (for rollback purposes, should things go wrong); if it was previously deployed, it will be redeployed automatically.

In addition, if a solution needs to be rolled back for some reason, administrators can retract the solution using either the browser interface in Central Administration or the STSADM.EXE operation retractsolution.

Creating WSS Solution Packages

Now that you understand the anatomy and deployment process, it is time to learn how to create a WSS solution package. As previously mentioned, a WSS solution package is a Microsoft cabinet file with a *.WSP filename extension. While there is a CAB Project template in Visual Studio, it is not a viable option for creating *.WSP files. The primary reason is that *.WSP files almost always contain subfolders for things such as Features or localized files for multilingual solutions, and the Visual Studio CAB Project template does not support subfolders.

In order to create Microsoft cabinet files, SharePoint developers can use the MakeCab.EXE utility included in the Microsoft Cabinet SDK. The MakeCab.EXE command-line utility accepts a few parameters. One parameter is the name of a file containing the instructions for MakeCab.EXE, such as how to compress the files, subdirectories that should be created in the cabinet file, and the files that should be included in the cabinet, including to which subfolders files should be added. This file is a *diamond directive file* (*.DDF). Other parameters passed into MakeCab.EXE are for things such as the name of the cabinet to create and where the file should be created.

> *The Microsoft Cabinet SDK is available from Microsoft's Knowledge Base for download* (www.andrewconnell.com/go/210).

The first thing to create is the DDF file. Create a new text file in Visual Studio named BuildSharePointPackage.ddf in a new folder called DeploymentFiles. This contains a few configuration settings that are used for nearly all packages, followed by a list of all the files to include in the package, including any subfolders that should be created. Each file listed in the DDF file points to the relative location of the file based on the location from which `MakeCab.EXE` is being executed. For example, if `MakeCab.EXE` were executed from the root of the project, in order to include the assembly created by building the project, the file would be listed in the following location:

```
bin\debug\MyFirstFeature.dll
```

To create a subfolder within a package, add a `.Set` command, changing the `DestinationDir` variable. All files following the command are placed in the folder. Listing 4-9 shows the DDF file to create a WSP file containing the `MyFirstFeature` Feature.

Listing 4-9: Diamond directive file

```
.OPTION Explicit
.Set DiskDirectoryTemplate=CDROM
.Set CompressionType=MSZIP
.Set UniqueFiles=Off
.Set Cabinet=On
;****************************************************
bin\debug\MyFirstFeature.dll

.Set DestinationDir=MyFirstFeature
TEMPLATE\FEATURES\MyFirstFeature\feature.xml
TEMPLATE\FEATURES\MyFirstFeature\elements.xml

;***End
```

There is another way to put files into folders within the `*.WSP` *file. Instead of using the* `.Set DestinationDir=[...]` *syntax, the source and target locations of the file are listed, separated with a space. This is not recommended, however, because each line in a DDF file has a maximum length. Using this method simply increases the chances of reaching the character limit. Instead, use the approach outlined above.*

The lines starting with a semicolon (;) are commented lines. Also notice that the full path to the files is listed in the DDF file, assuming `MakeCab.EXE` will be executed from the root of the project (the same folder where the project file, `*.CSPROJ`, is located).

The next thing to do is add the `manifest.xml` file to the DDF file. Keeping with the theme of using Visual Studio projects to organize everything, put the `manifest.xml` file previously created in the folder `DeploymentFiles`. Finally, add a line to the DDF file to include the `manifest.xml` file in the root of the package, as shown in Listing 4-10.

Listing 4-10: Diamond directive file with solution manifest.xml

```
.OPTION Explicit
.Set DiskDirectoryTemplate=CDROM
.Set CompressionType=MSZIP
.Set UniqueFiles=Off
.Set Cabinet=On
;****************************************************
DeploymentFiles\manifest.xml
```

```
bin\debug\MyFirstFeature.dll

.Set DestinationDir=MyFirstFeature
TEMPLATE\FEATURES\MyFirstFeature\feature.xml
TEMPLATE\FEATURES\MyFirstFeature\elements.xml

;***End
```

The Visual Studio project should now look like Figure 4-2.

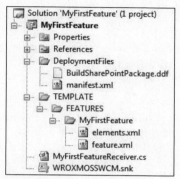

Figure 4-2

Finally, open a command prompt and change directory to the root of the project. Enter the path to `MakeCab.EXE` and the following parameters:

❑ `/F DeploymentFiles\BuildSharePointPackage.ddf` — Instructs `MakeCab.EXE` where to find the DDF file containing some setting information for all the files and folders to include in the package

❑ `/D CabinetNameTemplate=MyFirstFeature.wsp` — The name of the package to create

❑ `/D DiskDirectory1=wsp` — Where to create the package. In this case, a new folder named `wsp` is created at the root of the project.

```
MakeCab.exe /F DeploymentFiles\BuildSharePointPackage.ddf /D
CabinetNameTemplate=MyFirstFeature.wsp /D DiskDirectory1=wsp
```

This will create a new package named `MyFirstFeature.wsp` located in the `wsp` folder within the same folder containing the project. To add the solution to the SharePoint farm's solution store, enter the following command:

```
stsadm.exe -o addsolution -filename [path_to_package]\MyFirstFeature.wsp
```

To deploy the solution, browse to Central Administration ⇨ Operations ⇨ Solution management, select the `myfirstfeature.wsp` solution, and deploy the solution immediately. The Feature can now be deployed. To do so, browse to any SharePoint site and select Site Actions ⇨ Site Settings, and then select Site Features under the Site Administration section to load the Site Features administration page. From the Site Features page, `MyFirstFeature` is listed and available for activation.

If an error occurs when deploying the solution, it is likely the Feature was not uninstalled and deleted from the previous section covering Features. It is not possible to deploy a Feature on top of an existing Feature. To resolve this, uninstall the Feature and delete the MyFirstFeature *folder from the* [..]\12\TEMPLATE\FEATURES *folder.*

Automating the Building of Solutions with MSBuild

Creating a WSS solution package does require a few extra steps after building the project in Visual Studio. Some developers may realize they can create batch files, or post build actions, to automate the process of creating and deploying the packages to the SharePoint farm's solution store. Another option is to leverage the .NET Framework build process using MSBuild, the workhorse behind the build process triggered by Visual Studio.

*Entire books have been written about MSBuild, a subject beyond the focus of this chapter. For more information on MSBuild, refer to the official documentation on MSDN (*www.andrewconnell.com/ go/211*) or the official MSBuild wiki on Channel9 (*www.andrewconnell.com/go/212*).*

Instead of using a post build event script, add a custom MSBuild targets file to the project. This targets file contains instructions telling MSBuild what to do. The advantage to using MSBuild is that targets files are XML-based, thus providing a level of IntelliSense and validation when authoring them, unlike command-line scripts. In addition, similar to post build events, targets files can leverage some MSBuild reserved properties, such as replaceable tokens, for variable names.

In Visual Studio, create a new XML file named BuildSharePointPackage.targets and add it to the DeploymentFiles folder. Add the XML shown in Listing 4-11 to the BuildSharePointPackage .targets file (optionally, ignore the XML comments because they simply add documentation explaining the different pieces of the file).

Listing 4-11: MSBuild targets file used to call MSBuild

```xml
<?xml version="1.0" encoding="utf-8" ?>
<Project DefaultTargets="BuildSharePointPackage"
xmlns="http://schemas.microsoft.com/developer/msbuild/2003">
  <!-- Create a variable 'MakeCabPath' pointing to the location of MakeCab.EXE -->
  <PropertyGroup>
    <MakeCabPath>"C:\Program Files\Microsoft Cabinet SDK\BIN\MAKECAB.EXE"
</MakeCabPath>
  </PropertyGroup>

  <!-- Create a new target that will be called after the project has been build -->
  <Target Name="BuildSharePointPackage">
    <!-- Execute MakeCab.EXE from the root of the project directory,
         passing in the DDF file,
         creating the following package: wsp\[project_name].wsp -->
    <Exec Command="$(MakeCabPath) /F DeploymentFiles\BuildSharePointPackage.ddf /D
CabinetNameTemplate=$(MSBuildProjectName).wsp /D DiskDirectory1=wsp "/>
  </Target>
</Project>
```

With the MSBuild targets file created, the next step is to configure the Visual Studio project to tell MSBuild to call the custom target defined in the custom targets file after the project is successfully built. In order to do this, the project file (*.CSPROJ) needs to be edited. This can be done from Visual Studio or from any text editor. From within Visual Studio, right-click the project name in the Solution Explorer tool window in Visual Studio and select Unload Project.

If the option to unload a project isn't visible, Visual Studio probably isn't configured to show solutions. To change this, from within Visual Studio select Tools ⇨ Options, and then select Projects and Solutions ⇨ General page. Check the Always Show Solution option and click OK.

Right-click the project name in the Solution Explorer tool window and select Edit [project name].csproj and make the following changes:

1. At the end of the file some XML is commented out, preceded by an <Import> node. The <Import> node imports MSBuild targets files. Notice how it is already importing the C# targets file used to compile projects. Add a second <Import> node and set the Project attribute to point to the custom targets file created previously:

```
<Import Project="DeploymentFiles\BuildSharePointPackage.targets" />
```

2. Delete the commented XML except for the <Target Name="AfterBuild"></Target> node. This MSBuild target is called by MSBuild when the other targets have completed. Add a <CallTarget> node to the <Target> node, instructing MSBuild to call the custom target previously created:

```
<Target Name="AfterBuild">
  <CallTarget Targets="BuildSharePointPackage" />
</Target>
```

Save all changes, right-click the project in the Solution Explorer tool window, and select Reload Project. A security warning dialog will appear. This Visual Studio warning indicates that it is loading a project file that does not match any of the installed templates. Select Load Project Normally, uncheck Ask Me for Every Project in This Solution, and click OK.

Now, when the project is built in Visual Studio, MSBuild will automatically execute MakeCab.EXE to create WSS solution packages. If the build process reports an error in Visual Studio, the best way to debug the problem is to open the Output tool window in Visual Studio and inspect the error message reported from MakeCab.EXE. The Error tool window in Visual Studio only shows the generic error code returned by MakeCab.EXE, which is not very helpful in debugging the error.

Summary

This chapter covered WSS 3.0 Feature and solution frameworks, new additions to the SharePoint product offering in the most recent release. The Feature framework not only addresses many pain points associated with WSS 2.0, such as adding new functionality to existing sites and promoting code reuse, it also adds numerous new capabilities. These new capabilities include deployment of some custom code solutions such as event receivers, workflow templates created with Visual Studio, and providing even more possibilities by offering four events that can be handled with custom code. SharePoint developers will quickly find that a solid grasp of the WSS 3.0 Feature framework and creating custom Features is essential for anyone developing against the platform.

Addressing another pain point from WSS 2.0, Microsoft added the solution framework to the latest release of SharePoint, WSS 3.0. The solution framework can be thought of as SharePoint's internal installer capability, providing developers and administrators with the ability to deploy custom code, files, as well as some site changes (edits to the `web.config` and CAS policy files) natively through SharePoint. The solution framework even accommodates a multi-server farm, deploying custom code and files to all servers in the farm with no special input required by administrators. You also looked at the ins and outs of the solution framework, and learned how to create a WSS solution package (`*.WSP`).

In addition to covering both the WSS 3.0 Feature and solution framework, this chapter also demonstrated how to use Visual Studio as a development platform for building Features and automatically creating WSS solution packages.

5

Minimal Publishing Site Definition

Office SharePoint Server (MOSS) 2007 includes a Publishing Portal site definition that can be used to create new Publishing site collections. It includes all of the elements required by the MOSS Web Content Management (WCM) architecture, which consists of content types, master pages, page layouts, style sheets, images, and Web Parts, which together are used to perform various publishing tasks. It also includes a document library for holding the published pages, some default field controls, and sample content. Creating a new Publishing site typically begins by creating a new Publishing site collection based on the Publishing Portal site definition, and then carefully removing the parts not needed. This can be a tedious, error-prone, and time-consuming process.

At first glance, it is not obvious which parts are extraneous and which parts are critical to the underlying WCM framework. If the wrong file is deleted, either it has to be replaced or the process has to start from scratch by creating the site collection again. What is needed is a minimal site definition that can be used as a starting point to create new Publishing site collections. This template would contain all the essential elements, excluding the extraneous sample content. That is what this chapter is all about.

What are the available options for creating a minimal Publishing site definition? One approach might be to create a new Publishing Portal site, remove the parts not needed, and then save it as a site template from within the SharePoint browser interface. This is the general approach to use when creating a reusable site template for other sites. Unfortunately, this approach won't work, as Publishing sites cannot be saved as site templates. In order to understand why, this chapter takes a closer look at the fundamental elements of a Publishing site to see what happens when a new Publishing site is created. During this process, the chapter develops an alternate approach that fully leverages the tools provided by Windows SharePoint Services (WSS) 3.0 for building custom sites. The custom site definition created will tap into the special extensions for provisioning new sites that is used under the covers by the Publishing framework when a Publishing Portal is created.

Elements of a Publishing Site

The first step in the process of creating a minimal Publishing site definition is to look at what is included out-of-the-box (OOTB) with the Publishing framework in MOSS. When a new site collection is created based on the Publishing Portal template, the default site definition creates the content shown in Figure 5-1. Some of this content is critical to the operation of the Publishing sites within the collection, while other content is extraneous and can be removed. The critical parts are described in the following sections.

Name	Description	Items
Document Libraries		
Documents	This system library was created by the Publishing feature to store documents that are used on pages in this site.	0
Form Templates	This library contains administrator-approved form templates that were activated to this site collection.	0
Images	This system library was created by the Publishing feature to store images that are used on pages in this site.	0
Pages	This system library was created by the Publishing feature to store pages that are created in this site.	1
Site Collection Documents	This system library was created by the Publishing Resources feature to store documents that are used throughout the site collection.	0
Site Collection Images	This system library was created by the Publishing Resources feature to store images that are used throughout the site collection.	2
Style Library	This system list was created by the Publishing Resources feature to store custom XSL styles and cascading style sheets.	63

Figure 5-1

The Pages Library

Every Publishing site needs a document library to store the actual pages that are created in the site. This library is always called *Pages* so that it can be referenced easily from hyperlinks and other parts of the portal. When the site is first created, the Pages library contains a single entry named `default.aspx`, which defines the home page of the Publishing site. This page in turn references a page layout. As new pages are added to the site, they are created as items in the Pages document library.

Styles and Images

Many of the CSS style sheets, XSLT style sheets, images, and other files are specific to the default Publishing site definition and the sample content it includes. Of the 63 items in the default Style Library, only the core styles (about three files) are really needed.

Master Pages and Page Layouts

The SharePoint Publishing framework operates by leveraging the ASP.NET 2.0 architecture, which introduced the concept of master pages. Every Publishing page is associated with a page layout, which in turn is linked to a master page located in the master page gallery of the site collection. There can be any number of page layout and master page files associated with a given Publishing site. These can be viewed from the Site Settings ⇨ Master Pages and Page Layouts link in the Galleries section when a Publishing site is created. Figure 5-2 shows the master pages and page layout files that are created by default. Of these, the `PageLayoutTemplate.aspx` and the `VariationRootPageLayout.aspx` files are required because they are referenced by name from within the framework. The `default.master` file is therefore also required because it is referenced by these files.

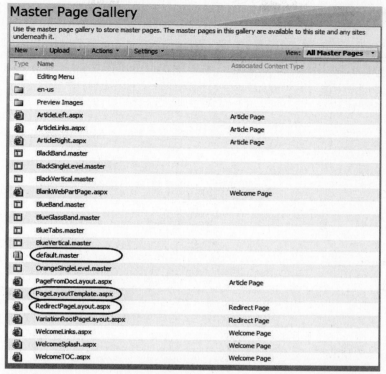

Figure 5-2

Content Types

Content types, in the context of a Publishing site, are primarily used to define the schema or structure of a type of a content page. Page layouts are then used, in conjunction with master pages, to define the rendering of the page defined by the content type. Content types enable developers to link specific workflows or policies with a type of a page regardless of where it is created throughout the site.

A page layout can only have one SharePoint content type associated with it. The only exception is the `PageLayoutTemplate.aspx` file, which is used as a starting point for creating new page layouts. Three content types are created by default: Welcome Page, Article Page, and Redirect Page. The `VariationRootPageLayout.aspx` is based on the Redirect Page content type and therefore must be accessible to all Publishing sites.

Examining the Publishing Portal Site Definition

Before building a custom site definition for creating Publishing sites, it helps to look at the site definition Microsoft provides OOTB to create Publishing sites: Publishing Portal. The site definition Microsoft provides will be virtually the same as the one created in the following sections. It is the Features used that do most of the work. When a site collection is created using the Publishing Portal template, the `PublishingWeb` Feature is activated. This Feature in turn activates other Features, which activate even more Features, as shown in Figure 5-3.

Figure 5-3

Each Feature is responsible for something different. The following sections describe the various things for which each Feature is responsible.

Publishing Feature PublishingWeb

The `PublishingWeb` Feature has it easy — it is simply responsible for activating the `PublishingSite` and `Publishing` Features and does nothing else.

Publishing Feature Publishing

The `Publishing` Feature adds the plumbing needed for a few of the unique capabilities of the Publishing framework. A new link is added to the Edit Control Block (ECB) menu for documents in document libraries to manage document conversions (covered in Chapter 18, "Offline Authoring with Document Converters"). New links are also added to the Pages library's General Settings page for scheduling items and customizing the Site Actions menu.

Finally, a few additional changes are made to the Site Settings page, including hiding two links: Master Pages (in the Gallery section) and Save Site as Template (in the Look and Feel section).

Publishing Feature PublishingSite

Just like the `PublishingWeb` Feature, the `PublishingSite` Feature also has it easy, as it simply activates four other Publishing Features and does nothing else: `PublishingPrerequisites`, `PublishingResources`, `PublishingLayouts`, and `Navigation`.

Publishing Feature PublishingPrerequisites

The `PublishingPrerequisites` Feature contains no element manifest files or activation dependencies; it simply contains a Feature receiver. The receiver ensures that all of the necessary WSS core Features have been activated. This includes the site collection Feature `BasicWebParts` and site Features `CustomList`, `DocumentLibrary`, `TasksList`, and `WorkflowHistoryList`. These are actually activated by the Publishing Portal site definition, and will also be activated by the Minimal Publishing Portal site definition.

Publishing Feature PublishingResources

The `PublishingResources` Feature adds a few components required for Publishing sites to function properly. The `PublishingColumns.xml` element manifest creates all site columns needed in Publishing sites for things such as chrome and page layouts, cache profiles, reusable content, and content query columns. A few system content types are created as well, including System Page, Page, System Master Page, Publishing Master Page, and Page Layout, among others.

After creating the site columns and content types, it then provisions a handful of files. Some of these are required for Publishing sites (`PageLayoutTemplate.aspx`, `PublishingMasterTemplate.aspx`, and `VariationRootPageLayout.aspx`) and one content page layout is used in many Publishing sites (`WelcomeLinks.aspx`).

In addition to ASP.NET 2.0 pages, other files provisioned are the Web Part definitions for the specific Publishing Web Parts such as the Table of Contents, Summary Links, and Content Query Web Parts, which are provisioned into the site collection's Web Part Gallery. The required XSLT style sheets used by these Publishing Web Parts are also provisioned into the site collection's Style Library.

Finally, the `PublishingResources` Feature also makes a few modifications to the Site Settings menu, such as adding the Master Page, Searchable Columns and Content, and Structure Logs links, as well as the following site collection links: Site Collection Output Cache, Variation Labels, Variation Logs, and Translatable Columns.

Publishing Feature PublishingLayouts

The `PublishingLayouts` Feature adds a few master pages, page layouts, style sheets, and a considerable number of images. It is responsible for things such as the Article Page page layouts. In addition, this Feature provisions eight master pages, including the default `BlueBand.master` master page that all Publishing Portal site collections start with. Ultimately, this is the sole Feature that requires the creation of a custom Minimal Publishing Portal site definition.

Publishing Feature Navigation

The Navigation Feature primarily makes a few modifications to the Site Settings page, adding and hiding some links.

Publishing Feature PublishingStapling

The PublishingStapling Feature uses the technique of Feature stapling to attach two of the Publishing Features to many of the MOSS 2007 site templates. The two Features, PublishingWeb and PublishingSite, are stapled to site definitions carried over from Microsoft SharePoint Portal Server 2003, the Collaboration Portal site definition, Search Center and Report Center site templates, Publishing Site, and Publishing Site with Workflow templates.

The Challenge with the Publishing Portal Site Definition

What is wrong with this site definition and the associated Features? One very common use for Publishing sites is an Internet-facing content-centric site. These Internet-facing sites usually have their own look and feel, which is customized quite a bit from the stock SharePoint design. To implement this custom branding, developers have to first create the site collection using the Publishing Portal template and then they usually remove all the branding files that were added as part of this template. This includes things such as various images, style sheets, and master pages.

It would be much easier to create a new SharePoint site with the entire Publishing infrastructure and no branding. This is the goal of the Minimal Publishing Portal site definition. How is it different from the stock Publishing Portal site definition? Most everything can be traced back to the PublishingLayouts Feature, which is responsible for adding most of the stock branding. Unfortunately, it is not terribly easy or straightforward because, as previously shown in Figure 5-3, the PublishingLayouts Feature is activated by another Feature, which is activated by yet another Feature, which is activated by the site definition. This means a new Feature is needed that replaces some of these other Features. In addition, it will add the minimal branding required to have a working site collection.

Creating a Publishing Site Definition

A SharePoint site definition consists of a tree of CAML elements that describe the different parts of the site and how they relate to one another. The topmost element is the template element. It is declared in a special file called WEBTEMP, which contains one or more template Configuration elements that reference associated site definition Configuration elements declared within the ONET.XML file associated with the site definition. Figure 5-4 shows how these files are related.

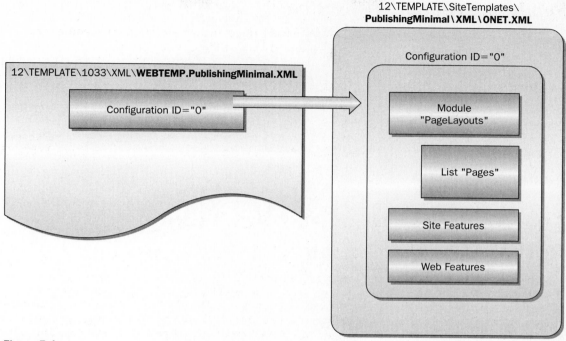

Figure 5-4

When thinking about site definitions and how they are used, it is important to understand the difference between *template* Configuration elements and *site definition* Configuration elements. When users create a new SharePoint site or site collection through the user interface, they are given the opportunity to select from the available site templates. What they are seeing onscreen are the visible template Configuration elements as specified in the WEBTEMP.[name].XML file, where [name] is the template name. The site definition Configuration elements are contained within the ONET.XML file that describes the actual components of the site.

The Significance of Site Definitions

This terminology can be a bit confusing. Sometimes site definitions are incorrectly called site templates and vice versa. While both terms refer to the general capability provided by SharePoint to reuse a particular configuration of lists and other content, the mechanisms are quite different.

SharePoint users can create *site templates* from the user interface to save an existing Web site into a file so that it can be recreated easily at a different address. This is a powerful tool that makes it easy to set up a site with all of the lists and other content needed to perform a given task. *Site definitions* are much more powerful than site templates and are used primarily by developers to build SharePoint applications that typically involve custom coding.

Among the many pros and cons of using site definitions versus site templates to create reusable sites in SharePoint, the most obvious are related to the relative complexity of the site to create. When doing anything beyond simple content modification, site definitions are typically the best choice because they offer much more flexibility and control. Conversely, sometimes simpler is better, especially in a case like this where the primary goal is to reduce the content that is created by default.

Why won't a site template work just as well for creating a minimal Publishing site? The problem is the complexity. First, many of the components that are used within a Publishing site are stored at the site collection. For instance, the master pages and page layouts are all stored in the Master Page Gallery associated with the site collection. These objects are then shared among all Publishing sites within the collection, with only the actual published pages and other content stored at the site level.

Another issue is the need to use content types to define the page layouts used for the Publishing pages. This requirement makes it impossible to simply use a site template to create a minimal Publishing site because content types can only be declared in a site definition or created using custom code. The default set of content types provided by the Publishing framework may still need to modify or extend or be bound to custom lists. The only way to do this would be to use a site definition.

Custom Site Provisioning

Although not an absolute requirement for building a minimal Publishing site definition, it is worth mentioning an additional capability that SharePoint provides for controlling how sites are created. *Site provisioning* can be an essential tool for developers tasked with customizing OOTB functionality.

When a new Web site is created, the SharePoint site provisioning engine examines the selected template and then finds and loads the corresponding ONET.XML file. Then it searches for a site definition Configuration element within the project element that matches the ID of the template Configuration element associated with the selected template.

As part of the template Configuration element, the name of a custom assembly can be specified such that it contains a class derived from Microsoft.SharePoint.SPWebProvisioningProvider. When specified, this class is called after the site is created to apply the appropriate configuration and to perform any additional initialization needed for the site. To fully customize the initialization, pass a string argument to the provisioning provider. The code in Listing 5-1 illustrates this approach by passing the name of a separate XML configuration file containing post-site-creation options. Another idea would be to control the site creation process using data stored in an external database. In that case, the string argument might include the database connection details.

Listing 5-1: Creating a custom site provisioning engine

```
using System;
using Microsoft.SharePoint;
using Microsoft.SharePoint.Publishing;

namespace WROX.ProMossWcm.Chapter05 {
  public class ProvisioningEngine : SPWebProvisioningProvider {
    private const string TEMPLATE_ID = "0";
    private const string TEMPLATE_NAME = "PublishingMinimal";

    /// <summary>
```

```
    /// Called when a new site is created.
    /// </summary>
    public override void Provision (SPWebProvisioningProperties props) {
        using (SPWeb site = props.Web) {
            // Apply the actual Web template for the publishing portal.
            site.ApplyWebTemplate(TEMPLATE_NAME + "#" + TEMPLATE_ID);

            EnsureContentTypes(site, PublishingWeb.GetPagesListName(site));

            // props.Data = custom string passed in from ONET.XML file
            InitializePortal(site, props.Data);
        }
    }


    /// <summary>
    /// Ensures the correct content types are added to the
    /// Pages library associated with the Publishing Portal.
    /// </summary>
    private void EnsureContentTypes (SPWeb site, string pagesList) {
        SPContentTypeCollection pageCTs = site.Lists[pagesList].ContentTypes;
        foreach (SPContentType contentType in
    site.Site.RootWeb.AvailableContentTypes) {
            if (IsCustomContentType(contentType) && pageCTs[contentType.Name] == null)
                pageCTs.Add(contentType);
        }
    }


    /// <summary>
    /// Determines whether a given content type is a custom type for this Feature.
    /// </summary>
    private bool IsCustomContentType (SPContentType contentType) {
        if (contentType.Hidden) return false;
        if (contentType.Group.ToUpper() != TEMPLATE_NAME) return false;
        return true;
    }


    /// <summary>
    /// Initialize the portal based on settings provided in the configuration file
    /// associated with the site definition.
    /// </summary>
    private void InitializePortal (SPWeb site, string configFilePath) {
        // *** code omitted ***
    }
    }
}
```

Note a couple of gotchas related to using the built-in site provisioning Features to be aware of. First, understand that the site provisioning class is expected to perform the important task of applying the Web template to the new Web site. It is the SPWeb.ApplyWebTemplate() method itself that determines whether a custom site provisioning class is available, and then calls its SPWebProvisioningProvider .Provision() method to apply the template. This means that when providing a custom site provisioning class, the template must be applied explicitly in code. Failure to do this will cause the site creation process to fall into an infinite loop as it tries repeatedly to acquire the template when the root Web of the portal is being created. It also means that the template configuration applied to the Web must not have a custom site provisioning class associated with it.

The best way to handle this scenario is to declare two configurations as part of the site definition. The first (ID="0") will be a hidden configuration that represents the actual template to be applied to the site. The second (ID="1") will be the visible configuration that is associated with the custom site provisioning class. When the SPWebProvisioningProvider.Provision() method is called, it applies the hidden configuration to the Web, thereby avoiding an infinite loop when the SPWeb.ApplyWebTemplate() method searches for another provisioning provider. The diagram shown in Figure 5-5 illustrates this process.

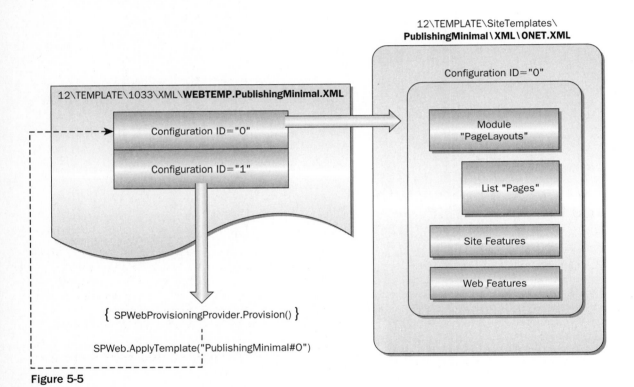

Figure 5-5

Why use site provisioning instead of a Feature receiver? The main reason is that a Feature receiver is called before the default lists and Web Parts, which are declared in the ONET.XML file, get created. This means that the list contents cannot be modified from within a Feature receiver. In the case of a Publishing Portal, it is precisely that content that may need to be modified in order for the Publishing Features to be properly initialized. Consequently, the custom code needs to be called after the lists and other components have been created. Some of those are custom components, but others are supplied by the Publishing framework Features that are referenced from within the custom site definition.

The following sections describe the different files and CAML elements needed to create a minimal Publishing site; but before diving into the actual site definition, create a SharePoint solution package that will tie everything together and act as a container for all the other files. Figure 5-6 shows the structure of the custom site definition solution documented throughout the remainder of the chapter.

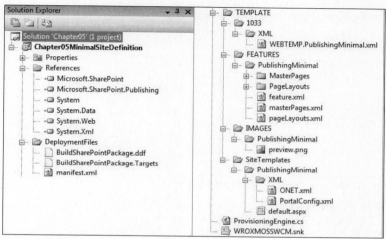

Figure 5-6

The WEBTEMP File

To create the Minimal Publishing Portal site definition, start by creating the WEBTEMP file (named WEBTEMP.PublishingMinimal.xml), which describes the configurations that make up the site. The configuration is not hidden from the user. It must not specify its own provisioning class because that would cause an infinite loop as SharePoint tries to resolve the template to be applied to the Web site. Instead, the ID attribute matches that of the complete configuration definition, which resides in the ONET.XML file located in the matching [..]\12\TEMPLATE\SiteTemplates subfolder. That configuration specifies the files and other Features of the new Web site. Listing 5-2 contains the hidden configuration.

Listing 5-2: Minimal publishing site configuration

```xml
<Configuration ID="0"
               Title="Minimal Publishing Site"
               DisplayCategory="Publishing"
               Hidden="FALSE"
               ImageUrl="/_layouts/images/PublishingMinimal/Preview.png"
               RootWebOnly="false"
               SubWebOnly="true" />
```

Next is the visible configuration that the user sees when creating the Publishing Portal. It has all of the standard attributes such as `ImageUrl`, `Description`, `DisplayCategory`, and so on (see Listing 5-3). It also specifies a custom provisioning class that is called after the site is created to apply the template for the site. Once the template has been applied, then all of the lists and other Features of the site are created, so the provisioning class can populate them with default data.

Listing 5-3: Visible minimal publishing configuration

```
<Configuration ID="1"
               Title="Minimal Publishing Portal"
               DisplayCategory="Publishing"
               Hidden="FALSE"
               ImageUrl="/_layouts/images/PublishingMinimal/Preview.png"
               ProvisionAssembly="Chapter05MinimalSiteDefinition, Version=1.0.0.0,
Culture=neutral, PublicKeyToken=c591e70cfdf9ce4f"
               ProvisionClass="WROX.ProMossWcm.Chapter05.ProvisioningEngine"
ProvisionData="SiteTemplates\\PublishingMinimal\\XML\\PortalConfig.xml"
               RootWebOnly="true"
               SubWebOnly="false" />
```

This markup declares that the PublishingMinimal site definition has a single configuration that is visible in the SharePoint user interface and is available for use to create a Publishing Portal. By setting the `RootWebOnly` attribute to `true`, the template is limited such that only top-level sites can be created.

Finally, a site configuration is needed to create Publishing sites with workflow that will automatically setup the Parallel Approval workflow association on the necessary libraries. Notice that `VisibleFeatureDependency` specifies that the PublishingMinimal Feature must be active for this configuration to be available. This Feature is defined later in the chapter.

Listing 5-4: Minimal Publishing Site with Workflow Configuration

```
<Configuration ID="2"
               Title="Publishing Site with Workflow"
               Hidden="FALSE"
               ImageUrl="/_layouts/1033/images/PublishingSite.gif"
               Description="A site for publishing Web pages on a schedule by using
approval workflows. It includes document and image libraries for storing Web
publishing assets. By default, only sites with this template can be created under
this site."
               SubWebOnly="TRUE"
               DisplayCategory="Publishing"
               VisibilityFeatureDependency="54A92CA1-4E7C-4B73-B03A-E93955E4E560" />
```

As indicated earlier, the creation of a Publishing site requires special code to be run each time the portal is provisioned. This code will create the additional elements that cannot be created via CAML.

The ONET.XML File

The `ONET.XML` file contains the CAML elements that declare the actual components that make up the site. The top-level element is the `project` element, which points to the appropriate schemas and provides a title for the site definition, as shown in Listing 5-5.

Listing 5-5: ONET.XML project element

```xml
<?xml version="1.0" encoding="utf-8" ?>
<Project xmlns="http://schemas.microsoft.com/sharepoint/"
         xmlns:ows="Microsoft SharePoint"
         Title="Minimal Publishing Site">
  <NavBars />
  <ListTemplates />
  <DocumentTemplates />
  <Configurations />
  <Modules />
</Project>
```

The NavBars element contains the individual navigation bar declarations. The NavBar elements shown in Listing 5-6 are copied directly from the standard Publishing site definition to provide the same basic navigation used for Publishing sites. No NavBars are needed in a Publishing site, so this node is empty.

Listing 5-6: ONET.XML NavBars element

```xml
<?xml version="1.0" encoding="utf-8" ?>
<Project xmlns="http://schemas.microsoft.com/sharepoint/"
         xmlns:ows="Microsoft SharePoint"
         Title="Minimal Publishing Site">
  <NavBars Name="SharePoint Top Navbar" ID="1002">"></NavBars>

  <ListTemplates />
  <DocumentTemplates />
  <Configurations />
  <Modules />
</Project>
```

Because no custom list templates are needed for a Publishing site, leave the ListTemplates element empty. Also include the standard set of document templates, as shown in Listing 5-7. Note that all are declared as referencing the default STS path, which provides out-of-the-box support for Word, Excel, PowerPoint, OneNote, FrontPage, and InfoPath documents.

Listing 5-7: ONET.XML DocumentTemplates element

```xml
<?xml version="1.0" encoding="utf-8" ?>
<Project xmlns="http://schemas.microsoft.com/sharepoint/"
         xmlns:ows="Microsoft SharePoint"
         Title="Minimal Publishing Site">
  <NavBars />
  <ListTemplates />
  <DocumentTemplates>
    <DocumentTemplate Path="STS" Name=""
DisplayName="$Resources:core,doctemp_None;" ... />
    <DocumentTemplate Path="STS" DisplayName="$Resources:core,doctemp_Word97;" ...
>
      <DocumentTemplateFiles>
        <DocumentTemplateFile Name="doctemp\word\wdtmpl.doc"
```

(continued)

Listing 5-7 *(continued)*

```
TargetName="Forms/template.doc" Default="TRUE" />
        </DocumentTemplateFiles>
      </DocumentTemplate>
      <!-- code omitted for readability -->
    </DocumentTemplates>
  <Configurations />
  <Modules />
</Project>
```

Configuration Elements

A site definition may contain several configurations, each declared in a separate `Configuration` element. This element declares the components that will be available within a given site definition as a group of settings. Using configurations separates the list and module declarations from the actual configuration of instances for a given site template within the site definition and makes it easy to reuse the same settings in multiple templates.

The `ID` attribute associates the `ONET.XML Configuration` instance with the WEBTEMP `Configuration` reference. Within each `Configuration` element, additional sub-elements are used to define individual site characteristics such as site Features, Web Features, modules, and property values that will be associated with the site immediately after it is created.

Now declare three configurations: one to match the configuration that is applied to the new Publishing Web site that mimics the Publishing Site without workflow site template; a second to match the visible configuration that is displayed in the SharePoint user interface for creating a Publishing Portal; and a third one to match the configuration that minics the Publishing Site with the workflow site template (see Listing 5-8).

Listing 5-8: ONET.XML Configurations element

```
<?xml version="1.0" encoding="utf-8" ?>
<Project xmlns="http://schemas.microsoft.com/sharepoint/"
         xmlns:ows="Microsoft SharePoint"
         Title="Minimal Publishing Site">
  <NavBars />
  <ListTemplates />
  <DocumentTemplates />
  <Configurations>
    <Configuration ID="-1" Name="NewWeb" />
    <Configuration ID="1" Name="Provisioner" />
    <Configuration ID="0" Name="PublishingMinimal">
      <Lists/>
      <Modules>
        <Module Name="Default"/>
      </Modules>
      <SiteFeatures />
      <WebFeatures />
    </Configuration>
  </Configurations>
  <Modules />
</Project>
```

The SiteFeatures and WebFeatures Elements

When creating a site definition, there may be additional Features that must be activated in order for the site to work. Consequently, the SharePoint site provisioning engine needs to know which Features to activate when the site is created and whether they must be activated at the site collection level or at the Web level. This is an important distinction, because it also determines when the activation occurs. Specifying them separately enables the provisioning engine to create the site more efficiently because it doesn't have to first load the Feature to determine its scope.

Use the `<SiteFeatures>` element to specify external Features that must be activated at the site collection level, and the `<WebFeatures>` element to specify Feature activation at the site level, as shown in Listing 5-9. Include the `ID` of the PublishingMinimal Feature that contains the custom master pages, page layouts, and images.

Listing 5-9: ONET.XML SiteFeatures element

```xml
<?xml version="1.0" encoding="utf-8" ?>
<Project xmlns="http://schemas.microsoft.com/sharepoint/"
         xmlns:ows="Microsoft SharePoint"
         Title="Minimal Publishing Site">
  <NavBars />
  <ListTemplates/>
  <DocumentTemplates />
  <Configurations>
    <Configuration ID="-1" Name="NewWeb" />
    <Configuration ID="1" Name="Provisioner" />
    <Configuration ID="0" Name="PublishingMinimal">
      <Lists/>
      <Modules />
      <SiteFeatures>
        <!-- Feature: PublishingMinimal -->
        <Feature ID="54A92CA1-4E7C-4B73-B03A-E93955E4E560" />
      </SiteFeatures>
      <WebFeatures />
    </Configuration>
  </Configurations>
  <Modules />
</Project>
```

Because the PublishingMinimal Feature is scoped to the site collection level, the other site collection Features required by the Publishing framework using `ActivationDependency` elements in the Feature definition itself can be included. This approach provides better Feature encapsulation, avoiding the need to add those dependencies directly to each site definition.

Conversely, because the PublishingMinimal Feature is not scoped to Web, it cannot use activation dependencies for the Web-scoped Publishing Features. Instead, it must specify them directly in the `ONET.xml` file within the `WebFeatures` element.

First, add support for custom lists, document libraries, picture libraries, task lists, collaboration lists, and the workflow history list, as shown in Listing 5-10.

Listing 5-10: Including site-scoped Features

```xml
<?xml version="1.0" encoding="utf-8" ?>
<Project xmlns="http://schemas.microsoft.com/sharepoint/"
         xmlns:ows="Microsoft SharePoint"
         Title="Minimal Publishing Site">
  <NavBars />
  <ListTemplates/>
  <DocumentTemplates />
  <Configurations>
    <Configuration ID="-1" Name="NewWeb" />
    <Configuration ID="1" Name="Provisioner" />
    <Configuration ID="0" Name=" PublishingMinimal">
      <Lists/>
      <Modules />
      <SiteFeatures />
      <WebFeatures>
        <!-- Feature: CustomLists -->
        <Feature ID="00BFEA71-DE22-43B2-A848-C05709900100" />
        <!-- Feature: DocumentLibrary -->
        <Feature ID="00BFEA71-E717-4E80-AA17-D0C71B360101" />
        <!-- Feature: PictureLibrary -->
        <Feature ID="00BFEA71-52D4-45B3-B544-B1C71B620109" />
        <!-- Feature: TasksList -->
        <Feature ID="00BFEA71-A83E-497E-9BA0-7A5C597D0107" />
        <!-- Feature: TeamCollab -->
        <Feature ID="00BFEA71-4EA5-48D4-A4AD-7EA5C011ABE5" />
        <!-- Feature: WorkflowHistoryList -->
        <Feature ID="00BFEA71-4EA5-48D4-A4AD-305CF7030140" />
      </WebFeatures>
    </Configuration>
  </Configurations>
  <Modules />
</Project>
```

Next, add the Publishing-specific Features to the `WebFeatures` element. The Publishing and Navigation Features support activation properties that enable values to be passed in to customize the Feature.

Feature Activation Properties

When activating a Feature from within a site definition, it is often necessary to provide additional property values that the Feature uses during its activation sequence. These properties are passed to the Feature receiver code so that it can initialize itself properly.

While this is a powerful capability of the Feature framework, it requires inside knowledge of how the target Feature is written. This information is often difficult to obtain and may not be well documented. If the target Feature changes, it may become necessary to modify the site definition to supply the correct property values.

As shown in Listing 5-11, pass these properties by name using the `Properties` element inside the `Feature` element, which configures the Office SharePoint Publishing Feature.

Listing 5-11: Publishing Feature utilizing activation properties

```
<!-- Feature: Publishing -->
<Feature ID="22A9EF51-737B-4ff2-9346-694633FE4416">
  <Properties xmlns="http://schemas.microsoft.com/sharepoint/">
    <Property Key="ChromeMasterUrl"
Value="~SiteCollection/_catalogs/masterpage/PublishingMinimal.master" />
    <Property Key="WelcomePageUrl"
Value="$Resources:cmscore,List_Pages_UrlName;/default.aspx"/>
    <Property Key="PagesListUrl" Value=""/>
    <Property Key="AvailableWebTemplates" Value="=*-PublishingMinimal#0;*-
PublishingMinimal#2"/>
    <Property Key="AvailablePageLayouts"
Value="~SiteCollection/_catalogs/masterpage/Minimal.aspx"/>
    <Property Key="AlternateCssUrl" Value="" />
    <Property Key="SimplePublishing" Value="true" />
  </Properties>
</Feature>
```

The activation properties of the Publishing Feature require a little more explanation:

❑ ChromeMasterUrl — Used to specify the default master page that will be used for new pages in the Publishing site. Unless this property is specified, the Publishing framework will use the default.master. This way enables referencing the masterurl easily from within the custom pages without having to use a hard-coded value. Changing it here changes it everywhere it is referenced.

❑ WelcomePageUrl — This is set to redirect the user to a specific page when the site's URL is requested.

❑ PagesListUrl — Specifies the name of the Pages document library that holds the actual Publishing pages. Leave the attribute blank to use the default value.

❑ AvailableWebTemplates — Limit the Web templates that are available to users from within this Web site by specifying a list of templates and configurations. The syntax of this attribute is the locale identifier (LCID) followed by a hyphen, template name, and optional configuration. To include all LCID values, use an asterisk for the LCID value, as shown here:

```
*-PublishingMinimal#0;1033-BLANKINTERNET#2
```

This says to display the #3 configuration of the PublishingMinimal template for all available locales, and to display the #2 configuration of the BLANKINTERNET template for LCID 1033. Leave the attribute blank to specify the default value.

❑ AvailablePageLayouts — Page layouts that should be displayed in the UI for selection can be specified when the user creates a new Publishing page. This attribute also uses a special syntax that must be a server-relative URL for each layout file, separated by a colon. To obtain the server-relative URL, use the special ~SiteCollection token.

❑ AlternateCssUrl — Specify an alternate CSS URL to reference custom styles.

❑ SimplePublishing — Setting this property to true causes the Publishing framework to relax its requirement that Published pages must go through an Approval workflow.

There is a separate Feature that controls the portal navigation for Web sites derived from `PublishingWeb`. Use it to set up the default navigation behavior of the portal. Turn on the `InheritGlobalNavigation`, `ShowSiblings`, and `IncludeSubSites` flags, as shown in Listing 5-12.

Listing 5-12: Navigation Feature utilizing activation properties

```
<!-- Feature: Navigation -->
<Feature ID="541F5F57-C847-4e16-B59A-B31E90E6F9EA">
  <Properties xmlns="http://schemas.microsoft.com/sharepoint/">
    <Property Key="InheritGlobalNavigation" Value="true"/>
    <Property Key="ShowSiblings" Value="true"/>
    <Property Key="IncludeSubSites" Value="true"/>
  </Properties>
</Feature>
```

The last configuration should be an exact copy of configuration #0 except its configuration `ID` should be 2 and the `SimplePublishing` property for the Publishing Feature should be set to `false`.

Enabling the Lockdown Feature

Under normal circumstances, a Publishing site has many more readers than contributors. This is the typical scenario for content publishing whereby a select group of content authors publish information for the rest of the world (readers) to consume. Because the readers are also using SharePoint, it may not be desirable for them to have access to other parts of the portal such as lists and document libraries unrelated to the published content. In order to support this scenario, the Publishing framework provides a special Feature called *ViewFormPagesLockDown* that restricts access for anonymous users to published content only. The lockdown Feature is explained in more detail in Chapter 15.

To activate the lockdown mode, include the `ViewFormPagesLockdown` Feature in the `SiteFeatures` section using the appropriate GUID. The adjusted `SiteFeatures` element is shown in Listing 5-13.

Listing 5-13: Including the lockdown Feature

```
<SiteFeatures>
  <!-- Feature: PublishingMinimal -->
  <Feature ID="54A92CA1-4E7C-4B73-B03A-E93955E4E560" />

  <!-- Feature: ViewFormPagesLockdown -->
  <Feature ID="7C637B23-06C4-472d-9A9A-7C175762C5C4" />
</SiteFeatures>
```

Modules

The `Module` element is used to declare a set of files that are automatically added to a site when it is created. This element, in conjunction with the File element, enables specifying the template file on the file system that will be used to create each file instance (in the content database). In the case of Web Part pages, specify the initial collection of Web Parts and their properties.

The `Module` element can be used in more than one place. In the `ONET.XML` file it is used to declare the home page for the site (`default.aspx`), as shown in Listing 5-14.

Listing 5-14: Adding modules to the minimal site definition

```xml
<?xml version="1.0" encoding="utf-8" ?>
<Project xmlns="http://schemas.microsoft.com/sharepoint/"
         xmlns:ows="Microsoft SharePoint"
         Title="Minimal Publishing Site">
  <NavBars />
  <ListTemplates />
  <DocumentTemplates />
  <Configurations />
  <Modules>
    <Module Name="Default" Url="" Path="">
      <File Url="default.aspx" NavBarHome="True" Type="Ghostable" />
    </Module>
  </Modules>
</Project>
```

The Feature Manifest

The final component is the custom Feature that is responsible for provisioning the master pages, page layouts, and other files used in the site definition. It is also responsible for activating any additional Features from the Publishing framework that may be required. The markup in Listing 5-15 shows the Feature manifest needed to accomplish this.

Listing 5-15: Feature manifest for setting up publishing

```xml
<?xml version="1.0" encoding="utf-8"?>
<Feature xmlns="http://schemas.microsoft.com/sharepoint/"
         Id="54A92CA1-4E7C-4B73-B03A-E93955E4E560"
         Title=" Minimal Publishing Feature"
         Version="1.0.0.0"
         Scope="Site"
         Hidden="FALSE">

  <ActivationDependencies>
    <!-- Feature: PublishingPrerequisites -->
    <ActivationDependency FeatureId="A392DA98-270B-4e85-9769-04C0FDE267AA" />
    <!-- Feature: PublishingResources -->
    <ActivationDependency FeatureId="AEBC918D-B20F-4a11-A1DB-9ED84D79C87E" />
    <!-- Feature: Navigation -->
    <ActivationDependency FeatureId="89E0306D-453B-4ec5-8D68-42067CDBF98E" />
  </ActivationDependencies>

  <ElementManifests>
    <ElementManifest Location="masterPages.xml" />
    <ElementManifest Location="pageLayouts.xml" />
  </ElementManifests>
</Feature>
```

The first thing to note is that the Feature is scoped to `Site`. One reason for this is that the publishing Features on which the site definition depends are also scoped to `Site`. In addition, the custom master pages and page layouts associated with the Minimal Publishing Portal site definition must be placed into the Master Page and Page Layout Gallery associated with the site collection. Any custom content types that need to be deployed would also have to be created at the site collection level.

The `ActivationDependency` elements refer to the three key publishing Features that must be activated in order for the Publishing site to work: `PublishingPrerequisites`, `PublishingResources`, and `Navigation`.

The Feature Elements

The Feature contains two element manifests that describe the remaining files that make up the solution: a single master page (with associated preview image) and two page layouts (with associated preview images). Refer to Chapter 7, "Master Pages and Page Layouts" or the code for this chapter for more information on how these files are provisioned into the Publishing site.

Deploying and Testing the Custom Site Definition

With the Minimal Publishing Portal site definition created, it is now time to package everything up into a WSS solution package for deployment. Like other chapters, this chapter uses the same automated solution package creation process that leverages MSBuild as demonstrated in Chapter 4. Refer to the code download associated with this chapter for the book to see the complete solution and sample WSP file. Add the solution to the SharePoint farm's solution store and deploy it. Finally, reset IIS in order to make SharePoint see the new site definition and WEBTEMP file.

Now, when creating new site collections, a new option will be present on the Publishing tab: *Minimal Publishing Portal*. After creating a new site collection using this site definition, the site will look virtually identical to a site created using the Blank Site site definition. This is because the master page used here is very slimmed down, taking the minimalist approach. However, a quick peek at the Site Actions menu will make users feel much more at home in the Publishing environment, as all the usual stuff is now visible. To validate this, check the Site Settings page to see the new cache and master page menus as well as the Manage Content and Structure page.

Summary

This chapter explained the structure of standard WSS 3.0 site definitions and dissected the out-of-the-box MOSS 2007 Publishing Portal site definition. In doing this, the challenge presented in most Publishing sites was uncovered. The Publishing Portal site definition adds a lot of branding files and content that is not needed or necessary within most Publishing sites. This extra content and files are typically cleaned out prior to starting the development process in creating new Publishing sites. To alleviate this task, the Minimal Publishing Portal site definition was described, including all the steps that need to be taken in the process of creating this site definition.

6

Site Columns, Content Types, and Lists

At the core, all content in a SharePoint site is stored in lists. This includes things such as master pages, images, style sheets, XSL styles, and content pages; even page layouts (in the case of Publishing sites) are stored in SharePoint lists. Similar to tables in a database, lists are composed of columns, or fields.

One of the challenges with Windows SharePoint Services (WSS) 2.0 with respect to lists was that the list templates were not very dynamic. In addition, many aspects of lists were not reusable. Such is the case when defining types of data within a list as well as the columns in lists. Microsoft addressed these issues by introducing a few new concepts. First, list columns can be defined as site columns, or templates, that can be used across multiple lists. Second, the type of data can be abstracted from a list into a new entity called a *content type*. Content types can then be added to a list either through the definition of the list or through the browser interface, by a site administrator. Lists can even contain multiple content types facilitating the storage of heterogeneous types of data within a single list. Finally, list templates can now be associated with sites not only at the point of site creation, but also at any time thereafter thanks to the addition of Features.

This chapter covers each of these three site elements in depth, including a detailed look at the different options available to administrators and developers for creating these different elements.

All three of these site elements are basic WSS 3.0 constructs found in all SharePoint sites. Regardless, Publishing site developers must have a solid grasp of these concepts in order to create professional solutions leveraging the capabilities of Microsoft Office SharePoint Server (MOSS) 2007 Web Content Management (WCM).

Site Columns

Columns are not new to WSS 3.0, they have been around in SharePoint for a while. However, site columns were introduced in WSS 3.0 in an effort to ease the maintenance of columns in a SharePoint site collection. In WSS 2.0, users could add and edit columns on a list-by-list basis. The challenge with this approach is that it was hard to standardize similar columns across lists. For example, if the field "First Name" was defined in one list as a certain data type, configured to have a minimum length, assigned a user-friendly description and default value, there was no easy way to ensure that other lists containing a "First Name" column conformed to the same specifications. Not only would this cause confusion with end users due to the lack of consistency, but it also created headaches for site owners and administrators to manage the various instances.

To address this, Microsoft introduced *site columns,* which are reusable column definitions/templates in WSS 3.0 that can be defined once in a SharePoint site and used in different lists in the same site or subsites. These site columns can also be used within content types. While the site columns are defined at the site level, they are available to all child sites of the site they are defined within. Therefore, creating site columns within the top-level site in a site collection effectively creates a site column definition that can be used throughout an entire site collection. All site column definitions are stored in the Site Column Gallery, accessible via Site Settings ⇨ Site Columns.

> *For more information on site columns, refer to the official documentation on MSDN* (www.andrewconnell.com/go/213).

Site columns alone cannot be used to store data. Rather, they are simply definitions. To use a site column it must be added to a list. This does not create a reference to the site column definition; SharePoint creates a copy in the list known as a *list column.* From here, the column can be customized in the list without affecting the underlying definition. Adding site columns to content types is treated a bit differently and is addressed later in the chapter. However, when updating the site column definition, users can propagate the changes everywhere the site column is being used.

Site Column Names and IDs

Site columns have two forms of identification: a unique name and a unique ID. The ID of a site column is simply a GUID. The ID of a site column may or may not be defined by an administrator or developer upon creation of the site column definition, depending on the method of creation. Each of the three options for creating a site column is covered in a later section. The name of a site column is a little more complex than the ID.

Site columns have two different names: an *internal name* and a *display name.* The display name is a user-friendly name that is shown in the user interface in all forms (new/edit/display) and lists pages. The display name can contain spaces, whereas the internal name cannot contain spaces. If the name entered contains a space when creating a new field using the browser interface or through code, SharePoint replaces the space with the hex value of the HTML space character: %20. This results in the string _x0020_ in the middle of a site column's internal name. If multiple spaces are entered as the name, it will contain multiple instances of _x0020_.

For example, if a new site column is created through the browser named "Company Full Name," the resulting internal name is Company_x0020_Full_x0020_Name. Why does this matter? As covered later in the chapter, the internal name is the one that is used when accessing a column in a list via the SharePoint object model. While not a problem, it causes undue pain when typing the code, as it feels too cryptic. The section on creating site columns demonstrates a few different ways to avoid the _x0020_ value in the internal name of a site column, depending on the method used to create the site column.

Creating Site Columns

SharePoint provides three options for creating site column definitions, each with its own advantages and disadvantages. Two of the options, creating site columns using the SharePoint browser interface or via custom code, can be classified as SharePoint customization. Recall from Chapter 2 that SharePoint customization is storing content within the content database. The third option for creating site column definitions is using WSS Features. A Feature can be used to define the site column template and upon Feature activation, the site column definition is created and added to the site's site column gallery. As covered in Chapter 2, the Feature approach is more along the lines of SharePoint development, making it very easy to package into a WSS solution for deployment across various environments.

The following three sections demonstrate the various techniques to creating site columns. All three techniques create the same site column, meaning if all three are performed on the same SharePoint site, errors will likely occur. The goal here is to show the equivalent process/code between the different approaches. In order to create or modify site columns, the user must have Design access rights to the site. If the user does not have the necessary rights within a child site that utilizes the site column, the update action does not succeed.

Creating Site Columns via the Browser Interface

Open a browser and navigate to a Publishing site. Select Site Actions ⇨ Site Settings ⇨ Modify All Site Settings and then select Site Columns under the Galleries column on the Site Settings page. On the Site Column Gallery page, select Create and use the following information to create a new site column:

- ❑ **Name and Type** — Column name — Press Release ByLine
- ❑ **Name and Type** — The type of information in this column is — Single line of text
- ❑ **Group** — New Group: WROX

That is all there is to creating a new site column using the browser! While incredibly simple and fast, this site column definition now only resides within the SharePoint content database. Create another site column that will store the body of the press release in a rich text field using the following values:

- ❑ **Name and Type** — Column name — Press Release Body
- ❑ **Name and Type** — The type of information in this column is — Full HTML content with formatting and constraints for publishing
- ❑ **Group** — Existing Group: WROX
- ❑ **Require that this column contains information** — Yes

Working Around _x0020_ in the Site Column Name

When creating a site column via the browser, the only name that can be specified is the display name. Recall that SharePoint takes this name and uses it not only for the display name, but also for the internal name; and if the name provided contains spaces, the spaces are converted to the hex value of %20. The way to avoid this is to first create the site column using the name with no spaces. Once the site column is created, go back in and update the definition via the browser and change the name to include spaces. This is effective because the internal name is never changed once the site column definition is created.

Creating Site Columns via Code

Creating the site column via code involves using the `Microsoft.SharePoint.SPField` and `Microsoft.SharePoint.SPFieldCollection` classes (site columns are referred to as *fields* within the SharePoint API). Each SharePoint site (`SPWeb`) contains a `Fields` property containing all site column definitions in the site's site column gallery. To add a site column definition to a site, use one of three overloads of the `Add()` method, the two most common of which are as follows:

❑   `SPFieldCollection.Add(SPField siteColumnDefinition)` — Adds an existing or previously created site column to the site's site column gallery.

❑   `SPFieldCollection.Add(string siteColumnDisplayName, SPFieldType fieldType, Boolean required)` — Creates a new site column using the provided display name, field type, and a flag indicating whether the site column is required or not.

Both overloads return a string value of the site column's display name. Similar to creating a site column using the browser interface, if any spaces are present in the display name when created, SharePoint will replace them with the _x0020_ string. To avoid this, use a similar technique to the one just described: Create the site column with a name containing no spaces and then immediately obtain a reference to it and change the display name, as shown in Listing 6-1.

Listing 6-1: Creating site columns via code

```
using System;
using Microsoft.SharePoint;

namespace WROX.ProMossWcm.Chapter06 {
  class Program {
    static void Main (string[] args) {

      using (SPSite siteCollection = new SPSite("http://wcm")) {
        using (SPWeb site = siteCollection.RootWeb) {
          // create field using desired internal name (no spaces)
          string prByLineFieldName = site.Fields.Add("PRByLine",
SPFieldType.Text, false);
          site.Update();

          // get reference to new site column
          SPField prByLineField = site.Fields[prByLineFieldName];

          // set display name & group
          prByLineField.Title = "Press Release ByLine";
          prByLineField.Group = "WROX";
          prByLineField.Update();
        }
      }

    }
  }
}
```

While providing additional flexibility and control in creating site columns over the browser, the site column created in Listing 6-1 still lives only in the SharePoint content database.

Creating Site Column Definitions via Features

The only way to provide the most flexibility in terms of control over the settings of the site column definition, promoting the easiest reuse, and portability to different environments is to use WSS Features. The CAML in Listing 6-2 reflects the element manifest that defines two site columns within a Feature. When the Feature that references this element manifest is activated, it is added to the SharePoint site.

Listing 6-2: Feature element manifest defining two site columns

```xml
<?xml version="1.0" encoding="utf-8" ?>
<Elements xmlns="http://schemas.microsoft.com/sharepoint/">
   <Field SourceID="http://schemas.microsoft.com/sharepoint/3.0"
             ID="{D8BCA662-8D3F-40B3-993D-408FF04FE264}"
             Name="PRByLine"
             DisplayName="Press Release ByLine"
             Group="WROX"
             Type="Text"
             Required="FALSE"
             ReadOnly="FALSE"
             Sealed="FALSE"
             Hidden="FALSE" />
   <Field SourceID="http://schemas.microsoft.com/sharepoint/3.0"
             ID="{249C1FED-EE2B-481A-89E0-A9041A359252}"
             Name="PRBody"
             DisplayName="Press Release Body"
             Group="WROX"
             Type="HTML"
             Required="TRUE"
             Sealed="FALSE"
             ReadOnly="FALSE"
             Hidden="FALSE" />
</Elements>
```

The site columns created in this listing are the same site columns created using the browser interface and custom code. Notice that some additional attributes are specified. Many of these can be set in the browser interface or custom code, as well as with a Feature. First, the Name (internal name) and DisplayName attributes are used to explicitly set these two values. Using each property gives developers full control without having to address the _x0020_ string in the internal name.

Two other attributes should stand out: ReadOnly and Sealed. A read-only site column is one that cannot be updated through the browser user interface, but it can be altered programmatically. A sealed site column is one that cannot be changed through the browser interface or programmatically; the only way to change a sealed site column is by changing the CAML in the Feature.

> ### Trick: Generating Site Column Element Manifest Files for Features
>
> Although creating site column definitions using Features provides the most flexibility, reuse, and portability, the challenge is that it takes longer to create Features. This is primarily so because of the lack of a "Feature designer"; all CAML must be written by hand. The browser approach of creating site columns has a leg up on the Feature approach because it is so much simpler. Thankfully, virtually everything in SharePoint is accessible via the SharePoint API. This enables developers to write custom code obtaining references to SharePoint objects — including site columns! Therefore, the SharePoint browser interface can serve as the "designer" tool for creating site columns in an isolated development environment; and with some custom code, the XML necessary for element manifest files can be generated.
>
> A sample project, AC's WCM Custom Commands for STSADM.EXE (`www.andrewconnell.com/go/214`), includes a custom `STSADM.EXE` command: `GenSiteColumnsXml`. After providing a few required and optional parameters, this command generates an element manifest file containing the CAML representation of site columns in the specified SharePoint site. The command does not produce the exact CAML that would be used to create the site column, but it comes close. It follows the 80-20 rule whereby 80% of the work is automated, leaving 20% for developer involvement.

Content Types

Content types were introduced to the SharePoint platform in WSS 3.0. In previous versions of SharePoint, each list schema was defined either in a template or on-the-fly. A limitation of this approach is that lists could only contain a specific type of information, which was always tightly coupled with a specific list. Microsoft added the concept of content types in WSS 3.0 to define the underlying schema, business rules, and other metadata on a particular type of information while not explicitly tying it to a specific list. Now a site owner can add multiple types of content to a list by adding content types to the list. This means that now heterogeneous data can be added to the same list. For example, a list named Proposals can now contain both Marketing Proposals and Sales Proposals, each having a unique schema and metadata associated with it.

One very important thing to keep in mind about content types is that by themselves, they store no data. In addition, content types are not defined within the scope of a SharePoint list. Instead, they define the structure of data. It is only when a content type is added to a list that data can conform to the content type. This separation of defining the schema of data from its storage facilitates more content standardization across SharePoint sites. Like site columns, content types are scoped at the SharePoint site level (`SPWeb`) and reside in a special gallery called the Site Content Type gallery.

For more information on content types, refer to the official documentation on MSDN (`www.andrewconnell.com/go/215`).

All content types must inherit from another content type. The lone exception to this rule is the root content type provided by Microsoft called *System*. The System content type is hidden from the SharePoint browser user interface and is not available when selecting a content type to inherit from when creating a new content type. It is recommended that content types be created to inherit not from System directly, but from Item, which inherits from System. All provided content types ultimately inherit from Item.

Developers can define various aspects of a content type. The most common things defined in a content type are site columns, but developers can also define things such as workflows, event receivers, policies, and even the document templates that should be loaded when a new item is created based on the content type. The document template is a URL pointing to a specific file on the server. This file can be in the format of a Microsoft Word template (as in the case of a marketing proposal) or a Web page (as in the case of the Page content type, which points to the Create Page page, `/_layouts/CreatePage.aspx`.

Content Type IDs

Unlike site columns, content types only have one form of identification. A content type ID uniquely identifies a content type within a site collection, as well as the lineage of that content type. Thankfully, SharePoint handles the creation of content type IDs when creating content types using the browser interface or with custom code. However, developers explicitly specify the content type ID when creating content types via Features. It is beneficial for developers to understand how content type IDs are structured in order to track the inheritance. By examining a content type's ID, one can determine the parent content type, its parent content type, and so on, going all the way back to the System content type. Content type IDs follow one of two conventions:

❑ [parent_content_type_ID] + [2-digit hex value not being '00']

❑ [parent_content_type_ID] + 00 + [GUID with no curly brackets or hyphens]

Why two conventions? Simply put, it provides more flexibility. Content type IDs are limited to a length of 1024 characters. The capability to include GUIDs in content type IDs provides the greatest flexibility, as it minimizes the chances for content type ID collision.

Consider the Page content type created by the activation of the Publishing Features — specifically, the Feature `PublishingResources`. Page layouts (used to create content/publishing pages) must use content types that inherit from the Page content type, and they can easily be used to demonstrate how the lineage is represented by the content type ID.

Figure 6-1 shows how the Page content type inherits from System Page (another content type created by the `PublishingResources` Feature), then Document, Item, and ultimately System. Each content type in the hierarchy has a specific purpose. For instance, the System Page content type defines the core site columns required on all publishing pages, such as scheduling and content owner information; and the Page content type defines the document template that should be loaded when a new item is created based on this template.

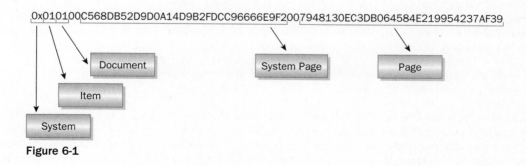

Figure 6-1

When should a custom content type use the two-digit hex value or GUID convention? Microsoft's recommendation is to use the GUID convention when creating a new content type that is based on a provided content type — provided by either Microsoft or a third party. Therefore, when creating custom content types for Publishing sites, it is recommended to start with the Page content type ID (to inherit from Page) and use the GUID convention to create something unique to the specific project. Then, all subsequent content types can use the two-digit hex convention. In effect, this creates a unique namespace for all content types for a particular project.

The following three content type IDs demonstrate this approach for a given project. Note that the Page content type is omitted for readability, the underlined portion represents the project uniqueness (or namespace), and the bold portion is the uniqueness for each content type:

❑ **Press Release** — `[Page content type ID]00242457EFB8B24247815D688C526CD44D01`

❑ **Executive Biography** — `[Page content type ID]00242457EFB8B24247815D688 C526CD44D02`

❑ **Product Detail** — `[Page content type ID]00242457EFB8B24247815D688C526CD44D03`

Creating Content Types

SharePoint provides the same three options for creating content type definitions that are available to create site columns. Just like site columns, the first two options (via the browser or custom code) store the content type definitions in the SharePoint site's content database, whereas the third option (via Features) keeps the content type definition on the file system until the Feature is activated, thereby offering the greatest reuse and portability. The following sections walk through the process of creating content type definitions using each of the three options. Similar to site columns, the user must have Design rights in order to create and manage site columns. All three options that follow create the same content type, so testing all three on the same site collection could result in an error. This makes it easier to see the differences between the various options.

Creating Content Types via the Browser Interface

Open a browser, navigate to a Publishing site's Site Settings page and select Site Content Type Gallery under the Galleries column. Then, from the Site Content Type Gallery page, select Create and use the following information to create a new content type:

❑ **Name** — Press Release

❑ **Select parent content type from** — Publishing Content Types

❑ **Parent Content Type** — Page

❑ **Group** — New Group: WROX

With a content type created, the next step is to add the site columns to the content type. To do this, from the Site Content Type: Press Release page, select Add From Existing Site Columns at the bottom of the page to select the site columns created previously in this chapter. On the Add Columns to Site Content Type: Press Release page, select the two fields from the WROX group named Press Release ByLine and

Press Release Body. These two columns should now appear in the list of the columns inherited from the Page content type (specifically, the System Page content type), as well as the two columns just added (see Figure 6-2).

Columns			
Name	Type	Status	Source
Name	File	Required	Document
Title	Single line of text	Optional	Item
Description	Multiple lines of text	Optional	System Page
Scheduling Start Date	Publishing Schedule Start Date	Optional	System Page
Scheduling End Date	Publishing Schedule End Date	Optional	System Page
Contact	Person or Group	Optional	System Page
Contact E-Mail Address	Single line of text	Optional	System Page
Contact Name	Single line of text	Optional	System Page
Contact Picture	Hyperlink or Picture	Optional	System Page
Rollup Image	Publishing Image	Optional	System Page
Target Audiences	Audience Targeting	Optional	System Page
Press Release Body	Publishing HTML	Required	
Press Release ByLine	Single line of text	Optional	

▫ Add from existing site columns
▫ Add from new site column
▫ Column order

Figure 6-2

At this point, the content type can now be used in association with a page layout to create new publishing pages. This content type is used in Chapter 7 to create new page layouts.

Creating Content Types via Code

Creating content types with custom code involves the use of the `Microsoft.SharePoint` `.SPContentType` and `Microsoft.SharePoint.SPContentTypeCollection` classes. Just like site columns, each SharePoint site (`SPWeb`) contains a `ContentTypes` property containing all content type definitions in the site's content type gallery. To create a new site column in code, first obtain a reference to the content type it inherits from, create the content type, add any desired site columns, and then add the content type to the site's `ContentType` collection, as shown in Listing 6-3.

Listing 6-3: Creating content types via code with site columns

```
using System;
using Microsoft.SharePoint;

namespace WROX.ProMossWcm.Chapter06 {
  class Program {
    static void Main (string[] args) {
      using (SPSite siteCollection = new SPSite("http://wcm")) {
        using (SPWeb site = siteCollection.RootWeb) {
          // get reference to "Page" content type this will inherit from
          SPContentType pageContentType = site.AvailableContentTypes["Page"];

          // create new content type
```

(continued)

Listing 6-3 *(continued)*

```
            SPContentType prContentType = new SPContentType(pageContentType,
    site.ContentTypes, "Press Release");
            prContentType.Group = "WROX";

            // add content type to the site
            site.ContentTypes.Add(prContentType);
            site.Update();

            // add site columns to content type
            SPField prByLineField = site.AvailableFields["Press Release ByLine"];
            prContentType.FieldLinks.Add(new SPFieldLink(prByLineField));
            SPField prBodyField = site.AvailableFields["Press Release Body"];
            prContentType.FieldLinks.Add(new SPFieldLink(prBodyField));

            prContentType.Update();

        }
      }
    }
  }
}
```

As the code in Listing 6-3 demonstrates, to add site columns to a content type they must be added as links, or references. This is done by obtaining a reference to an existing site column (`SPField`) and adding it as a new link (`SPFieldLink`) to the content type. Unlike lists, columns cannot be created within a content type on-the-fly — they must exist in the site column gallery and be referenced from a content type.

Creating Content Type Definitions via Features

Yet again, for the most flexibility and portability, create site elements such as content types with Features. Listing 6-4 shows the CAML in an element manifest in a Feature that, when activated, creates a new content type definition in a site that inherits from the Page content type. Notice that the content type ID inherits from the Page content type ID.

Listing 6-4: Feature element manifest defining a content type with two site columns

```
<?xml version="1.0" encoding="utf-8" ?>
<Elements xmlns="http://schemas.microsoft.com/sharepoint/">
  <ContentType ID="0x010100C568DB52D9D0A14D9B2FDCC96666E9F2007948130EC3DB064584E219
954237AF3900242457EFB8B24247815D688C526CD44D01"
               Name="Press Release"
               Group="WROX">
    <FieldRefs>
      <FieldRef ID="{D8BCA662-8D3F-40B3-993D-408FF04FE264}"
                Name="PRByLine" DisplayName="Press Release ByLine" />
      <FieldRef ID="{249C1FED-EE2B-481A-89E0-A9041A359252}"
                Name="PRBody" DisplayName="Press Release Body" />
    </FieldRefs>
  </ContentType>
</Elements>
```

Note two things from the CAML in Listing 6-4. First, when referencing a site column, both the site column's ID and Name (internal name) must be specified. Second, the content type can implement the site column using a different Display Name than that which is specified in the site column definition. In the case of Listing 6-4, the DisplayName attribute is not changed from the site column's original definition. This is where the Display Name can be overridden in the content type implementation of the site column.

Trick: Generating Content Type Element Manifest Files for Features

Similar to site columns, content types are also challenging to create using Features due to the amount of manual CAML coding required in element manifest files. However, like site columns, developers can use the browser interface as a designer for creating content types and then leverage the SharePoint API to generate the necessary CAML for use in Features. The same sample project mentioned previously in this chapter, AC's WCM Custom Commands for STSADM.EXE (www.andrewconnell.com/go/214), contains a custom command for generating the CAML for content types: GenSiteContentTypesXml. After providing a few required and optional parameters, this command generates an element manifest file containing the CAML representation of content types in the specified SharePoint site. It too follows the 80-20 rule that the previous command abides by.

Role of Site Columns and Content Types in Publishing Sites

While the title of this section might imply that site columns and content types have a special role or are used in some special way in Publishing sites (compared to standard WSS 3.0 sites), that is not the case. It is actually how content types are leveraged within a Publishing site — specifically, content pages — that warrants a bit of explanation.

When a content owner creates a new page, one of the first things selected is the page layout (see Figure 6-3). Selecting a page layout implicitly selects a content type as well: the content type the page layout is associated with. In this pairing, the content type is defining the schema, or the data elements, comprising the particular type of page. These data elements, or fields, are defined in the content type using site columns. The page layout serves the role of defining the rendering (when combined with the site's selected master page).

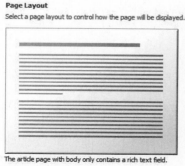

Page Layout

Select a page layout to control how the page will be displayed.

The article page with body only contains a rich text field.

Figure 6-3

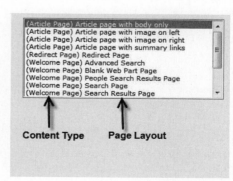

Content Type   Page Layout

With content types defining the schema of the page, not only can developers specify the site columns (also known as *data elements*) for a type of a page, everything else content types bring to the table can also be leveraged. For instance, special workflows or event receivers can be associated with types of content, not just the list the content resides within. This capability provides developers with the most control over a site's content.

Lists

The lowest level of a storage construct in SharePoint is a list. SharePoint lists are similar to database tables in many ways. In terms of the structure, lists have fields (columns) and items (records) just like databases. Database tables have *triggers*, events that fire under certain circumstances, such as when records are added, updated, or deleted. SharePoint lists also have triggers, known as *events*, that enable developers to write event handlers to execute custom code under certain circumstances. This analogy to a database table should be taken very loosely though, as there are some significant differences. For instance, database tables are optimized for multiple (and rapid) read/write operations, as well as to hold vast amounts of data, unlike SharePoint lists.

SharePoint lists also contain some additional capabilities. All SharePoint lists are capable of delivering their contents in the form of Really Simple Syndication (RSS), making it very easy to consume and present data stored within lists in other applications. Administrators can also associate pre-defined workflow templates with a list, as well as set unique permissions on the list, breaking the inheritance of permissions from the site in which the list resides.

Lists also have versioning capabilities. SharePoint lists can be configured to create a new version when an item is updated, optionally limiting how many versions can be retained. Document libraries, a type of SharePoint list, have enhanced versioning capabilities that enable administrators to configure not only whether the list allows versioning, but also the numbering scheme used. Administrators can elect to create only major versions or create major.minor versions. The minor versions are referred to as *draft revisions*. For instance, version 1.2 of a document means there is a published version (v1.#) of the document, but an updated draft version that is on the second revision (v#.2). When the document is published, the version is promoted to the next major version — 2.0.0 in this case.

All SharePoint sites contain at least a few core lists. Lists such as the Master Page Gallery, Web Part Gallery, User Information List, Site Template Gallery, and List Template Gallery are found in every single SharePoint site. These lists are created using the Global site definition that applies to all new SharePoint sites.

Special Publishing Lists

In addition to all the stock lists that every SharePoint site contains, Publishing sites create a few additional lists when the Publishing Features are activated. Some of these are special lists that reside only in the top-level site of the Publishing site collection, whereas others are found in every site that has the Publishing Feature activated.

Content and Structure Reports

The Content and Structure Reports list resides in the top-level site of the site collection. This list contains pre-defined CAML queries with a user-friendly name that content owners and administrators can use to find content meeting specific criteria. For instance, content owners can quickly see a list of all the content pages within a site that are checked out to them or those pages that are pending approval. Other reports might include lists of all the pages that are going live within the next seven days, as well as those which are expiring within seven days.

The reports contained in this list are available from the Site Actions menu for quick reference. Site administrators and developers can create additional reports and store them in this list for future use.

Images and Documents (and Site Collection Documents and Images)

The Images and Documents libraries are created in every site for which the Publishing Features have been activated. Content owners can manage the contents of these libraries, storing images used throughout a site, as well as documents and media files such as Window Media files, Flash movies, and ZIPs. When authoring a page, a content owner can select items from the Images and Documents libraries within the same site where the page is being created; content owners cannot select items from the Images and Documents in other sites, including parent sites.

While the restriction of only being able to select items from the same Images and Documents library is helpful in many cases, sometimes sites need some content in the form of images, documents, or media to be available across the entire site collection. To address this, the Publishing Features create two special galleries in the top-level site of the Publishing site collection: Site Collection Images and Site Collection Documents. Not only do content owners have access to the Images and Documents galleries within the site where the page is being created, they can also select items from the two special site collection galleries. These galleries are the ideal places to put things such as a company logo or a privacy policy.

Pages

The Pages list is created in every site where the Publishing Features have been activated. All content pages created by content owners are stored in each site's Pages list. Each content page, or list item, stored in the Pages list contains the data elements for each page, the title of the page, the file name of the page that appears in the URL, and the page layout selected to render the page.

Reusable Content

The Reusable Content list contains HTML or text content that can be added to content pages by content owners. This capability facilitates content reuse across a site, minimizing duplication. Content reuse enables site administrators to ensure that aspects of the site such as the company name, product name, or employee names are consistent across the site. When a new reusable content item is created, the creator has the option to automatically update the content in all pages where it is used. If this is selected, when the content is added to a page by an author, a read-only reference is added. Otherwise, if the item is not set to automatically update, the content is copied to the page, where it can then be updated. This list can be found in the top-level site of the site collection.

Style Library

The Style Library list resides in the top-level site of the site collection and contains images, style sheets, and XSL styles used throughout the site. Developers and designers should add files to this library that are used either in the branding of a site, such as CSS files and images used in the chrome of the look and feel, and XSL files that are used with the three Publishing Web Parts (covered in Chapter 11).

Creating Lists

While SharePoint creates many lists automatically for every SharePoint site (as well as some special ones depending on the type of site created, as in the case of a Publishing site), it also enables lists to be created by administrators, developers, and end users — granted they have the necessary rights to do so (specifically, Manage Lists). As with site columns, content types, and many other things within SharePoint, there are various ways to create a list within a SharePoint site. Again, just like site columns and content types, the way the list is created dictates how portable and reusable it is. The three options for creating SharePoint lists are using the browser, creating it through custom code, or using SharePoint Features to define the list schema and template, and optionally create an instance based on the template.

Creating Lists via the Browser Interface

To create a new list using the browser, navigate to a site and select Site Actions ⇨ Create or select Site Actions ⇨ Site Settings and from the Site Settings page select Site Libraries and Lists ⇨ Create New Content. The Create page contains a list of the various types of lists and libraries that can be created. The items on the Create page are lists and library templates previously defined. If none of the provided lists suit a project's needs, select the Custom List link in the Custom Lists column to create a minimal list with only a single column.

Next, on the New page, enter a title and optional description of the list and specify whether it should appear in the Quick Launch menu (left-hand navigation) and click Create. With the list created, the next step is to add some columns to it. With the list loaded in the browser, select Settings ⇨ List Settings to get to the list customization page. On the Customization [*list name*] page, note that the minimal columns have been added and some links are provided to add columns to the list. Adding columns to a list is similar to adding site columns to a content type.

By default, the Custom List template is not set to allow content types to be managed. To enable the list for content types, select Advanced Settings on the list's customization page and toggle the Content Types option at the top of the page.

Once a list has been created, it can be saved as a template for use in creating additional lists or to move the list template from one site to another in the same or different environments. This is done by selecting the Save List As Template option on the list customization page.

Creating Lists via Code

Creating a list via code involves using the `Microsoft.SharePoint.SPList` and `Microsoft.SharePoint.SPListTemplate` classes. Lists are created within the context of a SharePoint site. Therefore, the first step is to obtain a reference to a SharePoint site. Just like creating lists via the browser, an existing list template must first be selected. Therefore, the next step is to obtain a reference to an existing list template. Finally, create a new list using the `SPListCollection.Add()` method, which creates the list and returns the unique ID of the list. This unique ID, a GUID, can be used to obtain a reference to the list.

With the list created, developers can then customize it using the provided properties, as well as add columns to it. Columns can be added as list columns or as site columns. To add site columns, obtain a reference to an existing column in the site column gallery for the site and pass it in when creating the column.

The following code in Listing 6-5 demonstrates how to create a list programmatically, add it to the site's Quick Launch navigation, and add a few columns to it.

Listing 6-5: Creating lists programmatically with custom code

```csharp
using System;
using Microsoft.SharePoint;

namespace WROX.ProMossWcm.Chapter06 {
  class Program {
    static void Main (string[] args) {
      using (SPSite siteCollection = new SPSite("http://wcm")) {
        using (SPWeb site = siteCollection.RootWeb) {
          // get reference to the 'Custom Lists' template
          SPListTemplate customListTemplate = site.ListTemplates["Custom List"];

          // create a new list & retrieve a reference to that list
          Guid wroxListID = site.Lists.Add("WROX Publications", "List of SharePoint
books by WROX", customListTemplate);
          SPList wroxList = site.Lists[wroxListID];

          // set list to appear in left-hand navigation
          wroxList.OnQuickLaunch = true;

          // add a few columns
          wroxList.Fields.Add("ISBN", SPFieldType.Text, true);
          wroxList.Fields.Add("Authors", SPFieldType.Text, true);
          wroxList.Fields.Add("BookURL", SPFieldType.URL, true);
          wroxList.Update();

          site.Upda te();
        }
      }
    }
  }
}
```

Creating List Templates and Instances via Features

Notice that when creating a list using either the SharePoint browser interface or with custom code, one of the required first steps is to specify the template on which the list is based. How are these templates defined? As covered earlier in the discussion on creating lists using the browser interface, once a list is created it can be saved as a template. This template file is saved in the List Templates gallery and can be exported for use in other SharePoint sites. However, the template cannot be easily customized because it is packaged up into a SharePoint template file (*.STP), which is just a *.CAB file with a special extension. The contents of this file, manifest.xml, contains all the details for the template. Editing this file is quite challenging, however, and not a trivial task.

Another way to create list templates and instances is using a *list schema:* a sizeable CAML file defining the structure of a list. List schemas can be deployed using site definitions, as performed in WSS 2.0, but this is no longer recommended. The problem with this approach is that a list schema can only be added to a site upon site provisioning. Instead, the new and recommended way is to register the schema with a site and optionally create an instance of the list using Features. The Feature schema contains two site elements for use in element manifest files to create templates and instances based on templates: `<ListTemplate />` and `<ListInstance />`.

The core piece of a list template is the list schema file: `schema.xml`. This file resides within a subfolder in the Feature that makes the site aware of the list template. The `schema.xml` file contains all the information needed to define the characteristics of the list. At the root of the file is the `<List />` element, which specifies the information about the list (see Listing 6-6).

Listing 6-6: List definition file — schema.xml

```xml
<?xml version="1.0" encoding="utf-8"?>
<List xmlns:ows="Microsoft SharePoint"
      xmlns="http://schemas.microsoft.com/sharepoint/"
      Name="WroxPublications"
      Title="WroxPublications"
      BaseType="0"
      Direction="LTR"
      Url="Lists/WroxPublications">
  <MetaData>
    <ContentTypes />
    <Fields />
    <Views />
    <Forms />
  </MetaData>
</List>
```

In addition to basic information about the list contained in the `schema.xml` file, notice the `<MetaData/>` section in Listing 6-6. Within this section, developers can specify content types automatically bound to the list, all the fields within the list (including those defined in bound content types), all list views, and finally the new, edit, and display forms to be used for the list.

> *Unfortunately, not all CAML markup is included in the code samples for creating list templates. This is because list templates require a significant amount of CAML markup to define list views — so much CAML that due to space constraints and readability, not all markup is included in this book. The complete solution for creating the list template and instance by using Features is included. For additional information on the list schema file, refer to the official documentation on MSDN (`www.andrewconnell.com/go/216`).*

With the list schema created, the next thing to create is the `<ListTemplate />` element within the Feature that, when activated, makes the SharePoint site aware of the new list template definition (see Listing 6-7).

Listing 6-7: Element manifest for WroxPublications list template

```xml
<?xml version="1.0" encoding="utf-8" ?>
<Elements xmlns="http://schemas.microsoft.com/sharepoint/">
  <ListTemplate Name="WroxPublications"
                Type="10010"
                BaseType="0"
                DisplayName="WROX Publication List"
                SecurityBits="11"
```

```
                         VersioningEnabled="False"
                         Sequence="100"
                         Hidden="False"
                         Image="/_layouts/images/itcontct.gif" />
    </Elements>
```

A few attributes in the `<ListTemplate />` Listing 6-7 warrant some explanation:

❑ **Name** — This is the unique name of the list template within the Feature. The value in this attribute must match the name of the folder within the Feature containing the `schema.xml` file. Upon Feature activation, SharePoint looks in this folder within the Feature for the list schema file.

❑ **Type** — The list type is a unique ID of the list template that can be used by this Feature, or by other Features, to create list instances based on the template. It is recommended that you pick a number greater than 10,000, as the first 10,000 IDs are reserved for Microsoft's current and future use.

❑ **BaseType** — The value here points to the ID of an underlying list template on which the list is based. In the case of Listing 6-7, the WroxPublications list template is based on the Custom List (`Type=0`) template, which is the most bare-bones list template available and a great one to start with for custom list templates.

Now that the SharePoint site is aware of the list schema thanks to the `<ListTemplate />` node, the last thing to add to the Feature is a `<ListInstance />` site element, which creates an instance of the list based on the specified template upon Feature activation. Like the `<ListTemplate />` site element, add the CAML shown in Listing 6-8 to an element manifest in the Feature.

Listing 6-8: Element manifest to create a list instance

```
<?xml version="1.0" encoding="utf-8" ?>
<Elements xmlns="http://schemas.microsoft.com/sharepoint/">
   <ListInstance TemplateType="10010"
                 Id="WroxPublicationsList"
                 Title="Wrox Publications"
                 Url="Lists/WroxPublications"
                 OnQuickLaunch="True">
     <Data>
       <Rows>
         <Row>
           <Field Name="Title">Real World SharePoint 2007: Indispensable Experiences
From 16 MOSS and WSS MVPs</Field>
           <Field Name="ISBN">978-0-470-16835-6</Field>
           <Field Name="Authors">[... omitted for brevity ...]</Field>
           <Field Name="BookURL">http://www.wrox.com/WileyCDA/WroxTitle/productCd-
0470168358.html</Field>
         </Row>
       </Rows>
     </Data>
   </ListInstance>
</Elements>
```

Notice the TemplateType attribute in the <ListInstance /> in Listing 6-8. This is the ID of the list template defined in the <ListTemplate /> site element. In addition to creating instances of lists with Features, the <ListInstance /> site element can also define the default data to load into a list using the <Data /> node, as demonstrated in this listing.

Accessing Lists via the SharePoint API

One of the most common things SharePoint developers have to do is interact with lists programmatically when writing custom code, as virtually all SharePoint data lives within SharePoint lists. There are typically two ways to retrieve data from a SharePoint list programmatically: directly accessing the list or issuing a query against the list. The samples in this section are written to work with the WroxPublications list created in the previous section.

The first option, accessing a list directly, requires use of the SPList object. First a reference to the site containing the list must be obtained and then a reference to the list itself. From there, list items can be retrieved, created, or deleted. Keep in mind that any changes must be committed using the Update() method, as shown in Listing 6-9.

Listing 6-9: Directly accessing SharePoint lists

```
using System;
using Microsoft.SharePoint;

namespace WROX.ProMossWcm.Chapter06 {
   class Program {
     static void Main (string[] args) {
        using (SPSite siteCollection = new SPSite("http://wcm")) {
          using (SPWeb site = siteCollection.RootWeb) {
            // get reference to the list
            SPList spWroxBooks = site.Lists["Wrox Publications"];

            // add item
            SPListItem newItem = spWroxBooks.Items.Add();
            newItem["Title"] = "Professional SharePoint 2007 Web Content Management
Development";
            newItem["Authors"] = "Andrew Connell";
            newItem["ISBN"] = "978-0-470-22475-5";
            newItem["BookURL"] = "http://www.wrox.com/WileyCDA/WroxTitle/productCd-
0470224754.html";
            newItem.Update();

            // show all contents in the list
            foreach (SPListItem item in spWroxBooks.Items) {
              Console.Out.WriteLine(item.Title);
              Console.Out.WriteLine(item["ISBN"].ToString());
              Console.Out.WriteLine(Environment.NewLine);
            }
            Console.ReadLine();
          }
        }
     }
   }
}
```

Notice the code in Listing 6-9 where the fields in specific list items are accessed. The name used is the internal name. This is where the pains of the _x0020_ issue come into play, as this is the point where it would need to be included when referencing a field.

The second way to retrieve data from a list is by issuing a query. The SharePoint API offers many different options to query SharePoint lists. One way is using the Microsoft.SharePoint.SPQuery object and retrieving a collection of matching Microsoft.SharePoint.SPListItem objects. The SPQuery object enables developers to specify a CAML query and the maximum number of items to be returned from the query, as shown in Listing 6-10.

Listing 6-10: Querying SharePoint lists

```
using System;
using Microsoft.SharePoint;

namespace WROX.ProMossWcm.Chapter06 {
  class Program {
    static void Main (string[] args) {
      using (SPSite siteCollection = new SPSite("http://wcm")) {
        using (SPWeb site = siteCollection.RootWeb) {
          // get reference to the list
          SPList spWroxBooks = site.Lists["Wrox Publications"];

          // create query
          SPQuery query = new SPQuery();
          query.Query = "<Where><Eq><FieldRef Name='ISBN'/><Value Type='Text'>978-
0-470-16835-6</Value></Eq></Where>";
          query.RowLimit = 2;

          // get and display results
          SPListItemCollection results = spWroxBooks.GetItems(query);
          foreach (SPListItem item in results) {
            Console.Out.WriteLine(item.Title);
            Console.Out.WriteLine(item["ISBN"].ToString());
            Console.Out.WriteLine(Environment.NewLine);
          }
          Console.ReadLine();
        }
      }
    }
  }
}
```

Summary

This chapter has covered the core components within any SharePoint site: site columns, content types, and lists. Lists are the lowest-level storage construct within any SharePoint site, just as tables are in databases. Lists are primarily composed of columns but they can have additional characteristics such as custom workflows, event receivers, configurable versioning schemes, and policies. One of the challenges associated with lists in WSS 2.0 was that lists typically could only contain one type of data. This is because the schema of a list was not very flexible or portable. To address this, Microsoft introduced content types in WSS 3.0, which separate the schema of a type of information from the list. This enables administrators and developers to define a type of data, including some business rules and a process wrapped around it, that can then be associated with multiple lists.

All three of these different site elements (site columns, content types, and lists) can be created in various ways, such as using the SharePoint browser interface, using custom code, and using Features. In all three instances, however, Features provide the most code reuse and portability to implement the site elements in different environments.

Master Pages and Page Layouts

One of the biggest improvements to Windows SharePoint Services (WSS) 3.0 from the previous version of SharePoint is the adoption and utilization of ASP.NET 2.0 master pages. In previous versions of SharePoint, the look and feel customization of a site involved editing numerous files — depending upon the level of customization, that could involve hundreds of files! Thankfully, SharePoint's adoption of master pages dramatically reduces the number of files involved in customizing or branding a SharePoint site.

In addition to master pages, Microsoft had to come up with an easy way for content owners to choose among different page types and renderings without developer involvement. In effect, the content owner needed the capability to pick a template and fill in the content using a familiar Web interface. To achieve this, Publishing sites leverage page layouts, which act as templates. Developers and designers create page layouts that define where the editable regions of a page are placed, as well as the overall rendering of the page. Content owners then choose from the available page layouts when creating new pages.

This chapter covers the relationship of master pages and page layouts within Microsoft Office SharePoint Server (MOSS) 2007 Publishing sites. It also takes a look at a new capability in WSS 3.0 that enables developers to easily add or remove components to and from pre-defined areas within SharePoint sites.

Page Rendering Process Overview

Before jumping into master pages and page layouts, developers should understand how pages are constructed within a Publishing site, as it is a bit different from a typical SharePoint site. All content pages within a Publishing site are stored within a special list called Pages. This is the reason why the URL of Publishing sites always has /Pages near the end, just before the name of the requested page or file.

When a request is received for a URL within a Publishing site, SharePoint immediately goes to the list item of the requested Pages list. This list item contains some critical information related to the construction of the page:

- ❑ **Page Layout** — URL of the page layout associated with this page.

- ❑ **Associated Content Type** — Content type that defines the schema and business rules for a type of page.

- ❑ **Name** — URL name of the page requested (i.e., the default for the `default.aspx` requested page).

- ❑ **Metadata** — Data such as the page title, the description, the scheduling configuration, as well as contact information for the owner of the page.

- ❑ **Content Fields** — One or more fields containing content to be displayed on the page.

SharePoint first retrieves the URL of the page layout from the list item in the Pages list. Page layouts inherit from a specific class, `Microsoft.SharePoint.Publishing.PublishingLayoutPage`, that sets the master page for the request. Once SharePoint has retrieved both the page layout and the master page, the two are merged together. Finally, SharePoint pulls the content from the list item based on the various field controls defined in the page layout and adds it to the page.

Master Pages in Publishing Sites

Microsoft introduced master pages in ASP.NET 2.0. The concept is quite simple: A master page defines the general look and feel of a site, including CSS references, navigation, search, and the common top-branding most Web sites have. Master pages also contain content *placeholders,* which are sections of the page that can be replaced at runtime with other content. Developers create content pages that reference a specific master page, and the only markup these content pages contain are within content placeholders. The content placeholders in the master page are replaced at runtime with the contents defined within the content page.

SharePoint utilizes master pages a bit differently than a traditional ASP.NET 2.0 site. In ASP.NET 2.0, the master page is defined on a page-by-page basis. Instead, site owners and administrators specify the master page for a specific SharePoint site. All pages within that site are configured to use the master page specified for the current site. This is done using special *master page tokens,* which are covered later in the chapter. This advantage that SharePoint has over ASP.NET 2.0 enables site owners and administrators to change the master page of a site without touching the files on the file system or involving a developer.

Another difference between SharePoint's implementation of master pages and that of ASP.NET 2.0 is that the master pages in a SharePoint site are stored within a special document library: the Master Page Gallery. This is different from an ASP.NET 2.0 site where master pages are stored on the file system with the content pages. The Master Page Gallery is accessible by selecting Master Pages and Page Layouts under the Galleries section of a Publishing site's Site Settings page.

Types of Master Pages

Recall from Chapter 2 the discussion about two different types of pages within a SharePoint site: site pages and application pages. This topic applies to master pages as well and has a significant impact on the customization capabilities and limitations for SharePoint developers. As explained previously, unlike ASP.NET 2.0, content pages do not explicitly specify which master page they implement. Instead, the master page is set at the site level within a SharePoint site. This section explains how master pages are stored within a SharePoint site (`Microsoft.SharePoint.SPWeb`) and describes the two different types of master pages.

MasterUrl and CustomMasterUrl

Similar to ASP.NET 2.0, SharePoint sites are not limited to a single master page per site. A SharePoint site (`Microsoft.SharePoint.SPWeb`) contains two master page properties: `MasterUrl` and `CustomMasterUrl`. `SPWeb`. The `MasterUrl` property is used by all out-of-the-box (OOTB) content pages within WSS 3.0 and is the property that is set when changing the master page 3.0 using SharePoint Designer 2007. The `SPWeb.CustomMasterUrl` property is provided as a way for developers to use a different master page for custom content pages if desired.

Although WSS 3.0 sites do not utilize the `SPWeb.CustomMasterUrl` property, MOSS 2007 Publishing sites make heavy use of it. All page layouts are automatically configured to use the master page defined in the `SPWeb.CustomMasterUrl` property when rendering the site. The master page defined in the `SPWeb.MasterUrl` property is still used for standard SharePoint pages such as the list or form pages.

Unlike WSS 3.0 sites, Publishing sites contain a special Master Page Settings page, which is accessible from the Master Page link on the Site Settings page under the Look and Feel section. From the Site Master Page Settings page, shown in Figure 7-1, site owners and administrators can select a Site Master Page (the `SPWeb.CustomMasterUrl` property) and the System Master Page (the `SPWeb.MasterUrl` property). The master pages available for selection on this page are stored in the Master Page Gallery.

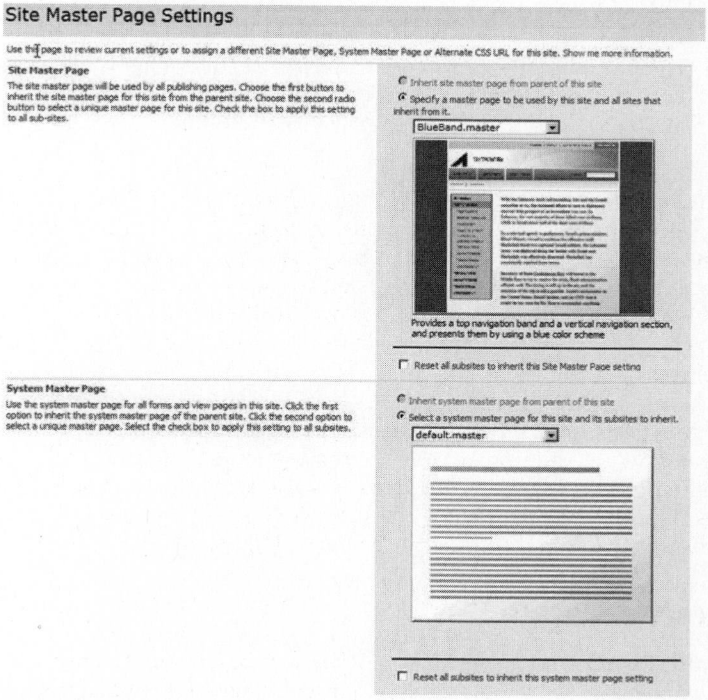

Figure 7-1

Site Master Pages Versus the Application Master Page

Aside from the two different master pages that can be specified, there are also two very different implementations of master pages within every SharePoint site. Recall from Chapter 2 that there are two different types of pages: site pages and application pages. Site pages support personalization and customization, can support themes, and contain Web Parts. The two master page properties on the SPWeb object, MasterUrl and CustomMasterUrl, are site pages, meaning they can be customized on a site-by-site basis. Application pages are found within http://site/_layouts and do not support personalization or customization. Site pages are found virtually everywhere else in a SharePoint site, such as list and form pages and Web Part pages. Site pages do support personalization and customization.

The difference between site pages and application pages also has an impact on master pages within a SharePoint site. As Chapter 2 explained, all application pages leverage the same master page, across all sites on the server. The application pages, which reside within the [..]\12\TEMPLATE\LAYOUTS folder, all contain hard-coded references to a specific master page: application.master. Because all SharePoint sites on a server share the same _layouts virtual directory path, does this mean that all SharePoint sites on the same server will look identical? Not necessarily. Developers can utilize SharePoint *themes*, a collection of CSS and image files, to influence the look and feel of application pages. Granted, CSS and images can only be taken so far, and sometimes customization of the underlying master page is the only option. Unfortunately, this is a limitation of application pages.

Are themes the only option for customizing application pages on a site-by-site basis due to the application.master limitation? No. One of the more common approaches users take is to create a copy of the [..]\12\TEMPLATE\LAYOUTS folder and change the _layouts virtual directory to point to the copied folder. That way, changes to application.master affect only a specific Web application and not all Web applications on a server. This option is not recommended because it has many downsides, one of which is that the _layouts virtual directory is set at the Web application level, meaning it is not possible to customize the application pages on a site-by-site or site collection-by-site collection basis: All site collections and sites within the Web application use the same _layouts virtual directory, and therefore the same master.

Another very large downside to this approach is that the _layouts folder is no longer in the SharePoint 12 folder structure. This means that any future hotfixes or service packs will not be applied to the copied folder. In addition, the capability to deploy files using WSS solution packages that contain files to be deployed to the [..]\12\TEMPLATE\LAYOUTS folder will not work for the copied folder. In addition, creating an additional copy of the _layouts folder is not supported by Microsoft.

Dynamically Switching application.master at Runtime

While there is no supported option for creating custom application.master pages on a site-by-site basis, some alternatives do exist. If creating alternate application.master pages is critical and necessary, consider creating a custom HTTP module that dynamically switches the application.master page out at runtime. The advantages to this approach are twofold: The original [..]\12\TEMPLATE\LAYOUTS folder is never moved, copied, or changed, and the HTTP module changes the master page at runtime from using the OOTB application.master to a custom application.master. Thus, no changes occur to the files contained in the SharePoint 12 folder.

An example of dynamically switching the `application.master` master page at runtime in application pages using a HTTP module can be obtained from `www.andrewconnell.com/go/217`. This sample not only contains an HTTP module that handles the dynamic switching, but it also creates a browser-based interface that enables site administrators to set the custom `application.master` page.

Be aware that this approach is not supported by Microsoft. This means if a SharePoint customer engages Microsoft's Customer Support Services (CSS) with a production issue, CSS will require that SharePoint be set back to a supported state before opening a case and investigating the issue. The advantage of using an HTTP module is that returning to a supported state can be quickly achieved by removing the single HTTP module registration line in the site's `web.config`. Therefore, this approach has no permanent downsides.

Master Page Tokens

As previously mentioned, SharePoint content pages do not contain references to explicit master pages. Instead, the master page is set at the site level using either the `MasterUrl` or the `CustomMasterUrl` property. If this is a dynamic reference that SharePoint switches out at runtime, what is stored in the content pages to tell SharePoint which master page to use? This is made possible using tokens that are interpreted as instructions by SharePoint at runtime to determine the URL of the master page to use. There are two types of tokens: *dynamic* and *static*.

Dynamic Master Page Tokens

Dynamic tokens are specific strings that tell SharePoint which master page to use — either the master page referenced in the `MasterUrl` property or the `CustomMasterUrl` property in the SharePoint site (`Microsoft.SharePoint.SPWeb`). There are two dynamic master page tokens:

❑ **~masterurl/default.master** — This token references the `Microsoft.SharePoint.SPWeb` `.MasterUrl` property. The entire string is read as the token. All pages within a WSS 3.0 site, OOTB, are configured to use this token by default. For example, if a content page has the directive:

```
<%@ Page MasterPageFile="~masterurl/default.master" %>
```

SharePoint would switch the token out at runtime with the following, which is the path to the default master page for an OOTB WSS 3.0 site:

```
<%@ Page MasterPageFile="_catalogs/masterpage/default.master" %>
```

❑ **~masterurl/custom.master** — This token references the `Microsoft.SharePoint.SPWeb` `.CustomMasterUrl` property. The entire string is read as the token. By default, no WSS 3.0 pages use this token, but developers are free to do so. However, this is not the case in Publishing sites, where it is heavily used. The `CustomMasterUrl` is used by all page layouts to define the look and feel of content pages.

Static Master Page Tokens

Static token strings, unlike the dynamic tokens, are not considered tokens; only the first part is considered a replaceable token. At runtime, SharePoint evaluates the first part of the token and replaces it with the URL specified, but it will not change the name of the master page. There are two different static tokens:

❑   ~sitecollection/default.master

❑   ~site/default.master

For example, if a content page had the following directive within the site http://site/subsite

```
<%@ Page MasterPageFile="~site/wrox.master" %>
```

SharePoint would switch the "~site" token out at runtime with the following:

```
<%@ Page MasterPageFile="/subsite/wrox.master" %>
```

Master Page Content Placeholders

Before creating master pages, developers need to be familiar with the use of content placeholders in creating master pages. In traditional ASP.NET 2.0 sites, developers define any number of content placeholders as desired. The SharePoint default master page contains 32 different content placeholders used by the content pages throughout SharePoint sites.

For a list of the content placeholders in the WSS 3.0 default master page, refer to the official documentation on MSDN (www.andrewconnell.com/go/217).

Note that not all of the 32 placeholders are required in all custom master pages. In fact, the eight provided master pages for Publishing sites only contain 21 of the 32 and one additional content placeholder. The following table contains all the content placeholders found in the eight provided Publishing master pages:

OSSConsole	PlaceHolderNavSpacer
PlaceHolderAdditionalPageHead	PlaceHolderPageDescription
PlaceHolderBodyAreaClass	PlaceHolderPageImage
PlaceHolderBodyLeftBorder	PlaceHolderPageTitle
PlaceHolderBodyRightMargin	PlaceHolderPageTitleInTitleArea
PlaceHolderCalendarNavigator	PlaceHolderSearchArea
PlaceHolderLeftActions	PlaceHolderTitleAreaClass
PlaceHolderLeftNavBar	PlaceHolderTitleAreaSeparator
PlaceHolderLeftNavBarTop	PlaceHolderTitleBreadcrumb
PlaceHolderMain	PlaceHolderTitleLeftBorder
PlaceHolderMiniConsole	PlaceHolderTitleRightMargin

Some of the content placeholders listed in the preceding table, while included in the eight Publishing master pages, are never rendered and shown. This is done by placing the content placeholders within an ASP.NET `Panel` control and setting the visibility to `false`, as shown in Listing 7-1.

Listing 7-1: Hiding content placeholder rendering

```
<asp:panel visible="false" runat="server">
  <asp:ContentPlaceHolder ID="PlaceHolderPageImage" runat="server" />
  <asp:ContentPlaceHolder ID="PlaceHolderBodyLeftBorder" runat="server" />
</asp:panel>
```

This technique enables site developers and designers to include content placeholders that are included within content pages, but keep any of the content defined in the content pages from being rendered. This is a common refactoring technique when implementing a rebranding campaign on a site. It enables designers to hide content placeholders with one simple action in the master page without going through all content pages to remove the content placeholder.

Creating Master Pages

Microsoft ships eight additional master pages with MOSS 2007 and provisions them into a new site when the site is created using the Publishing Portal site template. While these offer various unique layout and color schemes, the majority of MOSS Web Content Management customers will likely need to create custom master pages based on certain project requirements. Recall from Chapter 2 the discussion on customized versus uncustomized pages and SharePoint customization versus development. These topics are applicable in the context of master pages just as they are with any other type of SharePoint site. SharePoint master pages can be created in one of two ways: using SharePoint Designer or using Visual Studio (or some other text editor) and provisioning them into a SharePoint site using Features.

The differences between the two options are quite significant. In Chapter 2 you learned that customized files are those files whose source lives within the SharePoint site's content database. This can present a challenge for a large site, especially one in which the development process follows a structured software development life cycle that moves files and code through various environments such as testing and staging. When creating master pages with SharePoint Designer, the page starts as customized and resides exclusively within the content database; this is referred to as SharePoint customization.

If a project requires more control over the source of the files, as well as adoption within a structured software development life cycle and integration within a source control management system, developers can elect to create master pages using more of a template, and uncustomized, approach. To achieve this, developers create new master pages using a text editor, usually Visual Studio, and deploy using Features and WSS solution packages.

The next two sections document the two different approaches to creating master pages. A sample master page is provided in the code download associated with this book. The actual source of the master page is not important at this point; what is important is the process of creating master pages.

Creating Master Pages SharePoint Designer 2007

Open SharePoint Designer and an existing Publishing site by selecting File ⇨ Open Site. To create a new master page, select File ⇨ New. In the New dialog, select the Page tab, then ASP.NET in the first column, Master Page in the middle column, and finally click OK, as shown in Figure 7-2.

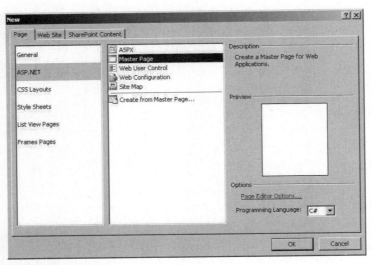

Figure 7-2

SharePoint Designer will create a new blank master page. One approach is to create the master page by copying an existing master page and customizing it. Another, and easier approach, is to start with what is commonly referred to as a "minimal master page." These are master pages that have the absolute bare minimum content and branding. Most contain the minimal CSS files to support the SharePoint administration interface such as the Site Actions menu or Page Editing Toolbar. A quick Web search using your search engine of choice will return numerous hits for some blogger's favorite minimal master. For simplicity, a minimal master page named minimal.master is included in the code download for this book. Open the minimal.master, or any master obtained from a search, in a text editor other than SharePoint Designer, select all the contents, and paste them into the master created by SharePoint Designer.

> ### Never Open Master Pages from the File System Using SharePoint Designer
>
> SharePoint Designer expects that all master pages it opens are contained within a SharePoint site, which includes additional information in the header. When a master page is opened from the file system, SharePoint Designer adds some extra code that it expected to be present. This extra code will cause the master page to throw an error at runtime in the SharePoint site. This is the source of a very common problem whereby a developer opens the WSS 3.0 default.master master page, makes no changes, but clicks Save regardless. The next time anyone browses to the SharePoint farm, nothing works because SharePoint Designer added extra code that corrupted the master page.

With the master page now created with the minimal content, save the master page to the Master Page Gallery by selecting File ⇨ Save As and browsing to `http://[site]/_catalogs/masterpage`.

At this point the master page is still checked out and unpublished. This is usually OK in a limited development environment, but if the master page was created in an environment that many people have access to, it is a good idea to check in and publish the page. Otherwise, after configuring the site to use the new master page, everyone else will receive a runtime error because the page is not published and thus they don't have the necessary permissions to see the site. To check in and publish the file, right-click the master page in the Folder List tool window and select Check In. Then select Publish a Major Version and click OK. A dialog will appear with the option to view/modify the approval status of the master page. Click Yes, which opens a new browser window that loads the Master Page Gallery with the master page at the top of the list. From the ECB menu of the minimal master page, select Approve/reject, as shown in Figure 7-3.

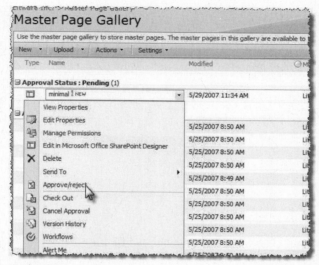

Figure 7-3

At this point the master page has been created, checked in, published, and approved, and can now be seen by anyone browsing the site. Configure the site to use the new minimal master page by browsing to the site and selecting Site Actions ⇨ Site Settings ⇨ Modify All Site Settings. On the Site Settings page, select Master Page under the Look and Feel column, then select the filename of the master page just created for the Site Master Page, and click OK. The Publishing site will now be using the new master page! Browse to the home page of the site (leaving the `http://[site]/_layouts` section) to see the master page in action.

When selecting the master page from the Site Master Page Settings page, notice that all the master pages had preview images associated with them, but the custom master page created with SharePoint Designer had a stock preview image. This is because SharePoint Designer does not have the capability to associate a preview image with a master page. After a master page has been created using SharePoint Designer, a preview image can then be associated with it by going to the properties of the master page list item within the Master Page Gallery and setting the Preview Image property to point to an existing image.

The master page created using SharePoint Designer resides exclusively within the SharePoint site's content database. The next section explains how to create a new master page as a file template living on the file system and provision it into a SharePoint site using a Feature as an uncustomized page.

Creating Master Pages Using Visual Studio and Features

Although creating master pages using SharePoint Designer is quite straightforward and provides developers and designers with a friendly WYSIWYG interface, it has its drawbacks. The most significant downside to creating master pages exclusively in SharePoint Designer is that the pages initially start out as customized, with no underlying template, meaning they reside exclusively within the database.

The other option is to go with more of the templated approach: Create the master page in a text editor, create a Feature that contains the master page, and upon activation it provisions the master pages as uncustomized instances into a SharePoint site, referencing the underlying template file on the file system. This approach enables developers to package the Feature and master page(s), as well as associated content, into WSS solution packages for easy deployment to other environments. This section walks through the process of adding a master page previously created to a Feature for deployment.

The first step is to create a new project in Visual Studio named Chapter7Pages for the Feature using the C# Empty Project template, as no code will be compiled in this Feature. Next, as recommended in Chapter 4, create the folder structure that will contain the Feature Chapter7Pages to mimic the SharePoint 12 folder structure, as shown in Figure 7-4.

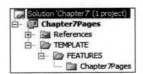

Figure 7-4

A sample master page, used throughout the remainder of the book, is included in the sample code download for this book. This master page, ACMETmp.master, contains a very simple user interface. In addition, a preview image named ACMEMasterPreviewTmp.gif is also included in the code download. It will be used as the preview image for the master page. Add these two files to a folder within the Chapter7Pages Feature folder named MasterPages (refer to Figure 7-4).

Next, create a new Feature definition XML file named feature.xml in the folder Chapter7Pages and add the CAML shown in Listing 7-2 to it.

Listing 7-2: Feature definition for the Chapter7Pages Feature

```xml
<?xml version="1.0" encoding="utf-8" ?>
<Feature xmlns="http://schemas.microsoft.com/sharepoint/"
         Id="D56F0D2D-0107-424d-AA0D-7120329A23E6"
         Title="Chapter 7 - Provisioning Master Pages and Page Layouts"
         Hidden="FALSE"
         Scope="Site"
         Version="1.0.0.0">

 <ElementManifests>
   <ElementManifest Location="elements.xml" />
   <ElementFile Location="MasterPages\ACMETmp.master" />
   <ElementFile Location="MasterPages\ACMEMasterPreviewTmp.gif" />
 </ElementManifests>

</Feature>
```

Note two things about the markup in Listing 7-2. First, the `Scope` attribute is set to `Site` (site collection) because only one Master Page Gallery exists in a site collection. Therefore, this Feature should not be available at each SharePoint site. Second, the `<ElementFile>` nodes are used to register the master page and preview image with the Feature definition. This will save time when packaging the Feature into a WSS solution package because each file won't need to be defined within the `manifest.xml` file.

With the Feature created, now the elements manifest file that will provision the files into SharePoint needs to be created. Create a new XML file named `elements.xml` in the `Chapter7Pages` Feature folder where the existing `feature.xml` file is located. The elements file will first provision the preview image and then the master page with a reference to the preview image. Add the CAML in Listing 7-3 to the `elements.xml` file to provision the preview image into the Master Page Gallery.

Listing 7-3: Elements manifest file provisioning a preview image

```xml
<?xml version="1.0" encoding="utf-8" ?>
<Elements xmlns="http://schemas.microsoft.com/sharepoint/">
  <Module Name="Master Page Preview Images"
          Url="_catalogs/masterpage/Preview Images/WROX"
          Path="MasterPages"
          RootWebOnly="TRUE">
    <File Url="ACMEMasterPreviewTmp.gif"
          Name="ACMEMasterPreview.gif"
          Type="GhostableInLibrary">
      <Property Name="Title"
                Value="ACMEMasterPreview.gif" />
    </File>
  </Module>
</Elements>
```

The CAML in Listing 7-3 needs some explanation. The `<Module>` site element, also referred to as a *file set*, groups similar files together. The attributes defined within the `<Module>` node are inherited by all the child `<File>` nodes. The following table details the various attributes in the `<Module>` element.

Attribute	Description
Name	Name of the file set.
Url	Site-relative path where the files will be provisioned. In Listing 7-3, the files will be provisioned to the Master Page Gallery within the subfolders `Preview Images/WROX`. If the folders are not present, SharePoint will automatically create them.
Path	Feature-relative path where the source files within the Feature are located. In Listing 7-3, the files are found within a subfolder named `MasterPages` within the root of the `Feature` folder.
RootWebOnly	When set to `TRUE`, the files in the file set are provisioned in the top-level site of the site collection.

File sets contain one or more files, as shown in Listing 7-3. Each `<File>` element represents a separate file to provision into a SharePoint site. The attributes in the `<File>` element are combined with those in the parent `<Module>` element. While some of the attributes have similar names to those in the `<Module>` element, they do not serve the same purpose. The following table details each of the attributes in the `<File>` element.

Attribute	Description
Url	Feature-relative path to the file. This attribute is combined with the `Path` attribute in the `<Module>` element. In Listing 7-3, the preview image would be found within the Feature at the following location: `MasterPages\ACMEMasterPreviewTmp.gif`.
Name	The name to assign the file when provisioned into the SharePoint site. This name becomes part of the URL to the file. In Listing 7-3, the URL for the file would be `http://[site]/_catalogs/masterpage/Preview Images/WROX/ACMEMasterPreview.gif`.
Type	When provisioning files into SharePoint libraries, this should always be set to `GhostableInLibrary`. When provisioning files into a SharePoint site but not adding the file to a library, this should be `Ghostable`.

The Master Page Gallery is just like any other SharePoint document library. It contains fields that are used to store metadata for each document added to the library. `<Property>` elements are contained within `<File>` elements. These elements are used to specify the value of the fields within the SharePoint library to which the files are being provisioned, such as the Master Page Gallery. Developers can use the `<Property>` element to set the values of the items added to the library. In the case of Listing 7-3, the `Title` field is assigned the value of `ACMEMasterPreview.gif`.

With a preview image provisioned, now the master page needs to be added to the element manifest file. Add the CAML shown in Listing 7-4 to the `elements.xml` file just after the `<Module>` element that provisioned the image.

Listing 7-4: Elements manifest file provisioning a master page

```xml
<?xml version="1.0" encoding="utf-8" ?>
<Elements xmlns="http://schemas.microsoft.com/sharepoint/">
  <Module Name="Master Page Preview Images"><!-- omitted for brevity --></Module>
  <Module Name="Master Pages"
          Url="_catalogs/masterpage"
          Path="MasterPages"
          RootWebOnly="TRUE">
    <File Url="ACMETmp.master"
          Name="ACME.master"
          Type="GhostableInLibrary">
      <Property Name="ContentType"
                Value="$Resources:cmscore,contenttype_masterpage_name;" />
      <Property Name="PublishingPreviewImage"
                Value="~SiteCollection/_catalogs/masterpage/Preview
Images/WROX/ACMEMasterPreview.gif, ~SiteCollection/_catalogs/masterpage/Preview
Images/WROX/ACMEMasterPreview.gif" />
      <Property Name="Title"
                Value="ACME.master" />
    </File>
  </Module>
</Elements>
```

The CAML provisioning a master page shown in Listing 7-4 is very similar to the same CAML that provisioned a preview image, with the exception of some extra field values being set. Two additional fields are set: `ContentType` and `PublishingPreviewImage`. The `ContentType` field specifies the content type of the master page list item in the Master Page Gallery (defining the schema and rules of the list item). The `PublishingPreviewImage` is a field of type URL that contains two values: the text value of a URL and the target of the URL. These two values are set by separating them with a comma.

Finally, with the Feature and necessary files created, the DDF file needs to be created in order to compile the Feature into a WSS solution package. Add a new text file named `BuildSharePointPackage.ddf` to a folder in the root of the project named `DeploymentFiles` and add the text in Listing 7-5 to it.

Listing 7-5: Diamond Directive File for Chapter7Pages Feature

```
.OPTION Explicit
.Set DiskDirectoryTemplate=CDROM
.Set CompressionType=MSZIP
.Set UniqueFiles=Off
.Set Cabinet=On
;*****************************************************
DeploymentFiles\manifest.xml

.Set DestinationDir=Chapter7Pages
TEMPLATE\FEATURES\Chapter7Pages\feature.xml
TEMPLATE\FEATURES\Chapter7Pages\elements.xml

.Set DestinationDir=Chapter7Pages\MasterPages
TEMPLATE\FEATURES\Chapter7Pages\MasterPages\ACMETmp.master
TEMPLATE\FEATURES\Chapter7Pages\MasterPages\ACMEMasterPreviewTmp.gif
```

Lastly, the `manifest.xml` file needs to be created and added to the project within the `DeploymentFiles` folder in the `Chapter7Pages` project. Add the CAML in Listing 7-6 to the `manifest.xml` file.

Listing 7-6: Manifest.xml for Chapter7Pages Feature

```xml
<?xml version="1.0" encoding="utf-8" ?>
<Solution xmlns="http://schemas.microsoft.com/sharepoint/"
          SolutionId="{7DFC3075-45C0-4946-9E5F-CA6BBC749C64}"
          DeploymentServerType="WebFrontEnd"
          ResetWebServer="FALSE">
  <FeatureManifests>
    <FeatureManifest Location="Chapter7Pages\feature.xml"/>
  </FeatureManifests>
</Solution>
```

Package the Feature into a `*.WSP` file by typing the following on the command line (the following assumes that it is being executed from the root of the project, the same place where the `Chapter7Pages` `.csproj` file is located):

```
[path_to_makecab]\MakeCab.exe /F DeploymentFiles/BuildSharePointPackage.ddf /D
CabinetNameTemplate=Chapter7.wsp /D DiskDirectory1=wsp
```

Now add the package to the SharePoint farm's solution store using `STSADM.EXE` (again, assuming it is executed from the root of the project):

```
[path_to_stsadm]\STSADM.EXE -o addsolution -filename wsp/Chapter7.wsp
```

Finally, deploy the solution to a Publishing site, navigate to the site and select Site Actions ⇨ Site Settings ⇨ Modify All Site Settings ⇨ Site Collection Features, and activate the Feature *Chapter 7 - Provisioning Master Pages and Page Layouts*. This provisions the master page and preview image to the Master Page Gallery, as shown in Figure 7-5, as uncustomized files referencing their templates on the file system in the Chapter 7 Feature. In addition, because the master page's Preview Image field was set, the preview image will now appear when the master page is selected in the Site Settings ⇨ Master Page administration page.

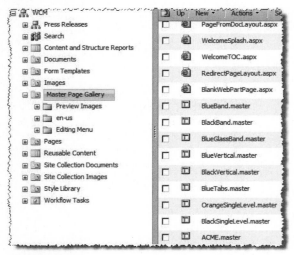

Figure 7-5

Incorporating Design Elements

Of course, provisioning a master page is helpful, but what about all the other files that make up the branding of the site? The master page likely references images and at least one site-specific CSS file, so how are these files added to the SharePoint site? Files related to branding, such as images and CSS files, should be added to a special SharePoint library, called the Style Library, that exists in the top-level site. This library has been assigned special permissions to ensure that even users with the most limited permissions can access the contents, as the files within it are usually referenced throughout the entire site topology.

Files can be added to the site collection's Style Library gallery by uploading them through the browser interface or using SharePoint Designer. Keep in mind that both of these techniques create customized files that reside exclusively in the SharePoint site's content database. The other approach is to provision the files using a Feature, as previously shown. For example, to add both the CSS and image files used by the sample master page included in the code download, add the two files (ACMETmp.css and ACMETmp.gif) to a new folder named Styles within the Feature and add the code shown in Listing 7-7 to the elements.xml file.

Listing 7-7: Element manifest file with branding files added

```xml
<?xml version="1.0" encoding="utf-8" ?>
<Elements xmlns="http://schemas.microsoft.com/sharepoint/">
  <Module Name="Master Page Preview Images"><!-- omitted for brevity --></Module>
  <Module Name="Master Pages"><!-- omitted for brevity --></Module>
  <Module Name="Styles"
          Url="Style Library"
          Path="Styles"
          RootWebOnly="TRUE">
    <File Url="ACMETmp.css"
          Name="ACME.css"
          Type="GhostableInLibrary">
      <Property Name="Title" Value="ACME.css" />
    </File>
    <File Url="ACMETmp.gif"
          Name="ACME.gif"
          Type="GhostableInLibrary">
      <Property Name="Title" Value="ACME.gif" />
    </File>
  </Module>
</Elements>
```

When referencing files within the Style Library from the master page, it is best to use a utility called SPUrl available to Publishing sites. SPUrl takes a string as an input and will automatically replace one of two tokens allowed with the URL equivalent: ~sitecollection (for site collections) or ~site (for SharePoint sites). For example, in Listing 7-7 where the image is provisioned at the root of the Style Library, use the following ASP.NET markup in the master page to reference the image:

```
<asp:image runat="server"
           ImageUrl="<% $SPUrl:~sitecollection/Style Library/ACME.gif%>" />
```

Page Layouts

The previous section covered master pages and a few different techniques for creating master pages in Publishing sites. Master pages enable developers and designers to define the overall look and feel of the Publishing site with just a single file, along with some additional branding files such as CSS or images. Just as in ASP.NET 2.0 sites, SharePoint sites also leverage content pages that fill in the content placeholders defined within a master page. Publishing sites take this a bit further by introducing a type of content page called a *page layout*. Page layouts, when combined with the master page, define the rendering and layout of a page. When the page layout is requested, SharePoint fetches the master page referenced within the SPWeb.CustomMasterUrl property and merges the two together. Developers and designers use page layouts to host editable regions of a page, implemented with Web Parts and field controls.

Page layouts have a special relationship with content types within a Publishing site. Each page layout must be associated with exactly one content type. This content type must inherit from the Page content type found in the Publishing Content Types group. Content types are used in a Publishing site to define the schema and rules for a particular type of content. For example, a Press Release content type may have fields for the title and byline, the date of the release, the press release body, optionally some reference links, as well as references with short bios for other companies mentioned in the press release. In addition, it may also have a special workflow associated with it defining a special approval process for the press release.

Keep in mind that the content type only defines the schema and rules for the type of content; it does not address the presentation in any way. This is where page layouts come into play. Page layouts, when combined with a master page, define the rendering/look and feel of a requested page. In addition, developers can associate multiple page layouts with a single content type to give content owners the utmost control in selecting different rendering options for a particular page type. When a content owner initiates the process of creating a new page within a Publishing site, the first thing he or she has to do is select a content type/page layout combination.

Moreover, content owners are not restricted to the page layout that is selected at the time of page creation. At any point in the future, even after the page has been published, a content owner can edit the page and change the selected page layout. The only limitation is that the only page layouts available are those associated with the content type selected when the page was created. This is because a page's content type cannot be switched from one content type to another after it has been created. In addition, page layouts can only be associated with exactly one content type; no one page layout can be associated with more than one content type.

Creating Page Layouts

The process of creating custom page layouts is very similar to the process of creating custom master pages. The same customization versus development or customized versus uncustomized debate comes into play when creating page layouts as it does with master pages. All the same concepts apply, so instead of rehashing them again, refer to the discussion earlier, as well as the full explanation in Chapter 2.

Developers are provided with one of two ways to create custom page layouts: using SharePoint Designer or using Visual Studio (or some other text editor) and provisioning them into a SharePoint site using

Features. Just like the previous sections on creating master pages, the following two sections cover both approaches to creating page layouts.

Creating Page Layouts Using SharePoint Designer 2007

Open SharePoint Designer and open an existing Publishing site by selecting File ⇨ Open Site. To create a new page layout, select File ⇨ New. In the New dialog, select the SharePoint Content tab, then SharePoint Publishing in the first column, and Page Layout in the center column. Before SharePoint Designer will create the page layout, it needs to know the filename, the name of the page layout, and the content type associated with this page layout (what defines the schema of the page). This page layout will be based on the Press Release content type created in Chapter 6, so use the following to complete the New dialog and click OK (see Figure 7-6).

- ❑ **Content Type Group** — WROX
- ❑ **Content Type Name** — Press Release
- ❑ **URL Name** — PressRelease.aspx
- ❑ **Title** — Default Press Release

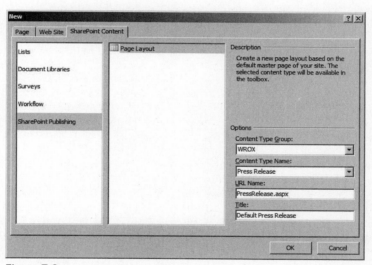

Figure 7-6

Now the page needs some structure. In the code download for this book, a sample page layout is provided named `ACMEPressTmp.aspx`. Open this file in a text editor, copy all the contents of the file, and paste it into the ASPX file SharePoint Designer created as the page layout while in the Code view of the page, replacing everything SharePoint Designer created. For now, skip the process of adding editable fields to the page, as the focus is on simply creating a new page layout. Adding editable regions to the page layout is addressed later.

Save the changes to the page layout. Just like master pages created using SharePoint Designer, the page layout is still checked out and unpublished. If development is happening in a local, isolated environment, then it is not important to check in and publish the file. However, if this is a shared development environment, then it is a good idea to go ahead and do so. Keep in mind that if the file is not checked in and published, then the person who has it checked out is the only one who will be able to render pages configured to use the page layout. The process of checking in and publishing the page layout is no different from doing the same thing with master pages.

With the page layout in the Master Page Gallery, content owners can now create pages based on the page layout and the associated content type. Browse to a Publishing site and select Site Actions ⇨ Create Page. On the Create Page page, use the following information to create the new content page and click Create:

❑ **Title** — Press Release 1

❑ **URL Name** — PressRelease1

❑ **Page Layout** — (Press Release) Default Press Release

SharePoint will create the page and the browser will refresh with the new page in Edit mote. Select Submit for Approval at the top of the page to start the page approval workflow process. On the Start "Parallel Approval": PressRelease1 page, click Start. The page will then load with the Press Release 1 page in Design mode. To advance the page through the workflow, select the Approve button in the Page Editing Toolbar. On the Workflow Tasks: Please approve DivisionArticle1 page, optionally enter any comments and click the Approve button. The page will refresh with the Press Release 1 page, published, in Display mode.

Just as with the SharePoint Designer–created master page, note that when selecting the page layout when creating a new page, all the page layouts had preview images associated with them, but the custom page layout created with SharePoint Designer had a more stock preview image. The same SharePoint Designer limitation exists with page layouts as with master pages. Therefore, to associate a preview image with the page layout, developers need to go to the page layout list item within the Master Page Gallery and set the Preview Image property manually.

Again, just like the master page created using SharePoint Designer, the page layout resides exclusively within the SharePoint site's content database. The next section describes how to create a new page layout as a file template living on the file system and provision it into a SharePoint site using a Feature as an uncustomized page.

Creating Page Layouts Using Visual Studio and Features

Like master pages, creating page layouts with SharePoint Designer is straightforward with the WYSIWYG interface and live preview of the page against the SharePoint site. However, like everything else that can be done in SharePoint Designer, it has a downside: All the assets created and modified are stored in the SharePoint content database, making it a challenge to integrate files into an organization's source control management system and software development life cycle, or to package changes up to move between environments. Again, just like master page development, another approach is to create page layout files as templates and provision them to SharePoint sites from the file system using a Feature. This section demonstrates how to provision a page layout using a Feature into a SharePoint site.

There are two files in the code download for this book that will be used in the provisioning of a page layout: `ACMEPressTmp.aspx` and `ACMEPressPreviewTmp.gif`. Copy these two files to a new folder named `PageLayouts` within the `Chapter7Pages` Feature folder in the Chapter7Pages project, as shown in Figure 7-7.

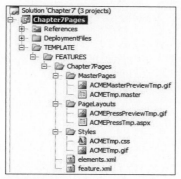

Figure 7-7

Now that the files are in the Feature, the next step is to modify the element manifest file, as shown in Listing 7-8. The section on master pages has already explained the different aspects of provisioning a preview image, so the focus is only on the page layout this time around.

Listing 7-8: Element manifest file provisioning page layouts

```xml
<?xml version="1.0" encoding="utf-8" ?>
<Elements xmlns="http://schemas.microsoft.com/sharepoint/">
    <Module Name="Master Page Preview Images"><!-- omitted for brevity --></Module>
    <Module Name="Master Pages"><!-- omitted for brevity --></Module>
    <Module Name="Styles"><!-- omitted for brevity --></Module>
    <Module Name="Page Layout Preview Images"
            Url="_catalogs/masterpage/Preview Images/WROX"
            Path="PageLayouts"
            RootWebOnly="TRUE">
      <File Url="ACMEPressPreviewTmp.gif"
            Name="ACMEPressPreview.gif"
            Type="GhostableInLibrary">
        <Property Name="Title"
                Value="ACMEPressPreview.gif" />
      </File>
    </Module>
    <Module Url="_catalogs/masterpage"
            Path="PageLayouts"
            RootWebOnly="TRUE">
      <File Url="ACMEPressTmp.aspx"
            Name="ACMEPress.aspx"
            Type="GhostableInLibrary">
        <Property Name="PublishingAssociatedContentType"
                Value=";#Press Release;#
```

(continued)

Listing 7-8 *(continued)*

```
0x010100C568DB52D9D0A14D9B2FDCC96666E9F2007948130EC3DB064584E219954237AF3900242457E
FB8B24247815D688C526CD44D01;#" />
        <Property Name="PublishingPreviewImage"
                  Value="~SiteCollection/_catalogs/masterpage/Preview
Images/WROX/ACMEPressPreview.gif, ~SiteCollection/_catalogs/masterpage/Preview
Images/WROX/ACMEPressPreview.gif" />
        <Property Name="ContentType"
                  Value="$Resources:cmscore,contenttype_pagelayout_name;" />
        <Property Name="Title"
                  Value="ACME Press Release" />
    </File>
  </Module>
</Elements>
```

Nearly everything in Listing 7-8 should be familiar with only one or two exceptions. First, the value of the ContentType field is different because page layouts in the Master Page Gallery conform to a different content type than master pages do. Second is the addition of a new field: PublishingAssociatedContentType. Recall that page layouts must be associated with a content type that defines the schema and rules of a particular page, while the page layout defines the rendering. When creating a page layout using SharePoint Designer, the first thing a developer must do is specify the associated content type. That is what the field PublishingAssociatedContentType does. This field expects values within a ";#" delimited string. The first value, "Press Release," as in Listing 7-8, is the name of the content type, while the second value, "0x010100...", is the ID of the content type.

Next, add the new files to the DDF file to be included in the package, as shown in Listing 7-9.

Listing 7-9: Diamond Directive File for Chapter7Pages Feature

```
.OPTION Explicit
.Set DiskDirectoryTemplate=CDROM
.Set CompressionType=MSZIP
.Set UniqueFiles=Off
.Set Cabinet=On
;**************************************************
DeploymentFiles\manifest.xml

.Set DestinationDir=Chapter7Pages
TEMPLATE\FEATURES\Chapter7Pages\feature.xml
TEMPLATE\FEATURES\Chapter7Pages\elements.xml

.Set DestinationDir=Chapter7Pages\MasterPages
TEMPLATE\FEATURES\Chapter7Pages\MasterPages\ACMETmp.master
TEMPLATE\FEATURES\Chapter7Pages\MasterPages\ACMEMasterPreviewTmp.gif

.Set DestinationDir=Chapter7Pages\Styles
TEMPLATE\FEATURES\Chapter7Pages\Styles\ACMETmp.css
TEMPLATE\FEATURES\Chapter7Pages\Styles\ACMETmp.gif

.Set DestinationDir=Chapter7Pages\PageLayouts
TEMPLATE\FEATURES\Chapter7Pages\PageLayouts\ACMEPressTmp.aspx
TEMPLATE\FEATURES\Chapter7Pages\PageLayouts\ACMEPressPreviewTmp.gif
```

Finally, update the `feature.xml` file to include the additional files that have been added to the Feature, as shown in Listing 7-10.

Listing 7-10: Feature definition for Chapter7Pages Feature

```xml
<?xml version="1.0" encoding="utf-8" ?>
<Feature xmlns="http://schemas.microsoft.com/sharepoint/"
         Id="D56F0D2D-0107-424d-AA0D-7120329A23E6"
         Title="Chapter 7 - Provisioning Master Pages and Page Layouts"
         Hidden="FALSE"
         Scope="Site"
         Version="1.0.0.0">

  <ElementManifests>
    <ElementManifest Location="elements.xml" />
    <ElementFile Location="MasterPages\ACMETmp.master" />
    <ElementFile Location="MasterPages\ACMEMasterPreviewTmp.gif" />
    <ElementFile Location="Styles\ACMETmp.css" />
    <ElementFile Location="Styles\ACMETmp.gif" />
    <ElementFile Location="PageLayouts\ACMEPressTmp.aspx" />
    <ElementFile Location="PageLayouts\ACMEPressPreviewTmp.gif" />
  </ElementManifests>

</Feature>
```

Follow the same steps as outlined earlier to create an updated WSP file, add it to the solution store, deploy the solution, and activate the Feature. If the solution was deployed in the master page module, use the `STSADM.EXE` operation `upgradesolution` to update what is already in the solution store. Because the Feature has already been activated, perform a forced activation using the `STSADM.EXE` operation `activatefeature` with an extra argument of `-force`, which reactivates the Feature even if it is already active.

Now when a content owner creates a new page, the new page layout is available in the selector, complete with a preview image, as shown in Figure 7-8.

Figure 7-8

Adding Content Regions: Field Controls and Web Part Zones

A page layout with zero editable regions is pretty close to being utterly useless unless the page layout contains some server controls that aggregate content or some static content. Therefore, with the page layout created, usually the next task is to add some editable regions to the page. Two types of controls can be added to a page: field controls and Web Parts.

Adding Web Parts to a page layout is no different than adding Web Parts to another SharePoint page or even an ASP.NET 2.0 page, for that matter: Add at least one Web Part zone to the page. A developer can then optionally add Web Parts to the page layout, or leave the Web Part zone blank. Content owners can drop Web Parts in the Web Part Gallery into the Web Part zone defined when creating and editing pages. This enables developers to give the content owners some flexibility in managing content.

Field controls, conversely, provide an additional level of control than that of Web Parts. Field controls, which are bound to a specific field in the Pages list, are added to a page layout by a developer. Content owners have the capability to manage the content within those controls, but cannot add, remove, or move the field controls around on the page layout. This enables developers to enforce a certain look and feel for sites requiring a more structured approach.

Web Parts and field controls enable both developers and content owners different levels of control and empowerment but there are many other differences between the two. The following table contains a list of some additional differences between Web Parts and field controls.

	Field Controls	Web Parts
Content Storage	In a field in the page's underlying SPListItem	Within the Web Part data of the page
Personalization	No	Yes
Versioning	Versioning tied to the page with complete history	Versioning tied to page without history
Who has ultimate control?	Page designer/developer	Page designer in placement of Web Part zones; content owner in managing of zone's contents (add/edit Web Parts within Web Part zones)
When to use?	Specific types of content must appear in specified places on a page; structured formatting/ branding	Structure of content on the page (in part of a page) is not important; gives content owners full control

While the preceding table contains a few differences between Web Parts and field controls, they all boil down to one very core difference: the content within Web Parts is stored separate from the actual page while content within field controls is stored within the page itself. Web Parts within a page layout, or more specifically a Publishing site, are treated no differently than the rest of SharePoint . . . or ASP.NET 2.0 for that matter. The data within a Web Part is stored separately from the page. When a page is loaded, the Web Part Manager is responsible for retrieving the data from the personalization store which is separate from the page. Field controls on the other hand store no data . . . they are used to simply provide an editing and display experience for data stored within a specific field in the underlying SPListItem of the page requested. When a page is updated, a new version is created. Because the data in field controls is stored in fields, this data is versioned however since the data within Web Parts is stored separately from the page, it is not versioned.

Where the data is stored with respect to Web Parts vs. field controls should be a very important factor for developers when creating Publishing sites. If a project calls for page versions to be retained due to industry regulation or company policy or if a project requires strict control of the placement and type of content on the page, field controls should be used. However, if the versioning of pages is not as important and / or content owners need to have an extra level of control on the content pages, then using Web Parts may make more sense. In addition, both field controls and Web Parts can be used on the same page layout.

The next two sections will demonstrate how to add Web Parts and field controls to page layouts. Later in the book a full chapter is devoted to each topic (field controls in *Chapter 10: Field Types and Field Controls*, Web Parts in *Chapter 11: Web Parts*) to go into more depth on such things like management, configuration as well as creating custom Web Parts and field controls. While the next two sections demonstrate adding Web Part zones and field controls to page layouts using SharePoint Designer, know that all SharePoint Designer is doing is adding text to the source of the page layout file. Therefore, these same changes can be made by hand to page layouts created as templates and provisioned into the Master Page Gallery using Features.

Adding Web Parts

If one is not already open, open a page layout through an existing SharePoint site using SharePoint Designer (using File ⇨ Open Site followed by opening the desired page layout. In order to add Web Part zones to the page, the Web Parts task pane needs to be loaded. If it is not present in SharePoint Designer, select Task Panes ⇨ Web Parts to load the Web Parts task pane. At the bottom of the page are two buttons: one for adding Web Parts and another for adding Web Part zones. Place the cursor somewhere on the design surface of the page layout where a Web Part zone is desired. Then click the New Web Part Zone button within the Web Parts tool window. The properties of the new Web Part zone can be modified using either the attributes on the `<WebPartPages:WebPartZone />` server control tag or the Tag Properties task pane when the Web Part zone is selected.

Adding Field Controls

If one is not already open, open a page layout through an existing SharePoint site using SharePoint Designer (using File ⇨ Open Site followed by opening the desired page layout). All the fields that have been defined in the content type associated with the page layout are displayed in the Toolbox task pane in SharePoint. Toward the bottom of the SharePoint Controls section notice two groups: Page Fields and Content Fields. The first group, Page Fields, contains a list of all the fields from content types the associated content type inherits from. The second group, Content Fields, contains a list of all the fields defined in the content type associated with the page layout.

Switch to Design view if it is not already selected and drag the Press Release Byline and Press Release Body field controls into the `PlaceholderMain` content placeholder from the Content Fields group within the SharePoint Controls section of the Toolbox task pane in SharePoint Designer, as shown in Figure 7-9.

Figure 7-9

Switch back to the Code view and notice the server control tags added by SharePoint Designer. SharePoint Designer uses the appropriate field control, which is used to edit and present the content stored in a field, depending on the type of the field. For instance, if a field is a single line of text such as the Press Release Byline, the `<SharePointWebControls:TextField />` is used. However, in the case of the Press Release Body field, which is of type Publishing HTML, SharePoint Designer adds the `<PublishingWebControls:RichHtmlField />` control. Notice that when the two controls were added to the page, two `<%@ Register %>` directives were added to the top of the page layout by SharePoint Designer. Like ASP.NET 2.0 pages, this is necessary to tell the .NET Framework which assembly contains the logic for the server controls on the page.

With the field controls added to the page layout, save all changes, check in, and publish the page. Using the browser, go back to the page previously created using the page layout (or create a new one), and switch to Edit mode by selecting Site Actions ➪ Edit Page. Notice the two new editable areas on the page added using the field controls!

When adding field controls to a page layout outside of SharePoint Designer, keep in mind that not only are the server control tags for the field controls required, such as `<SharePointWebControls: TextField />`, but the `<%@ Register %>` directives for the added field controls are required as well.

Building Master Pages and Page Layouts As Templates

This chapter has demonstrated two approaches to creating master pages and page layouts: one creating customized instances using SharePoint Designer and the other creating uncustomized instances using Visual Studio and Features. Thankfully, neither option is "right" nor "wrong," as it depends entirely on the project and development team implementing the Publishing site. However, some readers may assume that while the uncustomized, template approach provides better portability, the loss of WYSIWYG from the SharePoint Designer development approach is quite significant and therefore discard the Visual Studio and Feature approach too quickly.

Recall from Chapter 2 that one of the most significant downsides to adopting the SharePoint development approach (Visual Studio + Features) compared to the SharePoint customization approach (SharePoint Designer) is the lack of tools supporting the development approach. However, don't let this fact lead you to simply eliminate one approach. Developers can still use SharePoint Designer as a powerful development environment for creating new master pages, page layouts, CSS files, and other assets in a localized development environment. Those same developers can then save those files straight from the SharePoint site to the local file system, where they can be added to a Feature for provisioning.

Keep one thing in mind: The names of the files provisioned must be different from those that are already present in the SharePoint site. One way to get around this is to add an underscore ("_") as the prefix of the filename when creating files in SharePoint Designer. Then, when the files are saved locally and added to a Feature, remove the underscore prefix. This way, developers do not have to go through the process of cleaning up and removing files created in a development environment or maintaining two separate development environments.

Delegate Controls

Chapter 4 presented Features as a way to address the limitation in previous versions of SharePoint of not being able to easily attach new (or replace existing) functionality in SharePoint sites. Microsoft added yet another capability to easily inject custom user controls or server controls into pages for new content or to replace existing content defined by Microsoft in the out-of-the-box site templates or by custom developed templates and pages.

These replaceable areas within pages (master pages, content pages, page layouts, etc.) are implemented using delegate controls. Delegate controls are a special type of server control (`<SharePoint: DelegateControl />`). Each delegate control has a unique ID, specified using the `ControlId` attribute. This ID is used to register specific controls (user controls or server controls) using the site element `<Control />` within element manifest files in Features. The advantage of using Features is twofold. First, because Features are scoped, a delegate control can be scoped, so the addition/replacement can be as limited as the current site, or as far reaching as the entire SharePoint farm. Second, Features empower site owners to add/replace functionality via Feature activation. When controls are registered via

Features, one of the properties that must be set is the order in which to add the control. This is specified using the `<Control Sequence="" />` attribute.

How does it work? When a page is requested, the delegate control server tag is encountered by the .NET Framework when executing the compiled page. The delegate control looks at an internal list in SharePoint for all the controls registered for the specific `ControlId` specified in the `<SharePoint: DelegateControl />` server control tag within the current scope (site, site collection, Web application, or farm). If no controls are registered for the specific instance, then nothing is rendered and the delegate control acts as if it were never on the page. If one or more controls are registered for the specific instance, then the control with the lowest sequence number is added in place of the delegate control.

This enables developers to replace out-of-the-box functionality in SharePoint. In fact, this is exactly how Microsoft implemented the Search box in the upper right-hand corner of a SharePoint site. A quick search of the WSS 3.0 `default.master` page for the location of the Search box will yield no search-related controls; instead, a delegate control named `SmallSearchInputBox` is present. A farm-scoped Feature named `ContentLightup` registers the control `[..]\12\TEMPLATE\ CONTROLTEMPLATES\SearchArea.ascx` with a sequence number of 100. When MOSS 2007 is installed and the Standard license is applied, a Web application–scoped Feature named `OSearchBasicFeature` registers a server control with a sequence of 50. This replaces the out-of-the-box WSS 3.0 Search box with a more full-featured search interface, as MOSS 2007 Standard adds additional search capabilities to WSS 3.0. In addition, when an Enterprise license is applied to MOSS 2007, a Web application–scoped Feature named `OSearchEnhancedFeature` registers yet another server control with a sequence of 25, providing even more functionality than the MOSS 2007 Standard search control provides.

Creating Delegate Controls

Creating controls for use within a delegate control is quite straightforward. In fact, it is virtually no different from creating standard ASP.NET 2.0 user controls or server controls. Consider the following user control that does nothing other than write out a simple string:

```
<%@ Control Language="C#" %>
<div>hello world</div>
```

The file this code is stored in, `Chapter7DemoDelegateControl.ascx`, should be deployed to the `[..]\12\TEMPLATE\CONTROLTEMPLATES` folder on the server. In order to register this control a new Feature must be created. The Feature definition file contains nothing special, but the element manifest referenced in the `feature.xml` file contains the CAML shown in Listing 7-11 to add the sample user control in place of the existing search controls.

Listing 7-11: Feature registering a delegate control

```
<?xml version="1.0" encoding="utf-8" ?>
<Elements xmlns="http://schemas.microsoft.com/sharepoint/">
   <Control Id="SmallSearchInputBox"
            Sequence="20"
   ControlSrc="/_controltemplates/ProMossWcm/Chapter7DemoDelegateControl.ascx" />
</Elements>
```

Notice that the `<Control />` Id attribute is the string corresponding to the search delegate control defined in the default WSS 3.0 master page, and the `Sequence` is set to 20. This number will set the new control in front of all other search controls until the Feature is deactivated or another control is registered in front of this one with a lower sequence number.

What about using a server control as the delegate control? Consider if the code in Listing 7-12 is compiled into a strong-named assembly and deployed to the server's Global Assembly Cache (GAC).

Listing 7-12: Server control with public properties

```
namespace WROX.ProMossWcm.Chapter07 {
  public class SampleServerDelegateControl : Control {
    private string _textTitle = string.Empty;

    protected override void CreateChildControls () {
      base.CreateChildControls();

      Label label = new Label();
      label.Attributes.Add("style","border: solid 1px navy;");
      label.Text = "Server delegate control. Value TextTitle: " +_textTitle;

      this.Controls.Add(label);
    }

    public string TextTitle {
      set {
        _textTitle = value;
      }
      get {
        return _textTitle;
      }
    }
  }
}
```

The element manifest registering the server control would look like the code shown in Listing 7-13.

Listing 7-13: Element manifest using server controls in a delegate control

```
<?xml version="1.0" encoding="utf-8" ?>
<Elements xmlns="http://schemas.microsoft.com/sharepoint/">
  <Control Id="SmallSearchInputBox"
           Sequence="15"
           ControlAssembly="Chapter7, Version=1.0.0.0, Culture=neutral,
PublicKeyToken=c591e70cfdf9ce4f"
           ControlClass="WROX.ProMossWcm.Chapter07.SampleServerDelegateControl">
    <Property Name="TextTitle">Chapter 7</Property>
  </Control>
</Elements>
```

Notice the `<Property />` child element within the `<Control />` element. If the server control contains public properties, then the Feature can set the value of these public properties using this technique, as shown here. Completing the Feature containing a server control delegate, control registration, deploying, and activating it within a WSS 3.0 site will result in something similar to what is shown in Figure 7-10.

Figure 7-10

The complete code for both Features registering delegate controls using both user controls and server controls can be found in the code download for this book. Note that delegate controls implemented with server controls require the assembly containing the server control to be registered as a safe control in the Web application's web.config *file.*

Summary

This chapter explained how the plumbing works within SharePoint in the construction of a page when a request is received for a page within a Publishing site. The construction process is a bit different from a standard SharePoint request due to the addition of page layouts. Also covered in this chapter was master pages and how Microsoft leverages the master page model within SharePoint. Some of the more significant differences with master pages within a SharePoint site are that master pages are stored (customized or uncustomized) in the Master Page Gallery, rather than the file system, and content pages do not explicitly set the master page. Instead, dynamic tokens are used to tell SharePoint which master page to use from one of two options set at the SharePoint site level.

In order to provide a template page creation and rendering approach for facilitating content-centric sites on SharePoint, Microsoft added the concept of page layouts to MOSS 2007. Page layouts are used to define the rendering of a specific type of page, defined using SharePoint content types. SharePoint content types define the schema, special business rules, and workflow, while the page layout or multiple page layouts are, when combined with master pages, used to define the rending and look and feel of a page.

For both master pages and page layouts, two approaches were covered with respect to creating these assets within a SharePoint site. The first option for both, creating master pages and page layouts using SharePoint Designer, creates files within the SharePoint site as customized files residing exclusively within the SharePoint content database. The second option involves using Visual Studio and Features to define the files as templates and provision them into SharePoint sites as uncustomized files.

Finally, the chapter covered the concept of delegate controls, which provide developers with a very easy way to either add or remove functionality to or from an existing SharePoint site, but without customizing the original files provided by Microsoft out of the box. This approach, recommended by Microsoft, protects developers from having their files overwritten when a hotfix, service pack, or new version is released.

8

Navigation

Every Web site, regardless of the underlying technology used to implement it, uses some sort of navigation. Properly implemented navigation makes a Web site usable and the content within the site findable. SharePoint sites are no different, including Publishing sites. Thankfully, not much is unique when it comes to navigation in sites based on Windows SharePoint Services (WSS) 3.0, including Publishing sites, because SharePoint is completely dependent upon the navigation provider model included in ASP.NET 2.0.

This chapter explains what the ASP.NET 2.0 navigation provider model is and how SharePoint implements it. Also covered in this chapter are the various customization options available to site owners, administrators, developers, and designers. Because SharePoint is completely dependent upon the ASP.NET 2.0 navigation provider model, this chapter does not go into great depth about creating custom navigation components. Instead, readers are encouraged to review ASP.NET 2.0 documentation on this subject.

ASP.NET 2.0 Navigation Provider Model

Creating navigation components has traditionally been a requirement in every application. This was because each navigation component was tightly coupled to the underlying site architecture. For example, creating custom navigation components in WSS 2.0 sites was quite complicated, as developers were required to write the code that would walk through the SharePoint object model to determine the structure of the navigation.

The other component of all navigation controls was the rendering piece. This part was responsible for taking the navigation data structure and generating the HTML used to render the navigation control. Many third-party organizations were started that built navigation controls other companies could purchase to implement sophisticated navigation implementations. Unfortunately, these components were usually somewhat challenging to implement, as developers had to incorporate them into a project's code, which pulled the data part of the navigation out of the underlying site structure.

Microsoft addressed this challenge in ASP.NET 2.0, adding something called the *navigation provider model* to make it much easier to implement navigation in Web sites. The navigation provider model essentially divides the navigation into two pieces: the rendering piece and the piece responsible for getting the data from the underlying site architecture. Site map data sources are used to represent the hierarchical structure of a site, exposing the structure as a `SiteMapNodeCollection`. The `SiteMapDataSource` object is then associated with a navigation rendering control, which takes the `SiteMapNodeCollection` and uses it to generate the HTML necessary to render the navigation.

Site map data sources get the data from the underlying site architecture using the provider model approach. By default, ASP.NET 2.0 sites use the `XmlSiteMapProvider`, which assumes the site navigation is stored in the `web.sitemap` file.

Because WSS 3.0 is built on top of ASP.NET 2.0, it can leverage this navigation provider model by default. In the case of SharePoint, the navigation needs to be generated from the SharePoint site structure. To achieve this, Microsoft created a few custom site map provider objects that know how to walk the SharePoint object model. Specifically, WSS 3.0 includes a few providers, and installing Office SharePoint Server (MOSS) 2007 adds a few additional providers.

One big advantage to this model is that now it is very easy to incorporate new navigation rendering controls into a SharePoint site. Any navigation control that implements the ASP.NET 2.0 navigation provider model can now be used in a SharePoint site.

Customizing Site Navigation

While SharePoint's navigation will meet the needs of many projects, it is unlikely to satisfy all business requirements. Thankfully, SharePoint provides a few different vehicles for customizing the navigation, especially in Publishing sites. Some of these include browser-based changes that can be made by site owners, while others are things that can be done by designers or developers by modifying the markup of site map data sources and rendering controls or even by administrators configuring the underlying navigation providers.

Browser-Based Customizations

Publishing sites have an extra navigation customization capability that can be implemented by site owners through the browser. Navigating to the site's Site Settings page and selecting Navigation under the Look and Feel section takes the user to the Site Navigation Settings page (see Figure 8-1). From this page the site can be configured to include or exclude either subsites and/or pages from the main navigation. In addition to the scoping options, owners can also elect to manually or automatically sort the contents of the navigation.

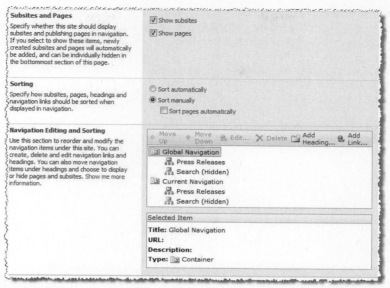

Figure 8-1

Site owners can also manually augment both the global navigation (typically the top navigation) and the current navigation (typically the left-hand navigation), such as manually reordering the items, and adding custom headings (seen as sections) and links. This facilitates adding custom links to the navigation that are not part of the existing site structure, such as links to partner companies or news articles.

Customizing the Navigation Control

Another type of customization available to site developers and designers is customizing the navigation rendering control and the site map data sources. This is done by customizing the markup associated with the master page containing the controls. The first customizations that can be done are to the rendering control. This does not affect what data is shown in the navigation; rather, it affects how the data is displayed.

Microsoft has included a customized implementation of the Menu control that ships with ASP.NET 2.0 for SharePoint sites, known as the Microsoft.SharePoint.WebControls.AspMenu control. This control directly inherits from the System.Web.UI.WebControls.Menu control. The reason for the custom SharePoint implementation is to simply fix a few known issues with the ASP.NET 2.0 Menu control, such as a localization issue whereby in right-to-left locales, the fly-out arrow continues to point in the left-to-right locale. When working with the SharePoint AspMenu control, it is best to rely on the ASP.NET 2.0 documentation for the Menu control (www.andrewconnell.com/go/219), as it is more complete and comprehensive.

Some of the customizations that can be implemented on the AspMenu control are to change the rendering direction of the navigation to either horizontal or vertical using the Orientation attribute, setting the number of levels to render using the StaticDisplayLevels attribute, and setting the number of levels of fly-outs to include the MaximumDynamicDisplayLevels attribute. Designers can also customize the rendering styles of the navigation control using CSS classes. All of these changes can be done in markup with no compiled code.

Customizing the Navigation Site Map Data Source

In addition to customizing the navigation rendering control, developers and designers can also customize the site map data source provided in SharePoint that is passed to the rendering controls. The site map data source used in Publishing sites, Microsoft.SharePoint.Publishing.Navigation .PortalSiteMapDataSource, has a few properties that are used to massage the site hierarchical data returned from the navigation providers. Some of the attributes developers can configure are as follows:

❑ ShowStartingNode — This attribute includes or excludes the starting node from the navigation. The starting node is usually the root node of the site collection.

❑ StartFromCurrentNode — This attribute should always be left set to true, as this value tells the data source to use its own logic to determine where to start.

❑ TreatStartingNodeAsCurrent — This attribute determines whether the data source's starting node is treated as the current node in the navigation. This is helpful when a section of a site needs to use its own navigation and not include portions of the site hierarchy above or parallel to it.

Three additional attributes can be used to provide context and node-type trimming of the site hierarchy. All accept a single value or a comma-delimited list of values. The values can be Area (meaning a SharePoint site), Page (meaning a Publishing page), Heading (meaning a manually created heading on the Site Settings ⇨ Navigation page), and AuthoredLink (meaning a manually created page on the Site Settings ⇨ Navigation page). The attributes are as follows:

❑ TrimNonCurrentTypes — The values listed in this attribute will remove those types of nodes that are not present directly beneath the current node. In other words, it removes all of those node types that are not in the child nodes collection of the current node.

❑ TrimNonAncestorTypes — The values listed in this attribute will remove those types of nodes that are not present directly beneath the current node or any of its ancestors.

❑ TrimNonAncestorDescendentTypes — The values listed in this attribute will remove those types of nodes that are not present directly beneath the current node or any of its ancestors or descendents.

Customizing the Navigation Provider

The site map data sources get their data from the navigation providers that ship with SharePoint. The WSS 3.0 installation contains a few navigation providers, but the ones included with MOSS should be used in Publishing sites because they are the ones that leverage the highly performant PortalSiteMapProvider object previously covered.

All the navigation providers are registered at the Web application level in the `web.config` file shared by all site collections in the Web application. The primary job of the providers is to examine the SharePoint site hierarchy and incorporate any changes made through the API or using the Site Navigation Settings page in each site's Site Settings page. In addition, they also perform any necessary security trimming on the navigation hierarchy before passing the structure back to the site map data sources.

Microsoft provides a few variations of the `PortalSiteMapProvider` control by passing in one of three navigation types, set using the `NavigationType` attribute. The three values are `Global`, `Current`, and `Combined`. `Global` is used to get the links from the top navigation bar collection. `Current` is used to get the links from the Quick Launch navigation collection. `Combined` performs a union of the two previous values.

Four additional public properties are available to configure what types of nodes are included in the navigation data. First, the `IncludeSubSites` and `IncludePages` properties accept one of three values: `Always`, `PerWeb`, and `Never`. These tell the navigation provider whether the settings on the Site Navigation Settings page should be applied (`PerWeb`), or ignored (`Always` or `Never`). The `IncludeHeadings` and `IncludeAuthoredLinks` properties are Boolean values that enable the site administrator to allow or block the inclusion of custom links and headings in the navigation.

Customizing Navigation with the API

Another navigation customization option available to developers is to use the SharePoint API. Each SharePoint site has a `Navigation` property that contains a reference to both the top navigation as well as the Quick Launch navigation. Adding new items to the navigation involves creating new `Microsoft.SharePoint.Navigation.SPNavigationNode` objects and adding them to the appropriate navigation collection, as shown in Listing 8-1.

Listing 8-1: Adding nodes to the top and Quick Launch navigation

```
SPWeb site = SPContext.Current.Web;

// get a reference to the top navigation
SPNavigationNodeCollection topNavigation = site.Navigation.TopNavigationBar;
// or get a reference to the Quick Launch navigation
// SPNavigationNodeCollection quickLaunchNav = site.Navigation.QuickLaunch;

// create new drop down menu in the navigation
SPNavigationNode newMenu = new SPNavigationNode("New Section", "", false);
// add the new menu to the end of the top nav bar
topNavigation.AddAsLast(newMenu);

// add a custom link
newMenu.Children.AddAsLast(new SPNavigationNode("Some Custom Link",
"http://www.wrox.com",true));
```

Creating Custom Navigation Components

At times the provided navigation rendering controls, site map data sources, and navigation providers may not suit the project's requirements. The most common custom development topic that comes up involves creating custom navigation rendering controls. However, developers and those implementing SharePoint sites should look to third-party component developers before building their own. The reason is simple: Most navigation controls can be purchased for a fraction of what it would cost to actually build the control. In addition, the purchased control usually provides significantly more functionality than what would normally be built into a component. Usually the only exception to this rule is when navigation uses images in the implementation, rather than text. No canned control can expect the exact images to be used; therefore, these are usually built from scratch.

Thankfully, there is nothing special about building custom navigation components for SharePoint sites. All the same rules apply that are involved when creating custom navigation controls for traditional ASP.NET 2.0 Web sites. Therefore, the recommendation is to rely on the ASP.NET 2.0 documentation, as well as any sources of assistance in creating custom components.

Performance and Usability Considerations

Because navigation controls appear on nearly every single page in a content-centric site, anyone implementing Publishing sites should exercise caution when creating such sites. A poorly performing navigation control can cripple a page and even an entire site. Attention should also be paid to the usability of the navigation controls. If the site's users cannot make sense of or easily use the site navigation, it is not serving its purpose and should be addressed.

PortalSiteMapProvider

The navigation controls provided in MOSS — specifically, the navigation providers — utilize a very powerful and performant object called `Microsoft.SharePoint.Publishing.Navigation.PortalSiteMapProvider`. The job of the `PortalSiteMapProvider` is to expose the SharePoint site hierarchy to site map data sources that can then massage the hierarchy before passing it along to the rendering controls. One of the unique characteristics of the `PortalSiteMapProvider` is the component's performance. It boasts a sophisticated, built-in caching mechanism to ensure that navigation controls are never the cause for a poorly performing site, and it has been optimized for cross-list and cross-site queries. However, like many other things in SharePoint, it cannot cross the boundaries of site collections.

When the `PortalSiteMapProvider` receives a request for data using one of the retrieval methods, it queries the data in SharePoint to obtain a set of results. It inserts these results into cache so that the next time the query is executed it will not have to issue the expensive results. Instead, it simply performs a few checks on the data and uses the results of the previous query. The three retrieval nodes most commonly used are as follows:

❑ `GetCachedList()` — This method returns a single SharePoint list as a `PortalListSiteMapNode` object.

❑ `GetCachedListItemsByQuery()` — By far the most commonly used, this method returns a collection of `PortalListItemSiteMapNode` objects from the results of a specific query passed in using the `SPQuery` object.

❑   `GetCachedSiteDataQuery()` — This method returns data from a specified SharePoint site as an ADO.NET `DataTable` from the provided query specified using the `SPSiteDataQuery` object.

These methods include all the necessary logic required to add and fetch the results from previously executed queries, so developers are free to just use the `PortalSiteMapProvider`; no special configuration is required. Using the `PortalSiteMapProvider` in code is fairly straightforward. Listing 8-2 contains the code to select all the pages in the Press Releases subsite that have been published since 2005.

Listing 8-2: Selecting all press releases published since 2005 with the PortalSiteMapProvider

```
PortalSiteMapProvider psmp = PortalSiteMapProvider.CurrentNavSiteMapProvider;

// get instance of the Press Releases site
PortalWebSiteMapNode prNode = psmp.FindSiteMapNode("/PressReleases") as
PortalWebSiteMapNode;

// get all Press Releases published since 2005
SPQuery query = new SPQuery();
query.Query = "<Where><Geq><FieldRef Name='ArticleStartDate'/><Value
Type='DateTime'>2005-01-01T12:00:00Z</Value></Geq></Where>"SiteMapNodeCollection
pages = psmp.GetCachedListItemsByQuery (prNode, "Pages", query,
SPContext.Current.Web);
```

When using the `PortalSiteMapProvider`, developers should consider a few things ahead of time, as there are two occasions when it is not suitable. First, because the `PortalSiteMapProvider` internally caches the results of previously run queries, it should only be used for queries that are run frequently, where "frequently" is defined as an interval less than that of the duration something remains in cache (by default, three minutes). Navigation fits this model very well, hence the reason why it is the workhorse for the navigation controls in Publishing sites.

However, leveraging cache to reduce or eliminate round-trips to the database comes at a cost: The results from previously executed queries are only kept in cache for a limited time. If the time between two queries is greater than the time the results are kept in cache, then the `PortalSiteMapProvider` is actually doing more harm than good. That's because it is incurring the overhead of adding the results to cache after retrieving them from the executed query. If the data in cache is invalidated before the query is run again, then no benefit is being realized; and in fact the process is actually slower than not using the `PortalSiteMapProvider` because it has the extra burden of dealing with the cache.

In addition, the `PortalSiteMapProvider` should not be used when the underlying data being queried changes very frequently. The reason for this is related to the behavior of the `PortalSiteMapProvider`, which checks the SharePoint change log to determine whether the data being queried has changed before using the results stored in cache. If the data has changed, then it invalidates the results in cache and reexecutes the query. If the underlying data is changing very frequently, then subsequent queries will not pull data from the cache but instead always reexecute the query against the SharePoint object model.

Table of Contents Web Part

Sometimes sections of a site can become quite populated with content. For example, the section that contains company press releases would likely grow to have quite a few pages within it over time. Some sites include the pages in the main navigation of the site. For sections with a large amount of content, this is not the best practice because navigation can quickly become unusable by site visitors. In this case, consider utilizing the Table of Contents Web Part on the default page of the site. Configure the main navigation for the site to exclude pages but display a link to the section. Then, on the home page of that section, configure the Table of Contents Web Part to show the content within the section.

Summary

This chapter has shown how to customize and manipulate SharePoint navigation in various ways, available to individuals serving different roles with respect to a Publishing site. Administrators can control the data passed back to the site map data sources through the providers, site owners can customize the navigation using the Site Navigation Settings page, and developers and designers can customize the actual rendering controls and data sources through markup. Developers can also create custom rendering controls, site map data sources, or providers. However, it is recommended that you look to third-party companies to purchase navigation rendering controls and to rely on the provided rendering controls.

9

Accessibility

Accessibility is a popular and relevant topic as more and more companies leverage the Internet as a vehicle for their business. With the growing popularity of SharePoint — specifically, Microsoft Office SharePoint Server (MOSS) 2007, used as both a collaboration tool and to facilitate the creation of content-centric sites — accessibility is now a very important factor in evaluating SharePoint for many organizations.

In the past, SharePoint has not had a great track record regarding creating accessible implementations. One challenge involved in creating accessible SharePoint sites was that it required modifying many files. In addition, some of the underlying rendering components could not be customized easily — and often it was not even possible.

While the latest release of SharePoint does not ship conforming to any specific standards out-of-the-box (OOTB), the new layered architecture makes it much easier to customize the rendered output. This makes it possible to create accessible solutions that meet accepted guidelines. In addition, Microsoft has teamed with one of their partners in order to provide a jump-start on creating accessible sites. The Accessibility Kit for SharePoint provides not only a significant number of components that can be reused, but also a fantastic educational opportunity to understand some different approaches to creating accessible Publishing sites.

This chapter does *not* walk through the process of creating an accessible site — each site is very different and such an exercise would turn into a discussion about HTML. Instead, the goal of this chapter is to provide insight into what it means to create an accessible site, outline how to read and understand the various guidelines, and suggest some techniques that can be leveraged in creating accessible Publishing sites.

What Is an Accessible Web Site?

The primary motivation behind having an accessible site is to ensure that users with a disability can consume a Web site without being put at a disadvantage. Disabilities in the context of Web sites fall into two categories: *visual* and *interactive*. Visual disabilities, of course, refer to those users who are blind and cannot see the screen. These users typically use either screen readers that verbally read aloud the content of a Web page for the user to hear or Braille displays.

Refer to the screen reader page on Wikipedia for more information on screen readers: www.andrewconnell.com/go/220.

Another visual impairment affects those who have problems with contrast, so Web pages that utilize different shades of colors that are not very distinct from one another can cause issues. Users may also be prone to photosensitive epilepsy caused by pages that contain flickering or flashing content in the range of three flashes per second (Hertz) or when screen elements change from dark to light very quickly.

The other types of impairment that accessibility covers involve interactive issues. For instance, users may not be able to use a mouse. In this case, users rely on the keyboard for all interaction, including navigating menus and entering values in forms. Other users may not have access to a keyboard and have to speak commands.

Note that creating accessible sites so disabled or impaired users can have the same or near-identical experience as those who are not impaired is not the only goal. Creating accessible sites also yields many other advantages that can go straight to the bottom line and have an economic impact on a Web site. These economic reasons are covered later in this chapter.

Many sites are not designed with accessibility in mind. However, many organizations and government entities require sites to meet certain accessibility standards. Recently, some countries have even adopted certain laws and standards that make a company liable if its site does not meet certain guidelines. With so many organizations, governments, and companies requiring accessible sites, the World Wide Web Consortium (W3C) has created a set of standards, or guidelines, for creating accessible Web sites. These guidelines are generally accepted by the community at large to be the standard for all accessibility requirements.

Keep one very important point in mind when creating accessible Web sites: It is not only developers and designers who need to be aware of Web accessibility standards, but also the content owners. Subject matter experts (SME) who author and edit content on Web sites need to be knowledgeable about what can cause issues with users who have trouble consuming non-accessible Web sites.

Measuring Accessibility

As mentioned earlier, the World Wide Web Consortium (W3C) has crafted some guidelines, standards, and measures for creating accessible Web sites, all published on their site: www.andrewconnell.com/go/221. As stated on their Web site, the W3C is

... an international consortium where Member organizations, a full-time staff, and the public work together to develop Web standards. W3C's mission is: To lead the World Wide Web to its full potential by developing protocols and guidelines that ensure long-term growth for the Web.

The consortium, through the hard work of many individuals, publishes standards otherwise known as *W3C recommendations* that developers and designers alike can use to create what are generally referred to as accessible or "valid" Web sites. It does so under the Web Accessibility Initiative (WAI), which works with people all around the globe to create standards and guidelines to make Web sites more accessible to people with disabilities. The WAI (www.andrewconnell.com/go/222) has identified three components of accessibility:

❑ **Web Content Accessibility Guidelines (WCAG)** — This set of guidelines is used by developers, designers, and Web authoring and accessibility evaluation tools.

❑ **Authoring Tool Accessibility Guidelines (ATAG)** — This set of guidelines pertains to Web authoring tools.

❑ **User Agent Accessibility Guidelines (UAAG)** — This set of guidelines is used by clients that consume Web sites, such as browsers and media players, including screen readers.

Because this book is targeted to developers and the developer experience in creating MOSS 2007 Web Content Management (WCM) Publishing sites, only the WCAG will be addressed.

The WCAG, originally published as v1.0 in 1999, will be replaced by the 2.0 version, which is in the late stages of review. The more current 2.0 version is designed to be easier to use and understand as well as easier to test with automated testing frameworks. However, because the WCAG 2.0 is so new, it is likely many organizations will still refer to WCAG 1.0 when measuring Web sites for accessibility, so developers should be familiar with both versions.

In addition to the WCAG, the United States (U.S.) government has something called Section 508, which requires all U.S. agencies to make all technologies, including Web sites, accessible to those users with disabilities.

With all these guidelines, determining whether a site meets specific requirements can become quite challenging. While many validation tools exist, the W3C has a validator that is the most popular and is the recommended validator to use.

WCAG 1.0

The Web Content Accessibility Guidelines (WCAG) 1.0 were approved in May 1999 and have been used ever since as the standard for measuring the accessibility capabilities of a Web site. The WCAG 1.0 consists of a few different components, broken down hierarchically. Everything is based on the concept of guidelines and checkpoints. The 14 guidelines in the WCAG 1.0 are as follows:

1. **Provide equivalent alternatives to auditory and visual content** — This includes instances where images are used, as they should contain a text equivalent.

2. **Don't rely on color alone** — When color is used to convey information, ensure that the information is available without using color as well.

3. **Use markup and style sheets and do so properly** — This includes the use of lists in HTML markup, and stresses that when possible, CSS should be used for formatting. For instance, bulleted lists should be represented with <UL> or <OL> elements and nested when appropriate.

4. **Clarify natural language usage** — Specify the natural language of the page and use the HTML <ABBR> and <ACRONYM> elements when appropriate.

5. **Create tables that transform gracefully** — This includes checkpoints that require the use of table heading elements (`<TH>`), column groupings (`<COLGROUP>`), and indicators whereby the table heading, body, and footer are `<THEAD>`, `<TBODY>`, and `<TFOOT>`, respectively.

6. **Ensure that pages featuring new technologies transform gracefully** — Specifies that pages using newer technologies such as JavaScript or Flash operate and offer data in an equivalent manner when these technologies are disabled or not available.

7. **Ensure user control of time-sensitive content changes** — Specifies that pages or elements within them should not flicker or flash so much that they cause seizures for people with photosensitive epilepsy. It also includes checkpoints to ensure that if the content on the page is timed (such as scrolling news), the user has a way to stop it or go back.

8. **Ensure direct accessibility of embedded user interfaces** — This ensures that programmatic elements such as client-side scripting are accessible. For instance, client-side image maps should be used in favor of server-side image maps.

9. **Design for device independence** — This includes some overlap with guideline 8, but also includes things such as using logical events — for instance, button click events instead of device-dependent events.

10. **Use interim solutions** — When older clients do not support something, use an alternate solution. For instance, do not create pop-up or spawned windows when only the more recent browsers support blocking them.

11. **Use W3C technologies and guidelines** — This guideline recommends that only W3C approved and recommended technologies are used, such as HTML, XHTML, CSS, and XML.

12. **Provide context and orientation information** — This ensures that when things such as framesets are used, each frame has a title. It also recommends associating labels with the control to which they are linked.

13. **Provide clear navigation mechanisms** — This ensures that navigation is not only intuitive and easy to use, but also consistent.

14. **Ensure that documents are clear and simple** — Use the simplest language images to supplement the content on the page. In addition, ensure that the styling, presentation, and branding is consistent across all pages of the entire Web site.

Each guideline contains one or more checkpoints, which are used to measure a Web page for different levels of conformity against the WCAG 1.0. Each checkpoint is assigned a priority level from 1 to 3, with Priority 1 checkpoints having the most significance and Priority 3 checkpoints having the least significance. According to the W3C, Priority 1 checkpoints are objectives developers must satisfy; otherwise, those with some sort of a disability defined by the W3C will find it impossible to use the Web site. Priority 2 checkpoints are objectives that developers should satisfy; otherwise, those with some sort of disability will have difficulty using the Web site. Finally, Priority 3 checkpoints are objectives developers may satisfy; otherwise, those with some sort of disability will find it somewhat difficult to use the Web site.

Priority 1 checkpoints include things such as ensuring that all `<img>` tags contain a text equivalent of the image in the `alt=""` attribute and that all information conveyed using colors is also available without color. Priority 2 checkpoints include things such as ensuring that when colors are used, there is sufficient contrast such that someone who views pages in black and white is not put at a disadvantage.

To help developers and designers, the W3C links various techniques that can be used to pass each checkpoint in the *WCAG 1.0 Techniques* document. The W3C breaks techniques down into multiple documents, such as core, CSS, and HTML techniques. In addition, developers and designers can work off of a checklist, *WCAG 1.0 Checklist*, provided by the W3C to speed up the process of creating accessible Web sites.

Conformance levels are used when defining the accessibility standards of a site. The W3C defines three different levels of conformance for WCAG 1.0:

❑ **Conformance Level A** — All Priority 1 checkpoints are satisfied.

❑ **Conformance Level AA** — All Priority 1 and Priority 2 checkpoints are satisfied.

❑ **Conformance Level AAA** — All Priority 1, Priority 2, and Priority 3 checkpoints are satisfied.

WCAG 1.0 References

❑ **WCAG 1.0** — www.andrewconnell.com/go/123

❑ **WCAG 1.0 Techniques** — www.andrewconnell.com/go/124

❑ **WCAG 1.0 Checklist** — www.andrewconnell.com/go/125

WCAG 2.0

The W3C — specifically, the Web Accessibility Initiative — created the WCAG 2.0, which is designed to build off the original WCAG 1.0 version. Differing from WCAG 1.0, the second version is intended to be more readable and usable, to apply broadly to different present and future technologies used to create Web sites, and, arguably most important, validated using a combination of automated test harnesses and manual checks.

The WCAG 2.0 is not a generally accepted standard because it is still in the draft stages, albeit very late in the process. However when it is ratified as an official W3C recommendation, it is likely that it the WCAG 1.0 will still be referenced and used as the standard for many organizations. This is no fault of the W3C or a slight to the WCAG 2.0 — history has just shown that standards take time to be generally adopted by the community.

One of the most significant differences in the WCAG 2.0 compared to the previous version is the structure of the guidelines. The WCAG 2.0 is organized around four design principles. Each design principle provides guidelines, just as the WCAG 1.0 has checkpoints; and, similar to the WCAG 1.0, each guideline is assigned a level of success criterion (see below). Also like the WCAG 1.0, the WCAG 2.0 includes a list of techniques that can be used in meeting the various guidelines outlined in the recommendation.

The four design principles that make up the WCAG 2.0 specify that the site should conform to all of the following:

❑ **Perceivable** — The content and user interface components on a Web page must be presented in ways that a user can understand. This includes guidelines to use text equivalents for all images, to make pages which leverage color implement a distinguishable contrast for users reading in black and white, and to make the content adaptable such that it can be presented in different ways without losing the data or structure.

❑ **Operable** — The user interface, including content areas and navigation, must be usable. For instance, a user should be able to navigate and interact with a Web page without the use of a mouse, and they should have enough time to read content that is timed or automatically refreshed. Timed implementations should also enable a user to pause, adjust, or extend the timer.

❑ **Understandable** — The content and user interface components must be easily understood by users. The site must be readable by both those who can see the page and those who are blind, and include things such as programmatically setting the language of the page and using the appropriate HTML markup for abbreviations and acronyms. In addition, the user interface of the Web site should be predictable and consistent across all pages. Finally, when prompting the user for input, the site should perform identifiable error checking and validation, as well as suggest potential solutions to errors.

❑ **Conformance** — A Web site's content must be robust enough that it can be consumed not only by unimpaired users but also by those who are disabled in one way or another.

Like the WCAG 1.0, conformance levels are used when defining the accessibility standards of a site. The W3C defines three different levels of conformance for WCAG 2.0:

❑ **Level A** — Meets all Level A success criteria.

❑ **Level AA** — Meets all Level A and Level AA success criteria.

❑ **Level AAA** — Meets Levels A, AA, and AAA success criteria.

Similar to the WCAG 1.0, the conformance levels can be applied to a specific Web page or according to a *complete process,* which is defined as a combination of Web pages used in a sequential process, such as placing an order on an e-commerce Web site.

WCAG 2.0 References

❑ **WCAG 2.0** — www.andrewconnell.com/go/126

❑ **How WCAG 2.0 Differs from WCAG 1.0** — www.andrewconnell.com/go/127

❑ **WCAG 2.0 Techniques** — www.andrewconnell.com/go/128

❑ **WCAG 2.0 Quick Reference** — www.andrewconnell.com/go/129

United States Rehabilitation Act of 1973 Section 508

While many companies, organizations, and governments meet the level of conformity requirements of the WCAG 1.0 or 2.0 for accessible Web sites, some elect to build their own standards. The United States (U.S.) is one such country that has elected to create their own standard. The U.S. first passed the Rehabilitation Act of 1973, which guarantees certain rights to people with disabilities. Section 508 of the Rehabilitation Act of 1973 was amended in 1998 by the U.S. government to require, among other things, that all U.S. federal agencies make Web sites accessible to those with disabilities.

Section 508 contains a series of standards that the U.S. Congress adopted for various forms of communication. *Subpart B: Technical Standards* — specifically, *Section 1194.22, Web-based Intranet and Internet Information and Applications* — applies to Web sites. This section contains 16 paragraphs, each defining a rule that Web sites must abide by in order to be considered in compliance with the law.

These paragraphs, noted with letters (a) through (p), contain references to the WCAG 1.0. In fact, paragraphs (a) through (k) map directly to WCAG 1.0 Priority 1 checkpoints, as indicated in the standards on the Section 508 Web site (see the following section for more information). The other paragraphs can be loosely associated with other checkpoints in the WCAG 1.0.

Rehabilitation Act of 1973 Section 508 References

❑ **Rehabilitation Act of 1973** — www.andrewconnell.com/go/230

❑ **Rehabilitation Act of 1973, Section 508** — www.andrewconnell.com/go/231

❑ **Rehabilitation Act of 1973, Section 508, Subpart B, Section 1944.22 Standards** — www.andrewconnell.com/go/232

W3C Markup Validation Service

How are Web pages and sites validated? Thankfully, the W3C provides a free validation service on their Web site (www.andrewconnell.com/go/233), including a list of other Web-based validators. *The W3C Markup Validation Service* enables users to enter a publicly accessible link, upload a file, or even paste in the raw markup to be processed and tested for validation against the W3C recommendations. When issues are found, users are presented with a comprehensive list of errors and warnings, including the exact markup that caused it.

Advantages to Creating Accessible Web Sites

So far, this chapter has presented accessibility as it relates to mandated rules that organizations and governments are required to follow in order to meet the needs of disabled users. However, accessibility is not something that should be considered only because an entity or law dictates it. Creating accessible Web sites actually yields numerous advantages for organizations, many of which are economic and can directly affect the bottom line in many ways, including development and maintenance of the Web site, as well as increased user traffic.

The most obvious advantage to creating accessible Web sites is that it makes them available to a larger audience. Users who have a disability that impedes them from using a non-accessible site can now use accessible sites. Consider an e-commerce site that is not accessible and doesn't conform to any recommendations. An entire segment of the potential customer base would be excluded from using the site, something the owners of any business would surely not desire. One of the prime goals in any business is to make it as easy as possible to a target customer demographic to buy the company's goods or services. Providing a Web site that conforms to generally accepted accessibility standards excludes no one from visiting and interacting with the site.

Building off the "broader audience" theme, another benefit to creating accessible Web sites is that they can be consumed by less mainstream devices. For example, as the use of mobile devices grew, the only sites that were easily consumed in these devices were those built specifically for mobile devices and accessible sites. For a site to be considered accessible, it must have well-formed HTML or XHTML. Because XHTML is simply a subset of XML, it can be easily transformed into a format that a mobile device can consume using extensible style sheets (XSL).

Accessible Web sites are also considered "future friendly" in the sense that future clients will most likely conform to accessibility standards and thus be able to read and render accessible Web sites. This is not only a benefit for site users because they can use any browser client they choose (including beta releases of new browser versions), it also means that an organization does not have to test and potentially modify the Web site markup to work in new browsers. The elimination of Web site maintenance yields a direct financial savings to an organization.

Keeping with the economic theme, following the best practices required for creating accessible Web sites generally means that less code needs to be written. For example, early (and non-accessible) Web sites used the HTML <FONT> element to define the styling of specific content. Larger Web pages typically contained numerous <FONT> elements defining the style of the text within them, including the font size, family, decoration, and color, to name a few. This bloated the page and made it very time-consuming to alter the site's appearance, such as changing a font size from 12-point to 10-point. Instead, accessible sites leverage cascading style sheets (CSS) and the <SPAN> element, which enable referencing a style by name, rather than duplicating the styling details repeatedly. This results in less markup in the source of the Web page, dramatically reducing the amount of time required to modify the presentation of a site.

Because accessible sites generally require less markup in the source of a Web page, that translates into a smaller page payload. The smaller the payload, the less markup there is to maintain for a developer and designer. Moreover, it results in faster page download times and reduced bandwidth expense.

Building off the "less markup" concept, another added benefit affects search results, as the Web site is indexed by the larger search engines. By centralizing the styling of a Web site to CSS files, which results in less markup, search engines can more effectively parse and index the content of a Web page. This results in better search results and higher page rankings.

Accessible Web sites are viewed by the general Web development community as the way things should be done. Granted, many organizations may not care about "doing the right thing," as they are more concerned about the bottom line. As shown here, however, even companies lacking a sense of responsibility can benefit from conforming to the accepted guidelines; and the goodwill created by designing accessible Web sites, even when not required, can set many developers, designers, and Web development firms apart from the crowd.

Creating Accessible SharePoint Sites

Enough about the advantages and details associated with creating accessible Web sites — this book is about developing SharePoint sites, so let's get to the part about implementing these techniques in MOSS Publishing sites. Out-of-the-box (OOTB), SharePoint does not generate accessible HTML markup. Accessible Web sites generally implement their layout using HTML <DIV> elements and CSS, compared to the traditional <TABLE>-based layouts. The HTML generated by SharePoint by default is primarily <TABLE>-based.

However, this is not just a SharePoint issue; the <TABLE>-based layout stems from the inherent architecture of Windows SharePoint Services (WSS) 3.0: It is built on top of the .NET Framework (specifically, ASP.NET 2.0). The controls included in ASP.NET 2.0, such as the GridView and Menu controls, are rendered using HTML <TABLE> elements. While it is possible to change the rendering of controls in ASP.NET 2.0 with control adapters, it is not a turnkey solution.

The new WSS 3.0–based architecture built on top of ASP.NET 2.0 is not all bad news when accessibility is considered. The fact that SharePoint can now fully leverage the master page model makes it much easier to centrally control the rendering.

As previously covered, creating accessible Web sites does not just fall in the domain of developers and designers. Content owners and editors also have a responsibility when managing content. For instance, adding images to an article on a site without including a text equivalent of the image using the `alt=""` attribute (breaking WCAG 1.0 checkpoint 1.1) is just as bad as a developer not including table column headings (`<TH>`) in data tables (breaking WCAG 1.0 checkpoint 5.1), as both are WCAG 1.0 Priority 1 issues.

Challenges to Creating Accessible SharePoint Sites

Aside from the general accessibility guidelines that should be followed when creating Web sites, a few aspects of SharePoint (and ASP.NET 2.0) present unique challenges.

First, consider ASP.NET 2.0. As previously mentioned, the ASP.NET 2.0 Web controls' default rendering is HTML `<TABLE>`-based. Thankfully, ASP.NET 2.0 introduced a new model for rendering controls that permits developers to plug in their own rendering implementation to change the default behavior. This is achieved using a custom `ControlAdapter`. In late 2006, Microsoft announced the CSS control adapters and eventually handed the project over to the community by posting the source on CodePlex: www.andrewconnell.com/go/234. This project changes the rendering of some of the ASP.NET 2.0 controls from `<TABLE>`-based to CSS-based, making it much easier to facilitate an accessible site. Unfortunately, the CSS control adapters do not include all ASP.NET 2.0 controls — and frankly, many enterprises have strong concerns about implementing a project that is not backed or supported by a sizeable entity.

Another issue with using a custom `ControlAdapter` deals with the ASP.NET 2.0 Web Part infrastructure. Web Parts are rendered within a two-row HTML `<TABLE>`, with one cell in each row, as shown in Figure 9-1. The top row contains the Web Part's header, where the title and Verbs menu is made available (depending on the `WebPart.ChromeType` property, as it may be set to not show a header). The second row contains the actual rendered Web Part. Similar to the HTML document object model (DOM), WSS 3.0 provides a SharePoint-specific DOM called the *Web Part Page Services Component (WPSC)*.

The WPSC can be leveraged by client-side script to listen for Web-Part-specific events, and to interact with the Web Parts already on the page, such as setting the values of public properties. The HTML `<TABLE>` containing the Web Part is assigned a unique ID, as is the `<DIV>` that contains the rendering of the Web Part in the second row. The WPSC is written with the expectation that this `<TABLE>` is present, so implementing a custom `ControlAdapter` for Web Parts that strips the `<TABLE>` rendering would break the WPSC.

Each project team can debate whether solving one issue by introducing another is a valid solution, but this simply demonstrates a challenge in creating accessible SharePoint sites. Granted, many Publishing sites will utilize field controls instead of Web Parts, but a Publishing site with zero Web Parts is unlikely.

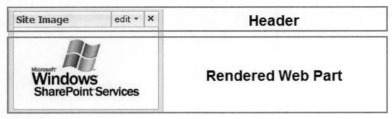

Figure 9-1

One of the most challenging aspects of SharePoint sites deals with the navigation. Many of SharePoint's menus require JavaScript, such as the Site Actions menu, the Edit Control Block (ECB) menu, and toolbar menus. These menus also facilitate a very mouse-centered user interface. Accessible sites should provide a way to perform the same actions when JavaScript has been disabled, as some clients do. Some of these menus are not as prevalent within Publishing sites for most site consumers because things such as Site Actions are not visible or available to anonymous users, which Publishing sites typically have more of compared to traditional collaborative SharePoint sites. However, the site authoring experience in Publishing sites is still heavily driven by these JavaScript and mouse-driven menus.

Another issue with Publishing sites involves the content authoring components experience. The Rich Text Editor (RTE) provided OOTB in Publishing sites is supported only when using Internet Explorer. In addition, it does not produce compliant markup. Thankfully, this can be easily addressed by implementing the Telerik RadEditor Lite for MOSS, which has a compliant interface and produces compliant markup. However, the Telerik RadEditor Lite is not fully accessible in that it contains a mouse-centered user interface and does not work when JavaScript has been disabled. Refer to Chapter 14, "Authoring Experience Extensibility," for more information on the Telerik RadEditor Lite for MOSS.

Aside from all these issues, one of the most significant things that will need to be done is to modify the OOTB markup provided by the Publishing Portal template. While Chapter 5 and Chapter 7 demonstrate how to create a minimal master page with no branding, the OOTB markup provided by the Publishing Portal template is a perfect example of the work in store for developers and designers when creating accessible Publishing sites. When validated using the W3C Markup Validation Service, the default Publishing Portal template (with zero customizations after creating the site collection) yielded 102 errors.

In an effort to address accessibility issues and challenges with SharePoint — specifically, Publishing sites — Microsoft teamed up with another vendor, HiSoftware, to offer ways to facilitate the creation of accessible Publishing sites.

Accessibility Kit for SharePoint

While SharePoint does not ship OOTB conforming to any of the accessibility guidelines recommended by the W3C, Microsoft teamed up with a partner, HiSoftware (www.hisoftware.com), to help make WSS 3.0 and MOSS 2007 meet these requirements. The *Accessibility Kit for SharePoint (AKS)*, the result of this partnership, was created by HiSoftware on behalf of Microsoft and is available as a free download and install. Using the AKS, developers and designers can learn how to create accessible SharePoint sites, including Publishing sites. The AKS is available from CodePlex (www.codeplex.com).

Position and Goals of the AKS

Before factoring the AKS into a project plan, it is important to understand the position and goals of the AKS. First and foremost, the AKS is not intended to be used as a turnkey solution; simply installing the AKS does not make a site accessible. Instead, it is better to think of the AKS as more of an educational tool. It contains files and utilities that will help you create accessible SharePoint sites.

The stated goal of the AKS is to help build sites that meet the WCAG 1.0 AA standard, or sites that meet all Priority 1 and Priority 2 checkpoints. Developers can use the files and utilities included in the AKS as reference and sample materials in implementing accessible Publishing sites.

The AKS follows the recommendation of Microsoft in terms of not modifying the OOTB codebase installed by SharePoint. Instead, it is non-invasive in that it simply adds extra files to a SharePoint installation. This ensures that the AKS files will not be overwritten or modified by any service packs or patches distributed by Microsoft. It also enables developers to select which pieces of the AKS are used in a custom Publishing site.

The AKS is an open system in that it is fully documented and provides guidelines for developers and designers creating accessible sites. It is completely extensible by developers.

Installation and Implementation

After obtaining the AKS, installation is extremely simple, as it uses a standard wizard-driven experience with no prompts aside from the usual license acceptance screens. The installation will copy an AKS site-collection-scoped Feature to the `[..]\12\TEMPLATE\FEATURES` directory, but it is not installed. It also adds some PDFs containing documentation and the entire source of the AKS in a new directory in `c:\Program Files`, as well as adding a new program group in the Start menu on the server. One of the items in the new AKS program group is used to install the AKS Feature.

The AKS Feature provisions a handful of master pages and CSS files that mimic the OOTB files provisioned by the Publishing Portal site definition. Once the AKS Feature is activated on a site collection created using the Publishing Portal site definition, users can select one of the AKS-provided master pages that use the AKS-provided CSS files. Developers can then pick through these files to see how things were implemented.

The AKS contains sample files, code, utilities, and some reusable content. The sample files include master pages, CSS files, and page layouts. One of the most significant parts of the AKS are custom control adapters. As previously mentioned, these custom `ControlAdapter` classes enable developers to see how the rendering of Web controls is modified from the default rendering options.

Developers and designers working on Publishing sites that require some sort of accessibility compliance level should consider and spend time evaluating the AKS to determine whether it can help meet the project's demands.

Summary

This chapter introduced the concept of accessible Web sites. Creating accessible Web sites is not only something that should be considered to make the site more easily readable by users with disabilities. Accessible Web sites also offer positive economic and performance benefits, such as easier maintenance and better search capabilities. This chapter provided introductions to the most common Web accessibility guidelines: the WCAG 1.0, the WCAG 2.0, and the United States Rehabilitation Act of 1973 Section 508. Finally, the Accessibility Kit for SharePoint (AKS), backed by Microsoft and its partner HiSoftware, was introduced as a fantastic learning aid, in addition to offering reusable components for developers and designers embarking on creating accessible Publishing sites.

10

Field Types and Field Controls

Windows SharePoint Services (WSS) 3.0 and Office SharePoint Server (MOSS) 2007 include many common field types that can be used in site columns, content types, and lists. This list includes types such as single line of text fields, choice fields, date/time fields and Boolean yes/no fields. Chapter 6 demonstrated that developers must learn to utilize these fields in order to deliver the required functionality in any SharePoint application.

Specific to Publishing sites, these field types are used in site column definitions, which are then used within content types that define the schema for types of content pages created on the site. The Publishing Features add additional fields to SharePoint, such as the Publishing HTML field that is used to provide the rich text storage capabilities, or the Publishing Image field that stores an image with specific formatting and settings within a content page. Thankfully, the same infrastructure that Microsoft leverages when creating field types is available to developers to create custom field types when the provided field types do not satisfy the needs of a project.

In addition to creating custom field types that are used to store data, developers can also create custom field controls that define the presentation of certain fields and the editing experience. This enables developers to create the most unique and user-friendly content entry experience for content owners while at the same time optionally providing additional complex validation on the field during editing.

Creating custom field types and controls is a complex and complicated subject that does not have a vast amount of resources or documentation. Many aspects of this area — creating both field types and field controls — are not heavily documented, if at all. This chapter demonstrates how to create a custom field type that also contains a custom field control in order to define a customized editing experience, as well as adding a design-time preview of the control and customized validation upon saving data in the field type.

Overview of All the Moving Parts

Before diving into the complex (and seemingly confusing) world of custom field types and field controls, it helps to put things in perspective. This area of SharePoint can be a bit intimidating when developers first see all the moving parts: field type, field value type, field control, rendering control, and field type definition. Understanding all of these terms and their relationships helps when building a custom field type and control because it is easier to visualize the big picture — that is, how they all fit together. Figure 10-1 shows the relationships between the different moving parts in a custom field type and field control.

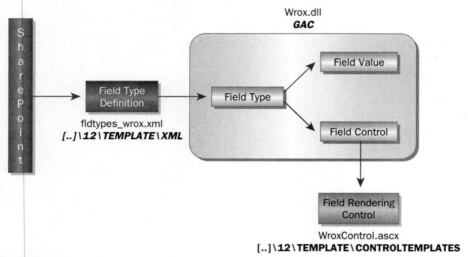

Figure 10-1

Each element within a custom field type and field control serves a unique purpose. The "hub" of the field type in Figure 10-1 is the *field type* class. This class is what SharePoint looks to for everything related to the custom field type. If the field type stores data within a custom data structure, rather than a simple string, the field type class will contain a reference to the *field value* class. To handle the editing experience, the field type will also contain a reference to the *field control* class. The field control class may optionally leverage a SharePoint `RenderingTemplate` found in an ASP.NET 2.0 user control file known as the *rendering control*.

With the field type, field value, and field control defined, SharePoint now needs to be made aware of the custom field type. This responsibility falls on the *field type definition* file. The field type definition file, an XML file containing CAML markup, provides SharePoint with enough meta information about the field type, as well as a pointer to the class, and the assembly containing the class, that defines the custom field type. SharePoint looks at all the field type definition files on the server when it initially loads (after recycling the Web services on a server) to generate a list of the valid field types.

Creating Custom Field Types and Controls

Creating a custom field type and field control requires creating numerous classes and files, packaging everything up, and deploying files to numerous locations. The following sections explain each of the components in Figure 10-1 in more depth, as they demonstrate how to create a custom field type and field control. First, it helps to see what the final result will look like and review the requirements for the field type and control.

The custom field type (CountryRegionField) and control (CountryRegionControl) that are built in this chapter enable a content author to select a country and then enter a state/region depending on the country selected. Initially, no country or state/region is selected. In fact, when no country is selected, the controls to select or enter the state/region are not shown. Upon selecting "United States," the page will issue a postback and refresh, presenting the content author with another selector to pick a state. If the content owner selects a country other than "United States," then the page issues a postback and renders a textbox to enter the region/county, rather than select a state from a selector. Figures 10-2 and 10-3 show what the field control looks like when editing a page in a Publishing site with "United States" or "United Kingdom" selected as the country, respectively.

Figure 10-2

Figure 10-3

In Display mode (when a page is not in Edit mode), the state/region should be displayed followed by the country, separated by a comma as shown in Figure 10-4.

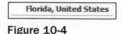
Florida, United States

Figure 10-4

The last requirement is that the field type should return its value as a custom object, rather than a delimited string. Therefore, when accessing a field via the API — named Location, for example — the code would look like what is shown in Listing 10-1.

Listing 10-1: Accessing a field of type CountryRegionField

```
SPListItem item = list.Items[0];
CountryRegionValue fieldValue = (CountryRegionValue)item["Location"];
Console.WriteLine("The country selected is: " + fieldValue.Country);
Console.WriteLine("The state/region selected is: " + fieldValue.Region);
```

To create a new custom field type and control, start with a new C# project in Visual Studio using the Class Library project template. Add references to `Microsoft.SharePoint` and `System.Web` and sign the project to create an assembly with a strong name.

Creating a Custom Field Type

The first step in creating a custom field type and field control is to create the field type class — the hub of everything related to the field. All field types must inherit from the `Microsoft.SharePoint.SPField` class or one that is derived from it. The `CountryRegionField` field type will inherit from `Microsoft.SharePoint.SPFieldMultiColumn`, which is an internal field that is not visible through the browser interface. It enables developers to store columns of data within a single field and provide an easy way (via the `Microsoft.SharePoint.SPFieldMultiColumnValue`) to serialize/deserialize the data to/from SharePoint into a custom value class.

The `CountryRegionField` class acts as the hub for everything related to the field type. It provides SharePoint with the desired value class, the rendering control that is used to generate the editing experience, as well as any custom validation that needs to be executed before saving data to the field. The class `CountryRegionField` inherits the `Microsoft.SharePoint.SPFieldMultiColumn` class, which enables multiple columns of data to be stored within the field type. All fields that implement the `SPFieldMultiColumn` class must have two constructors. Nicely, both constructors are always the same across all fields that implement this class. Listing 10-2 shows the contents of the `CountryRegionField.cs` file.

Listing 10-2: CountryRegionField.cs file containing the custom field type

```
using System;
using Microsoft.SharePoint;
using Microsoft.SharePoint.WebControls;

namespace WROX.ProMossWcm.Chapter10 {
  public class CountryRegionField : SPFieldMultiColumn {
    public CountryRegionField (SPFieldCollection fields, string fieldName)
      : base(fields, fieldName) { }

    public CountryRegionField (SPFieldCollection fields, string typeName, string
displayName)
      : base(fields, typeName, displayName) { }
  }
}
```

At this point, although the field type class has the minimal code it needs to function, it is not very useful. Later it will need to override a property and a few methods that tell SharePoint about the custom value and control classes, as well as implement the validation when saving data to the field. However, for now it is good enough as it is because these capabilities will be added when necessary.

Creating a Custom Field Type Definition

With a field type class created, the next step is to create the field type definition that will make SharePoint aware of the field. This is done by creating an XML file in the `[..]\12\TEMPLATE\XML` folder. When SharePoint starts up (when the server is rebooted or when the Web process has been recycled), it looks at the `[..]\12\TEMPLATE\XML` folder and loads all the field type-defined files named `fldtypes[_*].xml`. All the SharePoint fields provided in the WSS 3.0 install are found in the `fldtypes.xml` file. Other fields are added based on the MOSS 2007 installation. For instance, all the Publishing-specific fields are defined in the `fldtypes.publishing.xml` file. One of the most valuable aspects of this implementation is that developers have the source of the definitions for the Microsoft-implemented controls, which can be used for reference — the best documentation around!

The field definition file tells SharePoint a few things about the field type, including the name of the field and the underlying parent field type. The definition also tells SharePoint some of the rules associated with the type, such as whether it can be used to create new site columns or columns within survey lists, as well as the full name of the class and assembly containing the field type class. The other critical piece of the field type definition is the inclusion of a rendering pattern. The display rendering pattern defines how the field's content should be rendered when in a list or display mode. The CAML markup is shown in Listing 10-3.

Listing 10-3: CountryRegionField definition (fldtypes_wrox.xml)

```xml
<?xml version="1.0" encoding="utf-8" ?>
<FieldTypes>
  <FieldType>
    <Field Name="TypeName">CountryRegion</Field>
    <Field Name="ParentType">MultiColumn</Field>
    <Field Name="TypeDisplayName">Country, Region </Field>
    <Field Name="TypeShortDescription">Country and state/region</Field>
    <Field Name="UserCreatable">TRUE</Field>
    <Field Name="FieldTypeClass">WROX.ProMossWcm.Chapter10.CountryRegionField,
Chapter10, Version=1.0.0.0, Culture=neutral,
PublicKeyToken=c591e70cfdf9ce4f</Field>
    <RenderPattern Name="DisplayPattern">
      <Switch>
        <Expr><Column /></Expr>
        <Case Value="" />
        <Default>
          <Column SubColumnNumber="1" HTMLEncode="TRUE" />
          <HTML><![CDATA[,  ]]></HTML>
          <Column SubColumnNumber="0" HTMLEncode="TRUE" />
        </Default>
      </Switch>
    </RenderPattern>
  </FieldType>
</FieldTypes>
```

The first part of the field type definition (the `<Field>` elements) contains the metadata about the field that SharePoint needs to know about up front. Although the list seems somewhat limited, there are quite a few additional options that are not included in Listing 10-3. The following list explains each of the fields:

❑ **TypeName:** This is the unique name of the field used when creating items such as site columns using a Feature. For example, if a site column were created that was based on the field type created in this chapter, the element manifest's site element would look like the following (omitting the other required attributes):

```xml
<Field ID="..." Name="..." DisplayName="..." Type="CountryRegion" />
```

❑ **ParentType:** The parent type is the field type from which the custom field type is derived — in this case, `SPFieldMultiColumn` or just `MultiColumn`.

❑ **TypeDisplayName:** This name is used to display the field type on pages such as the Site Column Gallery or a content type's detail page.

❑ **TypeShortDescription:** The short description is the string used to display the field type as an option when creating new site or list columns (the long radio button list under the new column's title textbox).

❑ **UserCreatable:** This Boolean property tells SharePoint whether the field type can be used in the creation of a column in a list by a user. When `false`, developers can still use the field type in site columns within the definition of list templates created using Features.

❑ **FieldTypeClass:** This contains the strong name of the field type class and the assembly containing the class. This is also referred to as the five-part name: *namespace.type, Assembly, Version, Culture, PublicKeyToken.*

Following the fields is the rendering pattern. There are two rendering pattern options: `DisplayPattern` and `HeaderPattern`. The display pattern is used when the field type is displayed on a page such as a list view page or an item detail page. In Listing 10-3, the display pattern contains a CAML `switch` statement, which is similar to C#'s `switch` statement. It first checks whether the current column contains any data. If it is empty, nothing is rendered. Otherwise, the two values within the field (country and state/region) are rendered, with a comma and nonbreaking space separating the two. Notice how the `<Column />` node contains an attribute `SubColumnNumber`. This tells SharePoint to use a value from a specific column in this field type. The number to use is defined with the field type's custom value class.

The custom field type definition should be added to the Visual Studio project in the following location: `\TEMPLATE\XML\fldtypes_wrox.xml`.

Creating a Custom Field Value

One of the requirements of the `ContryRegionField` custom field type was to store the data within a custom data structure. While it sounds a bit complex, it is actually very simple. The custom field value class is very handy with field types that are derived from the `SPFieldMultiColumn` field because data is stored in the `SPFieldMultiColumn` field as a special delimited string using `;#` as the delimiter, and not just between two values but surrounding them. For example, using the examples in Figures 10-2 and 10-3 shown earlier, the two strings containing the data would be as follows:

```
;#United States;#Florida;#
;#United Kingdom;#Edinburgh;#
```

While it is entirely possible to write code that parses these strings, developers should instead create a custom field value class that knows not only how to serialize and deserialize the data between the raw string and a strongly typed property bag, but also enables users to specify the data's position within the string. This is helpful, as the index of the data within the raw string is directly related to the `<Column SubColumnNumber="" />` CAML element used in the rendering pattern within the field type definition.

The custom field type value class, `CountryRegionValue`, inherits from the `Microsoft.SharePoint.SPFieldMultiColumnValue` class. This class has three constructors but only two are necessary to override. The default constructor that accepts no parameters should be overridden to call the base constructor, passing in the number of data columns stored in the field. The second constructor should take a string and pass it to the base constructor that accepts the string value to parse. The SPFieldMultiColumnValue class then internally splits the string into an array. The last part to the custom value class adds properties that reference a specific position in the array representing the data in the delimited strings. Listing 10-4 shows the contents of the CountryRegionValue.cs file.

Listing 10-4: CountryRegionValue.cs file containing the field value

```
using System;
using Microsoft.SharePoint;
namespace WROX.ProMossWcm.Chapter10 {
  public class CountryRegionValue : SPFieldMultiColumnValue {
    private const int NUM_FIELDS = 2;

    public CountryRegionValue ()
      : base(NUM_FIELDS) { }

    public CountryRegionValue (string value)
      : base(value) { }

    public string Country {
      get { return this[0]; }
      set { this[0] = value; }
    }

    public string Region {
      get {return this[1];}
      set { this[1] = value; }
    }
  }
}
```

Although the value class is created, it is worthless until it is associated with the field type class. Refer back to Figure 10-1, which illustrates the relationship between all the moving parts in the custom field type and field value. In order to make the custom field type class aware of the custom value type, the SPField.GetFieldValue() method should be overridden; that should return an instance of the value type. The code in Listing 10-5 should be added to the CountryRegionField class.

Listing 10-5: Wiring the field type and field value together

```
public override object GetFieldValue (string value) {
  if (string.IsNullOrEmpty(value))
    return null;
  return new CountryRegionValue(value);
}
```

The next step is to create the control that will be used when interacting with the field type in Edit mode.

Creating a Custom Field Control

The requirements for the custom field type `CountryRegionField` are to have a customized and specific editing experience for content authors. Refer back to Figures 10-2 and 10-3 to see what the interface should look like. To add a custom editing experience for a custom field type, a developer would create a custom field control class. This class contains all the necessary information about the field control.

Thankfully, Microsoft did not stop there and leave developers with only a server control model to create the editing experience. The field control class can point to a new element called a SharePoint *rendering template*. This rendering template, similar to an ASP.NET 2.0 user control, enables developers to define the editing experience declaratively, rather than doing everything in managed code. However, unlike ASP.NET 2.0 user controls, the ASCX file is not loaded first, followed by the code-behind. Rather, the field control class tells SharePoint which rendering template to load. This presents a bit of a challenge for ASP.NET 2.0 developers who are used to the other model because it requires thinking a bit backwards at times.

The first piece in a custom field control is the control class. This class must inherit from the `Microsoft.SharePoint.WebControls.BaseFieldControl` class or one that derives from it. For the `CountryRegionField`, the `BaseFieldControl` will work. The control class, `CountryRegionControl`, will contain methods that override those defined in the `BaseFieldControl` class. At minimum, only three methods and properties need to be overridden. First, the control needs to make SharePoint aware of which rendering template to create by overriding the `DefaultTemplateName` property, as shown in Listing 10-6.

Listing 10-6: CountryRegionControl.cs custom field control

```csharp
using System;
using Microsoft.SharePoint.WebControls;
using System.Web.UI.WebControls;

namespace WROX.ProMossWcm.Chapter10 {
  public class CountryRegionControl : BaseFieldControl {
    private const string RENDERING_TEMPLATE = "ContryRegionControl";

    protected override string DefaultTemplateName {
      get { return RENDERING_TEMPLATE; }
    }
  }
}
```

Before going any further, it makes sense to switch gears here and create the rendering template — the ASCX control that will be used to declaratively define the editing experience. This file, `CountryRegionControl.ascx`, resides in the `[..]\12\TEMPLATE\CONTROLTEMPLATES` folder and can contain one or more rendering templates. A good example can be found in the `DefaultTemplates.ascx`, which contains WSS 3.0 field control rendering templates, and `SharePoint_Publishing_defaultformtemplates.ascx`, which contains Publishing field control rendering templates included with MOSS 2007. The name of the file doesn't matter — what matters is the ID of the rendering template within the file. It is this ID that is returned to SharePoint in the `CountryRegionControl` class using the overridden `DefaultTemplateName` property. The contents of the `CountryRegionControl.ascx` file are shown in Listing 10-7. (Some code is omitted here for readability. The full source can be found in the downloadable code for the book.)

Listing 10-7: CountryRegionControl.ascx custom field control rendering template

```
<%@ Control Language="C#" %>
<%@ Assembly Name="Microsoft.SharePoint, Version=12.0.0.0, Culture=neutral,
PublicKeyToken=71e9bce111e9429c" %>
<%@ Register Assembly="Microsoft.SharePoint, Version=12.0.0.0, Culture=neutral,
PublicKeyToken=71e9bce111e9429c" Namespace="Microsoft.SharePoint.WebControls"
TagPrefix="SharePoint" %>

<SharePoint:RenderingTemplate id="CountryRegionControl" runat="server">
  <Template>
    <table class="ms-form">
      <tr>
        <td align="right">Country:</td>
        <td><asp:DropDownList id="Country" runat="server" autopostback="true"
cssclass="ms-RadioText"><asp:ListItem>Select a
country...</asp:ListItem><asp:ListItem>United
States</asp:ListItem><asp:ListItem>Afghanistan</asp:ListItem><!-- omitted for
readability --><asp:ListItem>Zimbabwe</asp:ListItem></asp:DropDownList></td>
      </tr>
      <tr>
        <td align="right"><asp:literal id="RegionInputLiteral" runat="server"
text="Region:" visible="false"/><asp:literal id="RegionSelectorLiteral"
runat="server" text="State:" visible="false"/></td>
        <td><asp:textbox id="RegionInput" runat="server" visible="false"
cssclass="ms-input" /><asp:DropDownList id="RegionSelector" runat="server"
visible="false" cssclass="ms-RadioText"><asp:ListItem>Select a
state...</asp:ListItem><asp:ListItem>Alabama</asp:ListItem>
<asp:ListItem>Alaska</asp:ListItem><!-- omitted for readability -->
<asp:ListItem>Wyoming</asp:ListItem></asp:DropDownList></td>
      </tr>
    </table>
  </Template>
</SharePoint:RenderingTemplate>
```

The rendering control contains a single HTML table. Within this table are two rows. The first row is for the country selection. The first option in the `DropDownList` contains instructions for the user; the second option contains the country "United States," and all subsequent entries contain other countries in the world. The second row is a bit more interesting. In the first cell, two `Literal` controls are used to show labels for the second input: the state or the region. Both are initially set to be hidden (`visible="false"`). The second cell in the second row contains both a `TextBox` control and `DropDownList`. One is used by the contributor to select a state when the country "United States" is selected, whereas the other is used to enter the region of the country as a free-form text entry. Each `Literal` and entry control in the second row of the table is shown or hidden based on the selection of the Country `DropDownList`. This is handled in the `CountryRegionControl` class.

Now that the rendering template has been created, it is time to jump back to the `CountryRegionControl` class and add the necessary code to wire everything up. First, a few class-scoped fields are needed that will be used to reference the Web controls in the rendering template. Add two `DropDownList` controls, two `Literal`s, and one `TextBox` to the class, as well as a single constant to enforce consistency to the `CountryRegionControl` class, as shown in Listing 10-8.

Listing 10-8: CountryRegionControl.cs custom field control

```
namespace WROX.ProMossWcm.Chapter10 {
  public class CountryRegionControl : BaseFieldControl {
    private const string RENDERING_TEMPLATE = "CountryRegionControl";
    private const string UNITED_STATES = "United States";

    protected DropDownList _country;
    protected DropDownList _regionSelector;
    protected Literal _regionSelectorLiteral;
    protected Literal _regionInputLiteral;
    protected TextBox _regionInput;

    protected override string DefaultTemplateName {
      get { return RENDERING_TEMPLATE; }
    }
  }
}
```

The next step is to override the `CreateChildControls()` method, something that is done in almost all server controls. First, ensure that the current mode of the page is what is desired. In other words, the rendering template is only used in rendering the editing experience, not the display experience. The display experience is handled in the field type definition as outlined previously in Listing 10-3. Therefore, if the page is not currently in Edit mode, the control should "short-circuit" or stop doing any rendering.

Next, like all ASP.NET 2.0 server controls, a call to the base class' `CreateChildControls()` should be added before adding any custom logic. The main purpose of `CreateChildControls()` in the `CountryRegionControl` class is to wire up references of the Web controls in the class to those in the rendering template. This is necessary so that values can be set and retrieved later. Unfortunately, because the class is being processed before the ASCX file containing the rendering template, ASP.NET 2.0's capability to automatically wire up the controls is not an option. Therefore, each control must be retrieved and associated with the internal field created in Listing 10-8. This is done using the `BaseFieldControl.TemplateContainer.FindControl()` method. This object, `TemplateContainer`, is a reference to the template within the rendering template. After obtaining a reference, it is good practice for developers to test whether it is valid. This is done by simply checking whether the control retrieved is not equal to `null`. The `CreateChildControls()` method in the `CountryRegionControl` class is shown in Listing 10-9.

Listing 10-9: CountryRegionControl CreateChildControls() method

```
protected override void CreateChildControls () {
  if (this.Field == null ||
    this.ControlMode == SPControlMode.Display ||
    this.ControlMode == SPControlMode.Invalid)
    return;

  base.CreateChildControls();

  // get reference to Country selector
  _country = TemplateContainer.FindControl("Country") as DropDownList;
```

```
    if (_country == null)
        throw new ArgumentException("Country DropDownList not found. Possibly corrupt
control template.");

    _country.SelectedIndexChanged += new EventHandler(Country_SelectedIndexChanged);

    // get reference to State selector
    _regionSelector = TemplateContainer.FindControl("RegionSelector") as
DropDownList;
    if (_regionSelector == null)
        throw new ArgumentException("RegionSelector DropDownList not found. Possibly
corrupt control template.");

    // get reference to State selector's label
    _regionSelectorLiteral = TemplateContainer.FindControl("RegionSelectorLiteral")
as Literal;
    if (_regionSelectorLiteral == null)
        throw new ArgumentException("RegionSelectorLiteral Literal not found. Possibly
corrupt control template.");

    // get reference to Region textbox for free-form entry
    _regionInput = TemplateContainer.FindControl("RegionInput") as TextBox;
    if (_regionInput == null)
        throw new ArgumentException("RegionInput TextBox not found. Possibly corrupt
control template.");

    // get reference to Region textbox's label
    _regionInputLiteral = TemplateContainer.FindControl("RegionInputLiteral") as
Literal;
    if (_regionInputLiteral == null)
        throw new ArgumentException("RegionInputLiteral Literal not found. Possibly
corrupt control template.");
}
```

Notice the highlighted line in Listing 10-9. This line is used to wire up a server-side event handler with the country selector to handle when the value selected changes. This provides the capability to show and hide the necessary state/region Web controls and labels. This event wiring must be done within the CreateChildControls() method, rather than the markup within the rendering template, in order for the event to be correctly registered in the ASP.NET 2.0 page life cycle.

The next step in creating the field control is to override the BaseFieldControl.Value property. This property is used by SharePoint to set the value of the control when loading it in Edit mode, as well as to retrieve the values from the Web controls in the rendering template upon postbacks. When coding the Value property's get and set, developers should always call the EnsureChildControls() method first. This method checks whether the CreateChildControls() method has been called. If it has not been called, it is called at this time. It is only after an internal flag has been set in the .NET Framework indicating that CreateChildControls() has been called that the code will continue after calling EnsureChildControls(). It is critical that EnsureChildControls() is called first because the Value property is utterly useless without valid references to the Web controls in the rendering template.

The Value property returns a value of type object. The object returned should be the same custom field value that is part of the custom field type — CountryRegionValue in the case of the field type created in this chapter.

First create the `Value`'s `get` as shown in Listing 10-10. After a validation check, the purpose here is to retrieve the values from the Web controls in the rendering template and store them into a new object of type `CountryRegionValue`, returning this object back to SharePoint.

Listing 10-10: CountryRegionControl.Value property's get

```
public override object Value {
get {
  EnsureChildControls();
  CountryRegionValue field = new CountryRegionValue();

  if (_country == null || _regionSelector == null || _regionInput == null) {
    field.Country = String.Empty;
    field.Region = String.Empty;
  } else {
    // set country value
    if (_country.SelectedIndex == 0)
      field.Country = String.Empty;
    else
      field.Country = _country.SelectedValue;

    // set region value
    if (_country.SelectedValue == UNITED_STATES) {
      if (_regionSelector.SelectedIndex == 0)
        field.Region = String.Empty;
      else
        field.Region = _regionSelector.SelectedValue;
    } else
      field.Region = _regionInput.Text.Trim();
  }

  return field;
  }
  set {...}
```

In the `Value`'s `set`, shown in Listing 10-11, after a validation check the Web controls within the rendering template are set using the values provided by the value passed in by SharePoint. The last step in the set is to update the visibility of the controls. This is necessary because the editing experience should show either a state selector if the country selected is "United States" or a free-form textbox if some other country is selected.

Listing 10-11: CountryRegionControl.Value property's set

```
public override object Value {
  get {...}
  set {
    EnsureChildControls();

    if (value != null && !string.IsNullOrEmpty(value.ToString())) {
      CountryRegionValue field = new CountryRegionValue(value.ToString());

      _country.SelectedValue = field.Country;
      if (_country.SelectedIndex == 1)          // if UNITED STATES selected
```

```
         _regionSelector.SelectedValue = field.Region;
      else if (_country.SelectedIndex >= 2)  // if any other country selected
         _regionInput.Text = field.Region;
      SetRegionControlVisibility(_country.SelectedIndex);
   }
  }
}
```

```
private void SetRegionControlVisibility (int countrySelectedIndex) {
   switch (countrySelectedIndex) {
      case 0:   // if none selected
        _regionSelector.Visible = false;
        _regionSelectorLiteral.Visible = false;
        _regionInput.Visible = false;
        _regionInputLiteral.Visible = false;
        break;
      case 1:   // if UNITED STATES selected
        _regionSelector.Visible = true;
        _regionSelectorLiteral.Visible = true;
        _regionInput.Visible = false;
        _regionInputLiteral.Visible = false;
        break;
      default:   // if any other country selected
        _regionSelector.Visible = false;
        _regionSelectorLiteral.Visible = false;
        _regionInput.Visible = true;
        _regionInputLiteral.Visible = true;
        break;
   }
}
```

The last thing that needs to be added to the CountryRegionControl class is the server-side event handler that is called when the value of the country selector is changed, as shown in Listing 10-12.

Listing 10-12: Country selector event handler

```
protected void Country_SelectedIndexChanged (object sender, EventArgs e) {
   EnsureChildControls();
   SetRegionControlVisibility(_country.SelectedIndex);
}
```

With the field control finished, it now needs to be wired up to the field type (refer to Figure 10-1 at the beginning of the chapter). This is done by overriding yet another property on the "hub" class of the field type: CountryRegionField. The property, FieldRenderingControl, returns an object of type BaseFieldControl back to SharePoint when called. This is how SharePoint knows to load the field control for the custom field type. FieldRenderingControl is a read-only property, so only the get portion needs to be completed. Note that the underlying BaseFieldControl.FieldName property must be set with the internal name of the field instance that is using the custom field type. This is demonstrated in Listing 10-13.

Listing 10-13: Wiring field controls to field types

```
public override BaseFieldControl FieldRenderingControl {
  get {
    BaseFieldControl control = new CountryRegionControl();
    control.FieldName = this.InternalName;
    return control;
  }
}
```

The only thing left to do with the field control is to add a design-time experience. At this point, Office SharePoint Designer (SPD) 2007 doesn't have a clue what to show as a preview for the custom field control when it is dropped on the page. If the field control were dropped into a page layout in SPD and viewed in Design mode, it would show up as a gray box with an error, as shown in Figure 10-5.

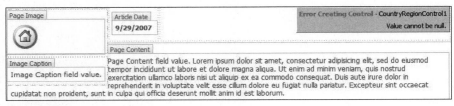

Figure 10-5

Adding Design-Time Rendering Preview

Figure 10-5 highlights the fact that page developers and designers will have no idea what the field control will look like based on the preview in SPD's Design mode as it is currently coded. The next step is to add a design-time preview. The control's Render() method is always called by SPD in an effort to generate the HTML that is shown in Design mode. However, in the case of a Publishing site, field controls are not going to be associated with any real underlying data in Design mode, as page layouts are the "source" of the data — they are used in conjunction with a master page to define the rendering of a page, which is just an item within the Pages list. Therefore, the Render() method is not ideal. Instead, developers should create a customized view of the control whenever it is rendered in SPD's Design mode.

To create the custom HTML used in a design-time experience, the control must implement the PMicrosoft.SharePoint.WebControls.IDesignTimeHtmlProvider interface. This interface contains a single method, GetDesignTimeHtml(), which returns a string. This string should contain the HTML used to render the control in SPD's Design mode. While a custom design-time interface can be implemented very easily with one line of code in GetDesignTimeHtml(), it would not provide a very clean or consistent experience compared to the out-of-the-box (OOTB) field controls shipped in MOSS 2007. For instance, the following code would present the Design mode experience shown in Figure 10-6:

```
public string IDesignTimeHtmlProvider.GetDesignTimeHtml () {
  return "Florida, United States";
}
```

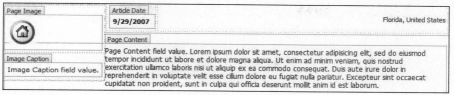

Figure 10-6

Notice how the text "Florida, United States" seems to be just floating on the page? It looks out of place compared to the other field controls. The design-time experience for these controls contains a significant amount of additional HTML that creates the tabbed interface with a border surrounding it. How does Microsoft do it with the OOTB field controls? Unfortunately, it is not possible to determine exactly how this is done because the methods that generate this interface are obfuscated and thus not available.

> *See for yourself how this is hidden. The method that implements this tab-like interface is* `Render()`. *Use the popular and free tool Reflector by Lutz Roeder (*www.andrewconnell.com/go/237*) to disassemble the* `Microsoft.SharePoint.WebControls.BaseFieldControl.Render()` *method in the* `Microsoft.SharePoint.dll` *assembly found in the* `[..]\12\ISAPI` *folder.*

However, with a bit of reverse engineering, by looking at the source of the rendered pages it is possible to simulate the same experience in custom field controls. By wrapping the preview HTML up in a few `<DIV>` tags and leveraging a few of the Microsoft- provided CSS classes, the `CountryRegionControl`'s design-time experience can look just like any other control. The code in Listing 10-14 will create the design-time experience in SPD shown in Figure 10-7. Note in particular that the interface name has been added to the class declaration.

Listing 10-14: Adding a design-time experience to the CountryRegionControl field control

```
public class CountryRegionControl : BaseFieldControl, IDesignTimeHtmlProvider {
   // omitted for brevity

string IDesignTimeHtmlProvider.GetDesignTimeHtml () {
StringBuilder designTimePreview = new StringBuilder();
   designTimePreview.Append("<div align=\"left\" class=\"ms-formfieldcontainer\">");

   designTimePreview.Append("<div class=\"ms-formfieldlabelcontainer\"
nowrap=\"nowrap\">");
   designTimePreview.Append("<span class=\"ms-formfieldlabel\"
nowrap=\"nowrap\">{0}</span>");
   designTimePreview.Append("</div>");

   designTimePreview.Append("<div class=\"ms-formfieldvaluecontainer\">");
   designTimePreview.Append("{1}");
   designTimePreview.Append("</div>");

   designTimePreview.Append("</div>");

   return string.Format(designTimePreview.ToString(),
                   this.Field.Title,
                   "Florida, " + UNITED_STATES);
   }
}
```

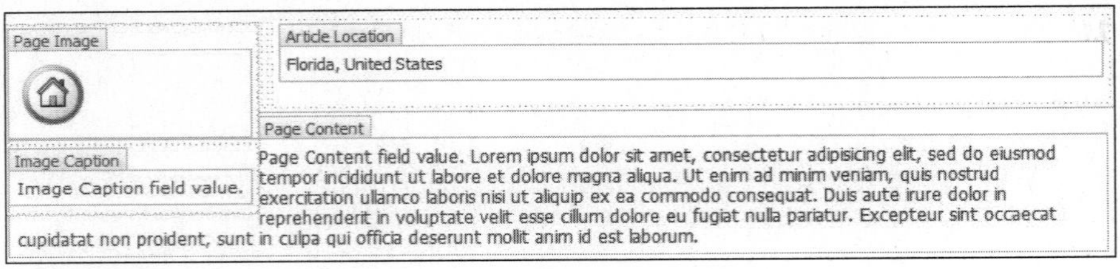

Figure 10-7

Now the `CountryRegionControl` looks just like any other field control provided OOTB. This completes the field control part of the custom field type. The `CountryRegionField` is almost finished. The last thing that is needed is some custom validation.

Adding Custom Data Validation

The requirements for the `CountryRegionField` dictate that content owners should not be permitted to select a country or region without selecting the other value. Fields marked as required that use the `CountryRegionField` must take into account what "required" actually means within the context of the field. In addition, whatever minimum information must be provided on nonrequired fields must still be entered. For instance, if the field is required, then both country and state/region must be submitted. However, if the field is not required, then the content owner can either leave both country and state/region unspecified or enter both values. This is because simply entering the country is not enough — even on optional fields, it is all or nothing.

Developers have two options in implementing validation of the data specified in the custom field type. The first option is to use ASP.NET 2.0 validation controls, either client-side or server-side, in the rendering template to validate the information provided. While this option would work, it leaves open a huge hole. What happens when a developer writes custom code that interacts with a field using the type `CountryRegionField`? The validation in the field control is not even taken into account because this approach of accessing the field through the API completely bypasses the field control that is only shown in the browser experience.

The other option is to implement purely server-side validation within the field type itself. This validation will be executed both when the field is accessed directly through the API and when content owners interact with the field using the Web-based authoring experience. It is recommended, at a minimum, to implement the second option in terms of validation on custom field types. The first approach, using ASP. NET 2.0 validation controls in the rendering template, is optional and can simply provide a better experience for content authors, as it can potentially eliminate the postback necessary to run the provided data through the validation controls if they are implemented as client-side validation.

To implement the recommended option, another method on the `CountryRegionField` custom field type class must be overridden. The `Microsoft.SharePoint.SPField.GetValidatedString()` method takes a single parameter of type `object`, which is the field value in the field type, and returns a string. It is the responsibility of this method to do all the validation checking; and if there is a problem with the data, it should throw the exception `Microsoft.SharePoint.SPFieldValidationException`. When SharePoint receives this exception it displays a user-friendly exception notice containing the message provided as a parameter when the exception is called. The code in Listing 10-15 contains the logic for the `CountryRegionField` field type data validation.

Listing 10-15: CountryRegionField.GetValidatedString()

```
public override string GetValidatedString (object value) {
  if (value == null) {
    if (this.Required) throw new SPFieldValidationException("Invalid value for
required field.");
    return string.Empty;
  } else {
    CountryRegionValue field = value as CountryRegionValue;
    // if no value obtained, error in the field
    if (field == null) throw new ArgumentException("Invalid value.");
    // if it is required...
    if (this.Required) {
      // make sure that both COUNTRY & REGION are selected
      if (field.Country != string.Empty && field.Region != string.Empty)
        throw new SPFieldValidationException("Both Country and Region/State are
required.");
    } else {
      // else, even if not required, if one field is filled in, the other must be
as well
      if (!string.IsNullOrEmpty(field.Country) !=
!string.IsNullOrEmpty(field.Region))
        throw new SPFieldValidationException("Both Country and Region/State are
required if one value is entered.");
    }
    return value.ToString();
  }
}
```

Notice that the code in the GetValidatedString() method takes into account whether the field is required or not using the SPField.Required property. Developers that elect to implement custom validation for the custom field type must take into account whether the field is required. If the value passes all validation checks, then it is passed back to the caller: SharePoint.

Creating Custom Field Controls without Custom Field Types

What happens when you need to simply provide a custom editing experience rather than a unique storage mechanism? While this chapter has focused on creating a custom field control that is paired with a custom field type, another option is to simply create a control that utilizes an existing field type. A possible use of this is when one of the existing field types works just fine for storing the data, such as a simple text field, but users want to modify the editing experience.

A classic example of this is the Telerik RadEditor Lite MOSS Editor control. This control is a feature equivalent control to the RichEditField control included OOTB in MOSS 2007. The primary difference between the two is that the RadEditor control supports multiple browsers, whereas the RichEditField only supports Microsoft Internet Explorer. The RadEditor control, a custom field control, utilizes the same Publishing HTML field type that the RichEditField does — the only difference is in the editing experience.

The Telerik RadEditor Lite MOSS Editor control is covered in more detail in Chapter 14, "Authoring Experience Extensibility."

Creating a custom control that leverages an existing field type is much simpler than linking one with a custom field type. Essentially, the only parts to build are the class that inherits from `BaseFieldControl` and the rendering template. Once the field control is built and deployed, a developer or designer can then manually add a `<% @Register %>` tag to a page layout and replace an existing field control with the custom field control's server tag.

For example, consider a project requirement to provide an editing experience that offers input fields for a content owner to enter a URL and title for a book on WROX's Web site. If the title and URL are entered, the display rendering should display the WROX logo followed by the book's title hyperlinked to the book's page on WROX's site. Otherwise, nothing would be rendered. The OOTB field type to be used would be the Hyperlink or Picture field type, as the only things that need to be stored are the book title and URL.

The first step is to create the rendering template, `WroxTemplates.ascx`, a simple table consisting of two textboxes, as shown in Listing 10-16.

Listing 10-16: WroxTemplates.ascx

```
<%@ Control Language="C#" %>
<%@ Assembly Name="Microsoft.SharePoint, Version=12.0.0.0, Culture=neutral,
PublicKeyToken=71e9bce111e9429c" %>
<%@ Register Assembly="Microsoft.SharePoint, Version=12.0.0.0, Culture=neutral,
PublicKeyToken=71e9bce111e9429c" Namespace="Microsoft.SharePoint.WebControls"
TagPrefix="SharePoint" %>

<SharePoint:RenderingTemplate id="WroxBookControl" runat="server">
  <Template>
    <table class="ms-form">
      <tr>
        <td align="right">Book Title:</td>
        <td><asp:textbox id="WroxBookTitle" runat="server" cssclass="ms-long" /></td>
      </tr>
      <tr>
        <td align="right">Book URL:</td>
        <td><asp:textbox id="WroxBookUrl" runat="server" cssclass="ms-long" /></td>
      </tr>
    </table>
  </Template>
</SharePoint:RenderingTemplate>
```

Next, add the WROX logo to the root of a C# project and set the build action to Embedded Resource. This will compile the image into the assembly. In order to retrieve the image out of the class library, it must be registered using an assembly attribute within the `AssemblyInfo.cs` file by adding the following code:

```
[assembly: System.Web.UI.WebResource("WROX.ProMossWcm.Chapter10.WROX.gif",
"image/jpg")]
```

With the rendering template and image addressed, the next thing to do is build the custom field control. Similar to the field control built previously in this chapter, this field control will have the standard protected fields used to reference the Web controls within the rendering template, the `DefaultRenderingTemplate` and `Value` properties, as well as the `CreateChildControls()` and `GetDesignTimeHTML()` methods, as shown in Listing 10-17. (Some code is omitted here for readability, but the full source can be found in the downloadable code for the book.)

Listing 10-17: WroxBookControl.cs

```
using System;
using System.Text;
using System.Web.UI.WebControls;
using Microsoft.SharePoint;
using Microsoft.SharePoint.WebControls;

namespace WROX.ProMossWcm.Chapter10 {
  public class WroxBookControl : BaseFieldControl, IDesignTimeHtmlProvider {
    private const string RENDERING_TEMPLATE = "WroxBookControl";
    private const string WROX_IMAGE_PATH = "WROX.ProMossWcm.Chapter10.WROX.gif";

    protected TextBox _wroxBookTitle;
    protected TextBox _wroxBookUrl;

    protected override string DefaultTemplateName {
      // omitted from book for readability
    }

    protected override void CreateChildControls () {
      // omitted from book for readability
    }
    public override object Value {
      get {
        EnsureChildControls();
        SPFieldUrlValue field = new SPFieldUrlValue();

        if (_wroxBookTitle == null || _wroxBookUrl == null) {
          field.Description = String.Empty;
          field.Url = String.Empty;
        } else {
          field.Description = _wroxBookTitle.Text.Trim();
          field.Url = _wroxBookUrl.Text.Trim();
        }
        return field;
      }
      set {
        EnsureChildControls();

        if (value != null && !string.IsNullOrEmpty(value.ToString())) {
          SPFieldUrlValue field = new SPFieldUrlValue(value.ToString());

          _wroxBookTitle.Text = field.Description;
```

(continued)

Listing 10-17 *(continued)*

```
            _wroxBookUrl.Text = field.Url;
        }
      }
    }

    string IDesignTimeHtmlProvider.GetDesignTimeHtml () {
      // omitted from book for readability
    }
  }
}
```

Finally, the last step is to implement the special rendering for the value in the control when the control is in Display mode, as shown in Listing 10-18.

Listing 10-18: Implementing custom display mode rendering

```
protected override void RenderFieldForDisplay (System.Web.UI.HtmlTextWriter output)
{
  // if nothing specified
  if (this.ItemFieldValue == null ||
string.IsNullOrEmpty(this.ItemFieldValue.ToString()))
    return;

  // get data from SharePoint
  SPFieldUrlValue field = new SPFieldUrlValue(ItemFieldValue.ToString());

  // create image control
  Image wroxImage = new Image();
  wroxImage.ImageUrl = Page.ClientScript.GetWebResourceUrl(this.GetType(),
WROX_IMAGE_PATH);
  wroxImage.AlternateText = "WROX logo";
  wroxImage.RenderControl(output);

  output.Write(" ");

  // create link to book
  HyperLink bookLink = new HyperLink();
  bookLink.Text = field.Description;
  bookLink.NavigateUrl = field.Url;
  bookLink.ToolTip = "WROX Book: " + field.Description;
  bookLink.RenderControl(output);
}
```

The implementation of the custom field control, covered in the next section, should result in an editing and display experience that look like Figures 10-8 and 10-9, respectively.

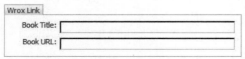

Figure 10-8

Figure 10-9

Implementing Custom Field Controls in Page Layouts

With a custom field type and/or field control created, now everything needs to be deployed into the proper locations before it can be used within content types and page layouts:

1. Deploy the assembly containing the field type, value, and control to the GAC.

2. Place the rendering template (`CountryRegionControl.ascx`) in the `[..]\12\TEMPLATE\CONTROLTEMPLATES` folder.

3. Copy the field type definition (`fldtypes_wrox.xml`) in the `[..]\12\TEMPLATE\XML` folder.

4. Add a safe control entry into the `web.config` file of the Web application of the site that will use the field type to indicate to SharePoint that the objects in the deployed assembly are safe.

> *Another option is to deploy the field type and all associated files using WSS solution packages. The downloadable code for the book demonstrates this approach.*

After deploying all the necessary files related to the field type and/or control to the appropriate locations, recycle the Web services on the server by typing the following at a command prompt: **iisreset exe**.

Recycling the Web server rather than the application pool is necessary because SharePoint loads field controls only when all the services start up. Once the Web services start, a developer can then designate a new field as a site column and add it to a content type. The custom field type will appear in the radio button list of field types when creating a new site column, as shown in Figure 10-10.

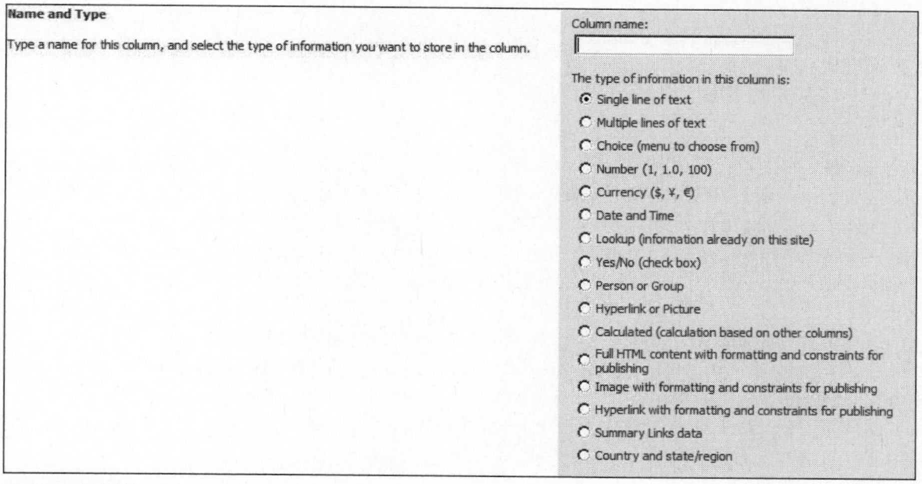

Name and Type	Column name:
Type a name for this column, and select the type of information you want to store in the column.	[ ]
	The type of information in this column is:
	⦿ Single line of text
	○ Multiple lines of text
	○ Choice (menu to choose from)
	○ Number (1, 1.0, 100)
	○ Currency ($, ¥, €)
	○ Date and Time
	○ Lookup (information already on this site)
	○ Yes/No (check box)
	○ Person or Group
	○ Hyperlink or Picture
	○ Calculated (calculation based on other columns)
	○ Full HTML content with formatting and constraints for publishing
	○ Image with formatting and constraints for publishing
	○ Hyperlink with formatting and constraints for publishing
	○ Summary Links data
	○ Country and state/region

Figure 10-10

With the content type updated with the new site column using the field type `CountryRegionField`, the last step is to add the column to a page layout. Open the page layout that uses the updated content type in SPD. Drag the new site column onto a page layout in Design mode. The first time it is pulled in, the control may render with the gray error box. If so, then save and close the page layout and reopen it. The field type's design-time rendering will now be shown when SPD is in Design mode, as previously shown in Figure 10-7.

When a site column is dropped on the page layout, SPD does two things:

❑ It adds a `<% @Register %>` directive to the top of the page layout for the new server control (field control).

❑ It adds a server control tag for the field control and sets the `FieldName` attribute to the internal name of the field.

The drag-and-drop approach does not work if a custom field control was created that leverages an existing field type. Therefore, developers must perform these two steps manually. Add a `<% @Register %>` directive to the top of the page layout and replace the existing field [server] control tag in the page layout to point to the custom field control. Listing 10-19 demonstrates the code that would be added for the `WroxBookControl` field control previously created in this chapter.

Listing 10-19: WroxBookControl added to a page layout

```
<%@ Page language="C#" Inherits="..."
        meta:progid="SharePoint.WebPartPage.Document" %>
<!-- omitted from book for readability -->
<%@ Register tagprefix="WROX"
            namespace="WROX.ProMossWcm.Chapter10"
assembly="Chapter10WroxBookControl, Version=1.0.0.0, Culture=neutral,
PublicKeyToken=c591e70cfdf9ce4f" %>

<!-- omitted from book for readability -->
<WROX:WroxBookControl FieldName="WroxLink"
                    runat="server" id="UrlField1"></WROX:WroxBookControl>
```

Summary

Creating a custom field type, field value, and field control is one of the more complicated and complex SharePoint subjects. SharePoint ships with many OOTB field types, otherwise known as *field controls.* Each has its own editing experience. While these field types provide solutions for many data storage needs in SharePoint projects and applications, sometimes they don't meet a project's requirements. In these cases, creating custom field types and controls makes the most sense.

This chapter explained how to create a custom field type that stores a complex data type. The two values are country and state/region (depending on the country selected). The field type contains special validation to ensure that the minimal and/or required fields are entered when editing a field that utilizes the type. The complex field value is represented in a custom class that other developers can utilize when interfacing with fields that use the custom field type.

To provide a custom editing experience, this chapter demonstrated how to create a custom field control. Not only does the control include the capability to provide a unique editing experience for content owners, it also includes a special rendering when the control is viewed in a design-time experience in a tool such as SPD. In addition, this chapter demonstrated how to create a custom field control utilizing an existing field type. After creating the custom field control, with either a custom or out-of-the-box field type, the chapter demonstrated how to utilize the control within a page layout.

11

Web Parts

Microsoft first introduced Web Parts in Windows SharePoint Services (WSS) 2.0. Information workers and developers quickly adopted Web Parts because they enable end users to modify the content, appearance, and behavior of pages through a browser. Not only could users easily modify the content and experience with the browser, but they could also modify pages for just their own experience, rather everyone's shared experience. In addition, developers could create two Web Parts that could be connected and pass data back and forth. A common use of Web Part connections is the Microsoft SQL Server Reporting Services Web Parts. One Web Part displayed a list of the available reports while the other took the selected report from the first Web Part and displayed the rendered report.

Web Parts became so popular that the ASP.NET team decided to add a Web Part Framework to ASP.NET 2.0. The ASP.NET 2.0 implementation is different from the WSS 2.0 implementation in that ASP.NET 2.0 adds a new component to the page: the `WebPartManager`. The `WebPartManager` control is responsible for managing all aspects of Web Parts on the page. It knows what Web Parts are allowed on the page, what Web Parts are already on the page and which Web Part zones they are in, any connections that have been established between two Web Parts, as well as the personalization data for each Web Part. Personalization data contains all the settings, or values, set on the public properties, for a Web Part. This is very different from the WSS 2.0 Web Part Framework in that each Web Part maintained its own connection and personalization information and Web Part zones managed which Web Parts were in each zone.

With ASP.NET 2.0 adding a Web Part Framework, the SharePoint team had yet another reason why they could change SharePoint's architecture (specifically, WSS 3.0) to be built on top of ASP.NET, rather than in a side-by-side model that was glued together using an ISAPI filter, as covered in Chapter 2. However, Microsoft could not turn its back on all the Web Parts developed for WSS 2.0, so it modified the existing `WebPart` and associated classes in the `Microsoft.SharePoint` namespace to serve as a backwardly compatibility wrapper to the new ASP.NET 2.0 Web Part model. In fact, the `Microsoft.SharePoint.WebPartPages.WebPart` class' inheritance hierarchy has completely changed to inherit directly from the ASP.NET 2.0 `WebPart` class, `System.Web.UI.WebControls.WebParts.WebPart`.

Microsoft Office SharePoint Server (MOSS) 2007 includes three special Web Parts that are available exclusively to Publishing sites. These three Web Parts are covered in the section "MOSS 2007 Publishing Web Parts" later in the chapter.

Adding Web Parts to Web Part Zones

What happens when a Web Part is dropped into a Web Part zone on a page within a SharePoint site? SharePoint adds some XML to the Web Part zone that contains information about the assembly containing the Web Part and the Web Part class itself. This XML also contains the values of the public properties on the Web Part class. This XML, shown in Listing 11-1, is then stored as personalization information for a specific user (if the personalization scope is set to User) or for all users who access the page (if the personalization scope is set to Shared) depending on the mode of the page. The next time a page is requested, SharePoint loads the personalization information for the Web Part, which tells it which class to load from which assembly and the values of the public properties to set on that class. The Web Part is then loaded within the ASP.NET 2.0 page life cycle, which generates the rendered HTML output. Figure 11-1 demonstrates what the XML in Listing 11-1 would produce. Knowing how this process works can prove to be a powerful tool for developers, as demonstrated later in this chapter.

Listing 11-1: XML in a Web Part zone for the WSS 3.0 Image Web Part

```
<WebPart xmlns="http://schemas.microsoft.com/WebPart/v2"
         xmlns:iwp="http://schemas.microsoft.com/WebPart/v2/Image">
  <Assembly>Microsoft.SharePoint, Version=12.0.0.0, Culture=neutral,
PublicKeyToken=71e9bce111e9429c</Assembly>
  <TypeName>Microsoft.SharePoint.WebPartPages.ImageWebPart</TypeName>
  <FrameType>None</FrameType>
  <Title>Watch My Gears Run</Title>
  <iwp:ImageLink>/_layouts/images/GEARS_AN.GIF</iwp:ImageLink>
</WebPart>
```

Figure 11-1

Using Web Parts in Publishing Sites

Web Parts are not only available within ASP.NET 2.0 and WSS 3.0 sites, but within MOSS 2007 sites as well, including Publishing sites! Although Web Parts are available within Publishing sites, developers and site owners should carefully evaluate whether it makes sense (i.e., meets the business requirements) to leverage them because Publishing site developers have another way to add content to pages that non-Publishing sites do not have: field controls. Chapter 7, "Master Pages and Page Layouts," covered the main differences between field controls and Web Parts, such as storage and the retention of content in previous versions.

When should Web Parts be used in a Publishing site? There is no correct or incorrect answer to this question, but consider the following as prescriptive guidance based on real-world implementations and deployments of Publishing sites by the authors of this book.

Most content-centric sites — specifically, MOSS 2007 Publishing sites — demand some level of versioning or maintaining historical content. At times, project requirements dictate retaining a certain number of versions or content over a period of time. For projects that require the retention of old, now unpublished, content, best practice suggests using field controls for content and Web Parts for functionality.

What does "functionality" mean? Because the data within Web Parts is not versioned, but just associated with the page separately from the page itself, Web Parts should not be used to store data when the history of a page is important within the scope of a project. Web Parts should instead be used to provide some sort of functionality. Examples of this include content rollup Web Parts (the section "MOSS 2007 Publishing Web Parts" covers this in more depth later in this chapter), pulling live content from an outside source such as a news RSS feed, or providing some sort of functionality to the consumer, such as signing up for e-mail notifications when the page is updated. Another use for Web Parts in a Publishing site is to target content to a specific audience, a capability of MOSS 2007. As covered in Chapter 7, Web Parts support personalization of content, whereas field controls do not.

The only data stored in the Web Part should be settings or configuration information that the Web Part uses to collect or display data, not actual content. Of course, developers are free to use Web Parts however they choose within a Publishing site. Page layouts will often contain a mixture of field controls and Web Parts, but typically field controls dominate the page to enforce and control branding by developers and designers.

Creating Custom Web Parts

Like the previous version of SharePoint and ASP.NET 2.0, developers are not limited to the Web Parts provided "out of the box" (OOTB). Developers are free to create custom Web Parts — for use within Publishing sites or any SharePoint site, for that matter.

Web Parts are ASP.NET 2.0 server controls, so creating Web Parts involves working in a pure code model, rather than defining the presentation experience declaratively as is done with markup in *.ASPX and *.ASCX files. This is often frustrating to ASP.NET 2.0 developers who are used to working with markup or a design surface within Visual Studio. Even though Web Parts are server controls, developers are not excluded from building Web Parts as ASP.NET 2.0 user controls (*.ASCX). One option is to use the *SmartPart*, an open-source project hosted at www.andrewconnell.com/go/238. The SmartPart is a Web Part that acts as a wrapper for user controls. This project effectively lowers the bar of Web Part development, enabling developers to work with visual designers creating user controls instead of adding all rendering logic in a server control.

Jan Tielens, the developer behind the SmartPart, has written a fantastic chapter on the subject of ASP.NET 2.0 user controls for use within Web Parts. See Chapter 7 of Real World SharePoint 2007: Indispensable Experiences from 16 MOSS and WSS MVPs *(Wrox, 2007).*

The other option is to create a custom Web Part wrapper for a specific user control. The custom Weather News Web Part created in this chapter is built using the pure server control approach, rather than the ASP.NET 2.0 user control approach.

Creating ASP.NET Web Parts, Not SharePoint Web Parts

The previous sections outlined the history of Web Parts as they were first introduced in WSS 2.0 and ultimately moved to the ASP.NET 2.0 Framework. Thanks to backward compatibility, developers can choose between two classes to inherit from when creating custom Web Parts:

❑ **ASP.NET 2.0** — `System.Web.UI.WebControls.WebParts.WebPart`

❑ **WSS / SharePoint 3.0** — `Microsoft.SharePoint.WebPartPages.WebPart`

Which one should developers inherit from? When creating a new Web Part, Microsoft's recommendation is to always create ASP.NET 2.0 Web Parts instead of SharePoint-specific Web Parts. Remember that the SharePoint Web Part class exists primarily for backward compatibility, so Web Parts developed for WSS 2.0 or SharePoint Portal Server (SPS) 2003 will still work in WSS 3.0 or MOSS 2007. The SharePoint Web Part class does contain some additional functionality that the ASP.NET 2.0 Web Part class doesn't, but Microsoft's advice is to not leverage those capabilities, such as connecting two Web Parts on different pages or creating client-side connections.

Advanced Web Part Techniques

When creating custom Web Parts within a SharePoint site developers are often tasked with solving some complex scenarios. In the case of Publishing sites, developers need to consider who will be responsible for placing and configuring Web Parts on the page. Many traditional SharePoint sites, such as pure collaboration team sites, assign to more sophisticated users the responsibility of managing the Web Parts on the page. Publishing sites are a little different because the users who will be placing Web Parts on the pages are the content owners. These content owners are frequently not as technically savvy as the developers who wrote the Web Parts, so extra care must be exercised regarding design, creation, and configuration management.

This section briefly discusses two techniques and how they relate to Publishing sites. Both techniques are utilized in the custom Weather News Web Part created in this chapter.

Creating Custom Edit Mode Panels

All Web Parts accept some minimal parameters that are exposed as public properties on the `System.Web.UI.WebControls.WebParts.WebPart` class. The default properties include things such as appearance settings — e.g., whether the Web Part rendering should include a border, whether the Web Part should be displayed minimized (only the header showing) or not, and so on. Developers can specify additional public properties on the Web Part that are used within the custom code. An example of this is the WSS 3.0 Image Web Part previously shown in Figure 11-1. The `ImageLink` property enables users to specify the image that the Image Web Part will display.

Public properties on a Web Part are exposed by SharePoint in the task page as long as they are decorated with the attribute `System.Web.UI.WebControls.WebParts.WebBrowsableAttribute`. This attribute tells SharePoint to include the property in the generic Editor Part, a control used in the task pane to edit Web Part properties. By default, all properties shown in the generic Editor Part are rendered as a standard input box unless the property is of type enum, in which case a selector is rendered. While this may be acceptable for many Web Parts, Publishing site developers will likely want to present a more robust and customized Web Part editing experience for end users, to minimize, if not eliminate, data entry error and server-side validation.

Creating custom Editor Parts is very much like creating custom Web Parts in that they are also ASP.NET 2.0 server controls. The primary difference is a little extra work required to associate the Editor Part with a Web Part. This is done by first overriding the `WebPart.CreateEditorParts()` method in the Web Part, which will add the custom Editor Part to the collection of Editor Parts for the Web Part. Then, within the Editor Part, two methods need to be overridden that will set/retrieve values to/from the Web Part: `EditorPart.ApplyChanges()` and `EditorPart.SyncChanges()`. The creation of a custom Editor Part is demonstrated in the Weather News Web Part created in this chapter.

Leveraging Asynchronous Programming Techniques

Web Part development, like all ASP.NET 2.0 server control development, introduces some additional challenges that typical ASP.NET 2.0 page developers do not need to be as concerned about. For example, when developing a Web Part, the developer has no true way of knowing exactly where this Web Part could be used. While it is true that a project plan may dictate that the Web Part will reside on a specific page, the whole point of Web Parts is to provide modular functionality that end users can implement. Furthermore, the developer may or may not be aware of the fact that the Web Part may exist on a page with many other Web Parts — even multiple instances of the same Web Part.

What happens if the custom Web Part contains a long-running process such as a complex calculation, retrieving data from a Web service or issuing a complex query against a database? That one Web Part will hold up the processing of the entire page. If there are multiple instances of that Web Part on the same page, a simple two-second task could now take up to eight or ten seconds just to run the long-running task! This obviously presents a challenge for developers, as one Web Part can bring an entire page to a crawl.

Developers need to create Web Parts with the mindset that they have no idea what else is going to be on the page or how many instances of the Web Part will be on the page. Long-running operations should be optimized to minimize their impact on the rest of the page. One approach to performing long-running operations is to leverage asynchronous programming techniques. Asynchronous programming involves firing off a long-running operation in parallel to existing processing. For instance, a query that takes five seconds to execute can be issued asynchronously, which would enable ASP.NET 2.0 to continue processing the rest of the page, including other Web Parts. When the long-running operation completes, ASP.NET 2.0 calls a method, a *callback method,* that picks up where it left off. When ASP.NET 2.0 reaches the `OnPreRender()` method in the ASP.NET 2.0 page life cycle, it waits for all pending asynchronous operations to either complete or timeout.

If a custom Web Part contains any complex calculations, database queries, Web service requests, or anything else that takes a considerable amount of time to process, then it is a good practice for developers to utilize asynchronous programming techniques to ensure that their Web Part is not the reason a page takes too long to load. Asynchronous programming is demonstrated in the Weather News Web Part created in the next section.

Creating a Weather News Web Part

This section demonstrates how to create a custom Web Part. The Web Part will be a 100% true ASP.NET 2.0 Web Part that works in an ASP.NET 2.0 Web site, but it will be deployed and tested within a SharePoint site. After creating an ASP.NET 2.0 Web Part, developers need to do a few extra things to make it function within a SharePoint site, as well as address deployment.

A common need people have for content sites is a weather Web Part. SharePoint used to include news, weather, and stock ticker Web Parts in SPS 2003 but they were dropped in the latest release of SharePoint. The Weather News Web Part, shown in Figure 11-2, will have a special capability to show a list of the last five weather reports in a Really Simple Syndication (RSS) feed, and when a user places the mouse over one of the reports, the contents of the report are shown below the reports.

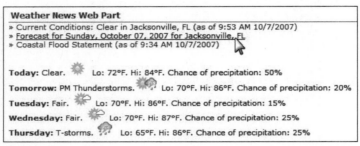

Figure 11-2

Users that add the Web Part to the page will be permitted to specify the URL of the RSS feed used to retrieve the weather reports and the degree of measurement: Fahrenheit or Celsius. This Web Part needs to take into account that the weather RSS feed may be not be returned in a timely manner; and if that is the case, the Web Part should not be responsible for holding up the processing of the entire page.

The first step is to create a new C# Class Library project in Visual Studio, add a reference to the `System.Web` assembly, and sign the project to create an assembly with a strong name. Next, create the Web Part by creating a new class named `WeatherWebPart` that inherits directly from the ASP.NET 2.0 `System.Web.UI.WebControls.WebParts.WebPart` class, as shown in Listing 11-2.

Listing 11-2: WeatherWebPart.cs file containing the WeatherWebPart class

```csharp
using System;
using System.Collections.Generic;
using System.Web.UI;
using System.Web.UI.WebControls;
using System.Web.UI.WebControls.WebParts;
using System.Xml;

namespace WROX.ProMossWcm.Chapter11 {
  public class WeatherWebPart : WebPart {
  }
}
```

Because the requirements of the Weather News Web Part dictate that it not hold up page processing while it retrieves the specified RSS feed, the Web Part will leverage asynchronous programming techniques. Although ASP.NET 2.0 pages have an `Async` attribute on the `Page` directive that developers can use to set the page to act as an asynchronous handler, it is not available within SharePoint sites when building Web Parts. The `Async` attribute defaults to `false`, and Web Part developers cannot tell users who add the Web Part to SharePoint sites to ensure that every page has this attribute set. Therefore, developers need to come up with another approach.

One solution is to use the `PageAsyncTask` class. This class enables developers to register tasks with the page to be processed asynchronously. The `PageAsyncTask` constructor requires a few parameters. These parameters include three callback methods, an object that represents the state of the task, and a Boolean value specifying whether the task should be processed in parallel with other tasks. When using the `PageAsyncTask` class, it is recommended that you create a worker class that contains the callback methods and provides an easy way to retrieve the results of the task. Putting this code in a separate class facilitates maintenance and readability.

Create a new class named `WorkerTask` in the project and create three callback methods, as shown in Listing 11-3.

Listing 11-3: WorkerTask.cs file containing the WorkerTask class

```csharp
using System;
using System.Xml;

namespace WROX.ProMossWcm.Chapter11 {
  internal class WorkerTask {
    private XmlNodeList _taskResults;
    delegate void WorkerTaskDelegate ();
    private WorkerTaskDelegate _task;

    private void ExecuteTask () {
    }

    internal IAsyncResult OnBegin (object sender, EventArgs e, AsyncCallback cb,
object data) {
      _task = new WorkerTaskDelegate(ExecuteTask);
      return _task.BeginInvoke(cb, data);
    }

    internal void OnEnd (IAsyncResult result) {
      _task.EndInvoke(result);
    }

    internal void OnTimeout (IAsyncResult result) {
      _taskResults = null;
    }
  }
}
```

The `WorkerTask` class is responsible for fetching the provided Weather RSS feed and returning the items within the feed. The three callback methods in the class are called under specific conditions:

☐ `OnBegin()` — This method is called when the asynchronous task is executed.

☐ `OnEnd()` — This method is called when the task completes.

☐ `OnTimeout()` — This method is called when the task does not complete in a timely manner.

The method `ExecuteTask()` is called via a delegate from within the `onbegin()` callback method. In addition, this class also needs to provide a way for the caller to specify the URL of the weather RSS feed. This is done using an internal field and forcing the caller to provide the URL when creating the object. The `WorkerTask` class needs to have a way to return the contents of the RSS feed. This is done using a public read-only property as shown in Listing 11-4.

Listing 11-4: Setting and retrieving values in the WorkerTask class

```
internal class WorkerTask {
    private string _rssFeedUrl = string.Empty;

    private XmlNodeList _taskResults;
    delegate void WorkerTaskDelegate ();
    private WorkerTaskDelegate _task;

    public WorkerTask (string rssFeedUrl) {
        if (string.IsNullOrEmpty(rssFeedUrl))
            throw new ArgumentException("The RSS feed URL must not be empty");
        _rssFeedUrl = rssFeedUrl;
    }

    public XmlNodeList TaskResults {
        get { return _taskResults; }
    }

    private void ExecuteTask () {
    }

    // omitted from book for readability
}
```

Finally, the `WorkerTask` needs to actually do some work when it is kicked off asynchronously. The `ExecuteTask()` method previously created is called when the task is started. This is where the real work happens, as shown in Listing 11-5.

Listing 11-5: WorkerTask.ExecuteTask()

```
private void ExecuteTask () {
    // fetch RSS feed
    XmlDocument rssFeed = new XmlDocument();
    rssFeed.Load(_rssFeedUrl);

    // get all items from the feed
    _taskResults = rssFeed.DocumentElement.SelectNodes("channel/item");
}
```

With the worker class complete, it can now be used within the Web Part. All the work of the WeatherWebPart class happens in the CreateChildControls() method. This method creates the asynchronous task, registers and fires it off, retrieves the results, and then creates the rendering experience based on the values returned. The requirements specified that the user of the Web Part needs to be able to specify the URL of the RSS feed as well as the degree measurement. These two values are stored in local fields (ignore the public properties that will expose these fields to the end users for now). The code in Listing 11-6 demonstrates creating a new instance of the worker class and using it to create an asynchronous task that is immediately executed.

Listing 11-6: Creating and executing asynchronous tasks in WeatherWebPart

```
public class WeatherWebPart : WebPart {
  private string _rssFeed = String.Empty;
  private bool _metricMeasurement = false;

  private string GetRssFeedUrl () {
    string result;

    if (_metricMeasurement) {
      result = _rssFeed + "&weadegreetype=C";
    } else
      result = _rssFeed + "&weadegreetype=F";

    return result;
  }

  protected override void CreateChildControls () {
    // if no RSS feed specified, do nothing
    if (String.IsNullOrEmpty(_rssFeed)) return;

    base.CreateChildControls();

    // create async task to go get RSS feed
    WorkerTask task = new WorkerTask(GetRssFeedUrl());
    PageAsyncTask asyncTask = new PageAsyncTask(task.OnBegin,
                                                task.OnEnd,
                                                task.OnTimeout,
                                                "RssFetcherTask",
                                                true);
    Page.RegisterAsyncTask(asyncTask);
    Page.ExecuteRegisteredAsyncTasks();
  }
}
```

The last step is to retrieve the results from the asynchronous task and render the HTML presentation. Each post in the Weather RSS feed is represented with a HyperLink control. As stated in the requirements, when the user hovers over a link, the contents of the post should be shown below the list of weather posts. Add the code in Listing 11-7 to the end of the CreateChildControls() method.

Listing 11-7: Rendering code in CreateChildControls()

```
protected override void CreateChildControls () {
  // omitted from book for readability

  Page.RegisterAsyncTask(asyncTask);
  Page.ExecuteRegisteredAsyncTasks();

  // loop through posts and display
  int postCounter = 0;
  HyperLink link;
  string displayID = "_WPQID_WeatherDisplay";
  if (task.TaskResults != null && task.TaskResults.Count > 0)
    foreach (XmlNode post in task.TaskResults) {
      postCounter++;

      // create new link
      link = new HyperLink();
      link.NavigateUrl = post.SelectSingleNode("link").InnerText;
      link.Text = post.SelectSingleNode("title").InnerText;

      // add rollover effects
      link.Attributes.Add("onMouseOver", "document.all." + displayID
          + ".innerHTML='" + post.SelectSingleNode("description").InnerText
          + "';");
      link.Attributes.Add("onMouseOut", "document.all." + displayID
          + ".innerHTML=';");

      Controls.Add(new LiteralControl("&raquo; "));
      Controls.Add(link);
      Controls.Add(new LiteralControl("<br />"));

      // only show last 5 posts in the feed
      if (postCounter >= 5) break;
    }

  // weather feed entry contents
  Controls.Add(new LiteralControl("<div id=\"" + displayID + "\"></div>"));
}
```

Note the generation of the <DIV> element's ID. The ID of an object on an HTML page must be unique in order to access it the way the rollover effects do using `document.all.[id]`. The code in Listing 11-7 uses the string `_WPQID_WeatherDisplay` as the unique identifier. The `_WPQID_` makes it unique, as SharePoint will replace that token at runtime with the Web Part's unique client-side ID. This token is one of a few tokens that can be used that are part of the Web Part Page Services Component (WPSC). The WPSC acts as a SharePoint-specific Document Object Model (DOM) on top of the existing HTML DOM.

For more information on SharePoint's Web Part Page Services Component, refer to the official documentation on MSDN (www.andrewconnell.com/go/239).

At this point the Web Part is now complete, but users of the Web Part need a way to manage the URL of the weather RSS feed, as well as specify the degree measurement. This is done by exposing the two local fields in the Web Part as public properties. If these properties were decorated with the `WebBrowsable` attribute, they would appear in the generic Editor Part in the task pane. Instead, these will not be decorated; they will be managed from a custom Editor Part. Therefore, create public properties that encapsulate the private fields, as shown in Listing 11-8.

Listing 11-8: Public accessors for Weather Web Part settings

```
public class WeatherWebPart : WebPart {
    private string _rssFeed = String.Empty;
    private bool _metricMeasurement = false;

    public string RssFeed {
        get { return _rssFeed; }
        set { _rssFeed = value; }
    }

    public bool MetricMeasurement {
        get { return _metricMeasurement; }
        set { _metricMeasurement = value; }
    }
}
```

In order to maintain complete control over how users will manage this data and to provide the most elegant experience, a custom Editor Part will be used for this task. As covered earlier in this chapter, Editor Parts are just ASP.NET 2.0 server controls. Thus, like other server controls, the rendering is defined within the `CreateChildControls()` method. Create a new class, `WeatherEditorPart`, that inherits from `System.Web.UI.WebControls.WebParts.EditorPart` and add a `CreateChildControls()` method that displays an input control for managing the RSS feed URL, and a selector for picking the degree measurement, as shown in Listing 11-9.

Listing 11-9: WeatherEditorPart.cs file containing the WeatherEditorPart class

```
using System;
using System.Web.UI;
using System.Web.UI.WebControls;
using System.Web.UI.WebControls.WebParts;

namespace WROX.ProMossWcm.Chapter11 {
    public class WeatherEditorPart : EditorPart {

        private DropDownList _degreeUnit;
        private TextBox _rssFeedInput;

        public WeatherEditorPart () {
            this.Title = "Weather Web Part Settings";
        }

        protected override void CreateChildControls () {
            base.CreateChildControls();

            // create textbox for RSS feed:
            Controls.Add(new LiteralControl("MSN Weather RSS Feed:<br />"));
            _rssFeedInput = new TextBox();
```

(continued)

Listing 11-9 *(continued)*

```
        _rssFeedInput.Width = new Unit("90%");
        Controls.Add(_rssFeedInput);

        Controls.Add(new LiteralControl("<br/><br/>"));

        // create degree measurement selector
        Controls.Add(new LiteralControl("Unit of measure to display:<br />"));
        _degreeUnit = new DropDownList();
        _degreeUnit.Items.Add(new ListItem("Fahrenheit", "F"));
        _degreeUnit.Items.Add(new ListItem("Celsius", "C"));
        Controls.Add(_degreeUnit);
    }


    }
}
```

With the core of the `WeatherEditorPart` created, it now needs a way to communicate back and forth with the `WeatherWebPart`. This is done via two methods:

❑ `SyncChanges()` — This is called when the Editor Part is first loaded into the task pane. Use this method to retrieve the values of the settings currently set on the Web Part.

❑ `ApplyChanges()` — This is called when either the OK button or the Apply button is clicked in the task pane, effectively setting the values on the Web Part.

In each of these methods it is important to first call `EnsureChildControls()` to verify that all controls in the Editor Part have been created before setting or reading their properties, as well as to get a reference to the Web Part the Editor Part is associated with, as shown in Listing 11-10.

Listing 11-10: Setting and retrieving settings from the Web Part within the Editor Part

```
public class WeatherEditorPart : EditorPart {
    // omitted from book for readability

    public override bool ApplyChanges () {
        EnsureChildControls();
        WeatherWebPart webPart = WebPartToEdit as WeatherWebPart;

        // get values from controls and set on Web Part
        webPart.RssFeed = _rssFeedInput.Text;
        webPart.MetricMeasurement = _degreeUnit.SelectedValue == "C" ? true : false;

        return true;
    }

    public override void SyncChanges () {
        EnsureChildControls();
        WeatherWebPart webPart = WebPartToEdit as WeatherWebPart;

        // set values within controls
        if (!string.IsNullOrEmpty(webPart.RssFeed))
```

```
        _rssFeedInput.Text = webPart.RssFeed;
        _degreeUnit.SelectedValue = webPart.MetricMeasurement ? "C" : "F";
    }
}
```

Last but not least, the Editor Part needs to be associated with the Web Part in some way because at present, the Web Part has no knowledge of the Editor Part. To do this, override the `CreateEditorParts()` method on the Web Part, as shown in Listing 11-11. The job of this method is to return a collection of Editor Parts back to the Web Part Framework. To get the new Editor Part added to the collection, create a new instance of the part and add it to the collection of existing Editor Parts.

Listing 11-11: Adding custom Editor Parts to Web Parts

```
public class WeatherWebPart : WebPart {
  // omitted from book for readability

  public override EditorPartCollection CreateEditorParts () {
    List<EditorPart> parts = new List<EditorPart>(1);

    EditorPart part = new WeatherEditorPart();
    part.ID = this.ID + "_EditorPart";
    parts.Add(part);

    return new EditorPartCollection(base.CreateEditorParts(), parts);
  }
}
```

That's it! The custom Weather News Web Part and associated Editor Part are now complete. At this point the Web Part and Editor Part can be used within an ASP.NET 2.0 Web site.

Making ASP.NET Web Parts Work in SharePoint Sites

As previously stated, it is recommended that you build ASP.NET 2.0 Web Parts when building Web Parts for SharePoint sites. These Web Parts will run within SharePoint without a problem — well, except for one small issue: SharePoint typically runs in a lower level of trust than ASP.NET 2.0 Web sites do. This lower level of trust is managed using code access security (CAS).

For more information on CAS, refer to Chapter 2, "Windows SharePoint Services 3.0 Development Primer."

The .NET Framework does not allow an assembly that is not fully trusted to call another assembly that is not fully trusted. This is the case with custom Web Parts — they are not fully trusted and thus cannot be called. To get around this issue, Microsoft provides an assembly attribute that developers can add to their projects to tell the .NET Framework that it is OK for assemblies that are not fully trusted to call their assembly. This attribute, `System.Security.AllowPartiallyTrustedCallers`, is typically added to the `AssemblyInfo.cs` code file in a project. Add this attribute to the `AssemblyInfo.cs` file in the project that contains the `WeatherWebPart` class:

```
[assembly:System.Security.AllowPartiallyTrustedCallers]
```

In addition to decorating the assembly with an attribute so it can be called in a SharePoint site, SharePoint also needs to be explicitly told that the class within the assembly is safe. SharePoint's safe mode parser checks every class loaded in every page to ensure that it has been marked as OK to load in the site. Skipping this verification would open SharePoint sites up to a world of undesirable possibilities, as someone within an organization using SharePoint Designer could add a reference to a user control that has not been approved by the SharePoint farm administrators.

For more information on the safe mode parser, refer to Chapter 2.

Therefore, in order for the Weather News Web Part to run properly within a SharePoint site, SharePoint needs to be made aware that it is a safe control. This is done by adding a `<SafeControl />` entry to the site's hosting Web application's `web.config` file. Rather than do this manually, it should be done using WSS solution package deployment, as covered in the next section.

SharePoint Web Part Deployment Options

The last step in creating a custom Web Part is the deployment process. Deploying a custom Web Part involves four steps, two required and two optional.

The required steps are as follows:

1. Deploy the assembly containing the Web Part class to the site's hosting Web application's `\BIN` directory or to the server's GAC.

2. Add a `<SafeControl />` entry to the site's hosting Web application's `web.config` file, telling SharePoint the control has been approved to run in SharePoint sites hosted within that Web application.

Here are the optional steps:

3. Deploy any resource files (images, CSS, JS, etc.) used by the Web Part.

4. Make the Web Part discoverable within SharePoint so users can add it to SharePoint pages within sites.

The last optional step may cause a double-take. *How else would it get on a page?* Recall what happens when a Web Part is added to a Web Part zone on a page from the section "Overview of Web Parts" at the beginning of this chapter: XML is added to the Web Part zone. Provided a Web Part has been deployed and marked as safe, someone with the Add and Customize Pages permission can import a Web Part definition file into a specific page without selecting it from the catalog. This is a neat technique, enabling site owners to strategically place Web Parts on specific pages but allowing those with the Add and Customize Pages permission to add a specific Web Part from the Web Part Gallery.

In order to make the Web Part discoverable, or enable users to pick the Web Part from a list of available Web Parts, a Web Part definition file must exist in one of two places: the Web Part Gallery in a top-level site of a site collection or the `\wpcatalog` folder within the Web root of a site's hosting Web application. If the Web Part definition is deployed to the `\wpcatalog` folder, all sites within all site collections within the Web application will have access to the Web Part. However, if the Web Part definition is added to the Web Part Gallery, a special document library in the top-level site of a site collection, only the sites within that site collection will be able to add the Web Part to their pages.

The Web Part definition file for the Weather News Web Part is shown in Listing 11-12.

Listing 11-12: Weather News Web Part definition file

```xml
<?xml version="1.0" encoding="utf-8" ?>
<webParts>
  <webPart xmlns="http://schemas.microsoft.com/WebPart/v3">
    <metaData>
      <type name="WROX.ProMossWcm.Chapter11.WeatherWebPart,
Chapter11WeatherWebPart, Version=1.0.0.0, Culture=neutral,
PublicKeyToken=c591e70cfdf9ce4f" />
      <importErrorMessage>Error importing the Web Part.</importErrorMessage>
    </metaData>
    <data>
      <properties>
        <property name="Title" type="string">Weather News Web Part</property>
      </properties>
    </data>
  </webPart>
</webParts>
```

The Web Part definition file tells SharePoint the name of the class and assembly containing the class for the Web Part. The `<Properties>` section enables developers to set the values of the Web Part's public properties.

To deploy the Web Part definition to the entire Web application, use the `<DwpFiles>` element within the WSS solution package `manifest.xml` file. DWP files are what Web Part definition files were called in WSS 2.0, hence the name. However, this is not recommended because it is considered the WSS 2.0 way to deploy Web Parts. The recommended approach is to provision Web Part definitions to the Web Part Gallery using Features.

The other option is to deploy the Web Part to the Web Part Gallery. Deploying the Web Part definition to the Web Part Gallery is very similar to provisioning master pages and page layouts to the Master Page Gallery. WSS 3.0 Features are used to provision an uncustomized instance of the Web Part definition into the Web Part Gallery. Features also enable developers to specify the group within which the Web Part should be displayed in the Add Web Parts pop-up dialog that appears when adding a Web Part to a page in a SharePoint site. Listing 11-13 contains the CAML markup of an element manifest file used to provision the Weather News Web Part to the Web Part Gallery in a site collection.

Listing 11-13: Feature element manifest provisioning Web Part definition into the web part gallery

```xml
<?xml version="1.0" encoding="utf-8" ?>
<Elements xmlns="http://schemas.microsoft.com/sharepoint/">
  <Module Url="_catalogs/wp" RootWebOnly="TRUE">
    <File Url="WeatherWebPart.webpart" Type="GhostableInLibrary">
      <Property Name="Group"
                Value="WROX Professional MOSS 2007 WCM Development" />
    </File>
  </Module>
</Elements>
```

The last step is to ensure that the Web Part runs correctly within a SharePoint site. This Web Part has an extra deployment requirement in that it will not run in a SharePoint site that has been created using the default settings with no modifications. The Weather News Web Part retrieves the news via a remote RSS feed. The default CAS policy for SharePoint sites, WSS_Minimal, does not permit Web requests outside of the current domain. Therefore, in order for the Weather News Web Part to properly function, either the code access security (CAS) policy must be changed or the trust level needs to be changed to something more permissive.

The easy fix is to bump the trust level up to WSS_Medium or Full, but that changes the security settings for all assemblies in the site. The much more secure way to do it is to customize the CAS policy to grant the necessary permissions only to the Weather News Web Part without affecting anything else. Thankfully, WSS solution packages provide a way to modify the CAS policy. The CAML markup in Listing 11-14 demonstrates how to modify the CAS policy within the WSS solution package manifest.xml file.

Listing 11-14: Customizing CAS policy files via manifest.xml

```xml
<?xml version="1.0" encoding="utf-8" ?>
<Solution xmlns="http://schemas.microsoft.com/sharepoint/"
          SolutionId="AD86F73D-BA51-4918-98AD-97611A64CF90"
          DeploymentServerType="WebFrontEnd"
          ResetWebServer="TRUE">
  <Assemblies>
    <Assembly DeploymentTarget="WebApplication"
              Location="Chapter11WeatherWebPart.dll">
      <SafeControls>
        <SafeControl Namespace="WROX.ProMossWcm.Chapter11"
                     Safe="True" TypeName="*" />
      </SafeControls>
    </Assembly>
  </Assemblies>
  <CodeAccessSecurity>
    <PolicyItem>
      <Assemblies>
        <Assembly
PublicKeyBlob="002400000480000094000000060200000024000052534131300040000010001 00e976
fa6a4eee88a3c45604062a386210b1d51cfad35e83a9f3447c3e692c65db877bebff48056ab87f316be
505e15e8ec77353b748832ae16553b7e35dbb825b1d95b8c007a3003706544956b3add805d12d8ee9ec
d54f9051b306dcac388f20f861384594bdb05084eb27ee89e4ae3e76259d11b3a796779178f2ef807c7
2c8"/>
      </Assemblies>
      <PermissionSet class="NamedPermissionSet"
                     Description="ProMossWcmDevelopment" version="1">
        <IPermission class="System.Web.AspNetHostingPermission, System,
Version=2.0.0.0, Culture=neutral, PublicKeyToken=b77a5c561934e089"
                     Level="Minimal"
                     version="1" />
```

```
            <IPermission class="System.Net.WebPermission, System, Version=2.0.0.0,
    Culture=neutral, PublicKeyToken=b77a5c561934e089"
                        Unrestricted="true"
                        version="1" />
            <IPermission class="System.Security.Permissions.SecurityPermission,
    mscorlib, Version=2.0.0.0, Culture=neutral, PublicKeyToken=b77a5c561934e089"
                        Flags="AllFlags"
                        version="1" />
        </PermissionSet>
      </PolicyItem>
    </CodeAccessSecurity>

    <FeatureManifests>
      <FeatureManifest Location="Chapter11WeatherWebPart\feature.xml" />
    </FeatureManifests>
  </Solution>
```

The full source, including a Feature that deploys the Weather Web Part to the Web Part Gallery upon activation and the files needed to create the WSS solution package, can be found in the associated code download for this book.

MOSS 2007 Publishing Web Parts

The beginning of the chapter mentioned that Microsoft included three Publishing-specific Web Parts in MOSS 2007. These three Web Parts, Summary Links, Table of Contents, and Content Query are available only within sites that have the Publishing Features activated because they have a dependency on some XSL files provisioned in the activation of these Features. Two of these Web Parts are primarily used for rolling up links to content — to promote content reuse rather than content duplication. The other, Summary Links, is used primarily to add some ad hoc links to a page on a site. The following sections discuss and demonstrate each of these in more detail.

All three Web Parts can have the rendering styles customized beyond what is available out of the box. The most extensible and powerful of the three, the Content Query Web Part, provides some very advanced customization techniques that can eliminate most custom-built content rollup Web Parts that developers are building today. While this chapter only covers in detail some advanced customization techniques with the Content Query Web Part, the techniques demonstrated can be applied to all three, including the rendering style customization options.

All three Web Parts work the same way under the hood. Depending on the Web Part, it retrieves the links that should be shown as an XML structure. The Summary Links Web Part retrieves the links stored within the Web Part, whereas the other two (Table of Contents and Content Query) use the settings specified by the content owner to retrieve links to pages within the site. That XML structure is then processed with XSLT to generate the resulting HTML used for rendering the output.

Creating Placeholder Data for Testing Rollup Web Parts

When working with the Publishing Web Parts — specifically, the Table of Contents Web Part and the Content Query Web Part — it helps to have some pages already created that can be used in querying, filtering, grouping, and styling the content. The code download for this book includes a sample project, `WidgetContentBuilder`, that creates a new subsite within a site collection called *Widgets*, new site columns, a new content type, *Widget Product Page*, and page layout `ProductPageLeft.aspx`, which implements the Widget Product Page content type — all deployed using a WSS 3.0 Feature: *Widget Content Builder Feature*. When this Feature is activated, it not only creates the subsite and site artifacts, it also creates ten content pages using the content type and page layout within the Widgets subsite. These pages are all checked in and published and can be used for testing the configuration options of the Table of Contents and Content Query Web Parts.

Not only is this a helpful Feature for creating random content for testing, it is also a good code demonstration of how to programmatically create pages, check them in, and publish and approve them.

Summary Links Web Part (and Field Control)

The Summary Links Web Part is provided for developers and designers to enable content authors to add ad-hoc links to a content page. This simple Web Part enables content owners to enter headings and links and modify some settings on each. The sorting can be set to manual or automatic. If automatic is selected, the author specifies which field is used to base the automatic sorting logic on.

When is the Summary Links Web Part useful? Consider a product page on a Publishing site. Many of the product pages on the various sites today contain links to things such as press releases, news articles, and case studies related to the product. The Summary Links Web Part is ideal for this type of a requirement.

After adding the Web Part to a Web Part zone within a page layout, the authoring experience looks like what is shown in Figure 11-3. This editing experience enables content authors to add new links and groups (headings), reorder the links, and set the style rendering options. When creating links, content owners can also specify the tooltip shown when hovering over the link, as well as the `Alt=""` attribute for accessibility needs and an image URL to be associated with the link.

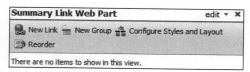

Figure 11-3

One thing unique about the Summary Links Web Part compared to the other two Publishing Web Parts is that it is provided not only as a Web Part but also as a field control. This flexibility enables developers to place the Summary Links field control on a page and associate it with a field in the page's content type. That way, the links entered in the control are versioned with the page, restricting content authors from add/removing/moving it on the page.

Table of Contents Web Part

The Table of Content Web Part is primarily used to keep the main navigation in a site from becoming too crowded or busy. Typically used on the home page of a site within the Publishing site collection, the Table of Contents Web Part displays links to pages within the site. It can be configured to show pages from a specific site and a set number of subsites (defined by an optional number of levels to include).

Content authors can elect to include hidden sites and pages in the results. This might seem a bit odd at first, but it enables content authors to hide links that would normally show in the main navigation and instead show them within the Table of Contents Web Part. Like the Summary Links Web Part and field control, content authors can specify sorting options and rendering styles, and the number of columns of links to show. Figure 11-4 shows the editing experience for the Table of Contents Web Part.

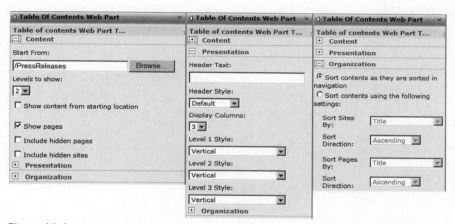

Figure 11-4

Content Query Web Part

Last but certainly not least in the trio of Publishing Web Parts is the Content Query Web Part (CQWP). This Web Part is by far the most powerful and flexible of all three Publishing Web Parts; think of the CQWP as the silver bullet for Publishing sites. Why? Many custom rollup Web Parts can be eliminated using the CQWP. This is very beneficial to a project, as it results in less custom code that needs to be maintained. The CQWP leverages some robust caching and performance optimization techniques to make it the most performant Web Part possible. If developers build custom rollup Web Parts, they need to include this caching infrastructure in their own custom code to achieve the same performance.

> *One of the caching and performance techniques the CQWP leverages is the* `Microsoft` `.SharePoint.Publishing.Navigation.PortalSiteMapProvider` *class. This class can be used by developers in custom code, as demonstrated in Chapter 19, "Performance Tips, Tricks, and Traps."*

In order to achieve the many different customization needs required for individual projects, developers need to be familiar with and proficient in the different customization capabilities and techniques available within a CQWP. However, before jumping into the advanced customization techniques take a look at what the CQWP can offer OOTB.

The CQWP is optimized to pull data from SharePoint lists across sites within a site collection. This means it can very quickly be configured to retrieve a certain type of pages no matter where the pages are within a site collection and regardless of where the CQWP is used. Once a CQWP is dropped into a Web Part Zone, content authors can configure multiple settings to customize the content that is displayed. The following list details the major functionality provided by the CQWP OOTB, and Figure 11-5 shows the configuration experience available in the task pane when editing the Web Part's settings:

- ❑ **Query Scope** — Set the scope of the query used to retrieve the data for the CQWP. The scope can be set to the entire site collection, a specific subsite (and all subsites within the specified subsite), or a specific list within a specific site.

- ❑ **List Type** — Retrieve data from a specific type of a list. This selector includes all list templates available within the site collection. When a template is selected, only content from that list is included in the query result set.

- ❑ **Content Type** — Filter the result set to optionally include content conforming to a specific content type and optionally all content types that are derived from the selected content type.

- ❑ **Audience Targeting** — Optionally include audience targeting when the query is executed; and, optionally, include items in the result set that are not targeted for the current user.

- ❑ **Custom Filters** — Similar to SharePoint list views, add up to three additional filters on specific fields to apply when executing the query to generate the result set.

- ❑ **Grouping and Sorting** — Similar to SharePoint list views, apply sorting and grouping logic on the result set returned by the query.

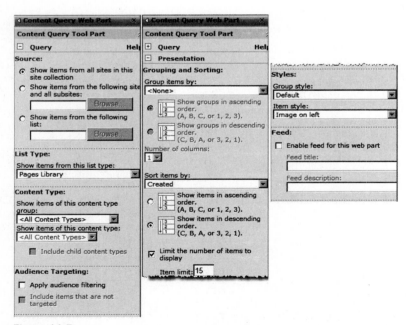

Figure 11-5

The CQWP, like the other Publishing Web Parts, also has styling options content authors can select. Both the group and item style can be configured using one of the OOTB styles. Developers are free to create custom styles as well. This is covered later in the chapter in the section "Implementing Custom Style Rendering Options."

The CQWP has one last capability that the other Publishing Web Parts lack: The results of the query can be published as an RSS feed. Site users can then subscribe to the RSS feed of the CQWP in their offline newsreaders, such as Office Outlook 2007. Developers can also use this RSS feed in other parts of the Publishing site, consuming it using either the XML Web Part and transforming the feed using XSL into HTML or in custom Web Parts.

Configuration of the CQWP is self-explanatory so this chapter instead focuses on advanced customization that can be implemented using the CQWP.

Advanced Content Query Web Part Customization

While the CQWP is quite powerful and flexible in most situations, developers will likely encounter business requirements that require some advanced customization of the CQWP. First, recall the discussion already covered in this chapter regarding how Web Parts are added to pages. The section "Overview of Web Parts" explained how adding a Web Part to a Web Part zone actually results in adding a block of XML that tells the Web Part Framework where the Web Part class and assembly containing the class can be found, as well as all the values of the Web Part's public properties. When the Web Part is loaded by the Web Part Framework, these values defined in the XML are assigned to the public properties, which the Web Part uses to create the desired rendering. All Web Parts work this way, including the CQWP.

How does this little bit of knowledge empower a Publishing site developer? Not all public properties of the CQWP are made available for editing in the task pane when modifying the Web Part. The trick is figuring out how to edit these values. Many developers first look to a custom code solution such as wrapping the CQWP up in a Web Part and setting these properties, but that just creates more custom code that needs to be maintained, deployed, and marked as safe.

There is a much easier way! Add the CQWP to a Web Part zone and make all necessary changes through the task pane. Then, after committing the changes, the next step is to get the XML that was added to the Web Part zone, the same XML that contains the values of all the properties just set in the task pane. To do this, when in Edit mode, click the downward-facing arrow in the upper-right corner of the CQWP (this is known as the Web Part Verbs menu) and select Export, as shown in Figure 11-6.

Figure 11-6

199

Internet Explorer will display a prompt to save a file named [CQWP_Name].webpart. Save this file and open it in a text editor. This is a Web Part definition file for the configured CQWP that is currently on the page! Notice the long list of properties, a significantly longer list than the Web Part definition for the custom Weather News Web Part created previously in this chapter. Armed with this Web Part definition, how can it be used? As shown earlier when creating the custom Weather News Web Part, it can be packaged into a Feature for deployment. Alternately, a developer can add it directly to the page. To do this, while in Edit mode, select Page ⇨ Add Web Parts ⇨ Import from the Page Editing toolbar, as shown in Figure 11-7. In the task pane, browse to the *.webpart file and click the Upload button. This adds the Web Part to the task pane, as shown in Figure 11-8, so it can be dragged back into a Web Part zone.

Figure 11-7

Figure 11-8

This technique provides developers with three very powerful capabilities. First, with access to all the custom properties, developers can now customize the CQWP beyond what is provided in the task pane. Some customizations are demonstrated later in this section. Second, the CQWP changes can be versioned and retained in source control because they are now refactored out of SharePoint and down to the file system. Once the file is on the file system, it can be added to any source control system — Visual Source Safe™, Team Foundation System™, Subversion . . . any SCM! Third, as demonstrated earlier when creating the custom Weather News Web Part, the Web Part definition file can be provisioned to the Web Part Gallery using a Feature and packaged using a WSS solution package. This enables developers to create predefined CQWP configurations that are easily deployable across sites and environments!

Modifying the CQWP Web Part Definition

Now it is time to dig in and learn how to customize the Web Part definition file for a CQWP. There are 89 properties that can be customized when the CQWP Web Part definition is exported from the browser. The following list contains some of the popular properties available for customization in the CQWP Web Part definition:

❑ Height and Width — When specified, the CQWP will occupy the set amount of space both vertically and horizontally on the page.

❑ Title — Name of the CQWP, shown in the Web Part header.

❑ DisplayColumns — Sets the number of columns to display the results within.

❑ UseCache — Boolean value specifying whether the CQWP should use the cache to retrieve results, or always perform live queries.

❑ ListOverride — Indicates to the CQWP what type of lists to filter by. Values here can be either the list's BaseType (e.g., Pages list = 1), ID (e.g., GUID of the list) or server template Type (e.g., Pages list = 850).

❑ QueryOverride — Provides developers with a way to use a custom CAML query instead of allowing the CQWP to create the query based on the values specified in the properties or task pane.

❑ WebsOverride — When specified, the CQWP does or does not recurse subsites, and only retrieves its results from the specified site.

❑ HeaderXslLink, ItemXslLink, and MainXslLink — Used to specify a custom XSL file that contains styles used in rendering (see the section "Implementing Custom Style Rendering" later in this chapter for more information on this).

❑ GroupStyle and ItemStyle — Specifies the style within the XSL file to use in creating the HTML used for rendering the results.

❑ CommonViewFields — Enables developers to specify additional fields beyond what the CQWP automatically retrieves. This property can contain multiple fields.

❑ ViewFieldsOverride — Enables developers to specify the exact fields to be returned by the query, rather than get the default queries returned by the CQWP.

For more information on the Content Query Web Part properties available for customization, refer to the official documentation on MSDN (www.andrewconnell.com/go/240). In addition, the MSDN article "How to: Customize the Content Query Web Part by using Custom Properties" (www.andrewconnell.com/go/241) contains additional information on using the filtering properties.

Setting the values on many of these properties is fairly straightforward, but others are not so obvious. For instance, using the ListOverride property is not a matter of simply entering the list's type within the value of the XML node in the Web Part definition. The ListOverride property is expecting a CAML string. The following example is setting the CQWP to only retrieve data from the Pages list type:

```
<property name="ListOverride" type="string">
<![CDATA[<Lists ServerTemplate="850"></Lists>]]></property>
```

The `WebsOverride` property is another one that needs a bit of explanation, as it is not as simple as setting it to a Boolean value. CAML is used to set the value, just like the `ListOverride` property. To retrieve data from the site(s) specified, use the following:

```
<property name="WebsOverride" type="string"><![CDATA[<Webs />]]></property>
```

If the CQWP should retrieve the data from the subsites of the site selected, then use the following:

```
<property name="WebsOverride" type="string">
<![CDATA[<Webs Recursive="True" />]]></property>
```

To retrieve specific fields using the `CommonViewFields` property, the internal name of the field and field type need to be included in the property. For instance, if the CQWP needed to pull the field Page Content (with an internal name of `PublishingPageContent`) from a page created using the Article Page template, the property would look like the following:

```
<property name="CommonViewFields"
type="string">PublishingPageContent,RichHTML</property>
```

Finally, if the `ViewFieldsOverride` property is used to select explicit fields for use in the display rendering, CAML similar to the CAML used to define the fields included in content types when creating content types via Features is used, such as the following:

```
<property name="ViewFieldsOverride" type="string">
  <![CDATA[
    <FieldRef Name="PublishingPageContent" Type="HTML" />
    <FieldRef Name="SummaryLinks" Type="SummaryLinks" />
  ]]>
</property>
```

Many of the files in the preceding list are demonstrated in the section "Implementing a Customized CQWP Solution," which creates a customized instance of the CQWP with custom styles. Before building a custom solution though, it is necessary to understand how the Publishing Web Parts are rendered using the different style options, including modifying and creating custom styles.

Customizing the CQWP Style Rendering

As previously explained, the Publishing Web Parts first create an XML structure of the content to be displayed. This XML structure is then run through the specified XSL file and template to generate the HTML (or RSS) that is used to render the results. These specified style sheets are all provisioned from the file system into a special gallery in the top-level site in a Publishing site collection: Style Library. These style sheets (XSL files) are all stored in the XSL Style Sheets folder in the Style Library.

When editing the CQWP properties through the browser in the task pane, two of the presentation options are Group Style and Item Style. The items listed in the Group Style selector are actually XSL templates defined in the `http://[..]/Style Library/XSL Style Sheets/Header.xsl` file. The items listed in the Item Style selector are XSL templates defined in the `http://[..]/Style Library/XSL Style Sheets/ItemStyle.xsl` file. The relationship between all the files is shown in Figure 11-9.

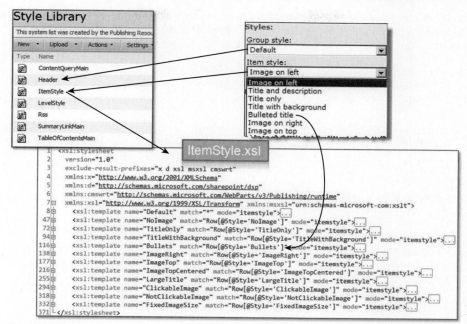

Figure 11-9

All three Publishing Web Parts use the same `Header.xsl` and `ItemStyle.xsl` file in their rendering (the Table of Contents Web Part uses another style sheet, `LevelStyle.xsl`, to define the different level styling options), but as expected, each Web Part has some subtle differences that need to be taken into account. This is all handled by special style sheets created for each Web Part.

Take a look in the `ItemStyle.xsl` file. This file contains a handful of `<xsl:template>` nodes that match the options in the Item Style selector in the task pane, as shown in Figure 11-9. The first portion of each template defines a handful of variables using the `<xsl:variable>` node. Within those variables, `<xsl:call-template>` nodes are used to execute XSL functions defined somewhere else. It is these functions that are defined within the special Web Part–specific style sheets. All the Web Part–specific style sheets reside in the same location as the other style sheets and are named for the Web Part they are used with: `ContentQueryMain.xsl`, `SummaryLinkMain.xsl`, and `TableOfContentsMain.xsl`. Each Web Part loads the appropriate XSL file so this is not something the developer needs to be aware of, although it is something that can be changed. To change the Web Part–specific style sheet, use the property `MainXslLink` in the Web Part definition file. For instance, to use the style sheet `CustomMain.xsl` found in the same location as the other style sheets, use the following code:

```
<property name="MainXslLink" type="string">/Style Library/XSL Style Sheets/
CustomMain.xsl</property>
```

The documentation Microsoft provides explains how to customize the existing styles using the existing XSL style sheets. This will work, but it isn't recommended. Why? Consider the following situation: A developer is working on a fairly large Publishing site implementation. Like most Publishing sites, this one uses multiple instances of the CQWP. However, one section needs to have a fairly customized CQWP implementation with some custom rendering. If the developer implemented this custom rendering by modifying one of the existing styles, all the other CQWP implementations on the site that use the modified style will get the same style customizations. Maybe that was not intended.

The other option would be to simply create a new template in the `ItemStyle.xsl` file and only select it in the customized CQWP implementation, but other implementations could also use it, which might not be desired. In addition, customizing the XSL file using SharePoint Designer, as demonstrated in the official MSDN documentation, is not easily replicated across multiple environments.

Instead of customizing the existing styles, it is recommended that you create brand-new XSL style sheets and configure the CQWP's properties to import the custom XSL file. This is demonstrated in the next section.

Implementing a Customized CQWP Solution

The next logical step is a demonstration of the advanced CQWP customization and styling options in order to see how all this works. A common requirement for companies is to create a rollup page that lists [x] number of product pages for a specific division (in the case of the demonstration, the division is *North America*). In addition, the rollup should show the name of the division of the product. OOTB, the CQWP cannot satisfy this requirement, but with a little customization and styling it is possible!

> *The CQWP customization demonstration that follows uses the content created by the* `WidgetContentBuilder` *Feature mentioned earlier in the chapter. This Feature creates some sample content in a new subsite within a Publishing site collection.*

Before going further, take a look at what needs to be implemented. Figure 11-10 shows what the resulting CQWP should look like.

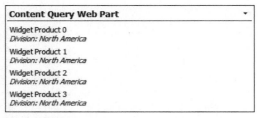

Figure 11-10

The first step is to add a CQWP to an existing page. By default, it will pull all the pages from the entire site collection, which is not what you want. Modify the CQWP's settings in the task pane by setting the following values (leaving everything not mentioned at their default):

❑ **Source** — Show items from the following site and all subsites: Widgets

❑ **List Type** — Show items from this list type: Pages Library

❑ **Content Type** — **Group** = Widget Content Builder; **Content Type** = Widget Product Page

Next, sort the result set by expanding the Grouping and Sorting section and set the following values:

❑ **Group items by** — None

❑ **Sort items by** — Name

❑ **Show items in ascending order**

❑ **Limit the number of items to display** — Checked

❑ **Item limit** — 4

After setting the minimal configuration settings on the CQWP, apply the changes by clicking OK at the bottom of the task pane. The resulting CQWP should look like Figure 11-11 — not what is required, as there is no mention of the division, but this is as much as you can do through the browser.

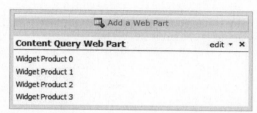

Figure 11-11

To display the product division it needs to be retrieved from the page. This is done by adding the field to the CQWP properties. Export the CQWP to a Web Part definition file and open the file in a text editor such as Visual Studio. To tell the CQWP to pull another field in addition to the other fields, use the CommonViewFields property, which should be on or near line 68. The body of the page is stored in the field named Division, which happens to be the same as the internal name of the field. The internal name is what is needed. The field type of the field is Choice. Modify the CommonViewFields property node in the CQWP definition as follows:

```
<property name="CommonViewFields" type="string">Division_WCB,Choice;</property>
```

Now that the CQWP is pulling the necessary field, it needs to display it. This is done within the style rendering. Instead of modifying an existing style, because this CQWP is so specific to this one part of the site, it makes more sense to create a completely new style. This involves doing two things: creating a new style and configuring the CQWP so that it is aware of the custom style sheet.

Create a copy of the ItemStyle.xsl file, as it is pretty close to what is desired — it's always easier to start with a copy than to start from scratch. Save this new XSL style sheet as WroxCh11.xsl in http://[..]/Style Library/XSL Style Sheets. The new style sheet contains more templates than necessary, so delete all the templates except the one named Default. Rename the template to WroxCh11.xsl and change the match attribute on the <xsl:template> node to Row[@Style='WidgetProductList']. The (George) file should now look similar to the markup in Listing 11-15 (the attributes in the opening <xsl:stylesheet> node have been omitted here for readability).

Listing 11-15: WroxCh11.xsl

```
<xsl:stylesheet>
    <xsl:template name="WidgetProductList" match="Row[@Style='WidgetProductList']"
mode="itemstyle">
            <xsl:variable name="SafeLinkUrl"><!-- omitted --></xsl:variable>
            <xsl:variable name="SafeImageUrl"><!-- omitted --></xsl:variable>
            <xsl:variable name="DisplayTitle"><!-- omitted --></xsl:variable>
            <xsl:variable name="LinkTarget"><!-- omitted --></xsl:variable>
            <div id="linkitem" class="item">
                <xsl:if test="string-length($SafeImageUrl) != 0">
                    <div class="image-area-left">
                        <a href="{$SafeLinkUrl}" target="{$LinkTarget}">
                            <img class="image" src="{$SafeImageUrl}"
alt="{@ImageUrlAltText}" />
                        </a>
                    </div>
                </xsl:if>
                <div class="link-item">
                    <xsl:call-template
name="OuterTemplate.CallPresenceStatusIconTemplate"/>
                    <a href="{$SafeLinkUrl}" target="{$LinkTarget}"
title="{@LinkToolTip}">
                        <xsl:value-of select="$DisplayTitle"/>
                    </a>
                    <div class="description">
                      <xsl:value-of select="@Description" />
                    </div>
                </div>
            </div>
    </xsl:template>
</xsl:stylesheet>
```

With the style sheet created, it is best to integrate it with the CQWP definition to ensure that the basics are working before adding any custom rendering logic. With the WroxCh11.xsl style sheet in the Style Library, the CQWP definition needs to be made aware of it. Go back to the definition file and find the ItemXslLink property. This property is used by the CQWP to load a custom style sheet in addition to the ones defined in ItemStyles.xsl. Modify the ItemXslLink property to point to the absolute URL of the style sheet, as follows:

```
<property name="ItemXslLink" type="string">/Style Library/XSL Style
Sheets/WroxCh11.xsl</property>
```

In addition, the CQWP needs to be configured to use the new (or renamed) style in the XSL style sheet. Find the ItemStyle property and change the value to be the name of the new style:

```
<property name="ItemStyle" type="string">WidgetProductList</property>
```

Save the changes, import the CQWP `*.webpart` definition file to the SharePoint site where it was exported, and add it to a Web Part zone. The new Web Part should look identical to the one that was exported. This is because although a new field is being pulled, the field is not being displayed in the rendering. To include the field in the rendering of the CQWP it must be added to the style.

Because the `WroxCh11.xsl` style sheet is a copy of the `ItemStyle.xsl` style sheet, it still contains a section where it displays the description of the product page returned in the results. This can be modified to display the content of the extra field *Division* that is retrieved by the CQWP. Find the following markup in the `WroxCh11.xsl` style sheet, which renders the `Description` field from the page:

```
<div class="description">
    <xsl:value-of select="@Description" />
</div>
```

Change it to return the field `Division`:

```
<div class="description">
    <em>Division: <xsl:value-of select="@Division_WCB" /></em>
</div>
```

The @ symbol is used to retrieve the value of a node in the XML that is transformed to HTML with the XSL. In other words, the @ selects the fields from the item in the result set of the query. After saving the changes, testing the page with the CQWP will show the results, as shown in Figure 11-12.

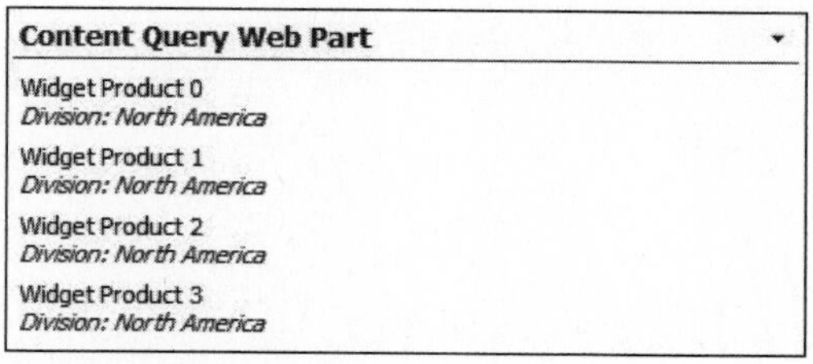

Content Query Web Part	▾
Widget Product 0 *Division: North America*	
Widget Product 1 *Division: North America*	
Widget Product 2 *Division: North America*	
Widget Product 3 *Division: North America*	

Figure 11-12

With the CQWP definition configured with the necessary settings and the custom style rendering created, the next step is to package everything up for deployment.

Deploying Customized Content Query Web Part Customizations and Renderings

The deployment of a custom CQWP definition is no different than deploying a custom Web Part definition file. The advantage with a custom CQWP is that there is no assembly to deploy and thus no safe control entry to add because the CQWP assembly has already been deployed as part of the MOSS installation. The only thing that is necessary is to provision the Web Part definition file into the Web Part Gallery for the site collection. The CAML markup in Listing 11-16 contains the contents of a site collection–scoped Feature's element manifest that provisions the Web Part definition into the Web Part Gallery.

Listing 11-16: Feature element manifest file provisioning a customized CQWP definition

```xml
<?xml version="1.0" encoding="utf-8" ?>
<Elements xmlns="http://schemas.microsoft.com/sharepoint/">
  <Module Url="_catalogs/wp"
          RootWebOnly="TRUE">
    <File Url="WidgetRollupWithDivision.webpart"
          Type="GhostableInLibrary">
      <Property Name="Group"
                Value="WROX Professional MOSS 2007 WCM Development" />
    </File>
  </Module>
</Elements>
```

Finally, the custom rendering style needs to be deployed as well. This is no different than provisioning the Web Part definition file to the Web Part Gallery or master pages, or page layouts to the Master Page Gallery, as shown in Listing 11-17.

Listing 11-17: Feature element manifest file provisioning a custom CQWP rendering style sheet

```xml
<?xml version="1.0" encoding="utf-8" ?>
<Elements xmlns="http://schemas.microsoft.com/sharepoint/">
  <Module Url="_catalogs/wp"
          RootWebOnly="TRUE">
    <File Url="WidgetRollupWithDivision.webpart"
          Type="GhostableInLibrary">
      <Property Name="Group"
                Value="WROX Professional MOSS 2007 WCM Development" />
    </File>
  </Module>
  <Module Url="Style Library/XSL Style Sheets"
          RootWebOnly="TRUE">
    <File Url="WroxCh11.xsl"
          Type="GhostableInLibrary">
    </File>
  </Module>
</Elements>
```

The complete code for the Feature and WSS solution package used to deploy this customized CQWP and style is included in the code download for this book.

Summary

Microsoft introduced the Web Part Framework in WSS 2.0 and later moved it to ASP.NET 2.0. By changing the architecture to build WSS 3.0 on top of ASP.NET 2.0 (compared to the previous architecture), Microsoft no longer needed to rely on SharePoint for the Web Part infrastructure but instead made it more broadly available. SharePoint developers benefit from this move, as many things in the Web Part Framework were simplified in the ASP.NET 2.0 version.

While most SharePoint 3.0 sites still use Web Parts quite extensively, MOSS 2007 Publishing sites offer an additional editing control for developers and content authors alike: field controls. This does not mean that Web Parts are no longer used in Publishing sites, but they are typically not used nearly as much as they are in traditional collaboration SharePoint sites. Instead, Web Parts serve more of a functional role, rather than storing content. This chapter demonstrated how to create a custom ASP.NET 2.0 Web Part that can be used within an ASP.NET 2.0 Web site, a WSS 3.0 site, or a Publishing site. It also demonstrated a few advanced techniques that developers may want to consider when implementing custom Web Parts such as custom Editor Parts and asynchronous programming techniques.

MOSS 2007 Publishing sites include a trio of Web Parts used primarily to aggregate content on a single page for navigation and organizational purposes, as well as to provide ad hoc links on a page without modifying the site's navigation. All three Web Parts — Summary Links, Table of Contents, and Content Query — retrieve the results to be displayed as XML. This XML is internally run through an XSL transformation to generate HTML that is used to render the results. Developers can tap into this process and customize the way these three Web Parts retrieve, filter, group, and sort the resulting data, as well as the rendering options for each.

12

Leveraging Workflow

Workflow has always been an important subject in the context of enterprise applications. Unfortunately, developers have historically been mostly limited to working with large and expensive workflow systems. Applications that did not rely on these third-party workflow engines required some form of workflow engine to be devised as their own implementations. These factors combined to make the workflow development story very murky for .NET developers.

Thankfully, Microsoft created the Windows Workflow Foundation (WF). Not only can WF be shared across applications, but developers can also utilize it within their own custom applications. Windows SharePoint Services (WSS) 3.0 is a prime example of this in that it added workflow to the SharePoint platform by leveraging WF.

This chapter begins by explaining the concepts and motivations behind WF in general. It then moves into the SharePoint WF story and how WF is incorporated within SharePoint. Finally, the steps for creating and deploying a custom workflow for use in a SharePoint Publishing site are covered. What this chapter does not contain is an in-depth discussion about WF or creating custom workflows that can be used outside of a SharePoint environment. Additional resources are provided at the end of the "Creating Custom Workflows" section for readers who want more information on WF or creating custom workflows.

The workflow development story within a SharePoint environment does not vary much between versions of Visual Studio (2005 vs. 2008). When appropriate, any differences between the two are described.

Understanding Windows Workflow Foundation

Before diving into how to leverage existing workflows or developing custom workflows, it is important for developers to have a solid grasp of WF and the motivation behind it. As with any software company, product teams develop new capabilities as they are needed within each product. At times this can result in two or more groups developing a similar component for use in different applications. The concept of workflow falls squarely in this camp. Applications such as WSS 2.0 and Content Management Server (MCMS) 2002 both had a need for workflow. At the time, the best option for adding extensible workflow to these products was to purchase a third-party solution that integrated into each of them. This was a costly proposition, both in terms of configuration and implementation, as workflow engines are typically quite sophisticated applications.

Microsoft recognized this problem of applications either developing their own workflow engine or having to rely on third parties. The logical solution was to create a core workflow engine that all applications could leverage and extend for their own specific uses and implementations. This was the motivation behind WF: to create a robust and extensible workflow engine that could be utilized not only by Microsoft's products but also by other independent software vendors (ISVs) and developers. The first release of WF was included in the .NET Framework 3.0 and is the primary reason why one of the few prerequisites of WSS 3.0 is installing the .NET 3.0 Framework.

The very core of the .NET Framework, the common language runtime (CLR), makes development easier in that it manages all memory tasks for the developer. When a developer creates a new object, the CLR allocates the necessary memory to create the object; and when the object is no longer used or is out of scope, the garbage collector (GC) handles releasing memory back to the system for other uses.

The challenge with building .NET applications is maintaining state across sessions. Consider an application that needs to run over an extended period of time. Traditional .NET development would usually involve creating some sort of loop that would constantly check for certain conditions. The challenge with this approach is that the process cannot sustain a server reboot, something that causes the process to stop and is not very scalable. To address this, developers would create a custom persistence engine that would store the state of the application so that the application could be interrupted and pick up where it left off. As previously mentioned in this chapter, different developers on various product teams (and in some cases, the same team) had varying implementations of this persistence. What WF brings to the table is the ability to create more reactive, or episodic, programs in the .NET Framework, building off the managed memory offering. Before diving into the architecture, however, it is helpful to understand some terminology in WF.

Windows Workflow Foundation Terminology and Architecture

Windows Workflow Foundation, included in the .NET Framework 3.0, is comprised of a few different components, as shown in Figure 12-1. The primary component is the WF *runtime engine*. The runtime is what oversees the execution and provides services to the running workflows. It is the runtime that initiates new instances of workflow programs, registers and fires specific events the workflow subscribes to, and manages the serialization and deserialization of the workflow to a persistent storage medium, enabling the workflow to exist across process interruptions.

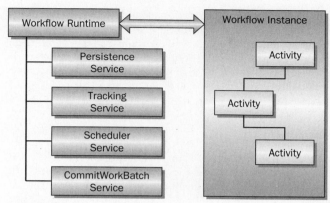

Figure 12-1

The WF runtime cannot operate independently. It requires an application to act as the *host* for the runtime. Both the application and the WF runtime execute within the same .NET `AppDomain`. Developers can create custom workflow programs by arranging a series of reusable components to perform the required task. These reusable components are called *activities*. The WF includes core activities, the base activity library (BAL), required to build most workflow programs. When the hosting application starts a workflow, it essentially hands a collection of activities (the workflow program) to the workflow runtime. The runtime in turn creates a new *instance* of the workflow.

The workflow runtime also provides four *services* that the hosting application can leverage:

❑ The *scheduling service* facilitates running workflows, by default, on asynchronous threads, and queues workflows that are waiting to be run. Developers can override the scheduling service to execute workflows in a synchronous manner by relegating all workflows to run on a single thread.

❑ The *CommitWorkBatch* service enables developers to configure how data is persisted. The runtime handles the persisting of data in the workflow, but by leveraging the service architecture it enables developers to implement custom logic for when the data is persisted.

❑ The *persistence* service enables the workflow runtime to persist workflows so that the workflow does not have to remain in memory until it terminates — for scalability reasons (as workflow instances can only execute on one server) and to survive periods when the host process recycles or terminates.

❑ The *tracking* service provides the workflow runtime with the capability to record performance and state information for monitoring the health of workflows. WF ships with default service implementations, but all of them are extensible, enabling developers to create their own implementation. For instance, the out-of-the-box (OOTB) implementation of the persistence and scheduling services included in the WF installation persists workflow data to a SQL Server database.

Activities

All workflows are comprised of activities. Activities are atomic units that perform a specific function. For instance, an activity may write a message to a log file, execute a command against a database, or send an e-mail message. Activities are similar to Windows Forms or ASP.NET 2.0 UI controls such as a `TextBox` or `GridView` or even an HTTP context in that they have states and parameters that are unique to the current point in time. These controls have been built by third parties and can be reused in other applications. They contain all the logic for both a design time and runtime experience as well as what to do when the activity is executed.

Activities can be as simple as performing a single action, such as pausing the workflow for a period of time (as in the `DelayActivity`), or complex, such as containing other activities. These complex activities, known as *composite activities,* include behaviors such as control loops, as in the case of `WhileActivity`, or they may control the execution of multiple activities such as the `SequentialActivity`, which requires that all child activities complete before moving on to the next activity. Each activity has properties that can be set through code or the designer interface, and an associated invocation event that developers can override in the workflow's code-behind file.

Developers use these activities to create a workflow program. Workflows are composed of activities that are arranged in a hierarchical tree formation. Each activity performs a specific function. In addition, developers are not limited to the activities provided by the WF. Similar to Windows Forms and ASP.NET 2.0 controls, developers are free to create custom activities and use them across an unlimited number of workflows. In fact, developers can share custom activities with other developers on the .NET 3.0 Framework community site (www.andrewconnell.com/go/242).

Types of Workflows

The WF supports building two different types of workflows in the context of SharePoint: sequential and state machine. A *sequential workflow* has one starting point, follows a generally predictable path or multiple paths, and may or may not have a termination point. These types of workflows resemble a flowchart. A *state machine* workflow is more suited to modeling real-world scenarios, as many business processes cannot be modeled using a flowchart. State machine workflows differ from sequential workflows in that they do not have a predefined path of execution. Instead, they rely more on the concept of conditions, and transition from one state to another.

At times it can be quite challenging to decide what type of workflow to build given a specific business case. One way to determine whether a sequential or state machine workflow is suitable is to ask who is in control of the business process. *If the workflow is in control,* such as when two people need to approve a page in a specific order before it is published, then a sequential workflow makes the most sense. This is because the workflow is defining the structure and linear flow of the process. However, *if the user or external inputs are in control,* such as when placing an order on an e-commerce site, a state machine workflow makes the most sense because the state of the order — such as Order Submitted, Inventory on Backorder, Pick List Submitted, and Order Fulfilled — is marked by transitions based on user input and input from other external systems.

Creating Custom Workflows

The WF does not provide a way to create custom workflows; instead, it simply acts as the host for the creation of instances of prebuilt workflows. This is similar to the .NET Framework, which does not provide a way to create custom applications. Instead, developers need to use some extra components to create custom workflows. The development experience varies a bit depending on the version of Visual Studio being used. Visual Studio 2005 was released well ahead of the general availability of WF, so extra components were needed for it to be used to develop custom workflows. Conversely, Visual Studio 2008 coincided with the .NET Framework 3.5 release, which included the WF and therefore the necessary hooks and components to create custom workflows.

Developing Custom Workflows with Visual Studio

When using Visual Studio 2005, developers need to download and install the Visual Studio 2005 for .NET Framework 3.0 (Windows Workflow Foundation): www.andrewconnell.com/go/243 (VSeWWF). The VSeWWF adds a few things to Visual Studio to enable developers to create custom workflows:

❑   A workflow designer interface that provides developers with a similar experience to building ASP.NET 2.0 or Windows Forms applications. Developers can easily drag and drop activities from the Visual Studio Toolbox onto the design surface and link them together.

❑   An activity data-bound parameter creator/binder wizard that makes it easy to bind the parameters of an activity to fields defined in the workflow class.

❑   It adds the base activity library, all activities included in the WF installation, to the Visual Studio Toolbox.

❑   The capability to create code-behind files associated with workflows and to override methods on the activity.

❑   It adds the capability to debug workflows.

Thankfully, Visual Studio 2008 does not require an extra download. It includes everything necessary to create custom workflows out-of-the-box. In fact, as covered later in the chapter, the entire process of creating and deploying the workflow in a development environment is much easier than in Visual Studio 2005.

> For more information on Windows Workflow Foundation, see the official MSDN documentation at www.andrewconnell.com/go/244. In addition, the following books are recommended: Microsoft Windows Workflow Foundation Step by Step by Kenn Scribner (Microsoft Press, 2007) and Professional Windows Workflow Foundation by Todd Kitta (Wiley, 2007).

Overview of SharePoint's Workflow Proposition

With a high-level review of the core WF concepts covered, it is time to shift attention to the SharePoint aspects of workflow. One of the biggest requests from customers using WSS 2.0 or SPS 2003 was for a much more robust and extensible workflow capability in the SharePoint platform. During the planning of WSS 3.0 and Microsoft Office SharePoint Server (MOSS) 2007, Microsoft was developing the WF, which was a logical platform on which the SharePoint team could base the next version. Microsoft's adoption of WF in SharePoint was driven by two design goals.

First, users needed the capability to easily tie workflows to documents and items in SharePoint document libraries and lists. This is accomplished by associating workflows within the context of a specific list, something covered later in the chapter.

Second, users needed the capability to interact and monitor the status of running workflows. Due to SharePoint's collaborative nature, most if not virtually all workflows have some sort of human element to them. At the very least, workflows can only exist within the context of items or documents in SharePoint lists or libraries. List items and documents are usually added to lists and libraries by a person, not a process. Users need to be able to not only complete a form when the workflow starts, but also to view the status of the workflow instance during its execution. They also need the capability to modify a workflow instance during execution and interact with tasks associated with it. To accomplish this, Microsoft created a status page for each running workflow instance. It provides links to do all of the things mentioned here, as well as view a log of the workflow history.

Microsoft ships one workflow with WSS 3.0 (Three-state) and another four with MOSS (Approval, Collect Feedback, Collect Signatures, and Disposition Approval).

Architecture

Earlier, you looked at the overall architecture of WF and what is needed to create and execute workflow instances within a .NET application. Specifically, the workflow runtime must be hosted by a .NET application and either utilize the out-of-the-box WF services or register custom implementations of its services. SharePoint meets these needs by acting as the hosting application for the workflow runtime. This saves developers the work of creating an instance and hosting the runtime within their custom code written for SharePoint — an added value to core workflow development.

SharePoint also handles customization of the runtime services. For example, SharePoint contains its own persistence service, `SPWinOePersistanceService`, which tells the workflow runtime to persist workflows that are not currently running to the current SharePoint site's content database instead of some external database. This is similar to the Web Part Framework implementation in SharePoint whereby the Web Part personalization data is stored within the content databases instead of an external database, as in a traditional ASP.NET 2.0 site. This is a fantastic demonstration of how pluggable and extensible the WF architecture really is!

Microsoft also adds a handful of SharePoint-specific activities to the WF. These activities are primarily used to interact with tasks created by the workflow (more on tasks in the "History and Task Lists" section) or to interact with SharePoint directly from the workflow program. For example, one activity, `SendEmail`, does not require the developer to provide the e-mail server or logon credentials to send e-mail messages. This information is automatically pulled from the Web application containing the site collection that contains the list the workflow template has been associated with.

Terminology

Before going too much further into SharePoint's implementation of the WF it is important to grasp a few concepts that are specific to SharePoint workflows. However, it helps to first review how traditional .NET applications utilize the WF. A .NET application hosts the workflow runtime. Developers can then build workflow programs that are created as new instances in the hosted workflow runtime and started. Because SharePoint adds a significant human element to workflow, Microsoft's implementation of the WF in SharePoint is a little different.

First, developers create a new workflows as a *workflow template*. These workflow templates are essentially the same as the workflow programs created for standard .NET applications. However, instead of creating workflow instances based on the template, SharePoint adds a layer of abstraction. Recall that SharePoint workflows are associated with items and documents within SharePoint lists and libraries; workflows running within the context of SharePoint must be tied to a list item or document. Workflow templates are installed and registered in a SharePoint site collection using site collection–scoped Features.

Once a workflow template has been installed and registered within a site collection, someone with the necessary permissions can then go into the settings for a list and create a *workflow association*. The workflow association is a named link that pairs the workflow template with a specific list, as shown in Figure 12-2. Associations also contain some parameters that are specific to the particular link. For instance, an administrator can specify whether the workflow can be started automatically when items are added or updated in a list or library or whether the workflow can be started manually. Developers can optionally create a special kind of form that the user creating the association must complete to provide information required by the workflow at the time of association.

Note that a workflow template can be associated with a SharePoint list multiple times because each association is seen as a separate entity in SharePoint. What makes the associations different is defined by the name given to the association, as well as the extra data collected by a custom form. Workflow associations are not exclusively tied to SharePoint lists. They can also be associated with SharePoint content types, enabling the workflow association to travel with the content type wherever it is used throughout the site collection.

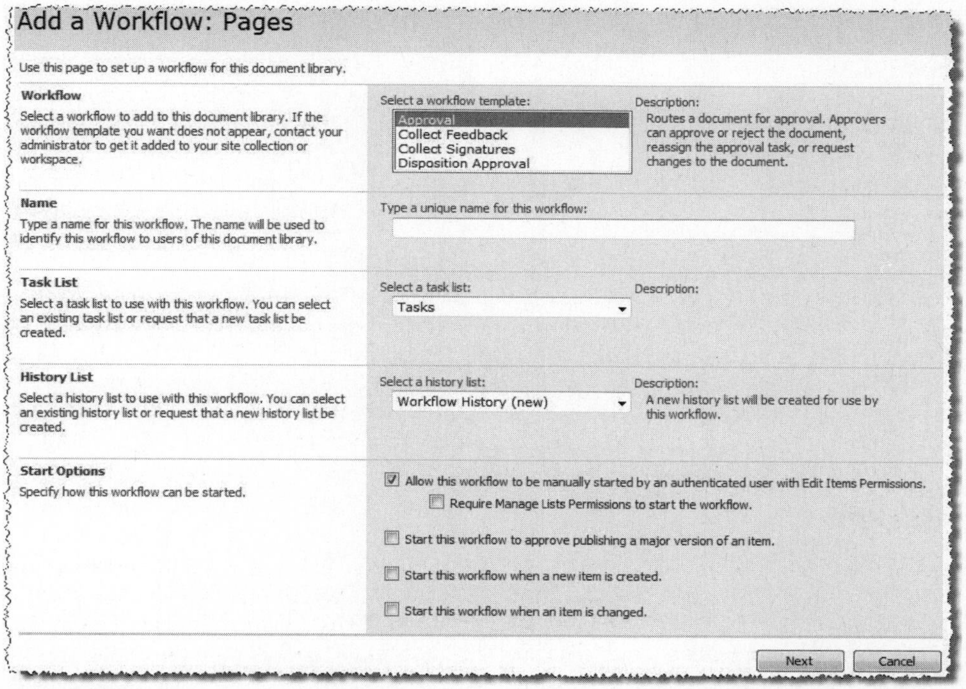

Figure 12-2

With the workflow template associated with a particular list, users can then start workflows (depending on the configuration options selected during the association) on specific items and documents within SharePoint lists and libraries. These running workflows are referred to as *workflow instances*. An item or document in SharePoint can have any number of workflow instances running at any given time.

History and Task Lists

One way SharePoint adds the human element to the WF is by heavily utilizing tasks. Because workflows are exclusively tied to specific list items and documents in SharePoint, users are generally going to assign tasks to someone as part of the workflow. While not required, it is by far one of the most common aspects for all workflows developed for use within SharePoint. Because SharePoint workflows make heavy use of tasks and even include special activities for interacting with tasks, one of the steps in associating a workflow template with a list is to specify the SharePoint task list where tasks will be created. If a task list does not exist when the workflow association is created, SharePoint automatically creates one. Now, when developers use the task-based activities within a workflow template, they don't have to worry about specifying the site or task list in which the tasks should be created. SharePoint handles this by saving that information as part of the association.

Another human element to SharePoint workflows is the history list. The history list gives developers a way to log information from the workflow that users can read to monitor the status and state of the workflow. This history information is shown on the workflow status page, another thing specific to the SharePoint implementation of workflow. Figure 12-3 shows an example of a SharePoint status page. One of the activities added to the WF by SharePoint is the LogToHistoryListActivity. This activity enables developers to write an outcome and description of a log message to the history. If a history list does not exist when creating the workflow association, SharePoint automatically creates it.

Workflow Status:

Workflow Information

Initiator:	MOSS2007\administrator		Document:	default
Started:	12/31/2007 12:34 AM		Status:	In Progress
Last run:	12/31/2007 12:34 AM			

If an error occurs or this workflow stops responding, it can be terminated. Terminating the workflow will set its status to Canceled and
▪ Terminate this workflow now.

Tasks

The following tasks have been assigned to the participants in this workflow. Click a task to edit it. You can also view these tasks in the list Workflow Tasks.

☐ Assigned To	Title	Due Date
	Approval requested for Press Releases ! NEW	1/7/2008
	Approval requested for Press Releases ! NEW	1/7/2008

Workflow History

The following events have occurred in this workflow.

Date Occurred	Event Type	☐ User ID	Description
12/31/2007 12:34 AM	Comment	System Account	Approval task created and assigned to users 'johndoe' and 'janedoe'. Both task due dates are set for 12:00:00 AM. The tasks contained the following instructions: Please review this page and approve.

Figure 12-3

Interacting with Users with Forms

What may be the biggest human element and value-added aspect of SharePoint within the context of the WF is the concept of adding forms to workflows. Developers are free to create workflow input forms that administrators can use when associating the workflow template with a list (*workflow association form*) or to modify a workflow instance when it is running (*workflow modification form*), a special form users are presented with when the workflow is started on a list item or document (*workflow initiation form*), and another form users are presented with when working with tasks created by the workflow (*workflow task form*), replacing the out-of-the-box task edit form. Not all forms are required and developers are free to implement none or multiple.

Note that if a workflow association is configured to start automatically when an item in the list or library is created or changed, the workflow initiation form is not displayed. The workflow initiation form is only shown when the workflow is started manually. Therefore, it is recommended to always create a workflow association form if the workflow template contains a workflow initiation form. The workflow association form should collect default information that the initiation form also collects so that even if the workflow is started automatically, the workflow template will still have the required information.

Developers have two options in creating workflow forms: ASP.NET 2.0 pages and InfoPath 2007 forms. Workflow forms created as ASP.NET 2.0 pages should be created as application pages that are deployed to a subfolder in the `[..]\12\TEMPLATE\LAYOUTS` folder and inherit the `LayoutsPageBase` class. Creating custom application pages is covered in detail in Chapter 2, "Windows SharePoint Server 3.0 Development Primer." ASP.NET 2.0 forms used in workflows must manually handle the serialization and deserialization of data from the form back to SharePoint from the page's code-behind. In addition, the workflow association form must also handle the case when the task list and workflow history list need to be created. That is, it must create those lists.

Using ASP.NET 2.0 pages for SharePoint workflows requires the developer to write a fair amount of custom code. One advantage of using ASP.NET 2.0 forms is that it enables the workflow to be used in any version of SharePoint derived from WSS 3.0, including MOSS 2007. However, the amount of custom code that needs to be written is an obvious disadvantage to using ASP.NET 2.0 pages as SharePoint workflow forms.

The other option is to create the workflow forms using Office InfoPath 2007. These forms are rendered in the browser using the MOSS 2007 Forms Services component. While Forms Services is only available for general use in MOSS 2007 Enterprise Edition, if the forms are used in the context of a SharePoint workflow form, they can be used in MOSS 2007 Standard as well without breaking Microsoft's licensing policies.

> *It is critical to understand this distinction: Only InfoPath 2007 forms used as SharePoint workflow forms can be used in any version of MOSS 2007, but if the InfoPath form is rendered in the browser for any other purpose, the MOSS 2007 Enterprise license is required.*

When InfoPath forms are used in SharePoint workflows, they are rendered in the browser and hosted within special ASP.NET 2.0 pages provided by Microsoft as part of the MOSS 2007 installation. There are many advantages to using InfoPath forms in SharePoint workflows. First, InfoPath forms require significantly less code than ASP.NET 2.0 forms. This is because SharePoint knows how to handle the serialization and deserialization of the data between the InfoPath form and SharePoint. This includes the creation of the task and history lists, as SharePoint handles this for the developer.

Second, compared to ASP.NET 2.0 pages, InfoPath forms can be constructed very quickly using the Office InfoPath 2007 client. InfoPath 2007 provides a rich design experience for developers.

Third, if users interacting with the workflow are using the Office 2007 clients, the clients can render the form without opening a browser. For instance, if a task is created and assigned to a user, that user is sent an e-mail notifying them of the assigned task. The user can then, from within Outlook 2007, interact with the workflow task form and complete the task — all without leaving Outlook 2007!

Because the focus of this book is MOSS 2007 Web Content Management and Publishing sites, only InfoPath 2007 forms are covered in detail; ASP.NET 2.0 pages used as workflow forms are omitted. When developing workflows exclusively for use in Publishing sites, it is recommended that you use InfoPath 2007 as the workflow forms technology.

> *For more information on using ASP.NET 2.0 pages in SharePoint workflow forms, the following books are recommended:* Inside Windows SharePoint Services 3.0 by Ted Pattison and Dan Larson *(Microsoft Press, 2007) and* Workflow in the 2007 Microsoft Office System *by David Mann (Apress, 2007).*

Workflow in SharePoint Publishing Sites

The site template Publishing Portal creates a new MOSS 2007 Web Content Management Publishing site. This is the common starting place most developers use when creating new Publishing sites. This template creates a new site and subsite (Press Releases) using the template *Publishing Site with Workflow*. This template is essentially an exact copy of a similar template, *Publishing Site*. The primary differences are that the *Publishing Site with Workflow* template simply turns on content approval for the Pages list and adds content scheduling.

It is the Feature receiver defined within the Publishing Feature that creates a workflow named *Parallel Approvers* that associates the *Approval* workflow template with the *Pages* list in Publishing sites.

Overview of the Parallel Approvers Workflow

The Parallel Approvers workflow association created on all Pages lists in a Publishing site when using the Publishing Portal site template forces all pages to go through an approval process before publishing the page. The workflow association dictates that the Approvers SharePoint group is assigned the task of approving the page. When the page is submitted for approval, a task is created and assigned to the Approvers SharePoint group. Someone from that group must then either approve or reject the page. When the page is approved, the content approval flag on the list item is set to Approved, which increments the version of the page to the next major whole number version, making the page published.

The Approval workflow template, added to the site collection from the Routing Workflows Feature (Feature ID 02464c6a-9d07-4f30-ba04-e9035cf54392 found in [..]\12\TEMPLATE\FEATURES\ ReviewWorkflows), contains a few InfoPath forms. One form is used as the workflow association form, another is used for the workflow initiation form, and a handful of other forms are used as the workflow modification forms and the workflow task forms.

Creating Custom Workflows for SharePoint Publishing Sites

While the Approval workflow template is very useful within Publishing sites, at times business requirements dictate a more complex solution than what is provided in MOSS 2007. In these cases, developers are free to create custom workflow templates for use within Publishing sites. Developers have two options when it comes to creating workflows in SharePoint sites (not just Publishing sites): creating workflows using Office SharePoint Designer (SPD) 2007 or Visual Studio 2005/2008. Each tool has advantages and disadvantages associated with it.

Creating Workflows with SharePoint Designer

As far as workflow development is concerned, SPD is targeted to information workers or those creating simple, one-off workflows. Workflows created with SPD are not templates; they are associated with a SharePoint list at design time. The first thing the user must do when creating a new workflow in SPD is to select the list it is associated with. SPD doesn't provide a way to either save the workflow to another list or copy it for use in another list. The workflow wizard SPD is very much like the Rules wizard Outlook offers when creating rules for e-mail. While workflows can be created fairly quickly and easily, in many ways they are limited when compared to those created using Visual Studio.

Workflows created in SPD are bound to a specific list at design time. This means that the workflows cannot be duplicated without manually repeating the same steps on another list or in another environment. In addition, SPD is limited to creating only sequential workflows; it cannot create state machine workflows. If users have trouble with the workflow, the only troubleshooting option is to monitor the inputs and outputs of the workflow, as SPD workflows are black boxes. This is very different from Visual Studio, which permits granular debugging by setting breakpoints and stepping through code. Two other important distinctions of SPD-created workflows is that they can only utilize ASP.NET 2.0 pages for workflow forms and they do not support any custom code.

SPD is not nearly as powerful as a workflow development environment as Visual Studio. The vast majority of workflows created for use in Publishing sites are built using Visual Studio. The rest of this chapter covers how to create workflows using Visual Studio, rather than SPD.

Creating Workflows with Visual Studio

Custom workflow templates can be created using either Visual Studio 2005 or Visual Studio 2008. The majority of the workflow development story is the same in Visual Studio 2008 as it is in Visual Studio 2005, but there are a few subtle differences. The steps and figures in this chapter demonstrate the process of creating workflows using Visual Studio 2008, but it is not reasonable to assume that everyone will be able to start using Visual Studio 2008 in their environment at the time this book is published. Therefore, any differences between the two versions are noted.

Neither version of Visual Studio has the limitations of SPD. For instance, developers are free to create either sequential or state machine workflows, as well as add custom code in a code-behind model similar to ASP.NET 2.0 pages. Visual Studio also provides a rich debugging experience for developers to troubleshoot defects in a custom workflow by setting breakpoints and watches, and stepping through code line by line. Workflows created using Visual Studio can also leverage either ASP.NET 2.0 pages or InfoPath 2007 forms as the workflow forms technology.

The biggest advantage to creating workflows with Visual Studio over SPD is that workflows developed with Visual Studio are templates that can be easily deployed to multiple sites or environments.

Required Components

In order to create workflows using Visual Studio 2005, developers need a few things. First, the .NET Framework 3.0 must be installed to provide the workflow runtime. Next, the Visual Studio extensions for Windows Workflow Foundation (VSeWWF) need to be downloaded and installed (`www.microsoft.com/downloads`). This adds the workflow designer and debugging capabilities, and add activities from the base activity library to the Visual Studio Toolbox.

At this point, developers can create the simplest workflows for the WF, but not within a SharePoint environment. The next step is to download and install the WSS 3.0 SDK (`www.andrewconnell/go/245`) and/or the MOSS 2007 SDK (`www.andrewconnell.com/go/246`). The two SDKs do a few things. First, they add SharePoint-specific activities to the Visual Studio Toolbox. They each also add two new project templates: one for creating sequential workflows for SharePoint sites and another for creating state machine workflows for SharePoint sites. Note that each SDK installs two templates each. The WSS 3.0 SDK project templates assume that ASP.NET 2.0 pages will be used for the workflow forms technology, whereas the MOSS 2007 SDK project templates assume that InfoPath 2007 forms will be used.

How is the Visual Studio 2008 experience different? Visual Studio 2008 was released in November 2007, well after the release of the .NET Framework 3.0 and WSS 3.0/MOSS 2007. This timeline enabled the Visual Studio team — specifically, the Visual Studio Tools for Office (VSTO) team — to include the necessary components and project templates into the most recent release. This means that developers only need to install Visual Studio 2008; they do not need to install anything else such as the VSeWWF extensions or the SharePoint SDKs.

Creating the Dual Approvers Workflow

Enough talk about the WF, workflow in SharePoint, and the different options developers have to create workflows! It is time to create something. The rest of the chapter demonstrates how to create a workflow that requires two people to approve a publishing request for a new page to be posted on a SharePoint site. The steps outlined assume that the developer is using Visual Studio 2008. However, extra notes are included when the experience or steps are dramatically different from Visual Studio 2008.

> *The primary difference between Visual Studio 2005 and Visual Studio 2008 is the testing experience. In Visual Studio 2005, the developer needs to manually deploy the workflow using a site-collection-scoped Feature (optionally using a WSS solution package or by copying the files into the necessary locations), manually install and activate the Feature, and then create the workflow association on a SharePoint list or document library to test it. Visual Studio 2008 gives developers the option to allow the IDE to do this for them. Regardless of the version used, developers need to package the workflow for deployment for use in production (or the central build server, staging server, etc.). Visual Studio 2008 just speeds up this process a bit.*

Create a new Visual Studio 2008 project using the SharePoint 2007 Sequential Workflow project template found under `Visual C#\Office\2007`, as shown in Figure 12-4. This project template is only visible when the .NET Framework 3.5 is targeted.

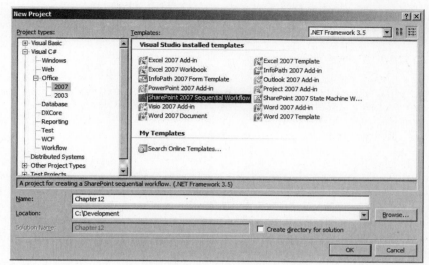

Figure 12-4

Set the name of the workflow to `Chapter12DualApprovers` and specify the URL of a local site to use in debugging to a Publishing site URL (e.g., `http://wcm/PressReleases`). In the next dialog, leave the Automatically Associate Workflow box checked to enable Visual Studio to create the workflow association automatically when F5 is pressed. Set the list to test the workflow to Pages and leave the history and task lists to the default values. Finally, set the configuration when the workflow should start. When testing within a Publishing site many people find it easy to only start the workflows manually.

Visual Studio 2005 Experience

Creating a new workflow project in Visual Studio 2005 involves fewer steps because it doesn't have the capability to handle creating the workflow association automatically. The project template to use in Visual Studio 2005 is the SharePoint Server Sequential Workflow, which is found under `Visual C#\SharePoint`.

The workflow project created in this chapter, like all the other chapters, is available in the download associated with this book from the publisher's Web site. Also implemented with this project is the approach of using MSBuild to package the workflow into a WSS solution package automatically with each project build for easy deployment. Unfortunately, the Visual Studio 2008 project expects the `feature.xml` *definition to be at the root of the project in order for the F5 debugging technique to work. For the sake of consistency, the downloadable project matches the others in terms of structure and therefore will not work with the F5 debugging capability offered in Visual Studio 2008.*

After creating the workflow, an optional step is to rename the `Workflow1` class to a more meaningful name. In this case, rename the workflow to `DualApprovers.cs`. This will likely cause some validation errors. Search the partial class `DualApprovers.Design.cs` for instances of `Workflow1` (even string references) and change them to `DualApprovers`. In addition, change the namespace in both the `DualApprovers.cs` and `DualApprovers.Design.cs` files to `WROX.ProMossWcm.Chapter12`:

```
namespace WROX.ProMossWcm.Chapter12 {
   public sealed partial class DualApprovers : SequentialWorkflowActivity {
      // existing code
   }
}
```

With the project now created, the next step is to model the workflow in the designer.

Modeling the Workflow Template

After creating the project, modeling the workflow is the best approach to make sure everything is well planned out. This is similar to using a modeling tool such as Office Visio 2007. The process of modeling the workflow involves dropping activities from the Toolbox onto the design surface. In addition to modeling the workflow, properties and correlation tokens should be created and set because it simplifies the process of adding code later. New workflows based on one of the SharePoint project templates start with the `OnWorkflowActivated` activity. This is how SharePoint initiates the workflow. The first thing the workflow will do is create two tasks, one for each person who needs to approve the page submitted for publishing.

Add a `Parallel` activity and two `CreateTask` activities within each branch, naming them `createAlphaTask` and `createBetaTask`. The `Parallel` activity will force all activities within it to complete before proceeding. Notice how both the `CreateTask` activities have a little red error icon in the upper right-hand corner. This is because they have no correlation tokens set. Correlation tokens enable workflows to create multiple tasks and keep related activities associated with specific tasks. Create a correlation token for each task (`aphaTaskToken` and `betaTaskToken`) by simply typing it into the `CorrelationToken` property in the Properties tool window. This will not eliminate the error, however, because correlation tokens also need owner activities. Set the owner activity for each activity to the name of the workflow class.

There is one more thing to do: set the `TaskID` and `TaskProperties` properties. The former is used to give the task a unique ID that can be used later in the workflow, and the latter enables the workflow to set specific values on the task that will be created. Click the builder button, the one with the ellipse, next to the `TaskID` property of the `createAlphaTask` activity to bring up the property binder. This dialog gives the developer a chance to create new public fields or properties in the workflow class and bind it to a property on the activity. Click the Bind to a New Member tab, enter the name `alphaTaskID`, and select the radio button Create Field. Fields should be chosen over properties because the data in a public field will be persisted to the content database. Do the same thing for the `TaskProperties` property on the `createAlphaTask`.

The workflow should now look like Figure 12-5.

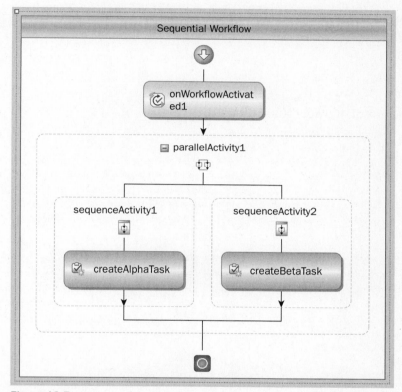

Figure 12-5

With the tasks created, the workflow should provide a little feedback by writing to the history list. Drag a `LogToHistoryListActivity` after the `Parallel` activity and the properties `HistoryOutcome` and `HistoryDescription`, the same way the `TaskID` property was set previously.

Now the workflow should go to sleep and wait for the two tasks to be completed. Add another `Parallel` activity and drop two `OnTaskChanged` activities onto it. Associate one of the `OnTaskChanged` activities to the alpha task by selecting the `alphaTaskToken` on one correlation token and the `betaTaskToken` on the other correlation token.

Also bind the previously created fields `alphaTaskID` and `betaTaskID` to the `TaskID` properties on each activity. Because the workflow needs to get values from the task after it has been modified, the code needs to get the values back from the `AfterTaskProperties` property on each `OnTaskChanged` activity. The `AfterTaskProperties` contains a snapshot of the task's properties after it has been changed. The `BeforeTaskProperties` contains a snapshot of the task's properties before it was changed.

Create two new fields (`alphaTaskAfterProperties` and `betaTaskAfterProperties`) and bind them to the `TaskAfterProperties` on the associated `OnTaskChanged` activity. After renaming the `OnTaskChanged` activities, the workflow should now look like Figure 12-6.

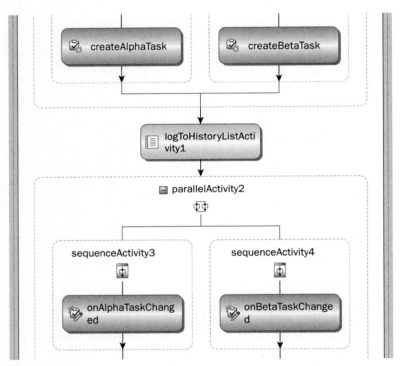

Figure 12-6

Finally, approve or deny the publishing request depending on the responses of the two tasks. Add an `IfElse` activity that contains two `Code` activities, one for each branch. Name these two `Code` activities `approveCodeActivity` and `denyCodeActivity`. Don't worry about the issues on these last three activities, as they can only be addressed by adding custom code, which will be handled later. The final workflow should look like Figure 12-7.

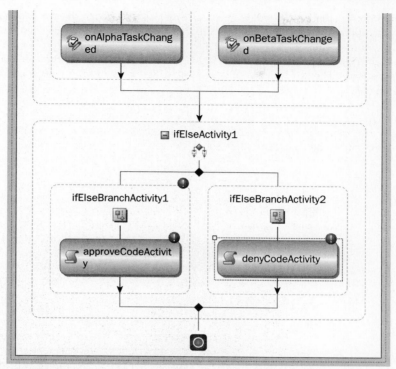

Figure 12-7

With the workflow modeled and fields bound to the various activity properties, the next step is to create the forms.

Creating the Workflow InfoPath Forms

The workflow needs some extra information passed into it from the user initiating it. Specifically, it needs to know which two users will be assigned the tasks. In addition, it would be nice to collect some instructions from the person initiating the workflow to display to the two people who will be assigned the approval or denial tasks. The two users should also have the ability to enter some comments when approving or denying the task.

To satisfy these requirements, it makes the most sense to create a few forms. This workflow needs an initiation form and a task edit form. It should also have an association form to collect some default data for the initiation form in case the workflow is configured to start automatically, but in this case it will be omitted.

First create the initiation form. In InfoPath 2007, create a new form by selecting Design a Form Template in the Getting Started dialog. In the Design a Form Template dialog, select Form Template, Based on: Blank and check the option Enable Browser-Compatible Features Only. The first thing to do when creating an InfoPath form is to define the data structure of the form. This is done by selecting Data Source in the task pane on the right-hand side of InfoPath. Right-click the `myFields` node . . . properties and rename it to `InitForm`. Create a new field by right-clicking `InitForm` and selecting Add. Set the

Chapter 12: Leveraging Workflow

Name to `alphaApprover`, the Type to `Field` (element), and the Data Type to `Text` (string); and Cannot Be Blank (*) should be checked. Repeat these steps for the beta approver field (`betaApprover`) as well.

Next, create the layout for the form. The quick way to do this is to right-click the `InitForm` node in the Data Source task pane and select Controls. Add a button control and then rearrange the form to make it look something like the layout shown in Figure 12-8.

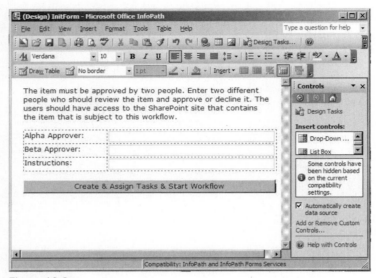

Figure 12-8

Now it is time to add some logic to the form. Right-click the button control and select Button Properties. Then select Click Rules ⇨ Add. On the Rule dialog, click Add Action. On the Action dialog, select Action: Submit Using a Data Connection, and then click Add. On the Data Connection Wizard, select Create a New Connection To: Submit Data and click Next. Then select To the Hosted Environment, such as an ASP.NET Page or Hosting Application, followed by Next and Finish. Click Add Action ⇨ Close the Form and click OK. Finally, click OK out of the dialogs.

The last thing to do is configure the security on the form so it can run within SharePoint. Select Tools ⇨ Form Options. In the Category for Security and Trust, uncheck Automatically Determine Security Level and select Domain, followed by OK. Save the form to a new folder in the Visual Studio project named `Forms_Design`. This retains the designed form for future updates. This is not the form that will be used in the workflow.

Publish the form by selecting File ⇨ Publish. In the Publishing Wizard, select To a Network Location and click Next. Browse to a new folder in the Visual Studio project named `Forms`. This is the form that will be used by the workflow. When prompted for a place to publish the form, use a different path than where the designed form was saved. It is recommended to publish forms to a subfolder named `Forms` within the Feature that will be used to add the workflow template to a site collection. When prompted by the wizard to enter the Alternate Access Path, clear the value and click Next. Ignore the warning InfoPath may display; if the warning does not appear, then the security was not set to Domain. Finally, select Publish. Include the new files in the Visual Studio project so that the project looks something like Figure 12-9.

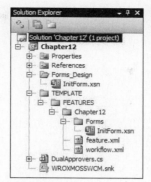

Figure 12-9

The data collected in the `InitForm` will be passed from InfoPath into the workflow by SharePoint and Forms Services. The data is passed into the workflow as XML. Because the XML conforms to the schema defined in the form, the data can be deserialized into a class to make it easier to work with. To do this, the schema needs to be extracted from the form, and the `xsd.exe` tool provided in the .NET Framework SDK is used to generate the class file. To extract the schema, select File ⇨ Save as Source Files (with the form open in Design mode in InfoPath). Save the source files to the `Forms_Design` folder the form was originally saved to. Rename the `myschema.xsd` file to `InitFormSchema.xsd`. To create the class that will be used in the project, open a Visual Studio 2008 Command Prompt window and enter the following command:

```
xsd.exe [path to /InitFormSchema.xsd]/InitFormSchema.xsd /c
```

Add the generated `InitFormSchema.cs` file to the root of the Chapter12 project open in Visual Studio. Add the `InitForm` class in the `InitFromSchema.cs` file to the same namespace as the workflow in Listing 12-1.

Listing 12-1: Adding the InitFormSchema-generated class to the project namespace

```
using System.Xml.Serialization;

//
// This source code was auto-generated by xsd, Version=2.0.50727.1432.
//

namespace WROX.ProMossWcm.Chapter12 {

    /// <remarks/>
    [System.CodeDom.Compiler.GeneratedCodeAttribute("xsd", "2.0.50727.1432")]
    [System.SerializableAttribute()]
    [System.Diagnostics.DebuggerStepThroughAttribute()]
    [System.ComponentModel.DesignerCategoryAttribute("code")]
    [System.Xml.Serialization.XmlTypeAttribute(AnonymousType = true, Namespace =
"http://schemas.microsoft.com/office/infopath/2003/myXSD/2007-12-30T05:14:38")]
    [System.Xml.Serialization.XmlRootAttribute(Namespace =
"http://schemas.microsoft.com/office/infopath/2003/myXSD/2007-12-30T05:14:38",
IsNullable = false)]
```

(continued)

Listing 12-1 *(continued)*

```
public partial class InitForm {
// existing generated code
}
```

```
}
```

Now the task edit form needs to be created. Go back to InfoPath 2007 and create a new form the same way the `InitForm` was created. Rename the `myFields` node to `TaskForm` and add three fields to the schema of the new file as shown in the following table.

Name	Type	Data Type	Cannot be Blank
Instructions	Field (element)	Text (string)	checked
Comments	Field (element)	Text (string)	checked
Decision	Field (element)	Text (string)	checked

Next, design the form as shown in Figure 12-10.

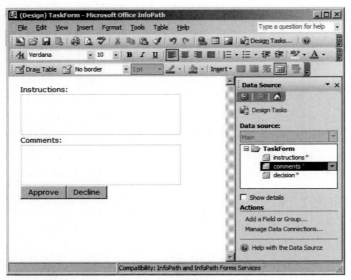

Figure 12-10

Unlike the initialization form, the task form needs some extra work in order for SharePoint to pass data back to it. This is because the form cannot know about any changes to the task list that may occur after development. This is done with an XML file named `ItemMetadata.xml`. Within Visual Studio, create the new `ItemMetadata.xml` file at the root of the project and add the following XML to it:

```
<?xml version="1.0" encoding="utf-8" ?>
<z:row xmlns:z="#RowsetSchema" ows_instructions="" />
```

Notice the field prefixed with ows_. This is the field used in the form that needs to be passed in by SharePoint. Now that the XML file is created, it needs to be added to the task form as a new data source. Jump back to InfoPath 2007 and select Tools ⇨ Data Connections ⇨ Add. Select Create a New Connection to: Receive Data and click Next. Specify that the form should receive data from an XML document and select Next. Click Resource Files ⇨ Add and then browse to and select the XML file. Select OK and Next to exit the wizard, accepting all the defaults.

With the data source created, the form needs to be configured to pull the instructions from the XML file and insert them into the field in the form. Right-click the instructions textbox and select Properties. Click the function button (shown in Figure 12-11) to the right of the Value textbox in the Default Value section.

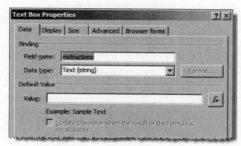

Figure 12-11

Click the Insert Field or Group, change the Data Source to ItemMetadata (Secondary), select :ows_instructions, and then OK to exit the dialog. From the Text Box Properties on the Display tab, check the Read-only checkbox, as those who are assigned the task should not be able to change the instructions.

Now some logic needs to be added to the two buttons. Each button will set the value of the decision field to approved or rejected and submit the data back to SharePoint. Right-click the Approve button and select Button Properties. Click Rules ⇨ Add ⇨ Add Action. Select the Action: to Set a Field's Value, pick the decision field from the Main data source, and click OK. In the Value textbox, type **approve** and click OK. Click Add Action on the Action dialog, and select Action: Submit Using a Data Connection ⇨ Add. From the Data Connection Wizard, select Create a New Connection To: Submit Data and click Next. Then select To the Hosting Environment, such as an ASP.NET Page or Hosting Application, and click Next followed by Finish. Now select Add Action ⇨ Close the Form and click OK to exit the dialogs. Repeat the same steps with the Decline button, setting the value of the decision field to decline.

Like the initialization form, set the security of the form to Domain by selecting Tools ⇨ Form Options ⇨ Security and Trust panel. Save the form to the Forms_Design folder as TaskForm.xsn. Then Publish the form using the same steps as the initialization form, making sure the alternate access textbox is cleared, to the Forms folder in the Feature.

Now both forms have been created and published for use in SharePoint and the workflow. The next step is to write the necessary code in the workflow to get the data back from the forms and perform all other custom coding tasks, such as setting field values and approving or declining the page.

Adding Code to the Workflow Template

With the workflow modeled, properties bound to fields, and the forms created, the next step is to add custom code that will perform all the business logic necessary in the workflow. Switch back over to Visual Studio, right-click the `onWorkflowActivitated1` activity, and select Generate Handlers. Within this method, add the code that will deserialize the data from the initialization form passed by SharePoint to the workflow through the `workflowProperties.InitializationData` property. Using the previously created class from the form's schema file, this task will be much easier. However, you first need to create a few class-scoped private fields that will be used to store the values from the form. Add the following fields to the class:

```
private string _instructions = default(string);
private string _alphaApprover = default(string);
private string _betaApprover = default(string);

private void onWorkflowActivated1_Invoked (object sender, ExternalDataEventArgs
e) {
}
```

Now add two `using` statements to the top of the class file for the namespaces `System.Xml` and `System.Xml.Serialization`, and then add the code in Listing 12-2 to the `onWorkflowActivated_Invoked()` method to pull the data submitted by the initialization form out of SharePoint and set the values of the local fields.

Listing 12-2: onWorkflowActivated1_Invoked() Method

```
private void onWorkflowActivated_Invoked (object sender, ExternalDataEventArgs e) {

    // load the data from the IP form 'InitForm' into a local object
    XmlSerializer serializer = new XmlSerializer(typeof(InitForm));
    XmlTextReader xrInitForm = new XmlTextReader(new
System.IO.StringReader(workflowProperties.InitiationData));
    InitForm frmInit = serializer.Deserialize(xrInitForm) as InitForm;

    // get approvers submitted
    this._alphaApprover = frmInit.alphaApprover;
    this._betaApprover = frmInit.betaApprover;

    // get instructions
    this._instructions = frmInit.instructions;
}
```

This code could be a bit more robust in confirming that the user is a valid user in the current site, but for the sake of brevity that step is omitted. The code also assumes that the user initiating the workflow is entering a fully qualified account name, such as DOMAIN\johndoe. Note also the highlighted lines in Listing 12-2. These four lines are deserializing the data provided by the initialization form into the class created using the XSD.EXE tool and the schema file from the initialization form.

The next step is to create the two tasks and assign them to the two users entered in the initialization form. The two tasks are created by the `CreateTask` activities. These activities have bound properties to fields in the workflow class. Because the handler method in action activities is executed before the activity, this is the best place to set values on the fields used to create the tasks. Right-click the activity `createAlphaTask` and select Generate Handlers, adding the code in Listing 12-3 to initialize the `alphaTaskID` and `alphaTaskProperties`.

Listing 12-3: createAlphaTask_MethodInvoking() Method

```
private void createAlphaTask_MethodInvoking (object sender, EventArgs e) {
   this.alphaTaskId = Guid.NewGuid();

   this.alphaTaskProperties.Title = "Approval requested for " +
workflowProperties.Item.Title;
   this.alphaTaskProperties.Description = "Please review the item, then approve or
reject it.";
   this.alphaTaskProperties.AssignedTo = this._alphaApprover;
   this.alphaTaskProperties.PercentComplete = 0;
   this.alphaTaskProperties.StartDate = DateTime.Today;
   this.alphaTaskProperties.DueDate = DateTime.Today.AddDays(7);
   this.alphaTaskProperties.ExtendedProperties["instructions"] = this._instructions;
}
```

Do the same thing for the `createBetaTask` activity, substituting the appropriate fields, as shown in Listing 12-4.

Listing 12-4: createBetaTask_MethodInvoking() Method

```
private void createBetaTask_MethodInvoking (object sender, EventArgs e) {
   this.betaTaskId = Guid.NewGuid();

   this.betaTaskProperties.Title = "Approval requested for " +
workflowProperties.Item.Title;
   this.betaTaskProperties.Description = "Please review the item, then approve or
reject it.";
   this.betaTaskProperties.AssignedTo = this._betaApprover;
   this.betaTaskProperties.PercentComplete = 0;
   this.betaTaskProperties.StartDate = DateTime.Today;
   this.betaTaskProperties.DueDate = DateTime.Today.AddDays(7);
   this.betaTaskProperties.ExtendedProperties["instructions"] = this._instructions;
}
```

With the tasks created, the next step in the workflow is to write some information to the history list so the user can see that the two tasks were created. Create a handler for the `logToHistoryListActivity1` activity and set the values of the history outcome and description by adding the code in Listing 12-5 to the handler.

Listing 12-5: logToHistoryListActivity1_MethodInvoking() Method

```
private void logToHistoryListActivity1_MethodInvoking (object sender, EventArgs e)
{
  this.HistoryOutcome = string.Format("Tasks created and assigned to '{0}' and
'{1}'.",
                        this._alphaApprover,
                        this._betaApprover);
  this.HistoryDescription = string.Format("Approval task created and assigned to
users '{0}' and '{1}'. Both task due dates are set for {2}. The tasks contained the
following instructions: {3}",
                        this._alphaApprover,
                        this._betaApprover,
                        DateTime.Today.AddDays(7),
                        this._instructions);
}
```

Now that the tasks have been created and an entry has been added to the history log, the workflow should go to sleep and wait for both tasks to be updated. The two OnTaskChanged activities are used for this purpose. However, before adding the necessary logic for these activities, create an enumeration to help determine the result of each task, as shown in Listing 12-6.

Listing 12-6: ApprovalDecision enumeration

```
using System;

namespace WROX.ProMossWcm.Chapter12 {
  public enum ApprovalDecision {
    Approved,
    Rejected,
    NoAnswer
  }
}
```

Next, a few class-scoped fields are needed to retain the answers of the tasks. In addition, add the handler for the onAlphaTaskChanged activity and pull the values from the task and save them locally into these fields, as shown in Listing 12-7. Keep in mind that the handlers for event-driven activities such as the OnTaskChanged activity are run after the activity is executed. This means that when the code runs, the local fields bound to the properties on the activity (such as AfterTaskProperties) will already be set so they can be referenced in the handler.

Listing 12-7: Code to acquire the values from the Alpha Task

```
private ApprovalDecision alphaTaskAnswer = ApprovalDecision.NoAnswer;
private ApprovalDecision betaTaskAnswer = ApprovalDecision.NoAnswer;

private void onAlphaTaskChanged_Invoked (object sender, ExternalDataEventArgs e) {
  // check if the task was approved
  string taskResult =
this.alphaTaskAfterProperties.ExtendedProperties["decision"].ToString();

  if (taskResult.ToLower() == "approve")
    this.alphaTaskAnswer = ApprovalDecision.Approved;
```

```
    else
       this.alphaTaskAnswer = ApprovalDecision.Rejected;
}
```

Add similar code in the highlighted method in Listing 12-7 for the `onBetaTaskChanged` activity handler.

At this point, everything has been handled except for the final piece: determining whether the two users assigned to the approval tasks either approved or rejected the page subject to the workflow. This is handled in the last portion: the `IfElse` and two `Code` activities. Conditional activities such as the `IfElse` have a `Condition` property that, depending on the Boolean result, determines the path to take. There are two types of Conditions:

❑ **Code Condition** — This requires a method that returns a Boolean value.

❑ **Declarative Rule Condition** — This creates a named rule based on properties, fields, or methods in the current class.

For the condition in the Dual Approvers workflow, select the if-else branch for the `approvalCodeActivity` activity and set the `Condition` property to `Declarative Rule Condition`, as shown in Figure 12-12.

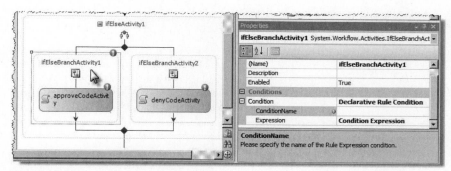

Figure 12-12

Now click the builder on the `ConditionName` property nested under `Condition` to bring up the Select Condition dialog. Click New and enter the following into the available field to determine whether both tasks were approved, because any other result should cause the publishing request to be rejected:

```
this.alphaTaskAnswer == ApprovalDecision.Approved && this.betaTaskAnswer ==
ApprovalDecision.Approved
```

Rename the condition to `Both Tasks Approved` and click OK to exit the dialog, setting the `Both Tasks Approved` condition on the Approved if-else branch. Repeat the same steps for the `denyCodeActivity` branch using the following as the contents of a new condition called `Both Tasks Not Approved`:

```
this.alphaTaskAnswer != ApprovalDecision.Approved || this.betaTaskAnswer !=
ApprovalDecision.Approved
```

Finally, the last step is to add the code that approves or denies the publishing request. Create handlers for the two `Code` activities and add the code shown in Listing 12-8 to the handlers.

Listing 12-8: Code to approve or deny the publishing request

```
private void approveCodeActivity_ExecuteCode (object sender, EventArgs e) {
    workflowProperties.Item.File.Approve("Approved by Dual Approvers workflow.");
}

private void denyCodeActivity_ExecuteCode (object sender, EventArgs e) {
    workflowProperties.Item.File.Deny("Denied by Dual Approvers workflow.");
}
```

At this point, the workflow has been completely modeled, forms have been built, and the necessary business logic has been added. Everything should compile without errors. The next step is to package and deploy the workflow for testing.

Deploying the Dual Approvers Workflow

As previously mentioned, Visual Studio 2008 includes a new capability: If the Feature definition file exists in the root of the project, then the developer can press F5 and the IDE will deploy and create the association automatically. That process is very straightforward, so this chapter instead presents the full life cycle of the workflow — including development, which involves packaging, deploying, and activating the Feature manually, followed by creating the association. What follows will work in both Visual Studio 2005 and Visual Studio 2008.

Deploying a workflow involves creating a Feature that is scoped for a site collection, as workflow templates must be deployed to a site collection; they cannot be deployed to a single SharePoint site. The workflow project templates in both Visual Studio 2005 (after installing the WSS 3.0/MOSS 2007 SDK) and Visual Studio 2008 include some boilerplate markup for both the Feature definition and the element manifest file.

First add the code in Listing 12-9 to the Feature definition file, `feature.xml`.

Listing 12-9: Feature definition for the Dual Approvers workflow

```
<?xml version="1.0" encoding="utf-8" ?>
<Feature xmlns="http://schemas.microsoft.com/sharepoint/"
        Id="4BDA238A-3B95-4974-8762-08B14A26656D"
        Title="Chapter12 - Dual Approvers workflow"

        Scope="Site"

        Hidden="False"
        Version="1.0.0.0"

        ReceiverAssembly="Microsoft.Office.Workflow.Feature, Version=12.0.0.0,
   Culture=neutral, PublicKeyToken=71e9bce111e9429c"
        ReceiverClass="Microsoft.Office.Workflow.Feature.WorkflowFeatureReceiver">

  <ElementManifests>
    <ElementManifest Location="workflow.xml" />
    <ElementFile Location="Forms\InitForm.xsn" />
    <ElementFile Location="Forms\TaskForm.xsn" />
```

```
    </ElementManifests>
    <Properties>

        <Property Key="GloballyAvailable" Value="true" />
        <Property Key="RegisterForms" Value="Forms\*.xsn" />

    </Properties>
</Feature>
```

Note a few things about the Feature definition file shown in Listing 12-9:

❑ The Feature is scoped for a site collection. This is a requirement for Features used in adding workflow templates to SharePoint.

❑ A specific Feature receiver is used when the workflow contains InfoPath 2007 forms. This receiver is provided by Microsoft and does the work of uploading the forms using the values in the `<Properties>` section of the Feature definition.

❑ The `GloballyAvailable` property tells the Feature receiver that the workflow forms should be shared across all SharePoint sites using the workflow. This should always be set to `true`.

❑ The `RegisterForms` property tells the Feature receiver where to find the forms, relative to the root of the Feature. In the case of the Dual Approvers workflow, the forms are in a subfolder named `Forms`.

Next, create the element manifest. Add the code in Listing 12-10 to the element manifest file, `workflow.xml`.

Listing 12-10: Element manifest for the Dual Approvers workflow

```xml
<?xml version="1.0" encoding="utf-8" ?>
<Elements xmlns="http://schemas.microsoft.com/sharepoint/">
  <Workflow Id="1BF29AF9-70D5-4DF8-BC22-837F4523902C"

            Name="Dual Approvers"
            CodeBesideClass="WROX.ProMossWcm.Chapter12.DualApprovers"
            CodeBesideAssembly="Chapter12DualApprovers, Version=1.0.0.0,
Culture=neutral, PublicKeyToken=c591e70cfdf9ce4f"
            AssociationUrl="_layouts/CstWrkflIP.aspx"
            InstantiationUrl="_layouts/IniWrkflIP.aspx"
            ModificationUrl="_layouts/ModWrkflIP.aspx"
            StatusUrl="_layouts/WrkStat.aspx"
            TaskListContentTypeId="0x01080100C9C9515DE4E24001905074F980F93160">

    <Categories />
    <MetaData>

      <Instantiation_FormURN></Instantiation_FormURN>
      <Task0_FormURN></Task0_FormURN>

      <StatusPageUrl>_layouts/WrkStat.aspx</StatusPageUrl>
    </MetaData>
  </Workflow>
</Elements>
```

Note the following about the element manifest in Listing 12-10:

❏ The `Name` attribute of the `Workflow` node is what will appear in the list of available workflow templates when creating a workflow association.

❏ The `CodeBesideClass` and `CodeBesideAssembly` point to the class in the assembly of the workflow template.

❏ The `AssociationUrl`, `InstantiationUrl`, and `ModificationUrl` attributes point to the URLs of the pages that contain the different workflow forms. When using InfoPath forms, these values should always be the same as what is shown in Listing 12-9. These three pages host the browser-rendered InfoPath forms. The form that is loaded is determined by values defined in the `<MetaData>` section of the element manifest.

❏ The `StatusUrl` is used to point to the status page in the workflow. Unless the workflow uses a custom status page, always use the value in Listing 12-9, which is the default status page provided by the SharePoint installation.

❏ `TaskListContentTypeId` refers to the content type of the task item to use in the task list. The one shown in Listing 12-9 is the default task list type to use for InfoPath forms.

❏ The `FormURN` nodes in the `<MetaData>` section point to the specific InfoPath forms that are used as the workflow forms. The forms are not referenced by an URL, but as unique IDs in the form. To get the unique ID of a form, open it in InfoPath in Design mode. The easiest way to do this is to right-click the published form in Windows Explorer and select Design. With the form open in InfoPath, select File ➪ Properties. The `FormURN` is in the ID field. Copy this value into the appropriate `FormURN` node in the element manifest.

The last step is to do the necessary things to package the workflow into a WSS solution package. Make sure the assembly is deployed to the server's GAC. Refer to the associated download for this book for the full source of the project. Add the WSS solution package to the SharePoint farm's solution store and deploy it. Once deployed, activate the Feature on the desired site collection.

Incorporating and Testing the Dual Approvers Workflow in a SharePoint Publishing Site

With the workflow deployed and added to a site collection, it can finally be tested. To test it, the workflow needs to be associated with a list. This can be a bit challenging with a Publishing site, as the Pages list is not the easiest one to access. Navigate to a Publishing site's Manage Content and Structure page, select the Pages library in the site, and select Edit Properties from the drop-down menu on the list itself in the Folder pane. On the Customize Pages page, select Workflow Settings. When working with a Publishing site's list that already has the Parallel Approvers workflow association, it can be challenging to test the custom workflow. To make life easier, configure the Parallel Approvers workflow to create no more new instances by clicking Remove a Workflow. On the Remove Workflow: Pages page, select No New Instances for the Parallel Approvers association and click OK.

Now create an association using the Dual Approvers template. Click Add a Workflow, select Dual Approvers and give it a name, leave the default list settings alone, and set the workflow to only start manually. Test the workflow by going to a page in the current site, checking it out, checking it back in, and then selecting Workflow ➪ Start a Workflow from the Page Editing Toolbar menu. Select the workflow association previously created. The workflow should then load the initialization InfoPath form, as shown in Figure 12-13.

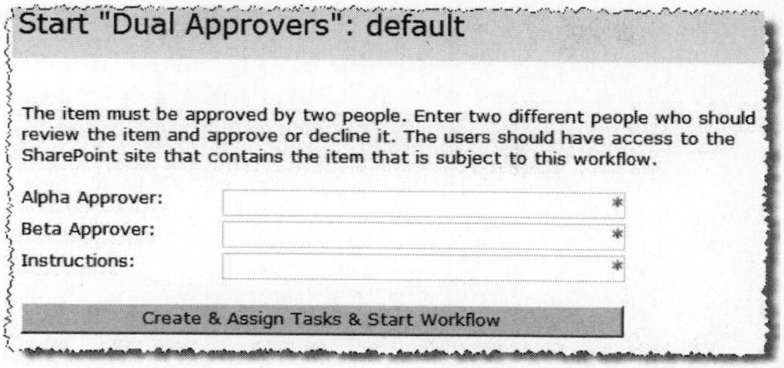

Figure 12-13

Before submitting this form, make sure two users are entered using their login accounts (such as DOMAIN\johndoe) and that they have access to the site containing the list. Once the workflow initiation form has been submitted, the workflow will start, the tasks will be created and assigned to the two users, and the page will return to the page that started the workflow. Because two tasks were created and assigned to two individuals, those individuals are sent an e-mail notifying them of the tasks.

To see the status page of the workflow, select Workflow ⇨ View Status from the Page Editing Toolbar on the page used to test the workflow. Click the running instance of the workflow to see a page that contains some information about the current workflow instance. The top portion of the page contains some general information about the workflow; the middle section contains a list of all the associated tasks; and the bottom section contains the contents of the workflow history list associated with this workflow instance. Clicking on a task will take the user to the workflow task edit form, shown in Figure 12-14.

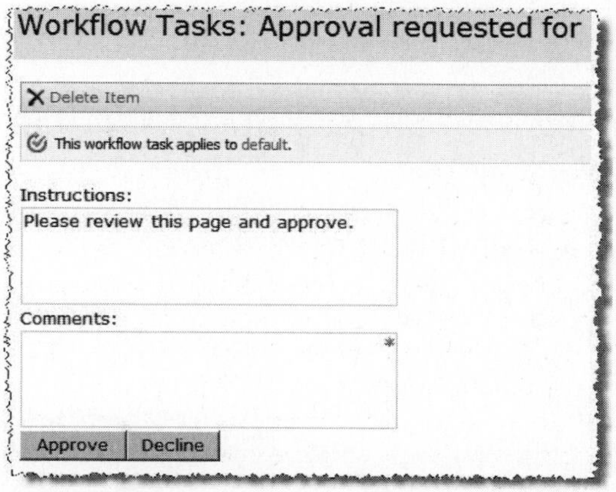

Figure 12-14

Debugging the Workflow Template

Sometimes a workflow needs to be debugged because of a code defect or to monitor it in the development phase. Debugging a workflow is very similar to any other type of debugging done with SharePoint projects. The developer must attach the Visual Studio debugger to a process manually and set a few breakpoints. Developers can even set breakpoints on the activities in the workflow designer! Refer to Chapter 2 for more information on attaching the debugger and debugging custom code in SharePoint environments.

Summary

This chapter covered the overall architecture and concepts of Windows Workflow Foundation (WF), a new component added to the .NET Framework in the 3.0 release. Microsoft realized over time that more and more of their products, as well as applications built by developers, required some form of workflow. At the time, products and developers were creating their own implementation or relying on expensive third-party solutions. Ultimately, Microsoft elected to build a free workflow engine so that applications could host workflows, as well as a framework for building custom workflow programs.

The SharePoint team, flush with customer experiences and requests for a robust workflow story included out-of-the-box, elected to leverage the WF as the workflow engine for the latest release: WSS 3.0. Taking the WF one step further, SharePoint hosts the workflow runtime and provides all the necessary services. In addition, SharePoint adds a human element to the WF by associating workflows with list items and documents, adding tasks and a history log, and introducing the concept of workflow forms, which facilitate user interaction with running workflows.

This chapter demonstrated the process of creating a custom workflow using Visual Studio. The workflow, Dual Approvers, is useful when a new page in a Publishing site requires signoff by two people before being published.

13
Search

Search is often an afterthought in an Office SharePoint Server (MOSS) 2007 Web Content Management (WCM) project. While the out-of-the-box (OOTB) features provided by SharePoint are a significant improvement over no search at all, understanding and planning the end user search experience will result in a search site that help users find not only what they are looking for but what site owners want them to find.

The decision to add search to a site should be considered carefully. Search is not a crutch to compensate for a poorly architected site. Proper planning of the site's hierarchy is vital to the user experience. A site that is hard to navigate by browsing will inevitably be a challenge to search. Conversely, a site that is well thought out and logically structured may not even need search. Consider that implementing search badly is worse than not providing search at all.

Properly implemented search is an opportunity for advertising and intelligence gathering. Think of search as a site's personal greeter, the nice person standing at the door saying, "Hi! What can I help you find today?" Visitors to the site will enter terms in the search box for things they want from the site whether it is provided or not! On an Internet site, this may present a competitive advantage and feature ideas; on an intranet it provides site managers with insight into what employees are looking for and thinking. For example, an employee who is searching for information about medical coverage for pregnancy may be considering expanding his or her family.

Because a well-planned search site helps users find what they are looking for and shows them what they should look for, this chapter dives into the issues related to implementing search as part of a WCM project, whether it is Internet facing or a corporate intranet.

Planning for Search

Planning a search site may be as simple as testing the OOTB site and deciding to use it as is or as detailed as gathering user requirements and developing an enterprise search strategy. This section covers the issues and questions that should be considered before embarking on a search implementation.

Issues

SharePoint is usually implemented by IT and then released to the corporation. Little thought is given to search. In some cases the planning for search starts with the question "What do we index?" Because SharePoint enables organizations to index SharePoint sites, file shares, Exchange Public Folders, and Lotus Notes databases, the most common answer is "everything!" The challenge for the user trying to find a specific document is that *quantity* of search results does not equal *quality* of search results.

Consider what users are looking for. This question drives the analysis of content sources and content types. One of the most powerful features of SharePoint search is the capability to filter a search result by metadata properties. Consider the different approaches of two searchers: the salesperson and the technical developer. The salesperson wants documents to help support a sale, whereas the developer seeks technical documentation. If users are offered an interface tailored for their particular role, they will be far more effective, and their search results will be far more relevant.

Questions to Ask

When planning for search, the project team should ask questions that help determine the scope of the search features. This means site owners should gather requirements for the search project. Sometimes the user community doesn't know what they want, in which case site owners may need to run a proof of concept and test ideas on a sample of users.

Who Are We As a Company?

This surprisingly simple question can reveal a lot about how search should be implemented. For a sales-driven, document-oriented company, intranet search should focus on sales documents. For a product company, Internet search should help users find product information. Frequently, Internet-facing sites offer a "search the Web" option on their home page. These companies are not search engines; they sell stuff. When searching the Web from their site, the results include their competitors! Search should focus the user on the site.

What Should Users Find?

SharePoint can index a great deal of content. The OOTB search results can be confusing to new users. This question can be asked another way: "Do we want our users to find list items and Web folders or should we tune the crawl rules and search results so the users only find pages and documents?"

Can SharePoint Find the Content?

Are there security or network barriers that prevent the use of crawling and indexing to find content? If the content is not stored in MOSS and the crawler cannot discover it, then the content cannot be indexed. One solution to this is to create links to the content in MOSS. Consider whether large binary files that were not stored in MOSS should be included in the search results. These files are 10–20GB in size and reside on a file share. Rather than crawl the file share, create links to the files in SharePoint and add verbose descriptions and keywords to the links to make them more findable.

Can SharePoint Read the Content?

Does the site contain standard document types that can be read by SharePoint or proprietary file types? If they are proprietary file types, then an IFilter may need to be either obtained or written to index the contents of those files. The alternative is to use SharePoint metadata to describe the content.

An IFilter is used by SharePoint to read the contents of a particular file type. The job of the IFilter is to extract the contents of a particular file type and return it to the search indexing engine.

How Should Results Be Handled?

How should users act on the information they find? The presentation of the search results can enable users to act on the results of their search. Properly managed search results can reduce additional work — for example, including a telephone number in company intranet search results can eliminate the need for a separate employee phone list.

What if no results are found? Often the empty result set is not considered in search implementations. Thankfully, SharePoint takes this case into account. When users can't find what they are looking for, it can be a minor inconvenience or a major hassle. One major e-commerce company offers a 10% discount if no results are found from a search query. To receive the discount, the user must call the company and speak to a representative about the zero result. If the company can find the item, then the user gets the discount. This is a great example of a company putting their money where their search is.

Where Do Users Go to Search?

While small organizations may have only one SharePoint site and one search center, large, geographically distributed organizations with more than one SharePoint farm may choose to have several distributed search centers. Each of these centers would index local content; the organization may implement a central "master" search center that indexes content from all regions on a regular basis. An organization may choose to have the search center as a subsite of the intranet `http://intranet.mycompany.com/search` or a separate site collection at `http://search.mycompany.com`. The great thing about SharePoint is that site owners have the flexibility to configure search for any of these scenarios.

Multiple search centers can be confusing to users. If the local index model is selected, developers should plan to implement search centers that provide options for "up-scoping." Up-scoping informs the user about local search center results and enables users to send their search to the master search site to broaden the scope of the query to the entire organization.

Search Is a Business Problem

So far this chapter has pointed out how organizations can go wrong when creating a search infrastructure. The bottom line is that search is a business problem, not a technical problem. The enterprise knows it cannot find anything. Users fight entering metadata because they don't see the value. A search project should advertise that it is *planning* to implement search. Additionally, it should demonstrate how tagging a document makes it more relevant and findable. Making a case to the stakeholder that metadata is valuable is a key consideration. The search project team needs to understand the following:

- ❏ What do we need to search? — Content sources, crawl rules.

- ❏ How do we search? — Search scopes, Search Center tabs, user interface, user experience.

- ❏ What do we do with the results? — Actions, search results configuration, keywords, and best bets.

Search Center Design and Configuration

The OOTB search experience for SharePoint is impressive. The search sites provided by SharePoint can be used without any additional configuration, though with very little effort the search site can be improved to provide users with a search experience that makes sense in the context of a site. The configuration of the search site depends on the results of the planning session.

Search Center vs. Search Site

SharePoint ships with two search site templates: Search Center (shown in Figure 13-1) and Search Center with Tabs (shown in Figure 13-2). The fundamental difference between the two site templates is that Search Center with Tabs is designed with the Publishing Features activated, meaning it is ready to accept the master page from the outset. A master page can be applied to the Search Center through the Site Settings page of the site.

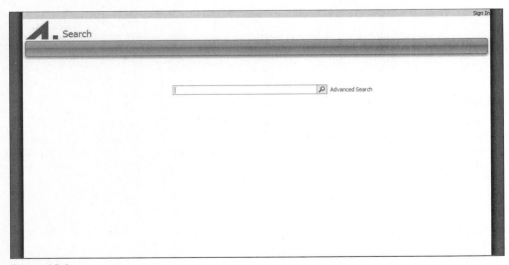

Figure 13-1

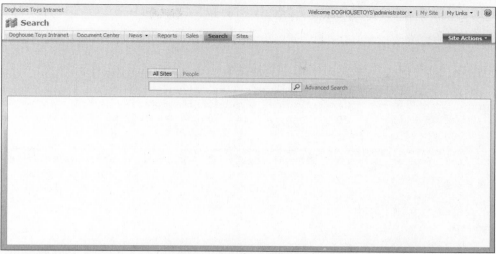

Figure 13-2

Creating a Search Center with Tabs Site on the Publishing Portal Template

New users are often confused by the use of the Search Center on the Publishing Portal template. When they try to create a Search Center with Tabs, the site template is not present in the list of available sites. A combination of settings and a Feature is required in order to enable the Search Center with Tabs site template on a Publishing site:

1. Select Site Settings ⇨ Modify All Site Settings ⇨ Site Collection Features in the Site Collection Administration section. Activate the Office SharePoint Server Standard Site Collection Feature.

2. Select Site Settings ⇨ Modify All Site Settings ⇨ Page Layouts and Site Templates in the Look and Feel section. Ensure that Search Center with Tabs is an available site template by moving Search Center with Tabs from the left text box to the right text box with the Add button.

3. Create a new search site using the Search Center with Tabs template on the Enterprise tab.

4. Optionally delete the original search site provisioned by the Publishing Portal template.

Page Layouts in the Search Center with Tabs

Once activated, the Office SharePoint Server Standard Site Collection Feature provisions four page layouts in the site collection. Each of the page layouts corresponds to a page in the search center. As the search center is enhanced by adding tabs and pages, the following page layouts are used (or, optionally, developers can create custom ones):

❑ `SearchMain.aspx` — The search center home page default.aspx with tabs for All Sources and People.

❑ `SearchResults.aspx` — The search center results page `results.aspx`.

❑   `PeopleSearchResults.aspx` — The results page for the People tab `peopleresults.aspx`.

❑   `AdvancedSearchLayout.aspx` — The advanced search page `advanced.aspx` sends the advanced query to `results.aspx`..

The default Search Center and Search Center with Tabs use page layouts to control the positioning of the Web Parts zones. If the master page designer does not understand how the default page layouts are constructed, SharePoint will encounter problems with the search center. For example, the content placeholder `PlaceHolderTitleBreadcrumb` is used to contain the Search Box Web Part on the search pages. Listing 13-1 demonstrates the Search Box in the `PlaceHolderTitleBreadcrumb`.

Listing 13-1: Search box in the PlaceHolderTitleBreadcrumb content placeholder

```
<asp:Content ContentPlaceHolderID="PlaceHolderTitleBreadcrumb" runat="server">
  <A name="mainContent"></A>
  <div style="height:100%;" align="center">
    <div style="width:390px">
      <SPSWC:ListBoundTabStrip ID="Tab" runat="server" ... />
      <WebPartPages:WebPartZone runat="server" ...>
        <ZoneTemplate>
          <SPSWC:SearchBoxEx runat="server" WebPart="true" ...>
            <WebPart ...>
              <Title>Search Box</Title>
            </WebPart>
          </SPSWC:SearchBoxEx>
        </ZoneTemplate>
      </WebPartPages:WebPartZone>
    </div>
  </div>
</asp:Content>
```

While some designers may not want to use the breadcrumb control, removing the `PlaceHolderTitleBreadcrumb` placeholder causes the search pages to lose their search box. Developers have two options if the site is not going to use the `PlaceHolderTitleBreadcrumb` placeholder:

❑   Hide it on the master and update all of the search page layouts, moving the Search Box Web Part into a visible section of the page.

❑   Simply remove the content from the `PlaceHolderTitleBreadcrumb` and leave the placeholder on the page for the Search site to use.

The control can be left on the master page by removing the content and closing the tag:

```
<asp:ContentPlaceHolder id="PlaceHolderTitleBreadcrumb" runat="server" />
```

CSS Issues

The Publishing Portal and Collaboration Portal templates use the Search Box Web Parts in the master page and in the Search Center pages. These controls share the same CSS classes, thus any CSS changes made to customize the OOTB search control will affect the controls on the search center. It is not uncommon to create a separate CSS file for the search center to undo all the styling on the master page. Simply create a new CSS file and save it to the Style Library. Then edit each search page layout by adding a link like the following to the `PlaceHolderAdditionalPageHead` placeholder:

```
<link rel="stylesheet" type="text/css" href="/Style Library/search.css" />
```

Results Page Anatomy

The Search Center pages default, results, and advanced contain Web Part zones that are pre-populated with the Search Box Web Parts. Placing the page in Edit mode reveals the Web Parts, enabling you to change the user interface of all of the pages, as shown in Figure 13-3.

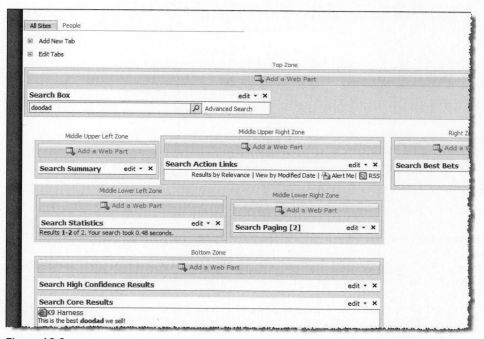

Figure 13-3

The standard results page for the Search Center is composed of eight Web Parts that work in concert to deliver the end user search experience. Each Web Part plays a role in delivering results to the user. While most of the time is spent working with the Search Core Results Web Part, it is good to understand how the other components work. The following table lists the MOSS OOTB Search Web Parts.

Web Part Name	Purpose
Search Box	Accepts user-entered queries and sends them to the results page address configured in the Web Part.
Search Summary	Provides summary information about the search and offers "Did you mean?" suggestions.
Search Action Links	Links to Alert Me, RSS, and ordering results by relevance or date.
Search Statistics	Displays the count of results and the time to query.
Search Paging	When search results span multiple pages, this Web Part facilitates the navigation from page to page.
Search High Confidence Results	Similar to the Best Bets, this Web Part displays exact matches on People results. It can be configured to return other classes of content.
Search Core Results	Search results are returned by this Web Part. This is the most important component of the results page.
Search Best Bets	Query terms that match best bets or synonyms are returned in this Web Part.

Search Results Configuration

Much of the work performed to customize the Search Center is done in the Search Core Results Web Part. The process involves editing XSLT to achieve the desired results. While it is possible to edit the search results Web Part XSLT in the editor dialog of the Web Part, this process is cumbersome and error prone. It is recommended that you use the XSL Link property of the Search Core Results Web Part to point to an XSL file in the site collection Style Library and edit the file with SharePoint Designer. This technique provides the benefits of SharePoint Designer's XSL editor, version control, and publishing.

One such change is to apply bold formatting and highlighting to the search results. First, set up the Search Core Results Web Part to use a file in the Style Library:

1. Execute a search that returns results on the search results page (`results.aspx`).

2. Switch to Edit mode by choosing Site Actions ⇨ Edit Page.

3. Edit the Search Core Results Web Part by choosing Modify Shared Web Part from the Web Part's Edit menu.

4. Click the XSL Editor button to display the default XSL for the Web Part.

5. Copy the entire contents of the Web Part to the clipboard and click Cancel to close the dialog.

6. In SharePoint Designer, create a new file in the `Style Library\XSL Style Sheets` folder. Name the file `defaultresults.xsl` and paste the XSL from the previous step into the file. Save and check in the file, publishing a major version.

7. Return to the Search results page (still in Edit mode) and expand the Miscellaneous section of the task pane. Enter the path to the new XSL file in the XSL Link property:

```
/Style Library/XSL Style Sheets/defaultresults.xsl
```

8. Click Ok to save to the changes and return to the search center results page. The results should look the same as before.

9. Return to SharePoint Designer, and open and check out the `defaultresults.xsl` file.

10. Edit the XSL file to change the hit highlighting by locating the section of templates that include the following code:

```
<xsl:template match="c0">
  <b><xsl:value-of select="."/></b>
</xsl:template>
```

11. Change each bold element to a `<span>` tag with a background color style as follows:

```
<xsl:template match="c0">
  <span style="background-color:lime; font-weight:bold"><xsl:value-of
select="."/></span>
</xsl:template>
```

12. Save the file and refresh the results page. The resulting hit highlighting is shown in Figure 13-4.

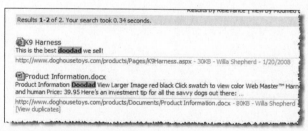

Figure 13-4

Just the Facts!

When working with the Search Core Results Web Part, it is helpful to see the details of the raw XML returned by the search engine. The markup in Listing 13-2 will return the search results in a nicely formatted style.

Listing 13-2: XSL used to display the raw XML query results

```
<?xml version="1.0" encoding="UTF-8"?>
<xsl:stylesheet version="1.0" xmlns:xsl="http://www.w3.org/1999/XSL/Transform">
<xsl:output method="xml" version="1.0" encoding="UTF-8" indent="yes"/>
  <xsl:template match="/">
    <xmp><xsl:copy-of select="*"/></xmp>
  </xsl:template>
</xsl:stylesheet>
```

1. Create a new file in the `Style Library/XSL Style Sheets` folder in the site and copy the code in Listing 13-2 into the file. Name the file `rawxml.xsl`. Save and check in the file.

2. Return to the Search Center and edit the results page. Set the XSL Link property of the Core Results Web Part to point to `/Style Library/XSL Style Sheets/rawxml.xsl`. Click OK to apply the change.

The output should look like Figure 13-5.

Figure 13-5

Search Term Stemming

The SharePoint search engine provides for search term stemming although the capability is turned off by default. The search term stemmer neutralizes the plurality and tense of a word. For example, a query for "work" will return results for "work," "works,""working," and "worked," as the word variations are based on the same root.

1. Edit the search results page (Site Actions ⇨ Edit page).

2. Locate the Search Core Results Web Part. From the Edit button, select Modify Shared Web Part.

3. In the task pane in the Results Query Options section, check Enable Search Term Stemming. Click OK to save the changes.

Sentences

The default Search Core results Web Part returns three sentences in the search results. This property can be changed when the need to display more content in the search results arises. To do this, change the Sentences in Summary property in the Search Core Results Web Part task pane.

Enhancing Search Results with Pivot

After executing a search, users may want to narrow their search based on the results received. For example, after seeing the results of the search, they may decide that they would like to see results only for a particular file extension. This process is called a *pivot*. Pivots can be created by adding a pivot link on any property returned in the search results.

The search results XSL contains several templates that are used to transform the results XML and render the search results. The primary section that is called by every result begins with the following:

```
<xsl:template match="Result">
```

The lines that follow the template declaration determine how the search results are rendered. For example, the following code calls a template that displays the author name:

```
<xsl:call-template name="DisplayString">
  <xsl:with-param name="str" select="author" />
</xsl:call-template>
```

The actual work is performed by the following template, whose results are shown in Figure 13-6.

```
<xsl:template name="DisplayString">
  <xsl:param name="str" />
  <xsl:if test='string-length($str) &gt; 0'>
    - <xsl:value-of select="$str" />
  </xsl:if>
</xsl:template>
```

Figure 13-6

The next few examples build up the XSLT `templates` and `call-templates` blocks to add more functions to the search results. Each template block should be added into its own space in the file, not inside another template. The `call-template` block should be added inside a template where the capability should appear.

Author Pivot

Create a pivot on the author with the following template:

```
<xsl:template name="SearchAuthor">
  <xsl:param name="str" />
  <xsl:if test='string-length($str) &gt; 0'>
    - <a title="Filter by author"
href="javascript:window.location='?k='+getParameter(window.location.search, 'k')
+'+author:{$str}'"><xsl:value-of select="$str" /></a>
  </xsl:if>
</xsl:template>
```

Call the template by adding the following code to the result template (see Figure 13-7):

```
<xsl:call-template name="SearchAuthor">
  <xsl:with-param name="str" select="author" />
</xsl:call-template>
```

Figure 13-7

Adding Fields to the Results

As the search project evolves, the fields returned by the default Search Core Results Web Part may not satisfy your requirements. Any managed property can be used in the XSL as long as it is included in the Web Part's Selected Columns property. The XML in Listing 13-3 can be found in the Search Core Results Web Part tool pane under the Results Query Options section inside the Selected Columns property. The default columns are shown here.

Listing 13-3: Default columns in the search results

```
<root xmlns:xsi="http://www.w3.org/2001/XMLSchema-instance">
  <Columns>
    <Column Name="WorkId"/>
    <Column Name="Rank"/>
    <Column Name="Title"/>
    <Column Name="Author"/>
    <Column Name="Size"/>
    <Column Name="Path"/>
    <Column Name="Description"/>
    <Column Name="Write"/>
    <Column Name="SiteName"/>
    <Column Name="CollapsingStatus"/>
    <Column Name="HitHighlightedSummary"/>
    <Column Name="HitHighlightedProperties"/>
    <Column Name="ContentClass"/>
    <Column Name="IsDocument"/>
    <Column Name="PictureThumbnailURL"/>
  </Columns>
</root>
```

Managed properties are configured in the Shared Services Provider Search Settings under Metadata Property Mappings.

File Extension Pivot

The following template is used to create a link for pivoting the search by file extension. Add the File Extension property to the Search Core Results Web Part. Open the tool pane, find the Results Query Options section, expand it, and add the following XML node to the Selected Columns XML property as follows:

```
<Column Name="FileExtension"/>
```

Add the code in Listing 13-4 to the Search Core Results Web Part XSL file after any
`</xsl:template>` tag.

Listing 13-4: Creating a file extension pivot

```
<xsl:template name="DisplayExt">
  <xsl:param name="str" />
  <xsl:param name="imageurl" />
  <xsl:if test='string-length($str) &gt; 0'>
    <span class="srch-Icon">
      <xsl:text> - </xsl:text>
      <a href="javascript:window.location='?k='
+getParameter(window.location.search, 'k') +'+fileextension:{$str}'" title="Filter
on documents of type: {$str}">
      <img align="absmiddle" src="{$imageurl}" border="0" alt="Filter on documents
of type: {$str}" />
    </a>
    </span>
  </xsl:if>
</xsl:template>
```

Call the template by adding the following line to the result template. Add this code into the XSL file after
the closing tag of the `<xsl:call-template name="DisplayString">` template that displays the field
"write," as shown in Figure 13-8. Notice that the FileExtension column includes the file extension and any
query string parameters that are part of the search result link. Therefore, if the file type is `"htm"` and the
URL for the result is actually `http://localhost/default.htm?profile=sales&departmentname=`
`service`, then the value of `FileExtension` will be `HTM?PROFILE=SALES&DEPARTMENTNAME=SERVICE`.
Add some XSL in order to ignore and fix query string values:

```
<xsl:call-template name="DisplayExt">
  <xsl:with-param name="str" select="fileextension"/>
  <xsl:with-param name="imageurl" select="imageurl" />
</xsl:call-template>
```

Figure 13-8

More from This Site

Add the Site Title property to the site columns by adding the following node to the Selected Columns
property:

```
<Column Name="SiteTitle"/>
```

Use the template in Listing 13-5 to display a link that filters the results on the site only from the results.

Listing 13-5: Adding a filter for the current site

```
<xsl:template name="DisplaySiteTitle">
  <xsl:param name="id"/>
  <xsl:param name="sitename"/>
  <xsl:param name="sitetitle"/>
  <xsl:if test="string-length($sitetitle) &gt; 0">
    <div class="srch-SiteName">
      <a href="javascript:window.location='?k='
+getParameter(window.location.search, 'k') +'&amp;u={$sitename}'"
id="{concat('CSR_',$id)}" title="{$sitename}">More results from <xsl:value-of
select="$sitetitle"/></a>
    </div><br />
  </xsl:if>
</xsl:template>
```

Call the template with the following code (see Figure 13-9):

```
<xsl:call-template name="DisplaySite">
  <xsl:with-param name="title" select="title" />
  <xsl:with-param name="url" select="sitename" />
  <xsl:with-param name="isdocument" select="isdocument" />
</xsl:call-template>
```

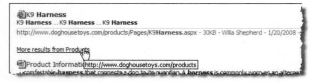

Figure 13-9

Go to Site

Often, it is useful to locate a site based on the results of a search. The documents and list items retrieved from a site provide valuable information about the site. A searcher wants an easy way to go straight to the site that contains the document. The code in Listing 13-6 demonstrates this process and accounts for the possibility that the "site" is actually a folder on a file share.

Listing 13-6: Adding a link to the hit result's containing site

```
<!-- Display the Site url as a clickable image -->
<xsl:template name="DisplaySite">
  <xsl:param name="title"/>
  <xsl:param name="url" />
  <xsl:param name="isdocument" />
  <xsl:if test='$isdocument = 1'>
  <xsl:variable name="siteUrl" select="foo"/>
  <xsl:if test='string-length($url) &gt; 0'>
    <xsl:choose>
```

```
        <xsl:when test="starts-with($url, 'file://')">
          - <xsl:element name="a"><xsl:attribute name="href">
          <xsl:call-template name="strip">
            <xsl:with-param name="relfile"><xsl:value-of select="url"/></xsl:with-
param>
          </xsl:call-template>
          </xsl:attribute><img src="/_layouts/images/folder.gif" alt="Open file
location" style="border:none; vertical-align:bottom;"/></xsl:element>
        </xsl:when>
        <xsl:when test="starts-with($url, 'http://')">
          - <xsl:element name="a"><xsl:attribute name="href">
          <xsl:call-template name="strip">
            <xsl:with-param name="relfile"><xsl:value-of select="url"/></xsl:with-
param>
          </xsl:call-template>
          </xsl:attribute><xsl:attribute name="target">blank</xsl:attribute><img
src="/_layouts/images/cat.gif" alt="Open file location" style="border:none;
vertical-align:bottom;"/></xsl:element>
        </xsl:when>
      </xsl:choose><br/><xsl:value-of select="$siteUrl"/>
      </xsl:if>
  </xsl:if>
</xsl:template>

<xsl:template name="strip">
  <xsl:param name="reldir"/>
  <xsl:param name="relfile"/>
  <xsl:choose>
    <xsl:when test="contains($relfile, '/')">
      <xsl:call-template name="strip">
        <xsl:with-param name="relfile">
          <xsl:value-of select="substring-after($relfile,'/')"/>
        </xsl:with-param>
        <xsl:with-param name="reldir">
          <xsl:value-of select="concat($reldir, substring-before($relfile,'/'),
'/')"/>
        </xsl:with-param>
      </xsl:call-template>
    </xsl:when>
    <xsl:otherwise>
    <xsl:value-of select="$reldir"/>
    </xsl:otherwise>
  </xsl:choose>
</xsl:template>
```

Call the template from the results with the following code (see Figure 13-10):

```
<xsl:call-template name="DisplaySite">
  <xsl:with-param name="title" select="title"/>
  <xsl:with-param name="url" select="sitename" />
  <xsl:with-param name="isdocument" select="isdocument"/>
</xsl:call-template>
```

Figure 13-10

Empty Results

What if users don't find anything when they execute a query on the site? They spelled it correctly, they just didn't find anything. This represents another opportunity to show how much attention is shown to the searcher. SharePoint provides a report in the Shared Services Provider (SSP) called Queries with Zero Results that indicates terms users entered that returned no results. Clicking the term in the report reexecutes the query.

Tell Users About It

The results XSLT provides a template for the no results case called dvt_1.empty. This section can be customized to provide a message to searchers when they fail to find what they are looking for, such as the message shown in Figure 13-11, whereby the Leave Feedback link takes the user to a survey about the site.

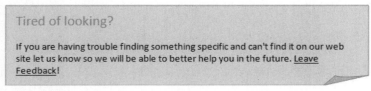

Figure 13-11

Up-Scoping the Search

Sometimes users unwittingly narrow their search, resulting in no returned results. In this case, it would be nice to suggest that the user "up-scope" their search. This can offer suggestions for a particular search configuration to help the user broaden the scope of the search. When working in a globally deployed search environment, the search may offer a link to the master search site, which provides a broader scope for their search.

Search Administration and Configuration

Effective search administration is a team effort. In distributed SharePoint environments where Central Administration and the SSP are controlled by IT and the site collection is managed by a departmental team, search administration is shared by members of each team. Understanding the administrative boundaries of search administration can be a challenge. Additionally, it is important to work as a team to plan the communication of changes that need to be made by the site collection owner versus changes that need to be made centrally by the farm administrator. Working together, these groups can produce an effective search experience for end users.

There are three principal areas where search is configured. A site collection administrator can make decisions for the site. This person can add scopes, keywords, and best bets, but not affect the content sources. The farm administrator can change farm-level search settings, view the status of the Query and Index Servers, and manage the SSP. SSP administrators control all indexing and search capability for the farm, affecting every aspect of search for the sites in the SSP. This section addresses the different roles and the features available to administrators. Note that every level of access affects the search results. Even end users can affect the capability to find their content by the proper use of tagging with metadata. The following table describes the SSP sections:

Section	Purpose
Content sources and crawl schedules	Create and manage the content sources for the SSP. Use this section to add new sources of content to the index.
Crawl rules	Change how content is indexed.
File types	Determine the file types to include in the index.
Crawl logs	View the results of a crawl. Tools for filtering and troubleshooting the crawl are included.
Default content access account	Manage the credentials of the default crawl account. This setting can be overridden for a specific source if desired.
Metadata property mappings	Once content has been crawled, map the properties found to common properties in the index.
Server name mappings	Allow the mapping of server names to affect search results.
Search-based alerts	Enable and disable search-based alerts. Use this option when making large changes to the index that may trip search alerts, e.g., when resetting the content index.
Search result removal	Find a little too much? Remove the results here (then fix crawl so it is not found it again).
Reset all crawled content	Allow the clearing of all content in the entire index. Be careful to turn off Search Alerts when resetting the content.

Server Mapping of Search Results

Change search results rendering with server mapping — for example, if the search results are returning `http://servername` and the results should render as `http://myserver.company.com`. Configure a server mapping from `http://servername` to `http://myserver.company.com`. An alternative to server mapping is to create a string replacement in the Search Core Results Web Part that handles the transformation. For example, if the file share `\\servername` is crawled and the users should see a drive letter instead, use XSL to perform the transformation of all instances of `\\servername` into `z:\`.

Search Scopes

Search scopes created and managed from the SSP are global to the sites that comprise the SSP. Search scopes enable searchers to narrow their search to scopes created globally in the SSP or locally in the site. The scopes can appear in the search scope drop-down and on the advanced search page. While it is common to create search scopes for each content source, consider the relevance of the scope for end users. Scopes can be created that cross content boundaries and focus the results on metadata properties (content types, file extension, etc.)

Authoritative Pages

Link depth, also known as *click distance,* is the distance of a page from the origin of the crawl, and it affects the relevance of the page. The deeper the pages are in the site, the less relevant they become to the search engine. The relevance of these deep pages can be enhanced with the help of *authoritative pages.* Pages that are linked to authoritative pages are more relevant than other pages. Authoritative pages only affect pages linked to them. Therefore, relevancy is not affected simply because pages have other pages under them in the site hierarchy. The authoritative page functionality ranks relevancy based on click distance, a calculation performed through links on the authoritative page itself.

Central Administration

The settings available to the farm administrator, from the Applications tab under Manage This Service, include farm-level search settings such as e-mail address, proxy settings, and timeout settings. The status of query servers, index servers, and the SSP search providers is shown on this tab.

Site Collection Search Settings

It is important that the site collection administrator understand the settings available within the site collection that effect search. The site collection administrator has a great deal of control over how search is delivered on the site. He or she also has control over what scopes are in use. For example, there is no control over when the scopes are compiled; this is controlled in the SSP. Site collection administrators still need to coordinate with farm administrators to achieve optimal search results.

Search Settings

The Search Center and Custom Scopes page is for configuring the location of the default search center for a site collection. This setting can be changed to point to another site collection if desired in order to have a centralized search center that is not part of the site collection.

View Scopes

The View Scopes page displays the search scopes for a site collection. The list includes scopes from the SSP and those configured locally in the site collection. Site collection administrators can create new search scopes for the site collection. The timing of the compilation of the search scope is determined in Central Administration.

Search Keywords

The Manage Keywords page enables the site collection administrator to create keywords and definitions and associate best bests with the keywords. When a searcher uses a keyword or synonym in the query, the Best Bets Web Part returns the keyword, definition, and links to the best bets. The effective use of keywords and best bets is an ongoing process. There may be seasonality to a business that necessitates a management strategy for keywords. Keywords can have a contact who is notified when the review date for the keyword is reached. In addition, keywords can be set to expire.

Search Reports

Two search-related reports are included with the site collection usage reports. The Search Queries Report displays a summary of query activity and top queries for the past 30 days. The Search Results Report displays Top Destination Pages, Queries with Zero Results, Most Clicked Best Bets, and Queries with Zero Best Bets. It is a good practice to regularly review the search reports to look for patterns in user query behavior. Understanding these reports can help in fine-tuning the query experience and significantly improve the quality of the search experience for a site.

Thesaurus File Configuration

Consider the case where a company produces a widget. The company Web site refers to the widget by the trademarked name: DooDad. Because the rest of the world thinks of them as widgets, that is how visitors will search for them. Entering the search term "widget" will result in zero results. The company wants to map the search term widget to the trademarked term DooDad. This is the purpose of the *thesaurus file*.

Thesaurus Files

Thesaurus files are used by the search engine to tailor the query for specific languages. The files are associated with the SSP Application ID in the following folder:

```
C:\Program Files\Microsoft Office Servers\12.0\Data\Office
Server\Applications\<Application ID (GUID)>\Config
```

Thesaurus files have a specific naming convention and XML format. The naming format is `Ts<lang id>.xml`. The U.S. English file is `Tsenu.xml`. The neutral English thesaurus file is `Tsneu.xml`. This file is a good choice if you are not creating a multilingual site, as it has a global impact on all English-language queries.

The default neutral English thesaurus file is shown in Listing 13-7.

Listing 13-7: Default neutral English thesaurus file

```xml
<xml id="Microsoft Search Thesaurus">
  <thesaurus xmlns="x-schema:tsSchema.xml">
    <diacritics_sensitive>0</diacritics_sensitive>
    <expansion>
      <sub>Internet Explorer</sub>
      <sub>IE</sub>
      <sub>IE5</sub>
    </expansion>
    <replacement>
      <pat>NT5</pat>
      <pat>W2K</pat>
      <sub>Windows 2000</sub>
    </replacement>
    <expansion>
      <sub>run</sub>
      <sub>jog</sub>
    </expansion>
  </thesaurus>
</xml>
```

The file is commented out on a new install. Remove the lines `"<!--  Commented out"` *and* `"-->"` *to enable the file.*

The XML indicates two functions of the thesaurus file. If the site uses the word "doodad" instead of the more common words "widget" or "thingamajig," then the thesaurus file can create a replacement set. The replacement set will not search for the pattern terms, it will substitute the subword in the query. This is an important distinction from expansion sets. The set would look like the following (see Figure 13-12):

```xml
<replacement>
  <pat>widget</pat>
  <pat>thingamajig</pat>
  <sub>doodad</sub>
</replacement>
```

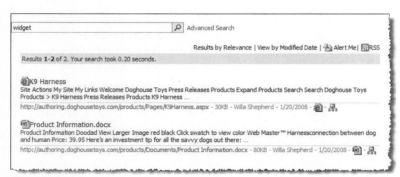

Figure 13-12

For example, if the site uses the word "run" interchangeably with the word "jog" and the goal is to include all references to each word when any of the words are included in a query, then the thesaurus file should use an expansion set. For instance, the following markup in a thesaurus file would yield the results shown in Figure 13-13:

```
<expansion>
   <sub>run</sub>
   <sub>jog</sub>
</expansion>
```

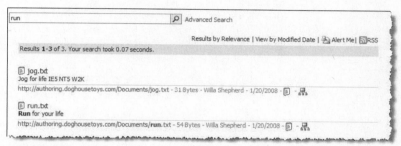

Figure 13-13

After editing the thesaurus file, the Office Search Service should be restarted to reflect the new terms using the following commands:

```
C:\>rem stopping search service
C:\>net stop osearch
The Office SharePoint Server Search service is stopping..
The Office SharePoint Server Search service was stopped successfully.
C:\>rem starting search service
C:\>net start osearchThe Office SharePoint Server Search service is starting..
The Office SharePoint Server Search service was started successfully.
```

Noise Word Configuration

"Noise" words are omitted from the query. The default English noise word file contains the following: *a, and, is, in, it, of, the,* and *to.* In contrast to the complexity of the thesaurus file, the noise word file is simple. Like the thesaurus files, noise word files are language specific. Noise words are listed on individual lines in the file.

Advertising OpenSearch Capability

OpenSearch is a standard for describing how to submit queries to a search engine and how the search results are returned. SharePoint can be configured to provide search results to a client that understands the OpenSearch schema file.

For more information on OpenSearch, see www.opensearch.org.

Telling the Browser Where to Search

Internet Explorer and Firefox provide in-browser search capability by routing the query to a search provider. These browsers detect sites that can participate as search providers by reading a tag in the page that indicates the site supports the OpenSearch standard. When a user browses to sites that support this standard for search, Internet Explorer advertises that search is available by turning the browser search button orange.

The OpenSearch standard defines a schema for an XML file that describes how to submit search queries to a site. The basic format of the file is as follows:

```
<?xml version="1.0" encoding="UTF-8"?>
<OpenSearchDescription xmlns="http://a9.com/-/spec/opensearch/1.1/">
  <ShortName>Short name</ShortName>
  <Description>Description</Description>
  <Url type="text/html" template="http://url?k={searchTerms}"/>
  <SyndicationRight>open</SyndicationRight>
</OpenSearchDescription>
```

Listing 13-8 contains the XML that would use a SharePoint Search Center site.

Listing 13-8: OpenSearch markup for a SharePoint Search Center site

```
<?xml version="1.0" encoding="UTF-8"?>
<OpenSearchDescription xmlns="http://a9.com/-/spec/opensearch/1.1/">
  <ShortName>Company Intranet</ShortName>
  <Description>Company Intranet Search</Description>
  <Url type="text/html" template="http://intranet.company.com/searchcenter/pages/
results.aspx?k={searchTerms}"/>
  <SyndicationRight>open</SyndicationRight>
</OpenSearchDescription>
```

The process for enabling this functionality is as follows:

1. Create the file by copying the preceding code. In editing the file, consider the `<ShortName>`, `<Description>`, and `<URL>`. The `<ShortName>` will appear in the browser, and the URL needs to be an absolute URL to your Search Center site. Name the file appropriately, such as `opensearch.xml`.

2. Copy the file to the server into the `/Style Library/XSL Style Sheets` folder. Check in and publish the file.

3. Open a master page and add the following line before the closing `</head>` tag:

```
<link title="Company Intranet" type="application/opensearchdescription+xml"
rel="search" href="/Style Library/XSL Style Sheets/opensearch.xml" />
```

4. Check in and publish the master page.

5. Open the site's home page in a browser. The search button in Internet Explorer 7 will turn orange, indicating it has found a search provider for the current page, as shown in Figure 13-14.

Figure 13-14

6. Select the drop-down button to see the site's title as one of the search providers, as shown in Figure 13-15.

Figure 13-15

7. Choose the Add Search Providers menu option to see the search provider listed, as shown in Figure 13-16.

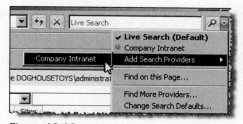

Figure 13-16

8. Select the search provider and then select Add Provider in the dialog shown in Figure 13-17.

Figure 13-17

9. Choose Add Provider and the Web site will be listed as an option for searching in Internet Explorer (see Figure 13-18).

Figure 13-18

SharePoint sites can have any number of search providers. The following example works for the OOTB People Search page:

```xml
<?xml version="1.0" encoding="UTF-8"?>
<OpenSearchDescription xmlns="http://a9.com/-/spec/opensearch/1.1/">
  <ShortName>People Search</ShortName>
  <Description>People Search</Description>
  <Url type="text/html"
template="http://intranet/searchcenter/pages/peopleresults.aspx?k={searchTerms}"/>
  <SyndicationRight>open</SyndicationRight>
</OpenSearchDescription>
```

Telling Applications Where to Search

SharePoint provides a search Web service that can be used by applications that understand how to submit queries and return results from a Web service. Microsoft Office applications and Internet Explorer are two examples of applications that can take advantage of the search service. In Microsoft Office applications such as Microsoft Word, users can Alt+click on a word and open the Research task pane. The Research task pane is also available through the menus. This task pane provides access to online resources such as dictionaries, thesauri, and other sites. The SharePoint Search Center can be added as a research service as well.

Search SharePoint from Microsoft Word

1. Open the Research task pane. At the bottom of the pane choose Research Options.

2. In the Research Options dialog, choose Add Services.

3. In the Add Services dialog, enter the address of the SharePoint server search Web service as follows: `http://server/_vti_bin/search.asmx`. Click Add and confirm the choice of the intranet site.

4. Click OK to return to the Research task pane.

5. Test a search against the SharePoint site by entering a term in the Search For: box in the Research task pane. Select the SharePoint instance from the drop-down menu. It is near the bottom under All Intranet Sites and Portals, as shown in Figure 13-19.

Figure 13-19

Custom Enhancements for Search

Many third-party companies have produced products that integrate into SharePoint to provide additional features and capabilities for search. Many of the products offer enhanced search tools such as wildcard search, image and video search, additional IFilters, and protocol handlers to return results from more content types and content sources than those provided out of the box.

The SharePoint community has stepped up and provided additional search capabilities and tools. Two projects freely available from CodePlex that stand out are *Faceted Search* and *MetaTagsGenerator*.

Faceted Search (www.andrewconnell.com/go/248) for SharePoint provides an enhancement to the standard search Web Parts that enables users to group search results by category or facet. The Web Parts display the total number of hits by facet and enable users to refine their search by clicking on the facet value.

The MetaTagsGenerator (www.andrewconnell.com/go/201) is a control that can be added to the master page to surface any metadata from the publishing page. Once the control is added to the page and configured, the metadata values from a specified group will be rendered in the page.

BDC Integration with Search

The Business Data Catalog (BDC) component of the enterprise version of SharePoint facilitates the indexing and searching of structured data through Web services and ADO.NET data connections. Configuration of the BDC involves authoring an application definition file. The application definition is an XML file that describes how the data is accessed, how the data is queried as a set of records and individual records, and how the entities within the data relate to one another. The BDC can help organizations surface information previously "trapped" in database systems by enabling users to query the data from the SharePoint search page and view the data through BDC Web Parts that can access it.

Business Value from Structured Data

A good example of the value of the BDC is providing access to a customer relationship management (CRM) system. Creating an application definition that defines the *customer, project,* and *prospect* information enables the searcher to find customers by name and then locate related projects and prospects. The key to a successful BDC implementation is understanding the data and the action that users will take upon locating the information. The application definition can create *actions* that are associated with BDC entities. The actions can direct users to any Web-enabled activity, such as sending an e-mail or getting more information based on a Web address.

The incorporation of the BDC into search design leads back to basic questions. Create a new Search Center or add tabs to the existing site? What actions will the user take after finding the content? The tabbed interface of the Search Center makes it very easy to add additional tabs for searching the BDC.

Microsoft Search Server 2008 Express

Microsoft Search Server 2008 Express (MSS) (www.andrewconnell.com/go/249) provides the power and flexibility of SharePoint search without the overhead of the collaboration features of SharePoint. MSS shares the search technology built by Microsoft for SharePoint but has added enhancements that will become available to SharePoint owners in 2008 as an upgrade.

The advantage of MSS is that if an enterprise search engine is needed but there is no need for the collaboration and Publishing capabilities of MOSS, a site can implement MSS Express free of charge. If more advanced features are needed, such as scalability to multiple servers, look to Microsoft Search Server 2008 (www.andrewconnell.com/go/250).

The major improvements provided by MSS include federated search and a simplified search configuration interface. The following table contains a list of the features as they compare to SharePoint:

	Microsoft Search Server 2008 Express	Microsoft Search Server 2008	Microsoft Office SharePoint Server 2007
Search Center	X	X	X
No Pre-Set Document Limits	X	X	X
Extensible Search Experience	X	X	X
Relevance Tuning	X	X	X

	Microsoft Search Server 2008 Express	Microsoft Search Server 2008	Microsoft Office SharePoint Server 2007
Continuous Propagation Indexing	X	X	X
Federated Search Connectors	X	X	X
Indexing Connectors	X	X	X
Security-Trimmed Results	X	X	X
Unified Administration Dashboard	X	X	X
Query and Results Reporting	X	X	X
Streamlined Installation	X	X	
High Availability and Load Balancing		X	X
People and Expertise Searching			X
Business Data Catalog			X
SharePoint Productivity Infrastructure			X

Summary

Though SharePoint offers great features for search results, this chapter has demonstrated that with very little work the interface can be greatly improved. This chapter looked at the various factors that can contribute to a successful search project. The most important factor is understanding the goals of search and how users will interact with a search site. The design of the search site can involve OOTB or custom Web Parts. Customizing the search results involves XML and XSLT. Configuration of the indexing jobs and content sources will affect users and the quality of their results. Integration with databases is also possible with SharePoint, and that integration can be surfaced through the search site. Finally, reporting and studying the search terms and the query results of users can lead to continuous improvement of the search experience and a satisfying experience for end users.

14

Authoring Experience Extensibility

All Web content management systems provide content authors with a user-friendly and easy way to create and manage content within a Web site. The capabilities offered in Microsoft Office SharePoint Server (MOSS) 2007 Publishing sites is no different. Content authors simply need to navigate to the section of the site where they want to add content, authenticate, and create new content using the provided browser interface.

What if this experience is not enough? Thankfully, SharePoint does not stop there. SharePoint, Windows SharePoint Services (WSS) 3.0, at its core is very extensible. Many opportunities exist for extending and replacing the functionality provided out-of-the-box (OOTB) in SharePoint. Thanks to the architecture of SharePoint 3.0, everything that WSS 3.0 has to offer is available to MOSS 2007 and thus, Publishing sites. Previous chapters have touched on the different customization options available to developers in providing a unique experience for content owners, such as page layouts, custom field controls, custom Web Parts, and custom workflows. This chapter takes the authoring experience a bit further and discusses some additional extensibility options available to SharePoint developers to customize the authoring experience.

Customizing SharePoint Navigation with Custom Actions

SharePoint has numerous system menus scattered throughout the product, such as the Site Actions menu, the Site Settings page, list pages (new/edit/display) with toolbars, as well as the edit control block (ECB) shown in Figure 14-1 for all list items. The menu structure is based on the concept of *actions*. Actions are registered to a specific menu within a specific context using WSS 3.0 Features. When a page loads, SharePoint interrogates the internal list of registered actions to get a list of the items that should appear in each menu.

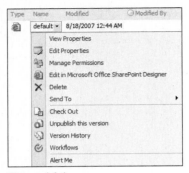

Figure 14-1

Thanks to WSS 3.0 and the Features framework it is quite easy to manipulate the SharePoint menus. In fact, Microsoft even used this model to implement the menus. If you have ever been curious about how the Site Settings page is created, take a look at the Site Settings Feature located in the[..]\12\ TEMPLATE\FEATURES\SiteSettings folder.

How does customizing SharePoint menus serve as a useful tool for developers in creating a customized authoring experience? The ideal time to modify the menus is when the desired customization does not directly affect the content the user is working on, but rather the overall experience. What if the content authors at one organization are not technically savvy in that they don't know HTML and primarily work within the Office client applications such as Word and Excel? No matter how hard developers try, the Web experience is always a little different than the thick client experience. What if some content management tasks need to be provided as tutorials for organizations with a high rate of turnover in the group that manages content in one section of the site? It is not very efficient to repeatedly have to hold training sessions with the new content authors. In these cases, developers could create some customized tutorials delivered as either a Web experience or an offline experience. Rather than send a bunch of links around to the content authors every time new employees join the company, developers could create a new link on the Site Actions menu that all authenticated users would see, linked to the tutorials, as Figure 14-2 demonstrates.

Figure 14-2

Adding items to SharePoint menu, like the Tutorials link at the bottom of the Site Actions menu shown in Figure 14-2, is achieved using Features. The site element `<CustomAction />` enables developers to create menu items and specify things such as title, description, image, and even permission rights indicating what users must have in order to keep the menu item from being "security trimmed" from their experience. The element manifest file to create the Tutorials menu item in Figure 14-2 is shown in Listing 14-1.

Listing 14-1: Element manifest file creating a menu item

```xml
<?xml version="1.0" encoding="utf-8" ?>
<Elements xmlns="http://schemas.microsoft.com/sharepoint/">
  <CustomAction Id="A4C9FEB8-D867-4045-BC17-083AED73E7E6"
                Location="Microsoft.SharePoint.StandardMenu"
                GroupId="SiteActions"
                Sequence="100"
                ImageUrl="/_layouts/images/lg_ICHLP.gif"
                Title="Tutorials"
                Description="Content author and owner online tutorials.">
    <UrlAction Url="/_layouts/WROX/Tutorials/default.aspx" />
  </CustomAction>
</Elements>
```

In addition to the `<CustomAction />` site element, WSS offers two additional site elements that are used to manipulate the SharePoint menus:

❑ `<CustomActionGroup />` creates a new group of menu items. For example, it can create a new column of links on the Site Settings page.

❑ `<HideCustomAction />` is used to hide actions created by other Features.

Offline Authoring with Document Converters

The remainder of the chapter details the different Web authoring extensibility options available in Publishing sites exclusively. However, before moving into Web authoring, let's briefly explore the offline authoring capabilities. Content authors are not limited to just the Web authoring capabilities MOSS 2007 Publishing sites offer. Pages can be created and managed using offline tools such as Office Word 2007 or InfoPath 2007. This capability is facilitated with *document converters*. Once a document converter is registered with a specified document library, SharePoint monitors the document library for new content. When new content arrives in the document library, it is passed to the registered document converter, which then creates a Web page and stores that page in the appropriate Pages library. This process does not bypass any security or workflow configurations; it simply automates the process of creating or updating an existing page in the Web experience.

Document converters are covered in detail in Chapter 18, "Offline Authoring with Document Converters."

Edit Model Panel

At some point in a Publishing site project, business requirements will dictate that the author's editing experience should be different from that of the display experience. For example, what if some fields on a page need to be edited by the content authors but not shown to people browsing the site? This technique comes in handy when a page needs to have some metadata associated with it at the same time that it would be used in classifying or grouping pages in a Content Query Web Part or for more advanced searching techniques.

The way to provide different editing and display experiences in MOSS 2007 Publishing sites is through the EditModePanel. The EditModePanel, used in page layouts, is an ASP.NET 2.0 composite control in that it can contain child controls. By default, it only renders the controls within the panel when the page is in Edit mode, but this is configurable using the PageDisplayMode property. When the PageDisplayMode property is set to Display, it displays the controls when the page is in Display mode. When the PageDisplayMode property is set to Edit (which it is by default), it displays the controls when the page is in Edit mode.

The EditModePanel is demonstrated in the page layouts included in the Publishing Portal site template — specifically, those associated with the Article Page content type (see Figure 14-3). A gray box is rendered at the bottom of a page containing a field control for a thumbnail image. The intention is to not use this image when viewing the content page but rather only in rollup Web Parts such as the Content Query Web Part as a thumbnail in a list of content.

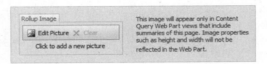

Figure 14-3

To add the EditModePanel to a page layout, either drag it from the SharePoint Controls section in the Toolbox task pane in SharePoint Designer onto the page layout or add the markup in Listing 14-2. In this case, the editor part will display its contents when the page is in Edit mode only.

Listing 14-2: Using an EditModePanel

```
<PublishingWebControls:EditModePanel runat="server" PageDisplayMode="Edit">
  <table cellpadding="10" cellspacing="0" align="center" class="editModePanel">
    <tr>
      <td>
        <PublishingWebControls:RichImageField FieldName="PublishingRollupImage"
                                               runat="server" />
      </td>
    </tr>
  </table>
</PublishingWebControls:EditModePanel>
```

Notice the CSS editModePanel class assigned to the table in Listing 14-2. This CSS class is what gives the EditModePanel the gray background presentation. It is included in the SharePoint style sheets provided in an OOTB install, so developers are free to implement a similar presentation in their own custom implementations.

Customizing the HTML Editor Field Control

The rich HTML Editor field control may be the most commonly used control on page layouts within Publishing sites. The control provides content authors with the capability to author rich content using formatting, tables, hyperlinks, and images, as well as modify the font color and size — all with a slick live preview of the rendered content. This control, shown in Figure 14-4, is very similar to the familiar formatting toolbars available in common word processing applications such as Office Word 2007.

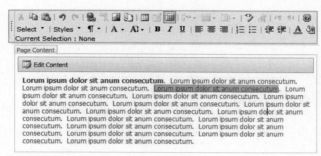

Figure 14-4

While the flexibility provided by the HTML Editor field control can be very useful in many cases, at other times it is necessary to restrict what content authors can and cannot do. For instance, it may not be desirable to allow content authors to pick the color or font size of the text, but should instead be defined using specific CSS classes. At other times, content authors might want to disallow the use of images or tables within a content field. To satisfy these needs, the HTML Editor field control provides a way to enable and disable buttons, as well as create custom buttons and specify the CSS classes available for use within a site.

Enabling and Disabling Buttons

Enabling and disabling buttons on the HTML Editor field control is very easy. There are two ways to control the buttons. One way is to open the page layout containing the control in SharePoint Designer in Design view and select the field control. The Tag Properties tool window shows all available settings on the control. Changing one of the values adds an attribute to the field control in the source of the page layout. The other way to control the `Enabled` state of a button is to manually add the Boolean attribute to the field control markup directly in the page. The code in Listing 14-3 shows the markup for a field control that has disabled the capability to add images and tables, as well as provide a way for the content author to view the raw HTML markup.

Listing 14-3: Customizing the HTML Editor field control

```
<PublishingWebControls:RichHtmlField id="Content" FieldName="PublishingPageContent"
runat="server" AllowImages="False" AllowTables="False" AllowTextMarkup="True"
AllowHtmlSourceEditing="False" />
```

The following table describes the available Boolean attributes:

Control Attribute	Description
AllowExternalUrls	Specifies whether the content can contain references to targets within the current site or external to the site.
AllowFonts	Specifies whether the content can contain `<font>` tags.
AllowHeadings	Specifies whether the content can contain HTML headings (`<h1>`, `<h2>`, `<h3>`, `<h4>`, `<h5>`, `<h6>`).
AllowHtmlSourceEditing	Specifies whether the content owner can view the raw HTML markup of the content and edit it.
AllowHyperlinks	Specifies whether the content can contain links (`<a>`).
AllowImages	Specifies whether the content can contain images.
AllowLists	Specifies whether the content can contain HTML lists (`<ol>` or `<ul>`).
AllowReusableContent	Specifies whether the content owner can add reusable content or not.
AllowTextMarkup	Specifies whether the content can contain formatting markup (`<b>`, `<em>`, `<u>`).
DisableCustomStyles	Specifies whether the content author can select from predefined CSS styles.
DisableBasicFormattingButtons	Specifies whether the content author can use the text formatting buttons for bold, italic, and underlined text, as well as indentation.

Adding Custom Buttons

Another bit of customization that can be implemented on the HTML Editor field control is the capability to create custom buttons in the floating toolbar. While not a trivial task, creating custom buttons can provide an even more specialized authoring experience. Creating a button involves writing JavaScript and registering it with the HTML Editor using XML.

Consider the following example of using a MOSS 2007 Publishing site that contains significant editorial content. The developers want to enable the content owners, the editors, to use a type of microformat called XHTML Friends Network (XFN). The XFN microformat provides a way to represent human relationships using HTML links.

What Are Microformats?

According to Wikipedia, "a microformat is a Web-based data formatting approach that seeks to reuse existing content as metadata, using only XHTML and HTML classes and attributes." In other words, today XHTML and HTML are used to define how content should be rendered (such as the <b>, <em>, or <u>tags) or what it should do (such as <a>). The goal of microformats is to add more structure to the data to define what the data is. For instance, there are proposed microformats for physical addresses, calendar items, and species (living things), to name a few.

For more information on microformats and the XHTML Friends Network (XFN), refer to the following pages on Wikipedia: www.andrewconnell.com/go/251 and www.andrewconnell.com/go/252.

XFN links are not very complicated. The main difference is that an XFN link contains an extra attribute rel, which contains a space-delimited list of specific identifiers such as *me, friend, met,* and *colleague.* Rather than tell content owners how to create these special links, the developers wanted to provide an easy and self-explanatory way for the editors to create them on their own. When the user has selected some text in the field control, a button should be enabled, allowing the content owner to enter a URL and rel values for the link, as shown in Figure 14-5 (notice the XFN button on the last row of the toolbar, just below the Select button).

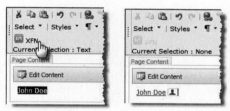

Figure 14-5

Clicking the XFN button will generate two JavaScript pop-up dialogs: one prompting for the URL and one prompting for the rel values. After the values for both pop-up dialogs have been entered, the button generates the HTML link. The result is shown in Figure 14-5. The extra image is rendered using a CSS trick:

```
a.xfnRelationship[rel~="me"]
{
 padding-right: 21px;
 background: url(/_layouts/xfn/xfn-me.png) no-repeat right;
}
```

To create this button, first create a new JavaScript file RTExfnMicroformat.js in the [..]\12\ TEMPLATE\LAYOUTS\1033 folder. This file contains the function that will create the button, as well as two additional functions. First, use the `RTE2_RegisterToolbarButton()` function to create the toolbar item as shown in Listing 14-4. This function has seven input parameters:

- ❑ **ID** — ID of the button.

- ❑ **IconURL** — Location of the image used in the button.

- ❑ **Text** — Text to appear on the toolbar for the button.

- ❑ **ToolTip** — Text to appear when a user hovers the mouse over the button.

- ❑ **ClickCallback** — Name of the JavaScript function to be called when the button is clicked. This function does all the work.

- ❑ **ResetStateCallback** — Name of the JavaScript function to be called when the state of the editor changes. This method would be called when the user enters, selects, or deselects text in the editor. This is used to change the enabled state of the button.

- ❑ **Arguments** — Array of arguments to pass to each of the callback functions when they are executed.

Listing 14-4: RTE2_RegisterToolbarButton() JavaScript function called to create custom button in the HTML Editor field control

```
RTE2_RegisterToolbarButton("xfnMicroformat",
                           "_layouts/xfn/xfn-small.png",
                           "XFN",
                           "Add XHTML Friends Network microformat link",
                           XfnButtonOnClick,
                           XfnButtonOnResetState,
                           new Array());
```

Next, create the two callback functions, as shown in Listing 14-5. The first one, `XfnButtonOnClick()`, does all the work when the button is clicked. The second, `XfnButtonOnResetState()`, is used to enable or disable the button. In this example, the button should only be enabled when text has been selected:

Listing 14-5: HTML Editor field control custom button callback functions

```
// The method that is called when the button is clicked.
function XfnButtonOnClick(strBaseElementID, arguments) {
  // get reference to document currently being edited
  var docEditor = RTE_GetEditorDocument(strBaseElementID);
  if (docEditor == null) { return; }
  // get reference to the selected text
  var selectedRange = docEditor.selection.createRange();

  // prompt user for url and microformat
  var url = prompt("Enter the person's URL:","http://www.someone.com");
  var xfn = prompt("Enter the XHTML friend (XFN) relationships:\nPossible values:
me, parent, child, colleague, friend, spouse, sweetheart, met", "");

  // create the <a> HTML for the blog link
```

```
  selectedRange.pasteHTML("<a href=\"" +url +"\" class=\"xfnRelationship\" rel=\""
+xfn +"\">" +selectedRange.htmlText + "</a>");

  // restore selection
  RTE_RestoreSelection(strBaseElementID);

  return true;
}

// The method that is called when the button's state is reset.
function XfnButtonOnResetState(strBaseElementID, arguments) {
  // get reference to document currently being edited
  var docEditor = RTE_GetEditorDocument(strBaseElementID);
  if (docEditor == null) { return; }

  // restore selection
  RTE_RestoreSelection(strBaseElementID);

  // if text is selected, show the button
  if (docEditor.selection.createRange().text.length != 0){
    RTE_TB_SetEnabledFromCondition(strBaseElementID, true, "xfnMicroformat");
  } else {
    RTE_TB_SetEnabledFromCondition(strBaseElementID, false, "xfnMicroformat");
  }
  return true;
}
```

Notice that a handful of predefined JavaScript functions are being called throughout the callbacks. Unfortunately, these functions are not documented, but developers can pick through the files that define them when creating custom buttons. The main JavaScript files involved in the HTML Editor field control are `HtmlEditor.js`, `FORM.js`, and `AssetPickers.js`, which are all found in the `[..]\12\TEMPLATE\ LAYOUTS\1033` folder.

With the JavaScript created, the next thing to do is make the HTML Editor field control aware of the custom button. When a page loads in Edit mode, the field control looks in a specific XML file within the master page gallery for all additional JavaScript files that should be loaded. The file, `http://[..]/ catalogs/masterpage/Editing menu/RTE2ToolbarExtension.xml`, contains a list of all the custom buttons to load onto the field control's toolbar. Each XML node in this file should point to the JavaScript file that contains the button registration function, as well as the callbacks. To register the XFN button, add the following to this file and then go through the save, check-in, publish, and approval process:

```xml
<?xml version="1.0" encoding="utf-8" ?>
<RTE2ToolbarExtensions>
  <RTE2ToolbarExtraButton id="XfnMicroformat" src="RTEXfnMicroformat.js"/>
</RTE2ToolbarExtensions>
```

After loading the JavaScript file, the HTML Editor field control will then call the `RTE2_RegisterToolbarButton()` function to register and create the button.

Depending on the custom button solution, extra steps may be needed, such as in the case of the XFN button, which needed extra CSS classes to display and deploy images. The code download available for this book contains the complete solution packaged up in a WSS solution package, including a Feature that provisions the CSS file to the Style Library. Another process for deploying the custom button via a Feature is discussed in detail in the section "Deploying Page Editing Toolbar Customizations" later in the chapter, as the process of registering HTML Editor field control buttons and page editing toolbar customizations are similar. The only manual step in the provided solution is to make the necessary changes to the `RTE2ToolbarExtension.xml` file to make the HTML Editor field control aware of the custom button.

Customizing Available CSS Classes

The previous section, "Enabling and Disabling Buttons," demonstrated how Publishing site developers and designers can enable or disable certain buttons on the HTML Editor field control toolbar to keep content owners from using certain formatting options. The downside to this approach is that it limits content formatting options when some content needs to be styled. The preferred way for designers to implement and maintain a consistent look and feel in a site is to use CSS classes. These style sheets contain the branding and layout information for the entire site. The best part about them is that they are typically global to an entire site, so branding changes only have to be made in one spot, enabling designers and developers to centrally manage the site's look and feel. This eliminates the need for inline styles or formatting that is defined on a case-by-case basis, such as the following:

```
<span style="font-weight:bold; color:red;">Company Name</span>
```

Instead, designers can use a specific CSS class. This specific class makes maintaining a common look and feel easy because the styling is defined in a single place.

The HTML Editor field control provides an another formatting capability in addition to turning on/off certain buttons (such as text formatting for bold, italic, underlined, or colored text). The HTML Editor field control will detect all CSS classes defined on the page that match a specific naming pattern and display them in the *Styles* selector in the toolbar of the field control. Any style with the class name containing the prefix of `ms-rteCustom-` is added to the list of possible CSS classes to choose from. The field control is intelligent enough to only display the classes that are available based on the context of the editor.

For example, add the following CSS class either to an existing CSS file loaded on the page or directly to the page layout (again, it does not matter how it gets on the page, only that it is defined in the page somewhere):

```
P.ms-rteCustom-ProWcmDev {font-weight:bold;}
```

This class only pertains to the HTML paragraph tag, so when an entire <p> element is selected, this class is available. Otherwise, this class will not appear in the Styles selector, as shown in Figure 14-6.

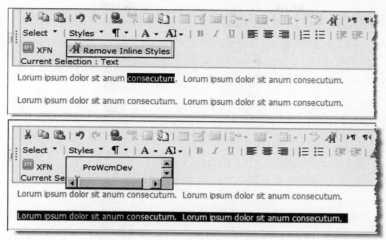

Figure 14-6

The HTML Editor field control also provides the capability to use specific CSS styles for a particular HTML Editor field control. The field control contains a `PrefixStyleSheet` property that can change the CSS class prefix for a particular field control instance from the default `ms-rte-Custom-` prefix.

Telerik RadEditor Lite for MOSS

The previous section covered the different customization options available to developers when using the HTML Editor field control. One of the most significant pain points associated with this control is that it is only supported for use within Internet Explorer. Other browsers, including the Mozilla-based browsers such as Firefox and Apple's Safari, are not supported and can't offer a full hassle-free experience. To address this issue, Microsoft has worked out an arrangement with Telerik (www.andrewconnell.com/go/253) to provide an HTML Editor field control feature equivalent, yet cross-browser, experience.

The Telerik RadEditor Lite for MOSS is available as a free downloadable add-on to anyone who has a valid MOSS 2007 license (it is not available for WSS 3.0–only installations). The RadEditor Lite for MOSS is a slimmed-down version of the more robust and commercial RadEditor for MOSS product. Like the HTML Editor field control, the RadEditor Lite can be customized in many of the same ways.

It is recommended that developers use the Telerik RadEditor Lite for MOSS in lieu of the Microsoft-provided HTML Editor field control. The RadEditor Lite for MOSS enables developers to provide a pure cross-browser authoring experience while leveraging the same customization techniques that the MOSS HTML Editor field control offers, such as custom CSS styles and custom buttons.

Go to the SharePoint 2007 section of the Telerik Web site (www.andrewconnell.com/254) to download and get more information about the RadEditor Lite product, as well as documentation on installation, customization tasks, and community support options.

Customizing the Page Editing Toolbar

All Publishing sites utilize the Page Editing Toolbar (PET). The PET provides content authors and owners with all the functionality needed to manage a page — from creating and editing pages to managing workflow, page settings, and more. The PET is divided into three sections:

❑ **Page Status Bar** — This is the top portion of the PET. It provides informational messages about the page, such as version, state, status, and when is it scheduled to start publication.

❑ **Page Editing Menu** — This is the lower-left portion of the PET. It includes menus of all the different actions that can be undertaken on the current page. If an action is not available (such as checking a page out because it is already checked out), then it is disabled.

❑ **Quick Access Buttons** — This is the lower-right portion of the PET. It includes buttons similar to the actions found in the Page Editing Menu section, but only actions that are available in the current context are shown.

The PET is very functional and essentially complete OOTB, with all the necessary tasks needed to create and manage a piece of content in a Publishing site, but it does provide a way for developers to create custom menus, menu items, and buttons. The process involves creating a class that will do the work and then modifying an XML file to make the PET aware of the new menus, items, and buttons. Luckily, the code for both new menu items and buttons is identical. The following sections demonstrate how to create custom editing menu items and custom buttons.

A common request from customers and designers is knowing which page layout ASPX file corresponds with a particular content page. While the ASPX can be determined by first checking the name of the page layout from the Page Settings page (PET: Page ⇨ Page Settings and Schedule) and using that title to find the corresponding page layout ASPX file in the master page gallery, an easier way can be provided. The solution is to create a new application page that provides additional publishing details about the current page, as shown in Figure 14-7.

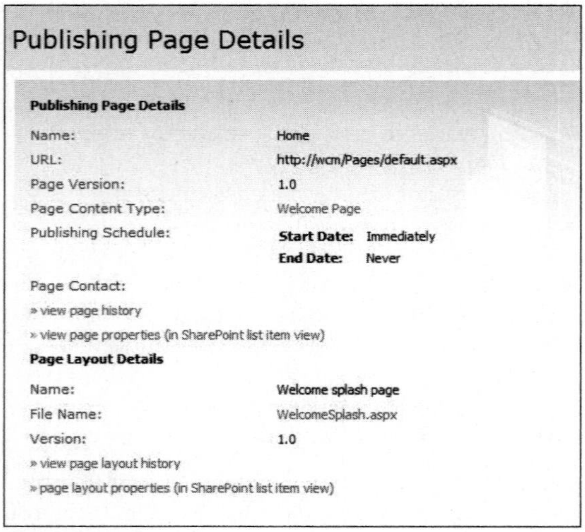

Publishing Page Details

Publishing Page Details	
Name:	Home
URL:	http://wcm/Pages/default.aspx
Page Version:	1.0
Page Content Type:	Welcome Page
Publishing Schedule:	**Start Date:** Immediately
	End Date: Never
Page Contact:	
» view page history	
» view page properties (in SharePoint list item view)	

Page Layout Details	
Name:	Welcome splash page
File Name:	WelcomeSplash.aspx
Version:	1.0
» view page layout history	
» page layout properties (in SharePoint list item view)	

Figure 14-7

To get to this page, content owners want to simply click a button in the PET Quick Access Button area or select an item from the PET Page Editing Menu, as shown in Figure 14-8.

Figure 14-8

The following sections create one of each to demonstrate both processes. These menu items and buttons center on the concept of PET actions, or console actions. The first step is to create a console action, as it can be used as either a menu item or a button.

Creating Page Editing Toolbar Actions

As previously stated, menu items and buttons in the PET are founded on the idea of actions — specifically, console actions. Creating a console action involves creating a new class that inherits from the `Microsoft.SharePoint.Publishing.WebControls.EditingMenuActions.ConsoleAction` class and overriding a handful of properties. Many of the properties can be set from the XML used to register the action in the PET Page Editing Menu or the PET Quick Access Buttons areas. However, developers can restrict the console action so that it doesn't accept values other than those defined within the console action by simply overriding the `get` portion of the property and ignoring the `set` portion. This way, the values specified in the XML are never applied.

To create a console action, create a new C# Class Library project in Visual Studio and add a reference to the `Microsoft.SharePoint` and `Microsoft.SharePoint.Publishing` assemblies. Next, create a new class, `PublishingPageDetailAction`, that inherits from `Microsoft.SharePoint.Publishing.WebControls.EditingMenuActions.ConsoleAction`. Set the default name of the action within the class constructor, as shown in Listing 14-6.

Listing 14-6: Page Editing Menu ConsoleAction class

```csharp
using System;
using Microsoft.SharePoint;
using Microsoft.SharePoint.Publishing.WebControls;
using Microsoft.SharePoint.Publishing.WebControls.EditingMenuActions;

namespace WROX.ProMossWcm.Chapter14 {
  public class PublishingPageDetailAction : ConsoleAction {
    public PublishingPageDetailMenuItem ()
      : base() {
      this.DisplayText = "Page Details";
    }
  }
}
```

The next thing to set is when the action is visible. This is done by overriding the `ConsoleAction.RequiredStates` property. This property returns either a single value from the enumeration `Microsoft.SharePoint.Publishing.WebControls.AuthoringStates` or a bitmask of multiple values. In this case, the Page Detail menu item and button should always be visible when the PET is active, so the `AuthoringStates.EditingMenuEnabled` is used. Add the property shown in Listing 14-7 to the `PublishingPageDetailAction` class.

Listing 14-7: ConsoleAction.RequiredStates property

```
public override AuthoringStates RequiredStates {
    get { return AuthoringStates.EditingMenuEnabled; }
}
```

Now the action needs to be configured to specify who can and cannot see the item or button. This is done by overriding the `ConsoleAction.UserRights` property. Similar to the `RequiredStates` property, `UserRights` returns a bitmask of the `Microsoft.SharePoint.SPBasePermissions` enumeration. In this case, everyone who has access to the PET should be able to see this action, so the `SPBasePermission.EmptyMask` is used, as shown in Listing 14-8.

Listing 14-8: ConsoleAction.UserRights property

```
public override SPBasePermissions UserRights {
    get { return SPBasePermissions.EmptyMask; }
}
```

All menu items and buttons can have an associated image (refer to Figure 14-8). In this case, the `PublishingPageDetailAction` will have a default image set but it will also allow for the image to be overwritten in the XML, as shown in Listing 14-9.

Listing 14-9: ConsoleAction.ImageUrl

```
private string _imageUrl;
public override string ImageUrl {
    get {
        if (string.IsNullOrEmpty(_imageUrl))
            return "~/_layouts/images/info16by16.gif";
        else return _imageUrl;
    }
    set { _imageUrl = value; }
}
```

Finally, the action must do something when it is clicked by the user! This can be accomplished on either the client side or the server side. To handle the click from the server side, override the `ConsoleAction.RaisePostBackevent()` method. If any errors are encountered in the postback, instead of throwing an exception, developers should call the `ConsoleAction.ShowError()` method, passing in the exception as well as a `Microsoft.SharePoint.Publishing.WebControls` `.ConsoleError` object. The server-side approach is helpful when performing some operation on the page, such as saving or checking-in, or some other server-side task.

In the case of the `PublishingPageDetailAction` console action, the user should be taken to a specific page. This does not require a postback; client-side script can be used. To do this, override the `ConsoleAction.NavigateUrl` property. When the menu item or button is clicked, the user should be taken to the Page Detail application page. This page needs to know what page it should show the details for, so the URL needs to contain some information such as the SharePoint site where the page resides and the ID of the page in the Pages list. Add the code in Listing 14-10 to the `PublishingPageDetailAction` class.

Listing 14-10: ConsoleAction.NavigateUrl override

```
public override string NavigateUrl {
  get {
    string pageDetailUrl = "_layouts/WROX/PublishingPageDetail.aspx";
    return String.Format("javascript:window.location='{0}/{1}?pageid={2}';",
                         SPContext.Current.Web.Url.ToString(),
                         pageDetailUrl,
                         SPContext.Current.ListItem.ID.ToString());
  }
}
```

At this point the console action is complete. The last two steps are to register a new menu item or button on the PET and perform the necessary deployment steps.

Adding Items to the PET Page Editing Menu

With the console action created, it now needs to be added to the PET. As shown in Figure 14-8, it is added as a menu item in a new menu called *Utilities*. The Page Editing Menu structure is defined by the XML file `EditingMenu.xml` located in `[..]\12\TEMPLATE\LAYOUTS\EditingMenu`. This is not the file developers should modify, however, to add custom menu items. Rather, this file contains a reference near the top where custom menu items are defined:

```
<?xml version="1.0" encoding="utf-8" ?>
<Console>
    <customfile FileName="CustomEditingMenu" />
    <references>
    <!-- omitted from the book for readability -->
```

This `<customfile />` node tells the PET to look for the file `CustomEditingMenu.xml` in a special location of the site hierarchy: `http://[..]/_catalogs/masterpage/Editing Menu`. This file is a customized instance in the site collection so it needs to be edited directly in SharePoint Designer. Another way to modify the file is covered in the section "Deploying Page Editing Toolbar Customizations."

This file contains two main areas: references and structure. The `<references>` section is similar to the `<% @Register %>` directive in `*.ASPX` and `*.ASCX` files. This where a reference is established to the console action class in the assembly previously created. The second section, `<structure>`, is where the new menu and menu item is created. Replace the markup in the `CustomEditingMenu.xml` with the markup in Listing 14-11.

Listing 14-11: CustomEditingMenu.xml

```xml
<?xml version="1.0" encoding="utf-8" ?>
<Console>
  <references>
    <reference TagPrefix="wrox"
               assembly="Chapter14PageEditingToolbar, Version=1.0.0.0,
Culture=neutral, PublicKeyToken=c591e70cfdf9ce4f"
               namespace="WROX.ProMossWcm.Chapter14" />
  </references>
  <structure>
    <ConsoleNode Sequence="500" ConfigMenu="Add" NavigateUrl="javascript:"
                 AccessKey="L"
                 DisplayText="Utilities"
                 ImageUrl="/_layouts/images/saveitem.gif"
                 UseResourceFile="false"
                 UserRights="EmptyMask"
                 ID="saPageLinks">
      <ConsoleNode DisplayText="Page Details"
                   ImageUrl="/_layouts/images/info16by16.gif"
                   UseResourceFile="false"
                   Action="wrox:PublishingPageDetailMenuItem"
                   ID="wroxPublishingPageDetailMenuItem">
      </ConsoleNode>
    </ConsoleNode>
  </structure>
</Console>
```

Notice in Listing 14-11 how the two <ConsoleNode /> elements are nested. This is what creates the new menu with a menu item. The only other thing to note in this code listing is the Action attribute on the inner <ConsoleNode />. This attribute is used just like an ASP.NET 2.0 server control in an *.ASPX or *.ASCX file, as it contains the tag prefix defined in the <references /> section above, and the name of the class of the console action.

Save all changes, and check in, publish, and approve the CustomEditingMenu.xml file. Because this file resides in the master page gallery, it conforms to the same approval and workflow settings as master pages, page layouts, and preview images. The new menu and menu item should now appear in the PET.

Adding Buttons to the PET Quick Access Buttons

Adding a new button to the PET Quick Access Button area is almost identical to creating a new menu item in the Page Editing Menu area. Similar to the Page Editing Menu, the PET uses the file QuickAccess.xml located in the [..]\12\TEMPLATE\LAYOUTS\EditingMenu folder to build the buttons. This file points to the CustomQuickAccess.xml file in the master page gallery for all custom buttons. The structure of this XML file, shown in Listing 14-12, is similar to that of the CustomEditingMenu.xml file except that there are no submenu options.

Listing 14-12: CustomQuickAccess.xml

```xml
<?xml version="1.0" encoding="utf-8" ?>
<Console>
  <references>
    <reference TagPrefix="wrox"
               assembly="Chapter14PageEditingToolbar, Version=1.0.0.0,
Culture=neutral, PublicKeyToken=c591e70cfdf9ce4f"
               namespace="WROX.ProMossWcm.Chapter14" />
  </references>
  <structure>
    <ConsoleNode Sequence="1"
                 ConfigMenu="Add"

HideStates="PageHasCustomizableZonesFalse|PageHasFieldControlsFalse"
                 Action="wrox:PublishingPageDetailAction"
                 ID="wroxPublishingPageDetailQuickAccessButton" />
  </structure>
</Console>
```

Notice an additional attribute in the `<ConsoleNode />` element: `HideStates`. This is a bitmask of the `AuthoringStates` enumeration, defining when the button should or should not be shown.

Just like the Page Editing Menu, this file conforms to all approval and workflow settings for the master page gallery, so it should be checked in, published, and approved for the changes to be seen by everyone. Otherwise, only the person making the changes to the XML will see the changes.

Deploying Page Editing Toolbar Customizations

Last step: deployment. The deployment of custom PET menu items and buttons is quite simple. The two XML files do not need to be deployed because the changes have already been applied to the site collection. However, the console action needs to be deployed. The assembly containing the console action can be deployed to the server's GAC or the targeted Web application's \BIN folder. The console action also needs to be flagged as a `<SafeControl />` in the `web.config` file regardless of where the assembly is deployed. All of this can be done with a WSS solution package.

One thing just doesn't feel right though: The two XML files defining the custom menu item and button were modified using SharePoint Designer. Does that mean in order to deploy the changes in multiple environments a developer or site owner needs to make this change on all environments manually? If the process followed in this chapter is what is used to implement the changes, then the answer is yes. However, this is not the only way!

Staying true to the theme of this book, whereby both SharePoint customization and development techniques are demonstrated, consider the following approach. The only part of the previously demonstrated process that requires manual intervention is the modification of the two XML files in the master page gallery. Does that mean these files can be replaced with uncustomized instances that point to the file system, just as master pages and page layouts can? Unfortunately, no — these files need to exist as customized instances in the master page gallery. This means that provisioning the files using WSS 3.0 Features is not possible, but deployment can still occur using Features with no manual work.

Instead of using the file provisioning technique, use Feature receivers to do the work of modifying the XML files. The associated code for this chapter demonstrates this approach. The process is as follows: A Feature is used to trigger the deletion of the existing XML files, replacing them with new, customized instances that contain the necessary XML to register the custom menu item and button in the PET. Sure, the files could be programmatically opened and modified using code, but that just adds complexity. Instead, the approach of deleting the old files and creating new files keeps the process simple.

The trick is to delete the old XML files before creating the new ones. One Feature, `Chapter14DeleteCustomizedPetFiles`, deletes the two XML files when activated (see Listing 14-13).

Listing 14-13: Chapter14DeleteCustomizedPetFiles Feature receiver deleting files

```
using System;
using System.IO;
using Microsoft.SharePoint;

namespace WROX.ProMossWcm.Chapter14 {
  public class Chapter14DeleteCustomizedPetFilesReceiver : SPFeatureReceiver {
    public override void FeatureInstalled (SPFeatureReceiverProperties props){}
    public override void FeatureUninstalling (SPFeatureReceiverProperties props){}

    public override void FeatureActivated (SPFeatureReceiverProperties props) {
      using (SPSite siteCollection = props.Feature.Parent as SPSite) {
        using (SPWeb site = siteCollection.RootWeb) {
          // delete the two customization files
          DeletePetCustomizationFiles(site, "CustomEditingMenu.xml");
          DeletePetCustomizationFiles(site, "CustomQuickAccess.xml");
        }
      }
    }

    private void DeletePetCustomizationFiles (SPWeb site, string fileName) {
      // delete the CustomEditingMenu.xml
      SPFile petCustomizationFile = site.GetFile("_catalogs/masterpage/Editing
Menu/" + fileName);
      petCustomizationFile.Delete();
    }
  }
}
```

Another Feature, `Chapter14CreatePetCustomizationFiles`, creates two new instances of the files programmatically upon activation (see Listing 14-14).

Listing 14-14: Chapter14CreatePetCustomizationFiles Feature receiver creating files

```
using System;
using System.IO;
using Microsoft.SharePoint;

namespace WROX.ProMossWcm.Chapter14 {
  public class Chapter14CreatePetCustomizationFilesReceiver : SPFeatureReceiver {

    private const string CUSTOM_EDITING_MENU = "<?xml version=\"1.0\"
```

```
encoding=\"utf-8\" ?><Console>" + /* omitted from the book for readability */ +
"</Console>";
    private const string CUSTOM_QUICK_ACCESS = "<?xml version=\"1.0\"
encoding=\"utf-8\" ?><Console>" + /* omitted from the book for readability */ +
"</Console>";
```

```
    public override void FeatureInstalled (SPFeatureReceiverProperties props){}
    public override void FeatureUninstalling (SPFeatureReceiverProperties props){}
    public override void FeatureDeactivating (SPFeatureReceiverProperties props){}
```

```
    public override void FeatureActivated (SPFeatureReceiverProperties props) {
      using (SPSite siteCollection = props.Feature.Parent as SPSite) {
        using (SPWeb site = siteCollection.RootWeb) {
          CreatePetCustomziationFile(site,
                                     "CustomEditingMenu.xml",
                                     CUSTOM_EDITING_MENU);
          CreatePetCustomziationFile(site,
                                     "CustomQuickAccess.xml",
                                     CUSTOM_QUICK_ACCESS);
        }
      }
    }

    private void CreatePetCustomziationFile (SPWeb site,
                                             string fileName,
                                             string content) {
      using (MemoryStream mStream = new MemoryStream()) {
        using (StreamWriter sWriter = new StreamWriter(mStream)) {
          sWriter.WriteLine(content);
          sWriter.Flush();

          // get reference to folder and create file
          SPFolder editingMenuFolder = site.GetFolder("_catalogs/masterpage/Editing
Menu");

          SPFile petCustomizationFile = editingMenuFolder.Files.Add(fileName,
                                                                    mStream);

          // check in & publish
          if (petCustomizationFile.Item.Level == SPFileLevel.Checkout)
            petCustomizationFile.CheckIn("");
          petCustomizationFile.Publish("");
          petCustomizationFile.Approve("");

          sWriter.Close();
          mStream.Close();
        }
      }
    }

  }
}
```

Both of these Features, Chapter14DeleteCustomizedPetFiles and Chapter14CreatePetCustomizationFiles, are hidden Features. They are activated by another visible Feature, Chapter14PageEditingToolbar, that activates each in the proper order, as shown in Listing 14-15.

Listing 14-15: Chapter14PageEditingToolbar Feature definition

```xml
<?xml version="1.0" encoding="utf-8" ?>
<Feature xmlns="http://schemas.microsoft.com/sharepoint/"
         Id="5116F0D5-8B50-4F42-A676-C44DFC9C6B93"
         Title="Chapter 14 - Page Editing Toolbar Customizations"
         Scope="Site"
         Hidden="FALSE"
         Version="1.0.0.0">

   <ActivationDependencies>
      <!-- Chapter14DeleteCustomizedPetFiles -->
      <ActivationDependency FeatureId="A168B00F-3E44-49A5-9911-959A29141910" />

      <!-- Chapter14CreatePetCustomizationFiles -->
      <ActivationDependency FeatureId="5BC41C2E-8BA7-4E96-B150-C8FC14734747" />
   </ActivationDependencies>

</Feature>
```

Activation of the Chapter14PageEditingToolbar Feature triggers the process of deleting the existing XML files and creating the new XML files that define the PET customizations. Figure 14-9 contains the process flow for the Feature activation.

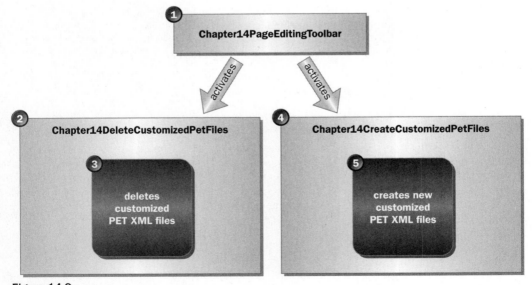

Figure 14-9

In addition, the Features contain logic to "undo" everything upon deactivation, as shown in Figure 14-10.

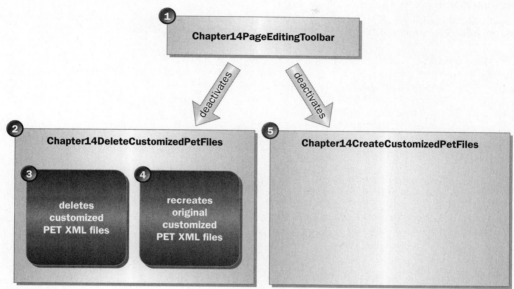

Figure 14-10

This is another example demonstrating that developers are not restricted to using the SharePoint customization approach to deployment. Rather, they can create a much more repeatable and automated deployment process using SharePoint development techniques.

> *Note that the deployment process demonstrated in this section also applies to the same customizations that need to be made in the HTML Editor field control XML files covered in the section "Adding Custom Buttons."*

Summary

MOSS 2007 ships with various capabilities developers can use to create very customized Publishing sites. These, as well as master pages, page layouts, custom field controls, and custom Web Parts, enable developers to craft a unique site on the MOSS 2007 platform using the Publishing Features. In addition to the many customization options, Microsoft has made WSS 3.0 and MOSS 2007 (as well as Publishing-specific aspects) extensible, enabling developers to extend and modify the OOTB experience for content authors.

This chapter discussed and demonstrated the various ways a Publishing site can be customized and extended. The most common field control, the HTML Editor field control, provides many options for customization, such as specifying selectable CSS classes, enabling and disabling the formatting buttons, as well as creating custom buttons. While the HTML Editor field control provides many opportunities for customization, it falls short in the area of cross-browser support. This chapter also touched on the recommended alternative to the HTML Editor field control: Telerik's RadEditor Lite for MOSS.

Finally, the subject of creating custom menu items and buttons for the Page Editing Toolbar was covered. Customizing the PET can provide a very specialized experience for content owners; thus, it is a very powerful technique in the Publishing site developer's toolbox.

15

Authentication and Authorization

A common component to all Web applications is authentication and authorization. Authentication is the process of ensuring that users are who they say they are, usually by looking up their account with a username and password combination. Authorization is the process of checking the specific rights indicating what a user can or cannot do within the provided context. Even in anonymous Web sites, the Web server authenticates users using a special anonymous user account that has been granted specific privileges.

SharePoint sites — specifically, Publishing sites — are no different. SharePoint relies on ASP.NET 2.0 for authentication, using the ASP.NET 2.0 authentication provider model. Internally, it handles the authorization piece with its own collection of components.

This chapter covers the details of the various components applicable to SharePoint security, as well as the process of customizing the ASP.NET 2.0 authentication provider model to change the default Windows authentication that SharePoint sites use to using a custom provider such as a Microsoft SQL Server database. In addition, some Publishing-specific security and permissions aspects are covered.

SharePoint Security Components

SharePoint deals with authorization using various interconnected components. The components enable site administrators and owners to specify what things users can see and do, to group these various rights into named sets, and to apply these named sets within the context of a securable object.

Permission Rights

At the very core of SharePoint authorization is permission rights. The various permissions are broken down into three categories: *list permissions*, *site permissions*, and *personal permissions*. List permissions are those things that apply to SharePoint lists, such as customizing the list's schema, content types, workflow settings, and versioning, among other things. Site permissions are those things that apply to SharePoint sites, such as creating subsites, managing permissions and creating new groups, connecting to sites using something other than the browser interface, such as SharePoint Designer, as well as customizing the pages within a site. Personal permissions include the capability to manage personal views and customize personalized pages with Web Parts.

All the individual permission rights can be viewed on the page where permission levels are created or customized. This is available from a site's Site Settings page by selecting Advanced Permissions ⇨ Settings ⇨ Permission Levels, from which you can either select an existing permission level or create a new permission level.

Permission rights can also be referenced from within the SharePoint API. The `Microsoft.SharePoint` `.SPBasePermissions` enumeration contains a list of all the permissions available. The values contained in this enumeration can be used in various places throughout SharePoint. For example, the custom action schema within a Windows SharePoint Services (WSS) Feature contains an attribute `Rights`, as shown in Listing 15-1. This attribute enables developers to specify a command-delimited list of the various rights required by the user in order to see the link in the user interface. If the collective permission rights of the current user, determined by combining all the assigned permission rights in all permission levels assigned to the user in various groups, does not contain all the permissions listed, the user will not see the item.

Listing 15-1: Configuring security trimming on custom actions

```
<CustomAction
    Id="0D62A8AE-1031-462e-8D01-EE734FA1AE8F"
    Location="Microsoft.SharePoint.StandardMenu"
    GroupID="SiteActions"
    Sequence="10"
    Title="Go to www.wrox.com"
    Description="Takes the user to http://www.wrox.com"
    Rights="ApproveItems,EnumeratePermissions">
    <UrlAction Url="http://www.wrox.com" />
</CustomAction>
```

The `SPBasePermission` enumeration contains two special values: `EmptyMask` and `FullMask` `.SPBasePermission.EmptyMask` is used to assign no permissions to something. `SPBasePermissions` `.FullMask` is used to assign all the permissions to something.

Permission Levels

Permission rights cannot be applied directly to a user or group in SharePoint. Instead, they are grouped together into something called a *permission level*. Permission levels, also referred to as *roles*, are then assigned to users or groups in the context of a SharePoint securable object (securable objects are covered later in the chapter).

Site administrators and owners can create and customize permission levels within a site. This is available from a site's Site Settings page by selecting Advanced Permissions ⇨ Settings ⇨ Permission Levels. Developers can also interact with SharePoint permission levels through the API using the `Microsoft .SharePoint.SPRoleDefinition` class. These `SPRoleDefinition` objects are not directly assigned to a user, group, or securable object. Instead, another object, `Microsoft.SharePoint.SPRoleAssignment`, is used to pair the permission level with a user or group. This is demonstrated later in the section "SharePoint Security via the API." All the permission levels defined within a particular SharePoint site can be obtained from the `Microsoft.SharePoint.SPWeb.RoleDefinitions` collection.

SharePoint Groups

SharePoint allows permission levels to be applied to site users as well as security groups, such as Active Directory groups, that have been added to the site. However, this is not the recommended approach. Rather, Microsoft recommends that site owners and administrators assign permission levels to SharePoint groups and then add site users and security groups to the SharePoint groups.

Site administrators and owners can create and edit SharePoint groups within a site. This is available from a site's Site Settings page by selecting People and Groups. Developers can also obtain references to existing SharePoint users and SharePoint groups using the `Microsoft.SharePoint.SPUser` or `Microsoft.SharePoint.SPGroup` classes. The users and SharePoint groups within a site are accessible using the `Microsoft.SharePoint.SPWeb.Users` and `Microsoft.SharePoint.SPWeb.Groups` properties.

Securable Objects

Until this point, only the permission rights, levels (or roles), and groups have been covered. These different components are used to define what a user can do within a provided context (using permission rights and levels) and how permissions can be applied to a group of users (using SharePoint groups). The next piece to this puzzle is assigning the permission to something in SharePoint, such as a site, a list, or a list item. Only certain objects can have permissions applied to them. These objects must implement the `Microsoft.SharePoint.ISecurable` interface.

Additional Publishing Security Components

So far everything discussed in this chapter applies to WSS 3.0. While the provided SharePoint permission levels and SharePoint groups offer enough control for most situations, Publishing sites demand a bit more granular control. Publishing sites contain additional permission levels and SharePoint groups beyond what is included in a standard WSS 3.0 site. The following sections explain the additional pieces included in Publishing sites.

Publishing Permission Levels

All SharePoint sites include a predefined default set of permission levels and SharePoint groups. For example, all WSS 3.0 sites include the permission levels listed in the following table:

Permission Levels	Description
Limited Access	This special permission level grants users the absolutely minimal rights to some objects in a site collection in order to browse a specific site. For example, consider a user given access to a subsite within a site collection. While this user has not been granted explicit permissions to the top-level site in the site collection, he or she must have access to things such as the master page gallery and the Style Library in order for the pages in the subsite to be constructed and rendered. All users on the site are granted this permission level. This permission level cannot be deleted or modified.
Read	Users granted this permission level are allowed to see but not change content.
Contribute	Users granted this permission level can not only see content, but also add, update, and delete items in SharePoint lists and libraries.
Design	Users granted this permission level have all the same rights as those granted the contribute permission level but also have additional list permissions such as customizing the list, overriding item checkouts, and approving items. In addition, they can apply themes and style sheets, and customize pages.
Full Control	As the name implies, users granted this permission level have unfettered access to the site. This permission level cannot be deleted or modified.

As mentioned earlier, when the Publishing Features are activated on a SharePoint site, they add some additional permission levels beyond what is included in a stock WSS 3.0 site. These additional permission levels are required to provide the necessary functionality and control over a content-centric site. The additional four permission levels are listed in the following table:

Permission Levels	Description
Approve	This permission level provides users with all the same permissions the contribute permission level provides but with the added capability to manage the approval state of an item.
Manage Hierarchy	This permission level allows users to create and manage the topology of a site collection by creating and editing subsites.
Restricted Read	This permission level is similar to the read permission level included in WSS 3.0 sites, but with one major difference: This permission level does not allow users to view previous versions of a list item, whereas those with the read permission level can view versions. In addition, users granted this permission level cannot browse user information on the site, whereas the WSS 3.0 read permission level does permit this.

Publishing SharePoint Groups

Similar to the permission levels, Publishing sites include a handful of additional SharePoint groups that traditional WSS 3.0 sites do not include. Most of them correspond to the additional permission levels added by the Publishing Features, but others are used to provide more granular control over a typical content-centric site.

The new groups that map directly to the additional Publishing permission levels include the Approvers, Hierarchy Managers, and Restricted Readers SharePoint groups. The other three SharePoint groups added by the Publishing Features provide additional control to site owners and administrators:

❑ **Designers** — This SharePoint group is meant for users who will have rights to customize the site and create custom master pages and page layouts. The Design and Limited Access permission levels are assigned to this SharePoint group.

❑ **Quick Deploy Users** — This SharePoint group is used in conjunction with content deployment, covered in more depth in Chapter 17.

❑ **Style Resource Readers** — This special SharePoint group grants the read permission level to the site collection's master page gallery, and the restricted read permission to the Style Library.

SharePoint Security via the API

Like everything in SharePoint, whatever can be done through the browser-based interface can also be done using the SharePoint API. Creating permission levels, assigning rights to these levels, creating SharePoint groups and applying permission levels to the groups, as well as adding users and security groups to SharePoint groups — all of this can be done through the SharePoint API. Unfortunately, like many other aspects of SharePoint, the object names in the API do not match the names used in the browser interface, which can be confusing to users.

Some of these classes have already been covered. For instance, SharePoint groups are represented as `Microsoft.SharePoint.SPGroups`, permission levels are `Microsoft.SharePoint.SPRoleDefinition`, and the collection of all permission rights is found in `Microsoft.SharePoint.SPBasePermission`.

In order to grant a permission level to a SharePoint group, the first step is to get an instance of the SharePoint group. The next step is to create an instance of a new `Microsoft.SharePoint.SPRoleAssignment` object. This object will allow the binding of a permission level to the group. This is done by adding the permission level binding to a collection of assignments using a special collection in the current SharePoint site, as shown in Listing 15-2.

Listing 15-2: Assigning permission levels to an existing group

```
using (SPWeb site = SPContext.Current.Web){
  // get reference to a group
  SPGroup group = site.Groups["WROX Members"];

  // create a new assignment for the group
  SPRoleAssignment roleAssignment = new SPRoleAssignment(group);

  // add two permission levels to the group
```

(continued)

Listing 15-2 *(continued)*

```
        SPRoleDefinition roleDefinition;

        roleDefinition = site.RoleDefinitions["Manage Hierarchy"];
        roleAssignment.RoleDefinitionBindings.Add(roleDefinition);

        roleDefinition = site.RoleDefinitions["Approve "];
        roleAssignment.RoleDefinitionBindings.Add(roleDefinition);

        // add the role assignment to the site assignments collection
        site.RoleAssignments.Add(roleAssignment);

        // update the site
        site.Update();
    }
```

The code in Listing 15-2 demonstrates how to add permission levels to a SharePoint group. Notice how the SPRoleAssignment object contains a collection of RoleDefinitionBindings and then adds the SPRoleAssignment back to the collection of role assignments for the site. Recall that all permissions are set within the context of a user or group and a securable object. This is why the association of the permission level is done with a group and then added to the collection of permissions for the SharePoint site.

Alternate Access Mappings

One common requirement for many Web sites, including SharePoint sites, is the ability to answer requests on multiple URLs. For example, an internal URL may be used by company employees to manage the content on the site while users of the site access it via a different, public URL. SharePoint addresses this requirement using Alternate Access Mappings (AAMs). Each AAM maps to a different zone. These can be used to create multiple paths of entry into a site collection, each path coming through a different Web application and URL. Because the different paths are segmented using different URLs, each site can implement different authentication providers as they are defined in the Web application's web.config, as shown in the next section.

Authentication Provider Model

When developers and companies build most applications, they traditionally tightly integrate the different security models into the project or product. However, the majority of the time these authentication models all have common tasks. These include authenticating the user with the provided username and password, creating new users, resetting passwords, providing some sort of "forgot my password" functionality, and so on.

Similar to site navigation, Microsoft saw this as a challenge and introduced the authentication provider model to ASP.NET 2.0. This provider refactors the implementation of authentication from the application and instead provides a common interface that applications can program against, leaving the implementation to the providers. Because SharePoint is built on top of ASP.NET 2.0, it can fully leverage this model. This provides SharePoint with two different models of authentication: Windows or

Forms-based authentication (FBA). However, these two options are misleading. Windows authentication really implies that users will get an NT Challenge Response dialog box like the one shown in Figure 15-1, which authenticates the username and password provided against Active Directory.

Figure 15-1

FBA simply changes the model to send users to a Web page where they can enter a username and password. This second option of FBA actually opens up a whole world of possibilities because now developers can configure any authentication provider. All SharePoint sites default to using Windows authentication, but they can be configured to use FBA.

Configuring Forms-Based Authentication

Configuring a SharePoint site for FBA is a multi-step process. While it is possible to change a newly created SharePoint site collection to use FBA instead of Windows authentication, it is usually a better idea to extend a new Web application from an existing one and configure the new Web application for FBA, leaving the original one set to Windows authentication. There are numerous reasons for this, one being that SharePoint's search uses NTLM (Windows authentication) to authenticate and crawl the site when indexing the content. In the following example, this is the model that is used.

The authentication provider model contains three different providers: *membership, role,* and *profile.* The membership provider is the one responsible for the users, including authentication. The role provider is used to determine which users are in which groups. Finally, the profile provider facilitates creating profiles for each user defined in the authentication store. These profiles can contain custom-defined properties along with the standard first and last name, among other properties.

At a minimum, a membership and role provider must be defined. The profile provider is not required, but be aware that omitting it can have adverse effects. For example, a common misperception is that FBA breaks SharePoint's My Site capability. This is not true. My Sites require a profile for the user in order to tie the My Site to the user. If no profile provider is defined, SharePoint cannot create a My Site for that user, which is why many people get the impression that FBA breaks My Sites.

Creating the SharePoint Web Applications

The process begins by starting with a new SharePoint Web application, `http://extranet`, in SharePoint's Central Administration. Select Application Management ⇨ Create or Extend Web Application ⇨ Create a New Web Application, just as you would with any other SharePoint Web application. After creating the Web application, create a new site collection using the Publishing Portal template (but any template will do). Next, extend a new Web application off `http://extranet` in Central Administration by selecting Application Management ⇨ Create or Extend Web Application ⇨ Extend an Existing Web Application. On the Extend Web Application to Another IIS Web Site page, select the `http://extranet` Web application and specify the URL of the new application as `http://internet`. Other than setting the zone to Internet, accept all default values on this page.

> *The name of the zone really doesn't matter. SharePoint is limited to only five zones: Default, Internet, Intranet, Extranet, and Custom. None of these names map to a specific configuration. They are just labels and could just as easily be called Zone 1, Zone 2, Zone 3, and so on.*

At this point, two Web applications are pointing to the same site collection.

Creating the FBA Authentication Database

The next step is to configure the data store for the FBA provider that will be used. Thankfully, Microsoft provides a Microsoft SQL Server authentication provider in ASP.NET 2.0. This provider stores all the user membership and profile information in a custom SQL database. Microsoft even ships a utility in ASP.NET 2.0 that will create the database. Launch this tool from the following location: `C:\Windows\ Microsoft.NET\Framework\v2.0.50727\aspnet_regsql.exe`. When prompted, enter the following values:

❏ **Server** — This is the name of the server to install the database to — usually the same one that contains the SharePoint content databases.

❏ **Windows Authentication**

❏ **Database** — SharePointFBA

With the database created, the next step is to grant a user access to the database. This will be the user account the SharePoint site uses to access the database. This is the identity of the application pool running the Web application hosting the previously created Publishing Portal site collection. Next, use SQL Server Management Studio and add the application pool identity account to the SharePointFBA database previously created and grant it the following roles: `db_datareader` and `db_datawriter`.

Creating the FBA Providers

With the SharePoint Web applications created and the FBA database set up, the next step is to create the providers. This is where things usually get complicated and most people run into problems. The authentication providers in ASP.NET 2.0 are specified in the site's `web.config` file. To configure SharePoint for FBA, not only do the providers need to be added to the `web.config` file, but SharePoint needs some additional configuration to make things work. Most people who run into problems do so by configuring the providers directly on the SharePoint site. Instead, it is recommended that you simplify things and create the providers using a vanilla ASP.NET 2.0 Web site instead of doing it within the context of SharePoint. The reason this simplifies the process is because the providers can be configured and tested without worrying about SharePoint at all. Later, if issues arise they can be isolated to the SharePoint configuration piece.

Create a new ASP.NET 2.0 Web site using Visual Studio. If a `web.config` file is not already present, add one to the project. The first step is to establish a connection to the FBA database. Replace the existing `<connectionStrings />` element in the `web.config` file with the following markup in Listing 15-3.

Listing 15-3: Database connection string for the FBA database

```
<connectionStrings>
  <add name="WroxFba" providerName="System.Data.SqlClient"
    connectionString="server=[SQL_SERVER]; database=SharePointFBA; Integrated
Security=SSPI;" />
</connectionStrings>
```

Next, add the markup shown in Listing 15-4 within the `<system.web>` nodes to define the membership and role providers.

Listing 15-4: FBA membership and role providers

```
<system.web>
  <!-- membership provider -->
  <membership defaultProvider="WroxFbaSqlMembershipProvider">
    <providers>
      <add name="WroxFbaSqlMembershipProvider"
        type="System.Web.Security.SqlMembershipProvider, System.Web,
Version=2.0.0.0, Culture=neutral, PublicKeyToken=b03f5f7f11d50a3a"
        connectionStringName="WroxFba"
        enablePasswordRetrieval="false"
        enablePasswordReset="true"
        requiresQuestionAndAnswer="false"
        applicationName="/"
        requiresUniqueEmail="false"
        passwordFormat="Hashed"
        maxInvalidPasswordAttempts="5"
        minRequiredPasswordLength="1"
        minRequiredNonalphanumericCharacters="0"
        passwordAttemptWindow="10"
        passwordStrengthRegularExpression="" />
    </providers>
  </membership>

  <!-- role provider -->
  <roleManager enabled="true" defaultProvider="WroxFbaSqlRoleProvider">
    <providers>
      <add name="WroxFbaSqlRoleProvider"
        type="System.Web.Security.SqlRoleProvider, System.Web, Version=2.0.0.0,
Culture=neutral, PublicKeyToken=b03f5f7f11d50a3a"
        connectionStringName="WroxFba"
        applicationName="/" />
    </providers>
  </roleManager>
</system.web>
```

With the connection string and providers configured, now Visual Studio can be used to launch a special Web application for testing the providers and managing the database. From within Visual Studio, select Website ⇨ ASP.NET Configuration. With the administration site open, switch the site from Integrated Authentication to Forms Authentication by selecting the Security tab ⇨ Select Authentication Type in the Users container. Make sure the option From the Internet is selected (also referred to as FBA) and click Done.

Now that the security is configured, test the providers. Select the Provider tab, then Select a Different Provider for Each Feature (Advanced), and click the Test link next to the two providers defined in the `web.config`: `WroxFbaSqlMembershipProvider` and the `WroxFbaSqlRoleProvider`. If there are any errors, go back and check the data entered into `web.config`.

Now is a good time to add some users who will be needed to test the FBA setup after it is configured in SharePoint. From the Security tab, select Create User within the Users container. On the Create User page, enter the following information for the new user, making sure the Active Use checkbox is checked:

- ❑ **User name** — George Washington
- ❑ **Password** — pass@word1
- ❑ **Confirm Password** — pass@word1
- ❑ **Email** — george.washington@foo.com

This user will be used for testing as a regular user of the site. Now add another user who will be added as a pseudo-administrator of the site:

- ❑ **User name** — FbaAdministrator
- ❑ **Password** — pass@word1
- ❑ **Confirm Password** — pass@word1
- ❑ **Email** — fba.admin@foo.com

At this point the providers have been created, configured, and successfully tested. In addition, two user accounts have been created in the database. This can be confirmed by looking at the `aspnet_Users` table in the SharePointFBA database. The next step is to add the providers to the `http://internet` SharePoint site and configure SharePoint to use the FBA providers.

Configuring SharePoint to Use the FBA Providers

Now it is time to add the FBA providers. In this case there are two Web applications pointing to the same Publishing site collection: `http://extranet` and `http://internet`. Both sites need to be able to talk to the FBA provider and the membership database in order to manage security from either site, but only the `http://internet` site will authenticate using the FBA provider.

Open the `web.config` file for the `http://extranet` site and use the markup in Listing 15-5 to add the database connection string information as well as the FBA providers.

Listing 15-5: FBA changes to the http://extranet web.config

```
<connectionStrings>
  <add name="WroxFba" providerName="System.Data.SqlClient"
    connectionString="server=[SQL_SERVER]; database=SharePointFBA; Integrated
Security=SSPI;" />
</connectionStrings>
<system.web>
  <membership defaultProvider="WroxFbaSqlMembershipProvider">
    <providers>
```

```
      <add name="WroxFbaSqlMembershipProvider"
          type="System.Web.Security.SqlMembershipProvider, System.Web,
Version=2.0.0.0, Culture=neutral, PublicKeyToken=b03f5f7f11d50a3a"
          connectionStringName="WroxFba"
          enablePasswordRetrieval="false"
          enablePasswordReset="true"
          requiresQuestionAndAnswer="false"
          applicationName="/"
          requiresUniqueEmail="false"
          passwordFormat="Hashed"
          maxInvalidPasswordAttempts="5"
          minRequiredPasswordLength="1"
          minRequiredNonalphanumericCharacters="0"
          passwordAttemptWindow="10"
          passwordStrengthRegularExpression="" />
    </providers>
  </membership>

  <roleManager enabled="true" defaultProvider="WroxFbaSqlRoleProvider">
    <providers>
      <add name="WroxFbaSqlRoleProvider"
          type="System.Web.Security.SqlRoleProvider, System.Web, Version=2.0.0.0,
Culture=neutral, PublicKeyToken=b03f5f7f11d50a3a"
          connectionStringName="WroxFba"
          applicationName="/" />
    </providers>
  </roleManager>
</system.web>
```

All of the markup added in Listing 15-5 can be copied straight from the web.config file created using Visual Studio in the previous step; in fact, this is recommended to reduce the chance of errors.

The same changes are required for the http://internet web.config file. Add the same markup in Listing 15-5 to the web.config for the http://internet SharePoint Web application. At this point neither Web application is authenticating using the FBA providers; they are still using Windows authentication. However, both can see and talk to the FBA membership database.

With the two sites' Web applications configured, the next step is to configure the Central Administration Web application because the need may arise to manage the security using FBA users on one of the Web applications from within Central Administration. Therefore, the web.config file for the Central Administration Web application needs the same changes. Add the same markup in Listing 15-5 to the web.config file for the Central Administration Web application. However, there is one difference in the Central Administration's web.config file: Change the defaultProvider attribute on the <roleManager> element to AspNetWindowsTokenRoleProvider so Central Administration will still use Windows Authentication for the role provider. This is required.

With all the web.config modifications complete, it is now time to configure the http://internet Web application to use the FBA membership provider. From within Central Administration, select Application Management ➪ Authentication Providers. On the Authentication Providers page, ensure that the Web application is set to `http://extranet` and select the Internet zone link. On the Edit Authentication page, use the following information to complete the form and then click Save:

❑ **Authentication Type** — Forms

❑ **Enable Anonymous Access** — checked

❑ **Membership Provider Name** — WroxFbaSqlMembershipProvider

❑ **Role Manager Name** — WroxFbaSqlRoleProvider

At this point the `http://extranet` Web application is not authenticating users with the FBA membership provider.

Now a user needs to be added to the site. Leave Central Administration and navigate to the `http://extranet` SharePoint site. Select Site Actions ⇨ Site Settings ⇨ Modify All Site Settings and select People and Groups. On the People and Groups page, click New, enter `george.washington`, and click the Check Names icon and grant the user rights to the Visitors group as shown in Figure 15-2.

Figure 15-2

Confirm that everything is working properly by browsing to the `http://internet` site. SharePoint should automatically redirect to the FBA login page. Enter the credentials for the `george.washington` account as specified previously to validate and gain access to the site.

Anonymous Access

One thing that was always tricky to configure in the previous version of SharePoint was anonymous access. Microsoft has made it much easier to support anonymous access in WSS 3.0. However, configuring a SharePoint site for anonymous access frequently trips up developers and administrators initially because first the Web application hosting the SharePoint sites must be configured to allow for anonymous access before the options for enabling and configuring anonymous access are available within the site.

As a general rule, administrators should never configure Web applications using the Internet Information Services Manager application. Instead, the majority of changes should be implemented using the SharePoint Central Administration Web site. There are many reasons for this but consider just one example: a load-balanced environment. When changes are made through Central Administration, all Web applications on all SharePoint WFE servers are changed at the same time.

To configure a Web application to allow anonymous requests, browse to Central Administration and select Application Management ⇨ Authentication Providers under the Application Security group. On the Authentication Providers page, select the desired Web application and the zone to be configured. Check the Enable Anonymous Access checkbox, shown in Figure 15-3, and click Save. Now the Web application has been configured to allow anonymous requests.

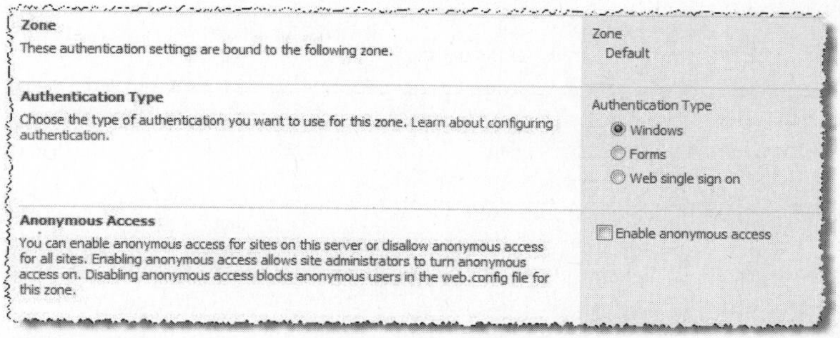

Figure 15-3

The next step is to enable a SharePoint site to allow for anonymous access. Browse to the desired SharePoint site's Site Settings page and select Advanced Permissions. On the Permissions page, select Settings ⇨ Anonymous Access.

> *If this option is not available, then the current site is likely inheriting permissions from its parent. Break inheritance by selecting Actions ⇨ Edit Permissions.*

On the Change Anonymous Access Settings page, select Entire Web Site and click OK. Now the entire site is configured for anonymous access. Users can now browse the site without logging in but they will be provided with a login control that enables them to log in to browse content and perform actions only authenticated users are permitted to do.

The Lockdown Feature

Traditional SharePoint sites permit all users to view the SharePoint application pages. This includes list form pages such as `http://[some URL]/Pages/Forms/AllItems.aspx`. Because Publishing sites are commonly used for Internet-facing anonymous sites, it is not ideal to have these SharePoint application pages accessible to the users of a site.

The capability to browse these SharePoint application pages is controlled using the View Application Pages permission right (`SPBasePermissions.ViewFormPages`). By default, the limited access permission level is granted this permission right. Unfortunately, this permission level is one of two that cannot be configured through the browser interface. However, it can be configured through the SharePoint API!

Microsoft has included a special SharePoint Feature named *Restrict Limited Access Permissions,* more commonly known as the Lockdown Feature. This Feature (`[..]\12\TEMPLATE\FEATURES\ViewFormPagesLockDown`) uses the `FeatureActivated()` and `FeatureDeactivated()` event receivers to add and remove the View Application Pages permission right from the limited access permission level. By default, this Feature is activated when a site collection is created using the Publishing Portal site definition, but administrators can easily activate the Feature via the command line using `STSADM.EXE`.

Summary

This chapter covered the details of the various components within a SharePoint site that are used for authorizing users and specifying what they can or cannot do. Publishing sites, while at the core are still just SharePoint sites, include some additional permission levels and groups that are specific to Internet-facing content-centric sites. This chapter also walked through the process of configuring a SharePoint site for FBA using a Microsoft SQL Server database.

16

Implementing Sites with Multiple Languages and Devices

It may not seem obvious that the same chapter would discuss both multilingual sites and sites for mobile devices, but both of these scenarios use the same capability built into the Office SharePoint Server (MOSS) 2007 publishing system: *site variations*. This feature enables the management of parallel site hierarchies for Web Content Management (WCM), and movement of content among them. First the multilingual scenario is examined, which explains how this is achieved; then their application in mobile device scenarios is addressed.

Developing Multilingual Web Sites

Douglas Adams' science fiction parody *The Hitchhiker's Guide to the Galaxy* describes a fanciful creature that might have made this section unnecessary. The Babel fish provided instant language translation, a service computer scientists have long sought to provide using software. If machines could reliably translate all the nuances of human language, there would undoubtedly be translation layers available on both client and server that could present any and all Web content in the language of each user's choosing. Alas, this vision has proven elusive — the services available on the Web produce obtuse and sometimes humorous results, and even the best machine translations must be checked by a human. For the foreseeable future, human translation will be a part of any multilingual Web site.

The translation problem is compounded in a WCM system because its text comes from so many places. In a typical SharePoint Publishing site, in addition to the authored content, an end user will see text that originates in the master page, in site metadata such as column and container names, as well as text that comes from SharePoint itself. Some text is simple string data, while other text is embedded in image files. In order for a user to have a good experience, all of this must be localized.

Many computer products claim to have multilingual capabilities, but this term is subject to a broad range of interpretation. The following table shows some of the possible capabilities and which are provided by SharePoint technologies. The table uses the term "content" to refer to authored content and configured metadata, and "user interface" to denote text that is displayed by the underlying platform — in this case by MOSS 2007 and any added extensions.

Capability	ASP.NET	WSS 2.0 and 3.0	SPS 2003	MOSS 2007
User Interface				
User interface runs in a chosen language (only one across the entire Web farm)	X	X	X	X
User interface runs in a mix of languages, but a given section of a Web site is always displayed in a single language	X	X		√
User interface is "language agile," meaning the same page is displayed in different languages depending on the user's preferences	X			
Content				
Supports content in any language. This mainly involves supporting a (normally double-byte) character set that can display the target languages	X	X	X	X
Supports content translations. This involves storing parallel content translated into each target language.				X

For the "user interface" — the part of each Web page that originates in MOSS 2007 and any developed extensions — utopia is language agility. That means both Japanese and Dutch users can visit exactly the same URL and see a page that is translated into their preferred language (without redirecting to a language-specific page).

ASP.NET enables language agility via the .NET Resource Manager. .NET resources are non-executable data that is compiled into an application. To create a Web control or page that is language agile, a resource file is created for each target language, containing all display text and the locations of localized images and other media. ASP.NET's Resource Manager will select the right resources when a page is rendered based on the thread culture, which the application sets to reflect the user's preferred language. The sample code in the section "Localizing Web Parts and Field Controls" demonstrates this concept.

Unfortunately, none of the SharePoint technologies are completely language agile. (This is not such a bad thing, actually, as most of the text on a typical SharePoint page is content, which does not lend itself well to language agility anyway.) Although MOSS 2007 supports many "language packs" that provide the capability to create SharePoint sites in a variety of languages, a given site's user interface will always be displayed in the single language that was chosen when the site was created. This is visible at the API level in the SPWebCollection.Add() method, which accepts a locale ID (LCID) as an argument; this locale defines a site's user interface language forever more.

None of this has any affect on content, however! A Korean document can be loaded into a Swedish site without any problem, or a page of English text can be added to a French Publishing site. This may well happen in collaboration scenarios where participants contribute in multiple languages and no translation is provided: Users need to be able to read more than one language on a page. In publishing scenarios, however, the content must be translated and presented with the corresponding user interface to present a single language to the viewer.

Language agility assumes that a resource will be available in all supported languages before it can be used. This is fine for a site user interface or Web Part, which has a finite and pre-determined set of resources to display, but it creates problems for user-created content. One reason for this is because translation takes time, and users often want to publish content in each language as soon as it's available. Another reason is that in practice, content often doesn't apply in every locale. It's sometimes desirable to simply drop inapplicable content for certain languages, rather than to provide a translation, or to replace content with something more relevant to a particular audience. Finally, certain languages may require layout changes that aren't easily accommodated by resource settings.

To address these needs, as well as to coordinate the translation effort, MOSS 2007 provides site *variations*. Variations are parallel site structures with a source site hierarchy and one or more parallel site hierarchies for the translations. When content is approved on the source site, the other variations are automatically updated with draft versions ready for translation. A translation workflow is provided to ensure that each variation is translated or otherwise addressed by a human translator. The use of parallel sites enables site designers to have as much flexibility as they need to choose the UI language, master pages, and other settings needed for each variation. Variations are explored in more detail in the "Using Variations" section.

Variations are not only for multilingual situations; they can be used whenever an alternative rendering is needed. A common example is the use of variations to create alternative renderings for mobile devices; this is covered in the section "Targeting Devices with Variations."

Installing the Language Packs

The first step in creating a multilingual Web site in MOSS is to install language packs that determine the user interface language:

❑ **SharePoint Language Packs** — These language packs are designed for Windows SharePoint Services (WSS) only. In a multi-server farm, each desired language pack must be installed on each server individually. These are not the language packs to use in a WCM scenario.

❑ **Server Language Packs** — These language packs are designed for MOSS 2007, and include all the resources from the SharePoint language packs, so there is no need to install both. These are the natural choice for a WCM scenario.

❑ **Server Multiple Language Pack** — This is a special Server Language Pack containing all of the language packs bundled together. This is the only way to add English language support to a non-English installation. This is the natural choice for a WCM scenario for which all available languages are to be accessible.

Installing the appropriate language pack(s) will make site definitions available in the target languages. This is necessary to enable the user interface to be displayed in the target language of each site variation. The following list contains links to download the language packs for the different versions of SharePoint. One point of common confusion is how to download different languages. By default, each of the following links loads in the browser's configured locale. Use the selector in the download box to switch to a different language, causing the page to postback and load in the selected language. Once in the desired language, the download link will trigger the download for the selected language. In addition, note that the release version of the language pack should be installed first, followed by the service pack:

❑ **WSS x32** — www.andrewconnell.com/go/255

❑ **WSS x32 Service Pack 1** — www.andrewconnell.com/go/256

❑ **WSS x64** — www.andrewconnell.com/go/257

❑ **WSS x64 Service Pack 1** — www.andrewconnell.com/go/258

❑ **MOSS x32** — www.andrewconnell.com/go/259

❑ **MOSS x32 Service Pack 1** — www.andrewconnell.com/go/260

❑ **MOSS x64** — www.andrewconnell.com/go/261

❑ **MOSS x64 Service Pack 1** — www.andrewconnell.com/go/262

Using Variations

The next step in creating a multi-lingual site is to set up the *variations* feature in Microsoft Office SharePoint Server 2007. A MOSS 2007 site collection can have at most one *variation hierarchy*, shown in Figure 16-1.

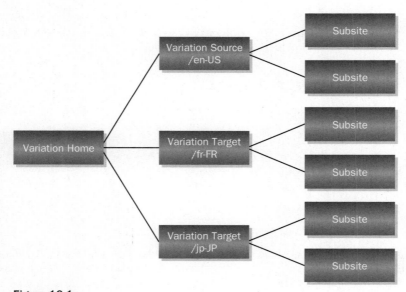

Figure 16-1

One site is designated as the *variation home*, and this is the root of the variation hierarchy. In most cases this will be the top-level site, but that's not necessary; a variation home can be any site in the site collection. It's best to plan ahead and set up variations correctly the first time, as changing or moving them afterward can be difficult.

Begin by creating a simple Publishing site to serve as the variation home; at first, this will behave as an ordinary site, but after the variation hierarchy has been created, this site will contain a redirect page (`VariationRoot.aspx`) to send users to the appropriate variation. The `VariationRoot.aspx` page can be replaced to customize the redirection logic, which by default redirects users to the variation label corresponding to their most preferred language in their browser language settings.

Next, click Variations in the Site Collection Administration section. Here, the variation home site can be set as well as other behaviors, such as whether or not to automatically create child sites in target variations to match new sites under the source variation, whether to re-create pages that have been deleted on target variations when the source page is updated, and so on.

The next step is to create the variation *labels*, which are the parallel sites for each variation. One of these labels will be the source, and the rest will be targets. Note that once the hierarchy is created, the source designation cannot be changed, so planning ahead and getting it right the first time is important. A language and culture can be defined for each label, and if the corresponding language pack is installed, this will generate a site containing that language.

To complete the setup, click the Create Hierarchies action on the Variation Labels screen. This will create a child site for each variation label and will set up the Relationships List in the variation home site.

Returning to the variation home site will redirect to the variation label corresponding to the preferred language. This is typically set in the Web browser — in Internet Explorer 7.0 it's on the Internet Options dialog box, and in Firefox 2.0 it is under the Advanced tab under Options. Users can choose a list of languages (first choice, second choice, etc.) and the redirector page will send them to the first one that has a variation label.

Master Pages and Page Layouts in Variation Sites

The master pages and page layouts provided with MOSS 2007 contain no visible text, so out-of-the-box (OOTB) there is no need to translate them. Each variation label inherits the master page setting from its parent, and all will be well. In practice, however, it is typical to create a unique master page for each variation for the following reasons:

❑   In a multilingual site, banners and other master page elements may contain text that needs to be translated, and in some cases the text flow will affect the whole layout. This is most easily managed by having a master page for each locale.

❑   If the variations aren't being used for multilingual sites but for branding or use on mobile devices, then each variation needs a master page with the appropriate branding or device layout.

In addition to master pages, page layouts may be affected, especially in device or branding scenarios, or when handling languages that flow text from right to left, for example. This is explained in the section "Targeting Devices with Variations" later in the chapter.

Maintaining Object Relationships

The variation feature tracks the variations of each child site and Web page in a hidden list called the *relationship list* in the variation home site. Whenever a new site or page is created, it is entered in the relationship list; and if a site or page is renamed or deleted, the relationship list is updated accordingly.

The relationship list tracks objects by their relative Web addresses in the `ObjectID` field; note that the `ObjectID` description holds the original address of the site or page. Now inspect the properties of a list item; note that the field also stores the latest and greatest Web address. This means you can change the site and page display names in the variation labels, as well as rename the subsite and page names to localize the URLs.

The actual copying of pages and sites from source to target variation labels is performed by the *variation job*, which by default runs every 20 seconds. When it wakes up, it copies any new sites or newly approved pages based on the rules specified under Variations in the Site Collection Settings.

This handles pages and sites, but what about other content on the page? A typical page includes images and possibly links to documents and other content that may need to be translated. This can be accommodated by specifying Copy Resources in the Resources radio button on the Variation Settings page. If this setting is selected, any images or documents in the source variation that are referenced on a page (by an image field control or hyperlink, for example) will be copied along with the page to each target variation, and their URLs will be adjusted on the target pages.

While this allows for the translation of images and referenced documents, note that these items are not managed in the relationship list and therefore won't be copied when they are updated, but rather when a page that references them is updated. Referenced items are copied every time a referencing page is copied, potentially overwriting localized versions stored in the target variations. Moreover, any change to the Web addresses of referenced items won't be tracked, so if a document is renamed in a target variation, a new copy with the old name will be copied the next time the referencing page is updated.

Web Parts in Variations

Web Part placement and metadata is not stored in the Pages list; it's stored separately by WSS. That is why Web Parts are not versioned along with the rest of a WCM page (though they are subject to approval), and it is no surprise that Web Parts require a little special handling when using site variations as well.

There is a setting on the Variation Settings page that enables the administrator to specify that Web Part changes will be propagated to target pages along with other changes; by default, this is set to true. This works fine for many but not all Web Parts. Some Web Parts, such as the Content Editor Web Part, do not reference any external data, so they work the same wherever they are moved. Other Web Parts are fully aware of variations, and will modify their metadata to handle their migration to a new site.

For example, the Content Query Web Part will re-target the content query to the target variation site when it is moved. Conversely, some of the Web Parts that ship with WSS are completely unaware of variations and will break. The standard List View Web Part used to show document libraries and other collaboration lists will break when it is moved because it references its list by a GUID, which is not present in the target variation. In some cases it may appear to work, but it will break if the Web Part is modified.

Building Language-Agile Features

This section demonstrates how to develop a custom Web part that is aware of variations and how to make entire Features language agile.

Variation-Aware Web Parts

The first example is a variation-aware Web Part for viewing lists and libraries. Figure 16-2 shows two Web Parts on a U.S. English-language Web page that is in the source variation site. The one on the left is the built-in List View of a task list, and the one on the right is the custom Variation List View Web Part. They look almost identical.

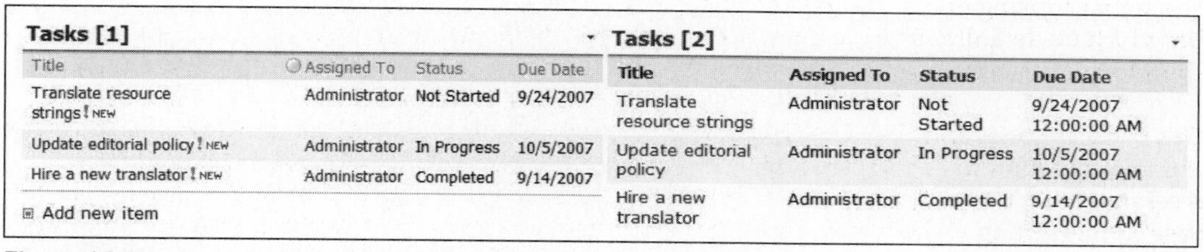

Figure 16-2

An interesting thing happens, however, on the target variation sites. Figure 16-3 shows the same two Web Parts on a French target variation site.

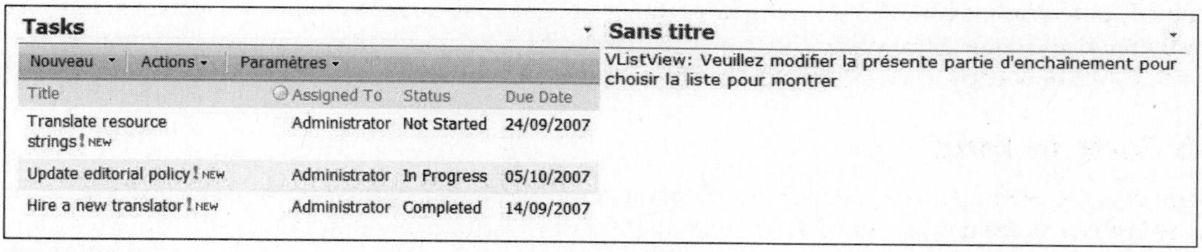

Figure 16-3

The Web Part on the left has not changed much, except it now has a French toolbar and the dates appear in the day-month-year style used in Europe. It is still displaying the task list from the English site, however, and will break if modified. In practice, the behavior of the built-in List View Web Part on a target variation is hard to predict. The Variation List View Web Part on the right knows that it is running on a new site, and is asking to be configured.

When the editor modifies the Variation List View Web Part and selects a list and view to show, as shown in Figure 16-3, the Web Part adjusts to show the French task list. Figure 16-4 illustrates that the task list has a French title, the tasks have been entered in French, and the column names from the French language pack are displayed.

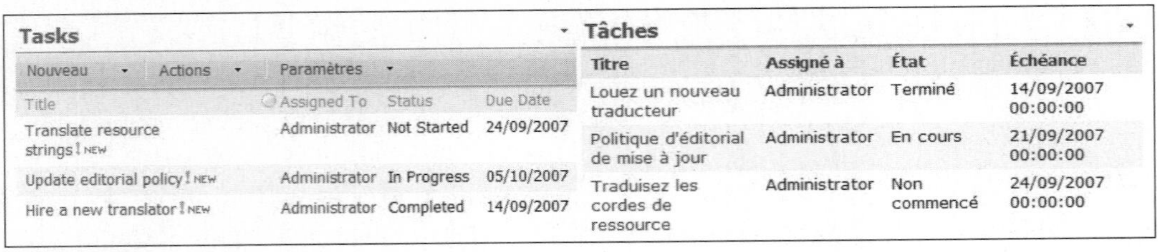

Tasks			▾		Tâches				▾
Nouveau ▾	Actions ▾	Paramètres ▾			Titre	Assigné à	État	Échéance	
Title	◯ Assigned To	Status	Due Date		Louez un nouveau traducteur	Administrator	Terminé	14/09/2007 00:00:00	
Translate resource strings! NEW	Administrator	Not Started	24/09/2007		Politique d'éditorial de mise à jour	Administrator	En cours	21/09/2007 00:00:00	
Update editorial policy! NEW	Administrator	In Progress	05/10/2007		Traduisez les cordes de ressource	Administrator	Non commencé	24/09/2007 00:00:00	
Hire a new translator! NEW	Administrator	Completed	14/09/2007						

Figure 16-4

Of course, the editor could have deleted the built-in List View and replaced it with one from the French site, and this would work initially; but whenever the source variation changes, the French Web Part will be overwritten and that Web Part will need to be re-created every time. Conversely, the Variation List View Web Part is smart enough to remember its settings, and won't need to be modified again.

How does this work?

It's really pretty simple. When the variation job copies a Web Part, it copies its metadata as well; and in the case of the built-in List View Web Part, that metadata is not relevant in the context of a target variation site. To get around that, the Variation List View Web Part stores the names of the lists and views to display in the site property bag rather than in the Web Part metadata. (Note that the sample Web Part uses the selected view to determine which columns to display, but does not respect other aspects such as filtering. All the rendering is in a child control to easily plug in another control to render a list.)

Listing 16-1 shows the Variation List View's properties. Notice that only the first one, the correlation ID, is stored in the Web Part metadata, as indicated by the `Personalizable` attribute. The first time this property is retrieved, it generates a new unique value, which it will retain from then on, even when the Web Part is copied to target variations.

`ListName` and `ViewName` are not decorated with the `Personalizable` attribute, so the SharePoint infrastructure leaves them alone. However, when the Web Part is configured, its Editor Part (the control used to configure the Web Part) will handle these properties as it would any other Web Part properties. This only requires that the properties be public for this purpose. These properties store their data in the site property bag, in properties whose names contain the correlation ID. This ensures that each Web Part's properties are kept separately, as more than one might be used in a particular site or page. Because the correlation ID is copied as part of the Web Part metadata, the target Web Part will pick up the right values even if it is moved around on the page in the source variation.

Listing 16-1: Web Part properties that survive variation page copies

```
private string _errorMessage = String.Empty;
private bool _errorSet = false;
private string _correlationID = String.Empty;

// This unique ID will propagate to target variations, so they can find the
// list and view properties in their SPWeb property bags.
[WebBrowsable(false)]
[Personalizable(PersonalizationScope.Shared)]
```

```
public string CorrelationID {
  get {
    if (String.IsNullOrEmpty(_correlationID))
      _correlationID = Guid.NewGuid().ToString();

    return (_correlationID);
  }

  set { _correlationID = value; }
}

// ListName - Stores the list to be displayed in site property bag
public string ListName {
  get {
    if (!String.IsNullOrEmpty(_correlationID))
      return (SPContext.Current.Web.Properties["listName_" +_correlationID]);
    else
      return (String.Emtpty);
  }

  set {
    try {
      SPContext.Current.Web.AllowUnsafeUpdates = true;
      SPContext.Current.Web.Properties["listName_" + _correlationID] = value;
      SPContext.Current.Web.Properties.Update();
    } catch (Exception ex) {
      _errorMessage = ex.Message;
      _errorSet = true;
    }
  }
}

// View name is stored in the same way ...
```

There is another approach to handling Web Part metadata across variations, but it currently only works in Web Parts derived from the `Microsoft.SharePoint.WebPartPages.WebPart` class and not the `System.Web.UI.WebControls.WebParts.WebPart` class used in this sample. The trick here is to implement an interface called `IWebPartVariationUpdate`, which requires a single method:

```
public void Update(PublishingWeb ownerWeb) {    }
```

If this is implemented, the variation job will invoke the `Update()` method on each Web Part on a page as it is copied to each target variation, thus giving it the opportunity to adjust any of its properties for the new site location.

Localizing Web Parts and Field Controls

That simple step makes the Web Part variation aware, but what about localization? There is not a lot of text in the Web Part — the majority of what it renders is content. However, there is some, such as in the Editor Part that is shown when a user selects a list or view to be displayed. Figure 16-5 shows the Editor

Part in English on the left and in French on the right. Notice that the title (Select View to Display in English) plus the "List:" and "View:" labels have been localized. This is UI, not content, and shows that the Editor Part is language agile.

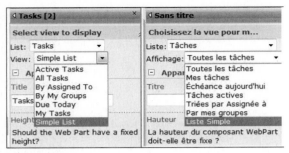

Figure 16-5

The standard .NET technique of using resource files was used to provide the localized text. In this case, `*.RESX` resource files are used to create a default set of resources in English that are bound into the Web Part assembly, and another set of French resources that are placed in a satellite assembly. Figure 16-6 shows the resources in Visual Studio; note that Visual Studio provides a simple design experience for the resource files. Basically, these are name-value pairs, where the name is used to look up the localized value at runtime.

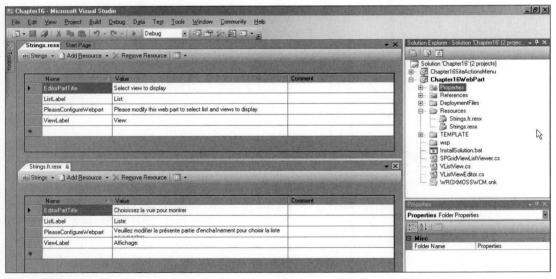

Figure 16-6

Accessing the resources in code is a simple affair, as shown in Listing 16-2.

Listing 16-2: Using resources at runtime for localization

```
using System.Reflection;
using System.Resources;

// ...

ResourceManager rm = new ResourceManager("WROX.ProMossWcm.Chapter16.Resources.
Strings",this.GetType().Assembly);

this.Title = rm.GetString("EditorPartTitle");
```

The resource manager is passed the base name of the resource file without the culture extension — the actual resource files are `Resources\Strings.resx` and `Resources\Strings.fr.resx`. The file-naming format is `basename.resx` for culture-neutral resources (the default), and `basename.cultureID.resx` for localized resources. The Culture ID can be a simple language identifier, such as "fr", or a language and region identifier such as "fr-CA" for Canadian French.

The resource manager will look for an exact match between the thread culture and the available resource file extensions. If it does not find an exact match, then it falls back to the language identifier (from "fr-FR" to "fr" in this example), and if *it* doesn't find the language identifier, it falls back to the culture-neutral resources (from "en-US" to the neutral resources in this example).

The resource manager bases its choice of resources on the thread culture, which SharePoint handles automatically. Therefore, whenever the resource manager's `GetString()` method is called with a resource name, the localized value is returned.

Note that this project creates an extra assembly for every localized resource file — in this example, the Web Part is in `bin\debug\Chapter16WebPart.dll` and the French resources are in `bin\debug\fr\Chapter16WebPart.resources.dll`. Both assemblies need to be deployed in the solution package or the Web Part will not work in French.

The same technique can be used in field controls and other assemblies. The key point is that these are runtime resources. However, there is another way to use resources in SharePoint: not at runtime but at deployment time.

Localizing SharePoint Features

In the Web Part example almost everything was localized, but the Web Part Gallery was not. After all, there is only one Web Part Gallery in the site collection, and because variations cannot span site collections, that one gallery is shared by all the variations. Thus, if a user were to add the Web Part to a new page, its name and description would be shown in the language of the top-level site. This is true of all the built-in Web Parts as well, for the same reason. This is less of an issue in variation hierarchies where Web Parts are configured only in the source variation, but what about adding menus, site settings, and other extensions to the Publishing sites?

Fortunately, SharePoint allows localizing Features and their elements. Resources are referenced directly from the Feature XML files, and are expanded at deployment time, when a Feature is activated. A Feature in any scope can be localized, but unless it is at site scope it will take on the language of its site collection, or of the SharePoint installation. Only a site-scoped Feature will localize its elements for individual variation sites.

This leads to another sample, this time a very simple Feature to add a button to the Site Actions menu. The button brings the user directly to the top-level site settings, which is always handy.

In Figure 16-7, the menu item is localized; the English menu is on the left and the French menu is on the right. In addition, the Feature's name and description are localized in the Site Features list.

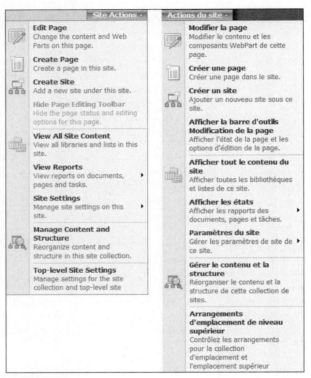

Figure 16-7

The same kind of resource files used in the Web Part will work in a Feature, but they are not compiled; instead, SharePoint interprets them directly. The default location for resources in a Feature is in a directory called Resources under the Feature directory; resource files must be named like

```
Feature Directory\Resources\Resources.xx-XX.resx
```

where xx-XX is the culture ID like before except that both the language and region portions are required. Here is the form for a "culture-neutral" resources file:

```
Feature Directory\Resources\Resources.resx
```

Listing 16-3 shows the elements.xml for the Site Actions menu.

Listing 16-3: Feature elements using resources for localization

```xml
<?xml version="1.0" encoding="utf-8" ?>
<Elements xmlns="http://schemas.microsoft.com/sharepoint/">
  <!-- Add Top-level Site Settings to Site Actions Menu -->
  <CustomAction Id="TopLevelSiteSettings"
                Location="Microsoft.SharePoint.StandardMenu"
                GroupId="SiteActions"
                Sequence="1000"
                Title="$Resources:MenuItemName;"
                Description="$Resources:MenuItemDescription;">
    <UrlAction Url="~sitecollection/_layouts/settings.aspx" />
  </CustomAction>
</Elements>
```

The menu title and description are localized, using the notation $Resources;name, where name is the name in the resource file. It is also possible to localize the Feature when it appears in the Site Features page on the Site Settings page. Listing 16-4 shows the feature.xml file for the menu item.

Listing 16-4: Feature XML using resources for localization

```xml
<?xml version="1.0" encoding="utf-8" ?>
<Feature xmlns="http://schemas.microsoft.com/sharepoint/"
         Id="DB844BB8-B4D5-4f00-B7EC-8712C24A40B9"
         Title="$Resources:FeatureName;"
         Description="$Resources:FeatureDescription;"
         Hidden="FALSE"
         Scope="Web"
         Version="1.0.0.0"
         RequireResources="FALSE">

  <ElementManifests>
    <ElementManifest Location="elements.xml"/>
  </ElementManifests>

</Feature>
```

The same notation works here as well. Another interesting thing about this XML is the RequireResources="FALSE" attribute. Setting this attribute to false (the default) instructs SharePoint to fall back to the culture-neutral resources file if no file is available for a site's locale. Setting this attribute to true will hide the Feature unless an exactly matching resources file is found.

This is useful when developing a Feature that will simply not show up unless the desired localization is available. For example, if this sample were added to a Japanese site, it would display in English, but if RequireResource="True" were set, it would be hidden to prevent sites with unsupported locales from using it entirely. In this case, there is no reason to provide a culture-neutral resources file because it will never be used. Note that this hiding is only provided at the SharePoint user interface; the Feature could still be activated on a Japanese site via the STSADM.EXE command line or the API, for example.

Targeting Devices with Variations

WSS 3.0 comes with built-in mobility support, which is intended to enable mobile users to access list data. The typical way to access this is via one of the two following URLs:

```
http://server/site/m
http://server/site/_layouts/mobile/default.aspx
```

Note that the first, simpler syntax is disabled by default in Publishing sites, but it can be re-enabled by activating a Feature called `MobilityRedirect` using the `STSADM.EXE` command:

```
stsadm -o activatefeature -name MobilityRedirect -URL http://URL
```

List views can be designated as "mobile" in the regular view editing screen, and these views will be offered to mobile users as well as regular Web browsers. Further customization of the rendering of mobile views is possible, but is beyond the scope of this book.

> *For more information on mobile device customizations in WSS 3.0, refer to the official documentation on MSDN:* `www.andrewconnell.com/go/263`.

In reality, this is most useful in collaborative environments. In Publishing sites, variations are a more useful tool for adapting authored pages to a mobile format.

Creating Variations for Mobile Devices

Creating a mobile device variation is as simple as creating any other variation label. Typically, the source and target variations have the same locale ID because there is no need to localize the user interface. In addition, developers may want to disable approval and the approval workflow, and set to major versions only, so that the target variation pages go live immediately without any human intervention.

Redirecting Mobile Users

When a variations hierarchy is created, a page called `variationroot.aspx` is created and set as the welcome page to the site. This page contains a user control called `VariationsRootLanding.ascx` that redirects the user to a variation based on the preferred language set in the client Web browser and the list of available variation locales. While this works well in multilingual sites, it is not especially helpful for redirecting mobile users to a special variation.

There are a few options for modifying the redirection logic. One is to create a new ASPX page (or page layout and a Publishing page) with the desired logic, ideally compiled into a control on the page, and set that as the new welcome page. Another option is to modify the provided page layout or the user control. Placing the logic in a compiled Web control is preferable for security reasons, even if it does require redeploying the assembly if the redirection logic changes.

Master Pages, Page Layouts, and Style Sheets

The mobile form factor will likely require the creation of custom master page(s), page layouts, and style sheets for the small screen. Creating master pages and page layouts is covered in Chapter 7, "Master Pages and Page Layouts." In general, mobile master pages and page layouts should avoid horizontal placement of elements so that users can stick to vertical scrolling when viewing the page on a small device.

Assigning master pages and style sheets to variations is as easy as selecting the desired settings in each variation's Site Master Page Settings and allowing child sites to inherit the master page from the variation site.

Assigning page layouts is slightly trickier. Directly changing the page layout of a page in a target variation will only be of temporary help, as the next time the source is modified the target page will have its layout overwritten. The key is to designate a "preferred" page layout so the variation job can assign the right layout every time it copies a page from the source variation.

The selection of preferred page layouts for variations is not done in the variation sites, but rather in the Master Page Gallery in the top-level site. Each page layout's properties page provides the capability to select one or more variations for which a page layout is preferred. When the variation job finds a source page that has changed, it will look for a page layout of the same content type marked as preferred for each target variation. If it finds one, it will set the target page to use the preferred page layout. Note that the language packs localize the content type names but still use the same underlying content types. For example, the Article Page content type is called *Page d'article* in a French Publishing site. Checking at the site-collection level, notice that these still map to the same underlying content types.

Care must be taken to designate only one preferred page layout for each content type/variation combination, or the results may be unpredictable. This is most easily done by creating a view on the Master Page Gallery that shows the associated content type and variations columns, and filters to only show Page Layout content type items.

Finally, note that using Web Part zones can affect the page layout processing if variations are set to propagate Web Parts. If a source variation page contains a Web Part in zones that don't exist in the preferred target page layout, the source's page layout will be reused in the target regardless of preferred page layout settings.

Summary

One of the more common requirements for content-centric Web sites is that they present the content in multiple languages to serve the largest audience possible. Fortunately, Microsoft included capabilities in MOSS 2007 Publishing sites to facilitate the creation and management of multilingual sites. This is primarily addressed using variations, a topic covered in depth in this chapter.

In addition, developers should also account for multilingual situations when building custom components, such as Web Parts, for sites that will be presented in multiple languages. This chapter demonstrated how to achieve localization with custom Web Parts.

17

Content Deployment

Content deployment is one of the key feature areas from Microsoft Content Management Server (MCMS) 2002 that has been brought over to and extended within Office SharePoint Server (MOSS) 2007 to enable flexible, powerful, fast, efficient, and secure deployment of Publishing sites. In a nutshell, content deployment is the copying of content from one site collection to another, either within the same SharePoint farm or across farms. The most common scenario that content deployment targets is that of enabling content authoring within the internal network (a read/write environment) and content delivery to the Internet (a read-only environment). Once configured by an administrator, content deployment can take place without any manual intervention.

While the main application of content deployment is for Internet-facing sites, it is an extremely flexible feature that can also be used with intranet sites and for deploying content across site collections on a single machine running MOSS. More complex uses include a three-tier deployment topology (authoring, staging, and production).

While MOSS provides a comprehensive administrative user interface for configuring, running, and monitoring content deployment, it also provides an API that enables developers to customize deployments to suit specific needs, such as deployment across disconnected environments.

Content deployment also features a capability called *Quick Deploy* that enables content authors to deploy single pages from within the authoring environment without having to wait for the next scheduled content deployment job to run.

This chapter covers the core concepts of content deployment, paths, and jobs, and how they can be combined to provide granular control over content publishing. It also describes the content deployment user interface, and includes examples and a look at the content deployment API. Finally, the Windows SharePoint Services (WSS) 3.0 content migration APIs are covered, a key infrastructure enabler for Publishing sites.

Content Deployment Fundamentals

The examples in this chapter mimic a simple content deployment topology consisting of an authoring (read/write) environment and a production environment (read only). This topology is shown in Figure 17-1.

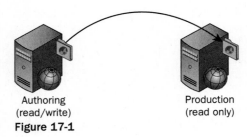

Authoring
(read/write)

Production
(read only)

Figure 17-1

However, to keep the samples simple and easy to follow, only two site collections within two separate Web applications on a single server are used.

A core concept of content deployment is that it follows a "single master" model. Deployment is always one way from source to destination; it does not provide replication or synchronization capabilities. In essence, content deployment has three phases of operation:

1. **Export content from the source** — Based upon the configuration settings, content deployment exports content by packaging it up as cabinet (CAB) files on the source server.

2. **Transport content from the source to destination** — The CAB files are then transferred to the destination server.

3. **Import content into the destination** — The destination server opens the CAB files and imports the content.

In large or heavily used environments, it may not be desirable or acceptable for the content deployment import and export processing to take place on machines that are serving end users. This is especially true within the read-only, production farm and when deploying large amounts of content. For these scenarios, content deployment can be configured to make use of dedicated import and export servers. These servers must be SharePoint Web Front End (WFE) servers, and only a single server can be specified for each role.

The CAB files are stored within a temporary folder on the export server and each one is 10 megabytes by default, but they can be configured if desired. After the files are sent to the import server, they are removed from the export server. Once the import is complete, the files are removed from the import server. There must be enough disk space on the import and export servers for the largest deployment that could take place.

Content deployment also takes care of the transport of the CAB files over the wire to the destination import server. This transport takes place over firewall-friendly HTTP. Transport layer security (SSL) can be configured to ensure that the data (including the credentials used to connect to the destination) cannot be intercepted. The use of SSL should be carefully considered, as there is a performance impact when leveraging it. When using content deployment within a trusted network, it is more appropriate to stick with HTTP or implement IPSec, rather than SSL.

Administration of content deployment configuration and operations takes place within SharePoint Central Administration and therefore requires SharePoint farm administrator rights. Content deployment operations cannot be delegated to a subset of users, as is the case for many of the shared service provider (SSP) features. This is usually appropriate, but as demonstrated later there is an alternative approach for content authors.

By default, content deployment is incremental; it will deploy only the changes since the last successful deployment. This approach avoids unnecessary processing and bandwidth. If a full deployment is required, this can also be configured.

Content deployment deploys the most recent major and minor versions of a content item. For example, if version 2.7 of a page is being deployed, the most recent major version (2.0) of the page (the published version), along with the most recent minor version (2.7), will be deployed to the destination.

A destination site collection for content deployment must be based upon the Blank Site template. If another template is used — for example, the Team Site template — then various elements will cause conflicts when the import is processed.

> For more information on the Blank Site template requirement, refer to the Microsoft Knowledge Base article # 923592 (www.andrewconnell.com/go/264).

Dependencies of the content deployed are picked up and handled by content deployment as long as those dependencies reside in the SharePoint content database. For example, if a page is dependent upon a Page Layout that has been updated since the last deployment or it includes other resources such as images or CSS files, these are packaged with the page itself and deployed. However, content deployment does not take care of the deployment of Features, assemblies, or configuration for which Features and solutions are the appropriate deployment mechanism. If the content being deployed depends upon files on the file system, such as assemblies containing Web Parts, custom field types or field controls, Features, or anything else for that matter, the files should be deployed as closely as possible to the same time when the content deployment jobs execute. This is another reason why SharePoint farm administrators should always enforce the deployment of custom code and files that are handled by WSS solution packages (*.WSP).

Content deployment also handles the activation of already deployed Features in the destination. Consider the scenario in which a new site is added within the source site collection and it uses a Feature not used elsewhere or that is otherwise available within the destination. Content deployment will take care of the Feature activation during deployment. For example, in the case of an initial deployment to a Blank Site, the Publishing Infrastructure Feature is activated.

Paths

A content deployment *path* defines a relationship between a source and a destination site collection for the purposes of deploying content. A path contains the details of both the source and the destination Web application and site collection. In addition, authentication details for the destination are necessary in order to connect and select the destination site collection. The application pool identity of the Central Administration Web application can be used or alternative credentials can be specified using either Windows or basic authentication. A path can also be configured to deploy the user names associated with the source content, and related security information, such as ACLs, roles, and membership, if desired.

A path itself does not perform any deployment of content; it is purely the mapping, or link, between the source and destination servers. Once a path is created and configured, jobs can be created and associated with a path to begin deploying content.

Jobs

Once a path is defined, a deployment *job* can be created and associated with a path. A job defines which sites within the source site collection are to be deployed, and the schedule indicating when to run the job. The job also specifies whether to deploy all content (full deployment) or just content that has been added or changed since the last time it ran (incremental deployment). When configuring a job, e-mail notifications can also be specified to indicate deployment success or failure. Jobs provide the capability to deploy content updates on a regular scheduled basis without the need for manual intervention.

A given path can have many jobs associated with it, each with its own schedule and configured to deploy specific sites within the source site collection. This granular control enables a common scenario whereby particular sections of a Publishing site have more aggressive deployment schedule than others.

For example, consider a site with two subsites, *About Us* and *News*. The *About Us* site should be deployed at the same time as the content within the top-level site, whereas the *News* site needs a more frequent schedule to enable news items to be published faster.

Quick Deploy Jobs

Because content deployment is managed via Central Administration, it requires Central Administration privileges. This is entirely appropriate for the initial configuration and ongoing management, but it does not address the need for content authors to be able to deploy certain pieces of content in an "on demand" fashion without having to wait for the next scheduled deployment to occur. This requirement is met by the Quick Deploy function.

Once a path has been created within a Publishing site collection, one that has the Office SharePoint Publishing Infrastructure Feature activated, a Quick Deploy job is automatically created for use on that path. The Quick Deploy job executes on a configurable schedule, which is set to every 15 minutes by default. The Quick Deploy job checks the Pages library for items that are marked for deployment since the last time it ran and then deploys these items.

By default, only site owners can mark pages for deployment using Quick Deploy. However, sites that have the Office SharePoint Publishing Infrastructure Feature enabled include a Quick Deploy Users SharePoint group, and members of this group (commonly content authors) can mark a page for deployment using the Quick Deploy item of the Tools menu within the Page Editing Toolbar, as shown in Figure 17-2.

Figure 17-2

If a path is created within a site collection before the Publishing Infrastructure Feature is enabled, the Quick Deploy job will not be created. To make use of Quick Deploy, delete and re-create the path after the Publishing Infrastructure Feature has been enabled.

Configuring Content Deployment

By default, content deployment is disabled in a farm and must first be configured before use. The destination farm needs to be configured to accept content deployment jobs and have a server selected as its import server. The import server must host the farm's Central Administration site, as the content migration packages are sent via the Central Administration site. The source farm requires a server to be configured as its export server. Development environments can simply be configured as a single server with all of these roles, which is the default configuration in a standalone or single-server scenario. Content deployment configuration is accessed via the Content Deployment section of the Operations tab within SharePoint Central Administration, as shown in Figure 17-3.

Content Deployment

- Content deployment paths and jobs
- Content deployment settings
- Check deployment of specific content

Figure 17-3

By clicking the Content Deployment Settings link, a number of farmwide settings for content deployment can be configured:

❑ **Accept Content Deployment Jobs** — This setting, shown in Figure 17-4, specifies whether incoming content deployment jobs should be accepted or rejected. When accept is chosen, the source farm stills needs to authenticate to Central Administration to deploy content.

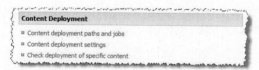

Accept Content Deployment Jobs

Specify whether you want to permit this server farm to receive content deployment jobs from another farm. Even with this setting enabled, the remote farm will need to authenticate to Central Administration to deploy content.

○ Accept incoming content deployment jobs
◉ Reject incoming content deployment jobs

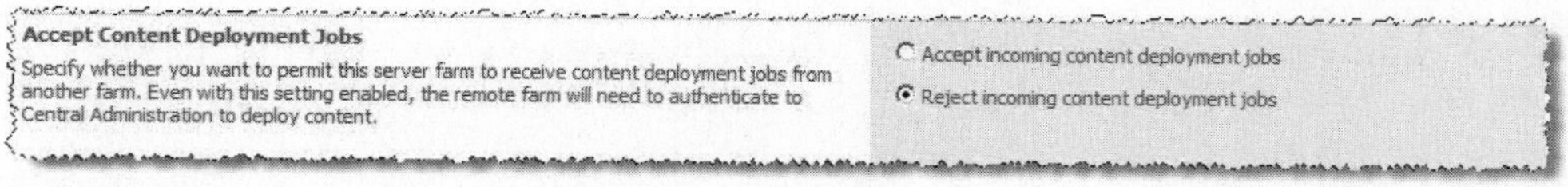

Figure 17-4

❑ **Import Server** — This setting, shown in Figure 17-5, specifies the server used to receive incoming content deployment jobs.

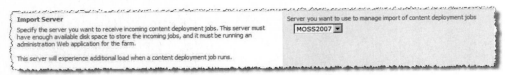

Figure 17-5

❑ **Export Server** — This setting, shown in Figure 17-6, specifies the server used to send outgoing content deployment jobs.

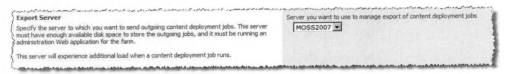

Figure 17-6

❑ **Connection Security** — By default, content deployment is only allowed if the connection between source and destination farms is encrypted by using the HTTPS protocol. This setting is shown in Figure 17-7.

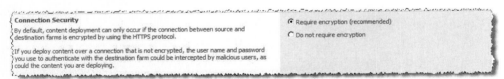

Figure 17-7

❑ **Temporary Files** — This setting, shown in Figure 17-8, specifies where the temporary files (CABs) for content deployment jobs are stored. These files are automatically deleted when the deployment job is finished.

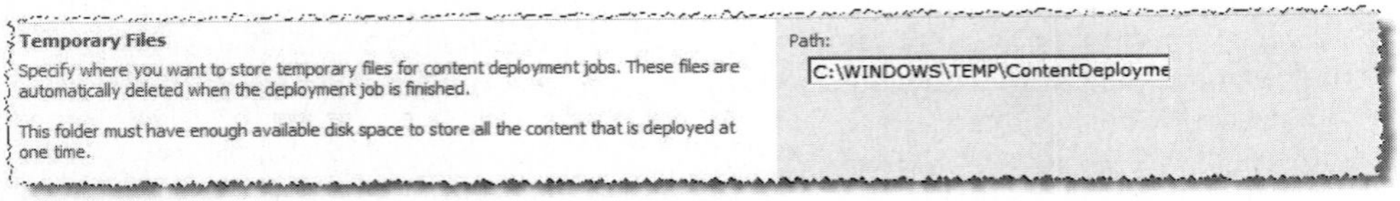

Figure 17-8

❑ **Reporting** — This setting, shown in Figure 17-9, enables administrators to specify the number of reports to keep for each content deployment job.

Reporting
Specify the number of reports you want to keep for each content deployment job that originates from this farm. The oldest reports will automatically be deleted to make room for new ones.

Number of reports to retain for each job:
20

Figure 17-9

Unfortunately, clicking OK to apply the changes does not return the user to the Operations page within Central Administration but rather to the Site Settings page. This is one of several esoteric glitches within the Central Administration application. To return to the Operations page, simply click the Operations tab.

Content Deployment Walkthrough

Once content deployment is enabled on the farm and configured, paths and jobs can be used to deploy content between site collections.

Example Scenario

For the purposes of demonstration, this chapter features a simple scenario that provides an overview of the capabilities of content deployment. Supporting the scenario are two SharePoint Web Applications:

❑ `http://cdsource` — Hosting a site collection based upon the Publishing Portal template. This mimics a read/write authoring environment (source).

❑ `http://cddestination` — Hosting a site collection based upon the Blank Site template. This mimics a read-only production environment (destination).

The source site collection has two subsites, *About Us* and *News*. The About Us site should be deployed at the same time as content within the top-level site, whereas the News site needs a more frequent schedule. This example scenario is shown in Figure 17-10.

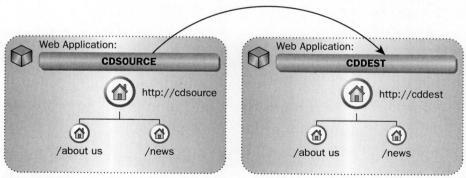

Figure 17-10

Creating Paths

Paths and jobs are created and configured using the Central Administration ⇨ Operations ⇨ Content Deployment Paths and Jobs page. Before jobs can be created, a path must first be created by clicking the New Path button. The Create Content Deployment Path page enables an administrator to define the relationship between the source and destination site collections:

❑ **Name and Description** — This setting, shown in Figure 17-11, provides basic information about the path, which is displayed on the summary page.

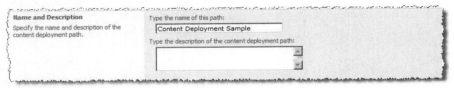

Figure 17-11

❑ **Source Web Application and Site Collection** — Use this setting, shown in Figure 17-12 to select the source Web application and site collection to use for content deployment.

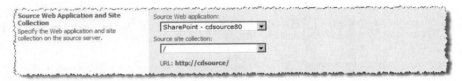

Figure 17-12

❑ **Destination Central Administration Web Application** — This setting, shown in Figure 17-13, specifies the URL to connect to for Central Administration on the destination farm.

Figure 17-13

❑ **Authentication Information** — These credentials settings, shown in Figure 17-14, are used to connect to the destination farm and must have Central Administration privileges. Clicking the Connect button connects to the destination to populate the Destination Web Applications and Site Collections selectors.

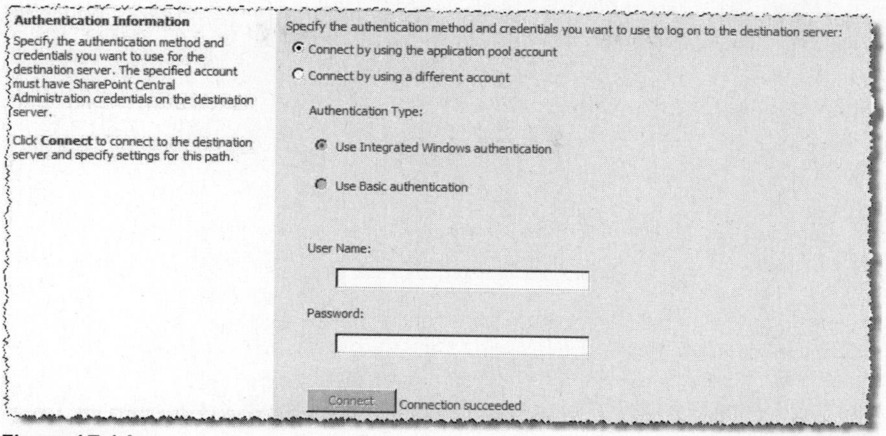

Figure 17-14

❑ **Destination Web Application and Site Collection** — Use these settings, shown in Figure 17-15, to specify the destination Web application and site collection to use for content deployment.

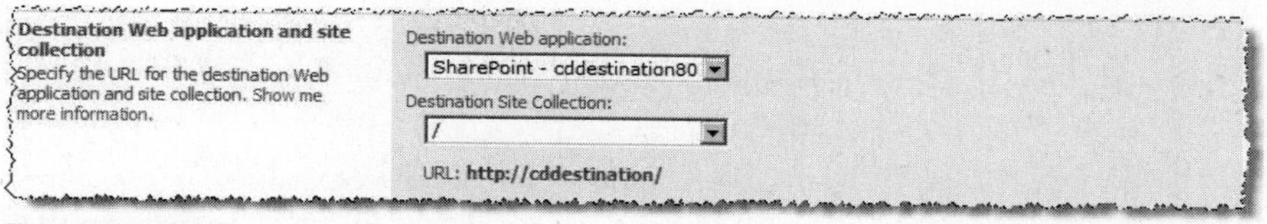

Figure 17-15

❑ **User Names** — This setting, shown in Figure 17-16, specifies whether the user names associated with content are also deployed.

Figure 17-16

❑ **Security Information** — Use this setting, shown in Figure 17-17, to specify whether ACLs, roles, or membership are deployed.

Figure 17-17

Clicking OK creates the path and redirects the administrator back to the Manage Content Deployment Paths and Jobs page, where the new path is shown. In addition to the path, a Quick Deploy job is automatically created and associated with the path, as shown in Figure 17-18.

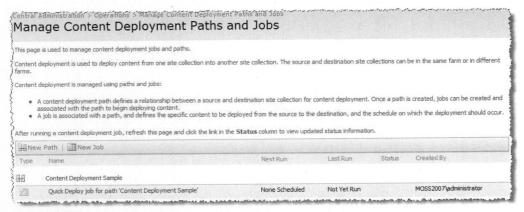

Figure 17-18

This configuration is required on both the source and the destination in a real-world scenario. Because this chapter uses a single server for the examples, this isn't necessary here.

Creating Jobs

With the path created, click the New Job button to create the two jobs needed in the scenario. The following settings can be configured:

❑ **Name and Description** — Use these fields, shown in Figure 17-19, to provide basic information about the path, which is displayed on the summary page.

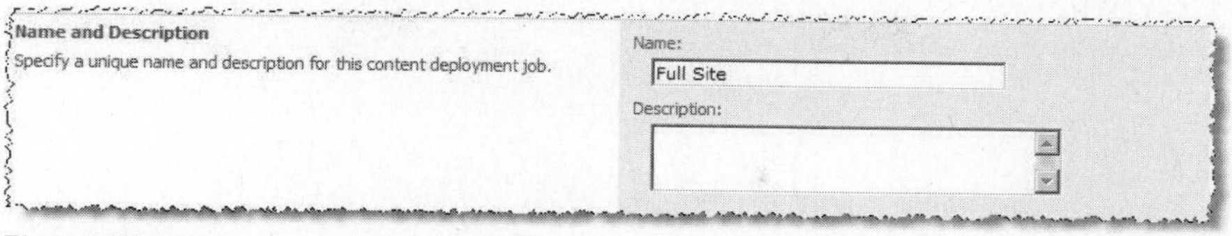

Figure 17-19

❑ **Path** — This setting, shown in Figure 17-20, specifies the content deployment path with which to associate this job.

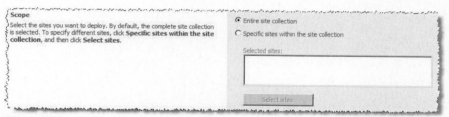

Figure 17-20

❑ **Scope** — This setting, shown in Figure 17-21, specifies the selection of content within the site collection to deploy.

Figure 17-21

❑ **Frequency** — These settings, shown in Figure 17-22, specify the publishing schedule for the job. If no schedule is configured, then the job can only be run manually from Central Administration.

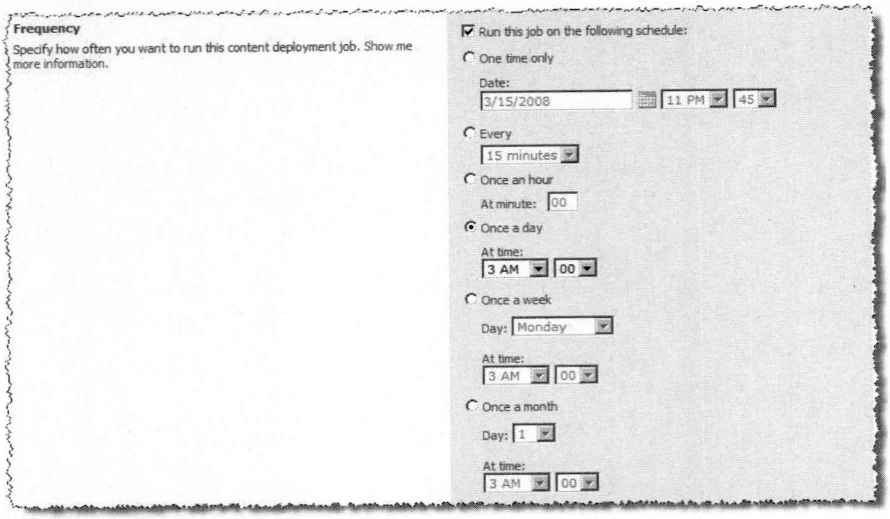

Figure 17-22

❑   **Deployment Options** — This setting, shown in Figure 17-23, specifies either incremental or full deployment.

Figure 17-23

❑   **Notification** — This setting, shown in Figure 17-24, enables configuration of an e-mail notification indicating whether content deployment has succeeded or failed.

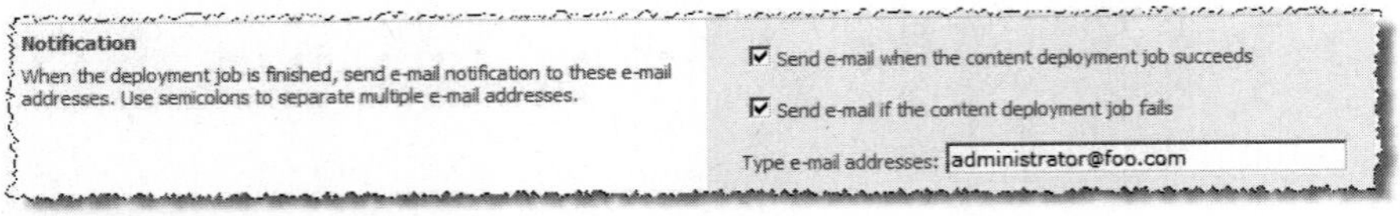

Figure 17-24

Clicking OK creates the job and takes the administrator back to the Manage Content Deployment Paths and Jobs page, where the new job is displayed.

Create another job for the News site. Within the Scope section, select Specific Sites within the Site Collection radio buttons and click Select Sites. A dialog will appear from which you can select the News site, as shown in Figure 17-25.

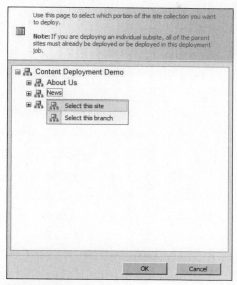

Figure 17-25

For the News site, specify a different frequency, this time deploying content every 15 minutes, as shown in Figure 17-26.

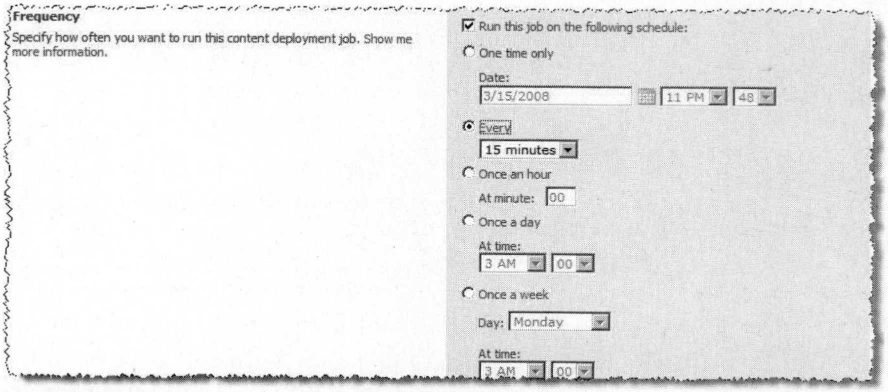

Figure 17-26

Clicking OK creates the second job and redirects back to the Manage Content Deployment Paths and Jobs page. Now wait until the scheduled deployment takes place or manually test or execute the jobs.

Running Jobs

Manually execute jobs from the Manage Content Deployment Paths and Jobs page by choosing Run Now or Test Job from the Job Item drop-down menu. The Test Job option simply tests the export and packaging of the content on the source and confirms that the destination can be reached. While this is a useful verification step it does not guarantee a successful deployment.

Selecting Run Now performs the deployment and the status of the job is updated. Initially, the status will be "Preparing" followed by "Running." Once Running is displayed, the status becomes a hyperlink, which when followed shows the Content Deployment Report depicted in Figure 17-27, summarizing the job's status.

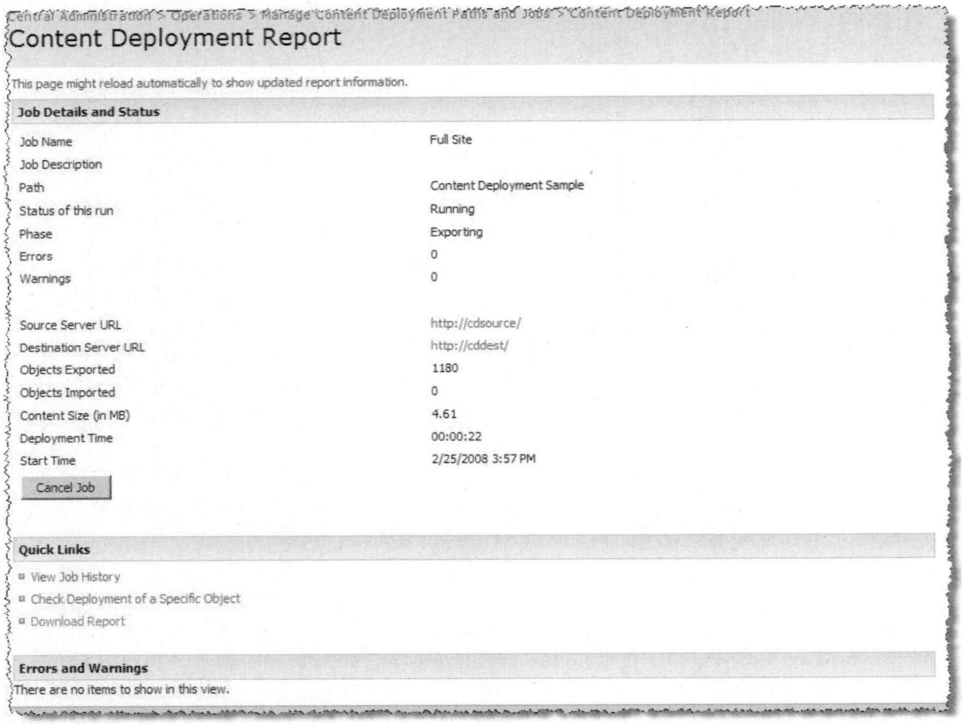

Figure 17-27

Once the job is complete, the status is changed to "Succeeded" or "Failed," both providing a link to the summary page shown in Figure 17-28.

Figure 17-28

This page enables the viewing of errors and warnings associated with the job; more information about each of these can be displayed by clicking the item. The job's history can also be accessed from the Content Deployment Report page.

In addition, deployment of a specific object can be checked by choosing the hyperlink and entering the URL to check.

Once the job has completed, administrators can then browse to the destination and see the deployed content. Notice in Figure 17-29 that the Publishing Infrastructure Feature has been activated on what was a Blank Site.

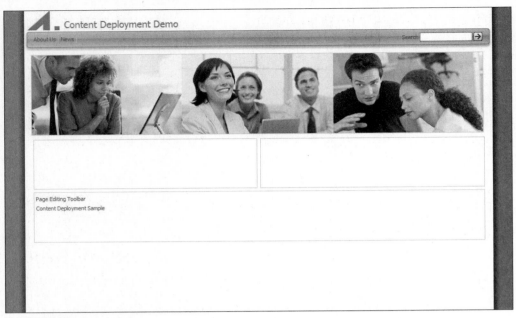

Figure 17-29

At this stage, verify the second job by creating a new page in both the About Us and News sites on the source site collection and running the News job. This will deploy just the new page within the News site, and not the page within the About Us site.

Unfortunately, if a new page is created within the top-level site and a new page is created within the News site, and then the News job is rerun, the new page within the top-level site is also deployed. This is a known issue with content deployment that means that content that's changed within the top-level site is always changed, regardless of which jobs are run. It is necessary for the capabilities of the top-level sites to be the same on both the source and destination; therefore, content deployment checks this every time a job is run. Unfortunately, as well as interrogating the Features, and so on, the content is also picked up and deployed.

Thus, while jobs can be leveraged to provide a different deployment schedule between subsites, the top-level site changes are always deployed. This unfortunate limitation can be overcome using the content deployment API, but it means that the automated capability can only be run with the understanding that the top-level site's content will be deployed.

Leveraging Quick Deploy Jobs

Once a path is created, a Quick Deploy job for that path is automatically created. However, the Quick Deploy job must be enabled before site owners or members of the Quick Deploy Users group can take advantage of the feature (the Quick Deploy option is grayed out within the Page Editing Toolbar). To configure the Quick Deploy job, choose Quick Deploy Settings from the Item menu on the Manage Content Deployment Paths and Jobs page.

The settings on the Quick Deploy Job Settings for Path page allow administrators to enable the Quick Deploy job, specify a schedule (which by default is every 15 minutes), and indicate which users can mark a page for Quick Deploy, as shown in Figure 17-30.

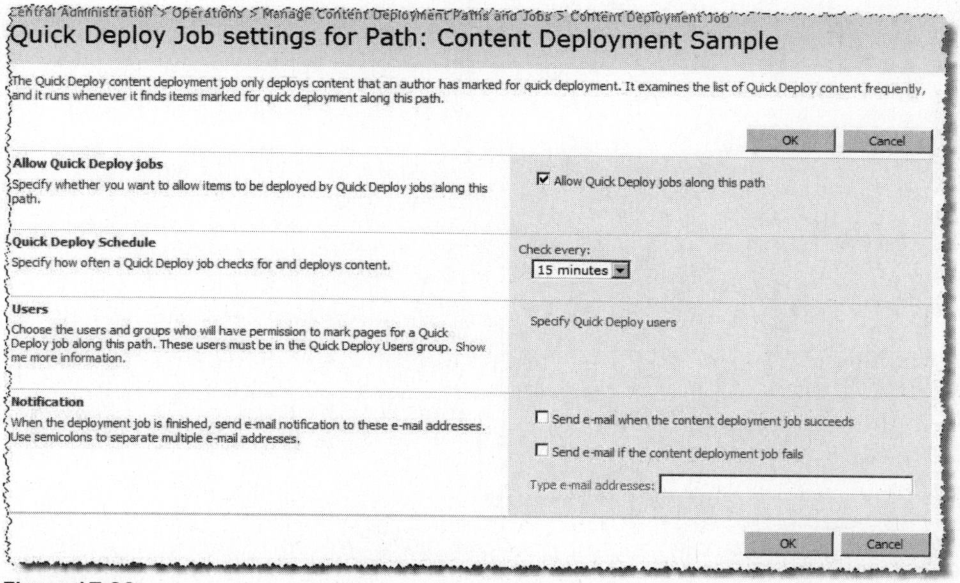

Figure 17-30

After the Quick Deploy job is enabled for a given path, content authors with the appropriate permissions can mark a page for Quick Deploy for all approved pages from the Page Editing Toolbar.

Using the Content Deployment API

In addition to the administration interface available from Central Administration ⇨ Operations, content deployment is exposed as an API via the `Microsoft.SharePoint.Publishing.Administration` namespace. This API is useful when administrators wish to provide an alternative user interface for managing content deployment paths and jobs.

The following simple example in Listing 17-1 shows how to enable content deployment in the source farm, create a path and job, and execute the job from a console application. The status of the job is output as the code executes. Once the operations are complete, the job and path are deleted.

Listing 17-1: Leveraging the content deployment API

```
using System;
using System.Collections.Generic;
using System.Text;
using Microsoft.SharePoint.Publishing.Administration;

namespace WROX.ProMossWcm.Chapter17 {
  class Program {
    static void Main(string[] args) {
      ContentDeploymentSample sample = new ContentDeploymentSample();
      sample.Invoke();
    }
  }

  class ContentDeploymentSample {
    public void Invoke() {
      // Path Settings
      string pathName = "Content deployment Sample 1";
      Uri sourceServerUri = new Uri("http://cdsource");
      string sourceSiteCollection = "/";
      Uri destinationAdminUri = new Uri("http://moss2007:8888");
      Uri destinationServerUri = new Uri("http://cddestination");
      string destinationSiteCollection = "/";

      // job Settings
      string jobName = "Full Site";

      ContentDeploymentPath path = null;
      ContentDeploymentJob job = null;

      try {
        // Configure Content deployment within the source farm...
        ContentDeploymentConfiguration config =
                  ContentDeploymentConfiguration.GetInstance();
        config.AcceptIncomingJobs = true;
        // credentials and deployment are in plain text over the wire
        config.RequiresSecureConnection = false;
        config.Update();

        // Create a deployment path using the settings above...
        ContentDeploymentPathCollection allPaths =
                  ContentDeploymentPath.GetAllPaths();
        path = allPaths.Add();

        path.Name = pathName;
        path.SourceServerUri = sourceServerUri;
        path.SourceSiteCollection = sourceSiteCollection;
        path.DestinationAdminServerUri = destinationAdminUri;
        path.DestinationServerUri = destinationServerUri;
```

```
        path.DestinationSiteCollection = destinationSiteCollection;
        path.Update();

        // Create a CD job associated with the Path created above...
        job = ContentDeploymentJob.GetAllJobs().Add();
        job.JobType = ContentDeploymentJobType.ServerToServer;
        job.Name = jobName;
        job.Path = path;
        job.Update();
        job.Run();
    }
    catch (Exception ex) {
        Console.Error.WriteLine(ex.StackTrace);
        throw;
    }
    finally {
        // Delete the job that was created.
        if (job != null) {
            job.Delete();
        }
        // Delete the path that was created.
        if (path != null) {
            path.Delete();
        }
    }
}
```

While the content deployment API can be useful for custom user interface development, it does not provide a solution for disconnected scenarios (i.e., when source and destination are unable to communicate over the wire). All three operations — export, transport, and import — are always performed when a job is executed. In addition, the API does not offer any capability to configure the granularity of deployment to anything other than the site collection defined in the path (i.e., the Select Sites to Deploy option within Central Administration).

This is because the underlying implementation of the Select Sites to Deploy option is a combination of the content deployment API and the content migration API available with WSS 3.0 (also known as PRIME). In order to provide a solution for disconnected scenarios and/or more granular content deployment, a combination of these APIs must be used.

Using the Content Migration API

The content migration API (`Microsoft.SharePoint.Deployment`) provides the capability to support disconnected and granular deployment scenarios by enabling different phases of the deployment to happen at different times. The exported content is packaged as a Content Migration Package (`*.CMP`) file, which can easily be transported to the destination environment via common mechanisms such as FTP or removable media such as DVDs. These CMP files are cabinet files with a different extension and by default their maximum size is 24MB. Content migration actually underpins a number of MOSS features, including content deployment, variations, the Manage Site Content and Structure tool, and the MCMS migration capability.

The following console application in Listing 17-2 shows how to use the content migration API to export content to a *.CMP file.

Listing 17-2: Exporting content with the content migration API

```csharp
using System;
using System.Collections.Generic;
using System.Text;
using Microsoft.SharePoint;
using Microsoft.SharePoint.Deployment;

namespace WROX.ProMossWcm.Chapter17 {
  class Program {
    private static string _sourceUrl = "http://cdsource";

    static void Main(string[] args) {
      try {
        SPExportSettings exportSettings = new SPExportSettings();
        // echo output
        exportSettings.CommandLineVerbose = true;
        // CMP file to export
        exportSettings.BaseFileName = "export.cmp";
        // Path to export CMP
        exportSettings.FileLocation = @"C:\windows\temp";

        exportSettings.OverwriteExistingDataFile = true;
        exportSettings.IncludeSecurity = SPIncludeSecurity.All;
        exportSettings.SiteUrl = _sourceUrl;
        exportSettings.IncludeVersions =
                    SPIncludeVersions.LastMajorAndMinor;
        exportSettings.FileCompression = true;

        SPExport export = new SPExport(exportSettings);

        // Run the export
        export.Run();
      }
      catch (Exception ex) {
        Console.Error.Write(ex.ToString());
        throw;
      }
    }
  }
}
```

To export only a subsite, some additional code is necessary. Use the Microsoft.SharePoint .Deployment.SPExportObject to create a reference to the particular site to be exported and add it to the Microsoft.SharePoint.Deployment.SPExportSettings.ExportObjects collection, as shown in Listing 17-3.

Listing 17-3: Exporting a specific site using the content migration API

```
using System;
using System.Collections.Generic;
using System.Text;
using Microsoft.SharePoint;
using Microsoft.SharePoint.Deployment;

namespace WROX.ProMossWcm.Chapter17 {
  class Program {
    private static string sourceUrl = "http://cdsource";

    static void Main(string[] args) {
      try {
        // get reference to specific site to export
        SPSite siteCollection = new SPSite(sourceUrl);
        SPWeb site = siteCollection.OpenWeb("/News");

        SPExportObject exportObject = new SPExportObject();
        exportObject.Id = site.ID;
        exportObject.IncludeDescendants = SPIncludeDescendants.All;
        exportObject.Type = SPDeploymentObjectType.Web;

        SPExportSettings exportSettings = new SPExportSettings();
        // echo output
        exportSettings.CommandLineVerbose = true;
        // CMP file to export
        exportSettings.BaseFileName = "export.cmp";
        // Path to export CMP
        exportSettings.FileLocation = @"C:\windows\temp";

        exportSettings.OverwriteExistingDataFile = true;
        exportSettings.IncludeSecurity = SPIncludeSecurity.All;
        exportSettings.SiteUrl = sourceUrl;
        exportSettings.IncludeVersions =
                SPIncludeVersions.LastMajorAndMinor;
        exportSettings.FileCompression = true;
        exportSettings.ExportObjects.Add(exportObject);

        SPExport export = new SPExport(exportSettings);

        // Run the export
        export.Run();
      }
      catch (Exception ex) {
        Console.Error.Write(ex.ToString());
        throw;
      }
    }
  }
}
```

The following console application in Listing 17-4 shows how to use the content migration API to import content from a *.CMP file.

Listing 17-4: Importing content with the content migration API

```
using System;
using System.Collections.Generic;
using System.Text;
using Microsoft.SharePoint;
using Microsoft.SharePoint.Deployment;

namespace WROX.ProMossWcm.Chapter17 {
  class Program {
    private static string destinationUrl = "http://cddestination";
    private static string destinationRootWebUrl;

    static void Main(string[] args) {
      try {
        SPImportSettings importSettings = new SPImportSettings();

        importSettings.CommandLineVerbose = true;
        importSettings.RetainObjectIdentity = true;
        importSettings.FileLocation = @"C:\windows\temp";
        importSettings.BaseFileName = "export.cmp";
        importSettings.SiteUrl = destinationUrl;
        importSettings.IncludeSecurity = SPIncludeSecurity.All;
        importSettings.UserInfoDateTime =
                   SPImportUserInfoDateTimeOption.ImportAll;
        importSettings.SuppressAfterEvents = true;
        importSettings.UpdateVersions = SPUpdateVersions.Append;

        SPImport import = new SPImport(importSettings);

        // Run the import
        import.Run();
      }
      catch (Exception ex) {
        Console.Error.Write(ex.ToString());
        throw;
      }
    }
  }
}
```

Incremental Deployment

Incremental deployment is supported with the use of *change tokens*. These tokens are used to quickly identify which content was part of the most recent import. They then look at only the content for anything that should be scheduled, such as something to be published or that will expire in the future. Without the change tokens, SharePoint would need to iterate all sites and pages within those sites after every import. The console application in Listing 17-5 demonstrates the use of change tokens.

Listing 17-5: Change tokens in the content migration API

```
using System;
using System.Collections.Generic;
using System.Text;
using Microsoft.SharePoint;
using Microsoft.SharePoint.Deployment;

namespace WROX.ProMossWcm.Chapter17 {
  class Program {
    private static string destinationUrl = "http://cddestination";
    private static string destinationRootWebUrl;

    static void Main(string[] args) {
      try {
        SPImportSettings importSettings = new SPImportSettings();

        importSettings.CommandLineVerbose = true;
        importSettings.RetainObjectIdentity = true;
        importSettings.FileLocation = @"C:\windows\temp";
        importSettings.BaseFileName = "export.cmp";
        importSettings.SiteUrl = destinationUrl;
        importSettings.IncludeSecurity = SPIncludeSecurity.All;
        importSettings.UserInfoDateTime =
                        SPImportUserInfoDateTimeOption.ImportAll;
        importSettings.SuppressAfterEvents = true;
        importSettings.UpdateVersions = SPUpdateVersions.Append;

        SPImport import = new SPImport(importSettings);

        SPChangeToken startChangeToken, endChangeToken;
        using (SPSite destinationSite = new SPSite(importSettings.SiteUrl)) {
          startChangeToken = destinationSite.CurrentChangeToken;
          destinationRootWebUrl =
                        destinationSite.RootWeb.ServerRelativeUrl;
        }

        // Run the import
        import.Run();

        using (SPSite destinationSite = new SPSite(importSettings.SiteUrl)) {
          endChangeToken = destinationSite.CurrentChangeToken;
        }
      }

      catch (Exception ex) {
        Console.Error.Write(ex.ToString());
        throw;
      }
    }
  }
}
```

The full capabilities of the content migration API are beyond the scope of this chapter, but it is hoped that the examples presented here convey how this powerful mechanism can be leveraged both to provide robust and flexible content deployment solutions for Publishing sites and to overcome the current limitations of the content deployment feature set.

Summary

This chapter covered the core concepts of content deployment, paths, and jobs, and how they can be combined to provide granular control over content publishing. You also saw the content deployment capability in action, along with the associated content deployment API. This chapter also covered the content migration API, one of the key infrastructure enablers for Publishing sites, and touched on how it can be leveraged to overcome the current limitations of content deployment.

18

Offline Authoring with Document Converters

When people think of Web-based content management systems, they are usually thinking of an authoring experience revolving around the browser. While this provides a very easy way for many content owners and subject matter experts to create and manage the content in a Web site, at times this approach cannot satisfy all needs. Another approach to content management is using the familiar approach of thick clients such as Microsoft Office Word.

Microsoft provided this capability in Microsoft Content Management Server (MCMS) 2002, the predecessor to Office SharePoint Server (MOSS) 2007 Web Content Management (WCM), by using something called the Authoring Connector, which worked with Word 2002. Unfortunately, the MCMS Authoring Connector was not widely used because it required a client installation. Even then, after it was installed, it was not the most reliable way to author content, and the browser-based approach was still the primary recommendation for content authoring a MCMS 2002 Web site.

Microsoft elected to go in a different direction with offline authoring in MOSS 2007. This new approach works with the default installation of the Office clients. The new approach enables users to upload documents authored in a thick client, such as Word 2007, and then manually trigger a conversion process. The conversion process parses the document, generating an HTML version of it, and automatically creates a new page in the configured Publishing site. This process does not circumvent any security or workflow configurations; it simply automates the process of authoring content through the Web browser.

Out of the box (OOTB), MOSS 2007 ships with four document converters, enabling administrators to configure the Open XML file formats for Microsoft Office Word 2007 — specifically, *.DOCX and the macro-enabled flavor, *.DOCM. InfoPath files (*.XSN) can also be used in document conversions, as can XML files with a provided extensible style sheet (XSLT). The document converter framework included in MOSS is not limited to just generating HTML content for Publishing sites utilizing the MOSS 2007 WCM capabilities. This component is a piece of the bigger Enterprise Content Management (ECM) strategy within MOSS 2007. This means developers can create document converters to transform one file type (e.g., *.XSN) to another (e.g., *.PDF). Because this book focuses on the Web Content Management aspects of MOSS 2007, this chapter covers only that section.

As with many other areas in this latest version of SharePoint, the document converter framework is completely configurable and extensible. Developers are free to create their own document converters with custom administrative and user settings pages so customers can meet the business needs of individual projects. The bulk of this chapter covers the process of creating a custom document converter, complete with custom settings pages. Before creating custom document converters, however, the chapter describes the process of configuring the document converter infrastructure and using the OOTB converters.

Document Converter User Experience

The end user experience in working with document converters is very simple and streamlined. Document converters are configured by being tied to specific content types. A user first uploads a document to a document library. After uploading, the user is taken to a page where he or she can enter metadata associated with the document, including specifying the content type. Once the document has been added to the document library and associated with a content type, it can then use the document converter(s) configured for use with that content type. To trigger the conversion process, select the Convert Document menu item in the ECB menu for the document in the library and then select the desired converter, as shown in Figure 18-1.

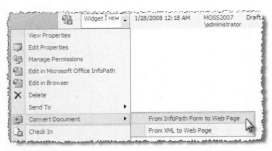

Figure 18-1

If the selected document conversion is configured to prompt the user for some additional settings information, the user is taken to that page. Upon submitting the settings page, the document converter is initiated using the highest priority (conversion priorities are covered in the section "Overview of the Document Converter Architecture"). Once the document converter has finished, the generated file (commonly referred to as the *copy*) is added back to the same document library as the document it was generated from (commonly referred to as the *original*). This file is not automatically checked in, approved, or published; the user would need to go through the typical workflow process of checking the file in, maybe making additional modifications and submitting it for publication.

One nice aspect of pages generated from a document is that a link is established between the original and the copy. If the original page is viewed in Edit mode, as shown in Figure 18-2, the author can elect to have the conversion process run again to refresh the content in the page with the updated content in the document.

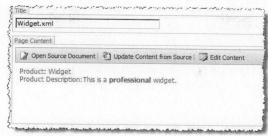

Figure 18-2

Overview of the Document Converter Architecture

Before diving into the intricacies of building a custom document converter, it is beneficial to understand the overall architecture supporting this capability. The document converter infrastructure is included as part of the Enterprise Content Management (ECM) strategy in MOSS 2007, thus it is included in the MOSS 2007 Standard license. The only limitation placed on the document conversion framework is that it can only run on member servers; it will not work on domain controllers. This is because the converters are executed under the context of a local account on the server. Domain controllers, by their very nature, do not have local accounts and thus will not work on a controller. This is one of the most common problems people run into, so be aware of this one simple fact: Document converters will not work on domain controllers, without a single exception.

The document converter infrastructure is run by two services: the Document Converter Load Balancer service and the Document Converter Launcher service. These two services are responsible for distributing the conversion load across the SharePoint farm and executing specific document converters on each server. When a conversion request is submitted, the Load Balancer service examines the registered servers in the farm that are running the Launcher service and the process queues for each. It determines which one has the lowest utilization and sends the conversion instructions to the Launcher service on the target SharePoint server using .NET Remoting.

The Launcher service then takes the request and the document to be processed and creates a locked-down environment and folder on the server in the following location:

```
C:\Program Files\Microsoft Office Servers\12.0\Bin\HtmlTrLauncher
```

It then takes the document to be processed and any configuration information and saves it to this locked-down folder. At this point the Launcher now has everything it needs to perform the transformation of the document. It initiates a .NET console application that accepts four parameters containing the logic specifying how to process the file submitted for conversion. These four parameters tell the console application the following:

❑ -in: The location of the file to be processed.

❑ -out: The location where the generated file should be saved.

❑ `-config`: The location of the XML configuration file containing any settings specified by the administrator when associating the document converter with the content type (covered in detail in the section "Document Converter Configuration"), as well as the settings submitted by the user when the conversion process was requested. While it is required to accept this parameter, it is not necessary to read from it. However, this means the converter is ignoring any settings specified by the administrator and user.

❑ `-log`: The location of the log file, provided the document converter contains logic to write to a log. While it is required to accept this parameter, it is not necessary to create the log file.

This console application must reside in a special folder on the servers running the Launcher service:

```
C:\Program Files\Microsoft Office Servers\12.0\TransformApps
```

The document converter, the console application, is executed under the context of a special, locked-down user account: HVU_<*machinename*>. This is the root cause for the limitation that document converters cannot execute on domain controllers.

After the original file has been run through the document converter to create the copy, the Launcher service then performs some post-processing on the resulting output. Specifically, it copies the metadata contained in the original file to the copy and then adds the file to the same document library containing the original that triggered the conversion process.

Once the copy has been added to the document library, the Launcher performs one last post-processing action: It establishes links and references between the original file and the copy file. The document library contains a few hidden fields that the document converter infrastructure utilizes, provided the document library is in a Web application that has configured document converters. Specifically, the ParentID field is updated on the copy to contain the unique ID of the original document used to generate the copy. The ParentVersionID field is also updated on the copy to contain the version of the original document used to generate the copy. Next, the document converter's ID is added to the Converter field on the copy to indicate which converter did the transformation. Finally, the Launcher service sends any e-mails that have been requested in the configuration of the document converter.

Developers are free to create additional post-processing that can replace or append the existing logic, as well as specify some pre-processing logic. This is covered in more detail in the section "Pre- and Post-Conversion Processing."

At this point the document conversion process is complete.

Updating Copy Files Post-Conversion and File Linkages

What happens when either the original file or the copy file is updated after the conversion process has executed? If versioning is not enabled for the document library, then the conversion process always runs, as it has no version to compare it to. Provided versioning is enabled, the copy file will be updated by a new requested conversion process by incrementing the version. This is true as long as the references are intact between the two files. If the original file is deleted or moved, then the link is severed because the copy file is the one containing all the references.

Conversion Priorities

A case may arise where some document conversion requests need to be executed with a higher priority than others. For instance, if the server is presently working on a large batch job of conversions, a user initiating a conversion request should take on a higher priority than the batch job so the user is not left waiting for the entire batch to finish.

Thankfully, the document conversion process provides such a prioritization capability. There are three priorities:

- ❑ **1 (High)** — All document conversion requests submitted through the browser interface default to this priority.

- ❑ **2 (Medium)** — All document conversion requests submitted via the API default to this priority.

- ❑ **3 (Low)** — This priority is ideal for times when batch document conversion requests are implemented.

Queued requests are sorted accordingly by priority by the Launcher service.

Using Document Converters to Create Publishing Pages

In most cases, the original file is left alone at this point and the links are only established on the copy file. However, in the case of conversions that generate an HTML copy, the object representing both files contains links in both the original file and the copy file that point both ways.

Some additional post-processing logic is performed in the case of document converters that are used to create new Publishing pages. The new page that is created is based on the specified page layout defined by the user when the conversion request was submitted. The generated copy file, containing HTML markup, is expected to contain a very simple structure matching the schema in Listing 18-1.

Listing 18-1: Schema of generated HTML

```html
<html>
  <head>
    <style>
      <!-- generated code goes here -->
    </style>
  </head>
<body>
    <!-- generated code goes here -->
  </body>
</html>
```

The Launcher service then extracts the content between the `<style></style>` elements and `<body></body>` elements and inserts it into the fields specified by the user when the document converter was initiated.

Document Converter Configuration

Before any document conversions can occur, the necessary services must be configured and started. In addition, a content type must be configured to support specific document conversions. The following sections describe how to do this with one of the OOTB configurations. To reiterate a point made previously, document converters can only be configured to run on servers that are not domain controllers due to the local account used to execute the actual converter requested.

Configuring Document Converter Services

The first task is to start the required services. This can be done from the Central Administration Web site. On the Operations page within Central Administration, select the Services on Server link. Select the server to configure, and then the Document Conversions Load Balancer Service. Specify whether the Load Balancer service should use HTTP or HTTPS to communicate with the Launchers associated with it, as well as the port number it will use to communicate with (see Figure 18-3).

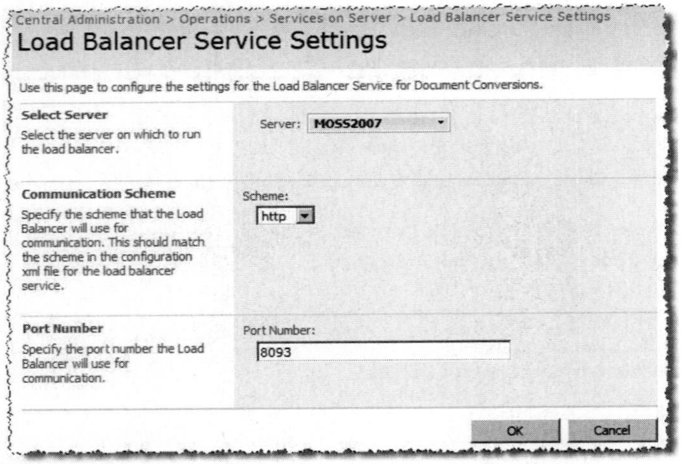

Figure 18-3

With the Load Balancer service started, now the Launcher service can be configured. On the same Services on Server page, select the server Document Conversions Launcher service. On the Launcher Service Settings page, select the server to configure and the load balancer service to associate with this Launcher, and then enter the port the Load Balancer service will use to communicate with the Launcher service (see Figure 18-4).

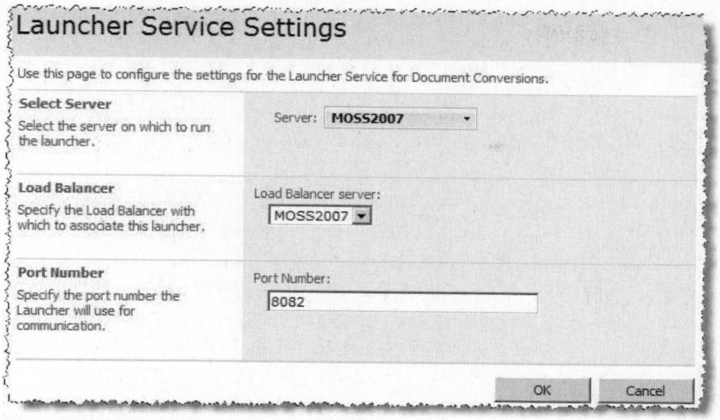

Figure 18-4

Because document conversions are configured at the Web application level, all site collections within the specified Web application will be able to utilize document converters configured here. However, simply turning these services does not allow users to start using the document converters.

The next thing to do is configure specific Web applications to allow desired document converters, as well as specify any additional settings required for each individual converter. On the Application Management page within Central Administration, select the Document Conversions link under the External Service Connections section. On the Configure Document Conversions page, select the desired Web application to configure. The page will then refresh with the available document converters installed on the selected Web application. When selecting a document converter, the administrator can elect to make the document converter visible to site owners and administrators in the site collections hosted by the Web application, as shown in Figure 18-5.

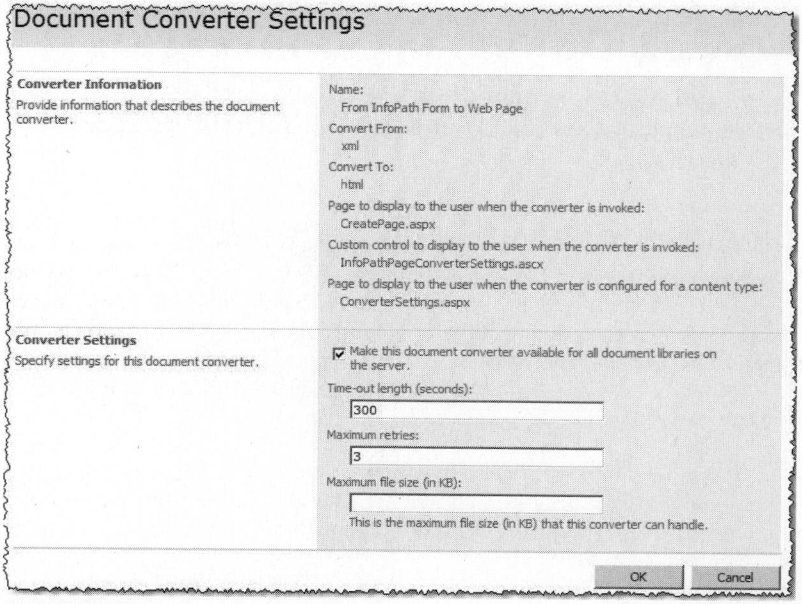

Figure 18-5

Administrators can also set the timeout duration allowed for the converters to complete their execution, as well as the maximum file size of the original file to be transformed and the maximum number of times it will attempt to process the file. Options include every x minutes, every hour between x and y minutes past the hour, or daily between x and y o'clock, which enables administrators to properly throttle the load imposed on the servers, as the conversion process can be quite processor intensive.

If the administrator elects to not make the document converter visible to the Web application, this only means it cannot be configured or triggered through the browser interface. It can still be initiated through the object model, as demonstrated later in the chapter.

With the document converter services initiated and the specified converters configured on a Web application-by-Web application basis, they can now be set up by site owners and administrators on a site-by-site level.

Configuring Document Converter Content Types

Now that all the configurations have been set up at the server and Web application level, site owners and administrators can configure specific content types within a site collection that can utilize the allowed converters. To do this, navigate to the content type gallery within a site collection and select an existing content type (or create a new one) and select the Manage Document Conversions for This Content Type link. The Manage Document Conversions for [*Content Type Name*] page enables site owners to select which document converters are allowed for the content type, as well as configure the nuances of each converter.

With the content type configured, the last step is to add the content type to the desired document library, such as a site's Pages library, so a content owner can upload a document and manually kick off the conversion process (refer to Figure 18-1).

Out-of-the-Box Document Converters

As previously mentioned, Microsoft includes four document converters OOTB in the MOSS 2007 installation. These converters are intended to be used to create HTML pages. The following sections describe these four OOTB document converters.

Word Document and Word Document with Macros to Web Page

These two document converters take one of the new Word Open XML file format documents and convert it to an HTML page. The two file types supported, DOCX and DOCM, can be authored in Word 2007, Word 2003 (when the Open XML file format add-in is installed), Word 2008 (the Apple Mac version of Word), or they can be programmatically created.

When administrators configure these document converters, they must specify the default page layout as well as the fields that should contain the generated styles and body content; whether the file should be created upon the request (synchronously) or in the background (asynchronously); and the location where the page should be created.

When a user initiates one of these document converters, they specify the page layout to use for the new page and whether the page should be generated immediately or in the background.

InfoPath Form to Web Page

This document converter takes an InfoPath 2007 form and converts it to HTML. The InfoPath form must be created using InfoPath 2007, not a prior version. If an InfoPath 2003 form is wanted, it must first be upgraded to the InfoPath 2007 file format by opening and publishing it from InfoPath 2007.

When an administrator configures this document converter he or she must specify the InfoPath form template and view to use in the rendering, as well as all the same things required in the Word Document to Web Page converter. Under the covers, the view in InfoPath 2007 is created using XSLT. This XSLT is extracted on-the-fly from the InfoPath 2007 form by the document converter, as is the XML file, and both are used to generate the HTML used in creating the resulting HTML page.

When users initiate this document converter they specify the same things required in the Word Document to Web Page converter.

XML to Web Page

This document converter takes an XML file and converts it to HTML using the specified extensible style sheet (*.XSL). If that sounds familiar, it is. The process is almost identical to that of the XSN to HTML document converter except that no InfoPath 2007 file is used. This converter can be quite helpful for automatically generated XML files from external applications.

When administrators configure this document converter they must specify the XSL style sheet to use in the transformation of XML to HTML, as well as all the same things required in the Word Document to Web Page converter.

When users initiate this document converter they specify the same things required in the Word Document to Web Page converter.

Creating Custom Document Converters

While the OOTB document converters provide a few options for converting files to HTML pages automatically, they surely won't meet every business need. What if a company has not yet upgraded to the Office 2007 clients and is still using Office 2003 or an earlier version? What about converting other file types to HTML? What if the generated file desired is not HTML but something else such as a *.PDF or *.XPS file?

Thankfully, Microsoft made the document converter infrastructure extensible, like so many other areas of SharePoint, enabling developers to create custom document converters to meet specific business needs. Developers can create converters that take any type of a file as an input and generate any file type as output. This is done by creating a custom console application. The custom converters may have special requirements to prompt both administrators and users for specific settings when configuring the document converter with a content type, as well as when users initiate the transformation process.

The following sections demonstrate how to create a document converter, as well as the special requirements involved when creating HTML pages for Publishing sites.

Creating the Document Converter

The document converter created in the following sections will take an XML file containing a dataset, shown in Listing 18-2, and transform it to an HTML table. When configured, the administrator needs to specify the formatting of the table as a custom setting and pass that to the converter.

Listing 18-2: XML file consumed by the custom document converter

```xml
<?xml version="1.0" encoding="utf-8" ?>
<root>
  <Title>US Presidents</Title>
  <Description>The first five Presidents of the United States</Description>
  <Data>
    <Columns>
      <Column>No.</Column>
      <Column>Term</Column>
      <Column>President</Column>
      <Column>Vice President</Column>
    </Columns>
    <Rows>
      <Row>
        <Column>1</Column>
        <Column>April 30, 1789 - March 4, 1797</Column>
        <Column>George Washington</Column>
        <Column>John Adams</Column>
      </Row>
      <Row>
        <Column>2</Column>
        <Column>March 4, 1797 - March 4, 1801</Column>
        <Column>John Adams</Column>
        <Column>Thomas Jefferson</Column>
      </Row>
      <!-- additional rows omitted for brevity -->
    </Rows>
  </Data>
</root>
```

While this could also be accomplished using the OOTB XML to HTML converter with a custom XSL file, it is a simple example that is easy to follow in order to understand how to create a custom document converter.

Creating the Document Converter Application

The first step to creating a custom document converter is to create the application that will do all the heavy lifting. This console application has a few requirements. First, as previously mentioned in the section "Overview of the Document Converter Architecture," it must expect four command-line arguments telling the converter where to find the file to process, where to put the generated copy, where the settings are stored, and the log file to write to. Second, the executable must be deployed to a specific folder on the SharePoint servers configured to run the Launcher service.

The code in Listing 18-3 shows the static `Main()` method that is called when the executable is created.

Listing 18-3: Document converter Main()

```csharp
using System;
using System.Collections.Generic;
using System.IO;
using System.Web.UI;
using System.Xml;

namespace WROX.ProMossWcm.Chapter18 {
  class Program {

    static void Main (string[] args) {
      Dictionary<DocConverterArgumentType, string> arguments =
DocConverterArgumentHelper.ParseCommandLineArguments(args); ·

      TransformXmlToHtml(arguments[DocConverterArgumentType.InputFile],
                 arguments[DocConverterArgumentType.OutputFile],
                 arguments[DocConverterArgumentType.ConfigurationFile],
                 arguments[DocConverterArgumentType.LogFile]);
    }
  }
}
```

Notice the highlighted line that uses the `DocConverterArgumentHelper` class, which contains logic to ensure that all the required arguments are passed in and loads them in an easy to use generic `Dictionary` collection. This reusable class can be used in any document converter to simplify the process of working with the arguments in custom document converters. It is not shown in the book for brevity, but it's available in the associated code that can be downloaded from the publisher's Web site.

After getting all the arguments, the next step is to process the file. That is the job of the `TransformXmlToHtml()` method, shown in Listing 18-4.

Listing 18-4: Document converter's TransformXmlToHtml() method

```csharp
private static void TransformXmlToHtml (string inputFile, string outputFile, string
configFile, string logFile) {
  using (StreamReader reader = new StreamReader(inputFile)) {
    using (HtmlTextWriter writer = new HtmlTextWriter(new
StreamWriter(outputFile))) {
      // write shell of HTML
      writer.RenderBeginTag(HtmlTextWriterTag.Html);

      // write out styles and body of HTML
      WriteHtmlStyles(reader, writer, configFile);
      WriteHtmlBody(reader, writer);

      writer.RenderEndTag(); // </HTML>
      writer.Close();
    }
  }
}
```

The `TransformXmlToHtml()` method first creates a reference to the original file to be copied, as well as the file in which to put the generated HTML. The method then writes out the basic `<HTML></HTML>` tags, as the generated file needs to conform to the same structure contained in Listing 18-1. Next, it calls a method, passing in references to the two files and the location of the configuration file. This is required because, as defined in the requirements, the administrator specifies the type of formatting to use when the HTML table is created from the provided XML. The `WriteHtmlStyles()` method is shown in Listing 18-5.

Listing 18-5: Document converter's WriteHtmlStyles() method, generating the styles

```
private static void WriteHtmlStyles (StreamReader reader, HtmlTextWriter writer,
string configFile) {
  // load the settings
  XmlDocument xDoc = new XmlDocument();
  xDoc.Load(configFile);
  XmlNode tableFormattingType =
xDoc.SelectSingleNode("/RcaTransformation/ConverterSettings/tableFormatting");

  // write <head> &<style> tags
  writer.RenderBeginTag(HtmlTextWriterTag.Head);
  writer.RenderBeginTag(HtmlTextWriterTag.Style);

  // write styles
  writer.WriteLine("TABLE {border-style:3px black solid;}");
  writer.WriteLine("TD {border-style:1px gray solid;}");

  switch (tableFormattingType.InnerText.ToLower()){
    case "raw":
      writer.Write("TH {font-weight:bold;}");
      break;
    case "gray":
      writer.Write("TH {font-weight:bold; color:black; background-color:gray;}");
      break;
    case "black":
      writer.Write("TH {font-weight:bold; color:white; background-color:black;}");
      break;
  }

  writer.RenderEndTag(); // </STYLE>
  writer.RenderEndTag(); // </HEAD>
}
```

This method is fairly straightforward except for one part, the highlighted portion. This part pulls the data out of the configuration file but the XPath query requires a little explanation. SharePoint uses a specific schema when creating the configuration file. The XML structure is displayed in Listing 18-6, which contains the content of the configuration file for the custom document converter.

Listing 18-6: Structure of the XML configuration file

```
<?xml version="1.0" encoding="utf-8"?>
<RcaTransformation>
  <ConverterSettings SourceDocLibUrl="/PressReleases/Pages">
    <tableFormatting>gray</tableFormatting>
  </ConverterSettings>
```

```
<TransformationContext>
   <TransformationStateStore xmlns:xsi="http://www.w3.org/2001/XMLSchema-instance"
xmlns:xsd="http://www.w3.org/2001/XMLSchema">
      <IsUpdate>false</IsUpdate>
      <LayoutBodyFieldId>f55c4d88-1f2e-4ad9-aaa8-819af4ee7ee8</LayoutBodyFieldId>
      <LayoutStylesFieldId>a932ec3f-94c1-48b1-b6dc-41aaa6eb7e54
</LayoutStylesFieldId>
      <PageSiteId>8524a11c-55b0-463f-89b5-215659fbc51d</PageSiteId>
      <PageWebId>88c41972-22a3-40fb-a13c-bdff0152a5f1</PageWebId>
      <PageUrl>Pages/Sample.aspx</PageUrl>
   </TransformationStateStore>
  </TransformationContext>
</RcaTransformation>
```

The structure of the configuration file is fairly static and is handled by SharePoint. However, when creating custom settings that should be passed into the converter, as demonstrated later in the section "Adding Settings to Document Converters," those settings are added to the section highlighted in Listing 18-6. The `tableFormatting` node is the custom node that will be added by a custom settings page created later.

With the styles written out to the HTML file, the next step is to write out the body of the page. This task is handled by the `WriteHtmlBody()` method, shown in Listing 18-7.

Listing 18-7: Document converter's WriteHtmlBody() method, generating the content

```
private static void WriteHtmlBody (StreamReader reader, HtmlTextWriter writer) {
  // load data
  XmlDocument xDoc = new XmlDocument();
  xDoc.Load(reader);

  string tableHeading = xDoc.SelectSingleNode("/root/Title").InnerText;
  string tableDescription = xDoc.SelectSingleNode("/root/Description").InnerText;
  XmlNode tableColumns = xDoc.SelectSingleNode("/root/Data/Columns");
  XmlNode tableRows = xDoc.SelectSingleNode("/root/Data/Rows");

  writer.RenderBeginTag(HtmlTextWriterTag.Body);

  // write table heading and description
  writer.WriteLine(String.Format("<h1>{0}</h1>", tableHeading));
  writer.WriteLine(String.Format("{0}", tableDescription));

  // write table
  writer.RenderBeginTag(HtmlTextWriterTag.Table);

  // write heading row
  writer.RenderBeginTag(HtmlTextWriterTag.Thead);
  writer.RenderBeginTag(HtmlTextWriterTag.Tr);
  foreach (XmlNode column in tableColumns.ChildNodes) {
    writer.RenderBeginTag(HtmlTextWriterTag.Th);
    writer.WriteLine(column.InnerText);
    writer.RenderEndTag(); // </TH>
  }
```

(continued)

Listing 18-7 (continued)

```
      writer.RenderEndTag(); // </TR>
      writer.RenderEndTag(); // </THEAD>

      // write data rows
      writer.RenderBeginTag(HtmlTextWriterTag.Tbody);
      foreach (XmlNode row in tableRows.ChildNodes) {
        writer.RenderBeginTag(HtmlTextWriterTag.Tr);
        foreach (XmlNode rowColumn in row.ChildNodes) {
          writer.RenderBeginTag(HtmlTextWriterTag.Td);
          writer.WriteLine(rowColumn.InnerText);
          writer.RenderEndTag(); // </TD>
        }
        writer.RenderEndTag(); // </TR>
      }
      writer.RenderEndTag(); // </TBODY>
      writer.RenderEndTag(); // </TABLE>
      writer.RenderEndTag(); // </BODY>
    }
```

At this point the document converter is complete. Developers can test their work by manually calling the converter, passing in the required parameters just as they would with any other console application, as this one does not do anything with respect to a SharePoint context.

At times the document converter needs to be tested "in flight," or when the Launcher service executes it. In this case, the developer needs to attach the Visual Studio debugger manually. This can be a bit tricky, as the console executable will be triggered by another application, SharePoint, and could possibly run very quickly. However, there is a technique that can stop the converter when it runs and give a developer the chance to attach the debugger to debug the code. To do this, add the following line to where the process should stop, ideally just inside the `Main()` method:

```
System.Diagnostics.Trace.Assert(false, "MOSS Document Converter currently
paused.");
```

This will display a dialog box on the server (shown in Figure 18-6) when executed and stop the document converter until addressed. Before addressing the dialog box, manually attach the debugger in Visual Studio as demonstrated throughout this book. Look for the name of the console application, which will appear after checking Show Processes From All Users, as it will be running under the context of the `HVU_<machinename>` account. Once the debugger is attached and a breakpoint set, click the Ignore button on the dialog to enable the document converter to continue. It should then hit the breakpoint. If it fails to do so, it is likely that the debugging symbols (`*.pdb`) are not located in the same directory as the console executable. Just copy that file into the directory and try again.

Figure 18-6

Another issue that may arise is that the document converter may not fire at all. In this case, check the ULS logs located in [..]\12\LOGS for entries in the category Launcher Service to help in troubleshooting the problem.

Deploying Custom Document Converters

With the document converter created, the next step is to package it up for deployment and registration with SharePoint. Document converters are registered with SharePoint Web applications using a SharePoint Feature. The Feature tells SharePoint what types of files can be converted, the name of the console executable previously created that should be triggered, and any extra information needed for document converter–specific settings.

Deploying, installing, and activating a Feature are not all that is required for implementing a custom document converter. In addition, the document converter executable should also be deployed to a specific folder on each server in the farm that has the Launcher service running:

```
c:\Program Files\Microsoft Office Servers\12.0\TransformApps
```

Unfortunately, the Windows SharePoint Services (WSS) solution package framework used throughout this book for deployment provides no such vehicle for deploying this file to the proper folder. Therefore, once the solution has been deployed, an administrator must manually copy the document converter executable to the required location on each and every server where the Launcher service is running.

For more information on some non-OOTB solutions addressing the deployment issue whereby document converter executables are not deployed, see www.andrewconnell.com/go/265.

Creating the Document Converter Feature

The SharePoint Feature schema includes a <DocumentConverter> element that is placed in an element manifest file. The Feature should be scoped for Web applications, as shown in Listing 18-8.

Listing 18-8: Feature used for registration with a SharePoint Web application

```xml
<?xml version="1.0" encoding="utf-8"?>
<Feature xmlns="http://schemas.microsoft.com/sharepoint/"
         Id="7E71F2BF-774F-4871-A3DC-B0E52B074E96"
         Title="Chapter 18 - XML Data to HTML Table Document Converter"
         Scope="WebApplication"
         Hidden="False"
         Version="1.0.0.0">

  <ElementManifests>
    <ElementManifest Location="XmlToHtmlConverter.xml" />
    <ElementFile Location="Chapter18XmlDataToHtmlConverter.exe" />
  </ElementManifests>

</Feature>
```

Shown in Listing 18-9 is the Feature's element manifest, which will register the document converter with a specific Web application.

Listing 18-9: Feature's element manifest, registering a document converter

```xml
<?xml version="1.0" encoding="utf-8" ?>
<Elements xmlns="http://schemas.microsoft.com/sharepoint/">
  <DocumentConverter Id="1937057B-51CC-4968-8D13-C1BC4DB67F39"
                     Name="XML Data to HTML (as HTML table)"
                     From="xml"
                     To="html"
                     App="Chapter18XmlDataToHtmlConverter.exe"
                     ConverterUIPage="CreatePage.aspx" />
</Elements>
```

Notice that Listing 18-9 includes references to the type of file that can trigger the conversion process (From="xml"), the file type generated (To="html"), and the name of the actual document converter executable (App="Chapter18XmlDataToHtmlConverter.exe"). In addition, because this converter will generate a page, the Feature needs to tell SharePoint the page that users should be directed to in order to specify any settings required for the conversion. This attribute, ConverterUIPage, is required for document-to-page conversions. In this case, the OOTB page will suffice.

While at this point the document converter could certainly be used in a real-world environment, what if the document converter needs some custom settings by the administrator or user? The next section looks at adding custom settings to document converters.

Adding Settings to Document Converters

Many document converters will require some sort of configuration information. Such settings could be set by an administrator, such as the name of the content type and page layout to use when creating the page, or by the user, such as the name of the Publishing page that is automatically generated by the conversion process. Following the extensibility theme, Microsoft added the capacity for developers to grant administrators and users the capability to enter custom settings consumed by a custom document converter. The custom settings are embedded in the configuration XML file, whose location is passed as one of the four arguments to the document converter.

Consider any of the OOTB document converters, such as the From InfoPath Form to Web Page document converter. When administrators configure the document converter on a content type, they can specify the view in the InfoPath file to be used when generating the HTML from the data in the form, as shown in Figure 18-7. This is a custom setting needed by the document converter.

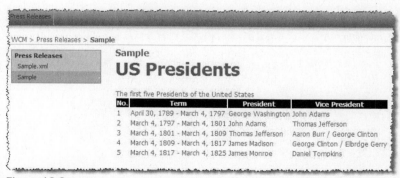

Figure 18-7

When users trigger the conversion process on the InfoPath file, they must specify the name of the page (the filename) to create as well as the title of the page. Generally, all document converters that generate HTML pages use the same settings page: `CreatePage.aspx`.

All the customization of specific settings pages for individual document converters is handled by creating custom ASP.NET 2.0 pages or user controls (`*.ASCX` files). These pages and controls are associated with the document converter within the Feature's element manifest. This was previously demonstrated in Listing 18-9, which set the user settings page to `CreatePage.aspx` using the `ConverterUIPage` attribute.

The custom settings data entered by the administrator and user is passed into the document converter via the configuration file parameter. The XML configuration conforms to the schema demonstrated in Listing 18-6. This includes not only the stock settings information, but also any settings introduced by the developer.

At this point the document converter can be deployed and tested. Use the `sample.xml` file in the provided code for this chapter to generate a new Publishing page that will look like the one shown in Figure 18-8.

Press Releases

WCM > Press Releases > **Sample**

| Press Releases |
| Sample.xml |
| Sample |

Sample
US Presidents

The first five Presidents of the United States

No.	Term	President	Vice President
1	April 30, 1789 - March 4, 1797	George Washington	John Adams
2	March 4, 1797 - March 4, 1801	John Adams	Thomas Jefferson
3	March 4, 1801 - March 4, 1809	Thomas Jefferson	Aaron Burr / George Clinton
4	March 4, 1809 - March 4, 1817	James Madison	George Clinton / Elbrdge Gerry
5	March 4, 1817 - March 4, 1825	James Monroe	Daniel Tompkins

Figure 18-8

Adding custom settings to a document converter is a little different, varying according to who will enter the configuration information: the administrator or the user requesting the conversion.

Implementing Administrator Settings

Adding custom settings information to a document converter for an administrator to enter takes place at the content type configuration level. Developers are given two options for adding custom settings information. They are free to define a custom ASP.NET 2.0 page that the administrator is presented with when they select the Configure link on the Manage Document Conversion for [*content type name*] page that can be reached by selecting the Manage Document Conversions for this Content Type link on the content type's settings page. This is done by setting the value of the `ConverterSettingsForContentType` attribute in the document converter's Feature element manifest file.

Another option is to use an existing converter settings page, such as the OOTB `ConverterSettings` `.aspx`, and inject a new section into the page. This is done by specifying the name of a user control in the `ConverterSpecificSettingsUI` attribute. When this technique is used, the `ConverterSettingsForContentType` attribute must also be set to tell SharePoint what settings page should be used. The settings page must have a `ConverterSpecificControl` master page content placeholder control, which SharePoint will use to dynamically inject the settings user control into.

This user control's code-behind must implement the `Microsoft.SharePoint.Publishing` `.IDocumentConverterControl` interface. This interface provides the minimal plumbing, such as the name to display for the custom section in the settings page and code to serialize/deserialize the custom settings to/from SharePoint in order to include them in the XML configuration file.

The custom converter created in this chapter is going to have a special administrator-specified setting: the formatting to use when generating the HTML table of the data. The administrator should select one value among three: Raw, Gray, or Black. These options will simply be used when defining the styles that are automatically generated by the converter.

Create a new user control named `XmlToHtmlConverterSettings.ascx` in the project (see Listing 18-10). This file will be deployed to the `[..]\12\LAYOUTS` folder, so mimic the structure in the Visual Studio project. The file will inherit a code-behind class created later and utilize some of the SharePoint-provided controls. Next, use these SharePoint-provided form controls to create a simple ASP.NET 2.0 drop-down list, as shown in Figure 18-9.

Listing 18-10: XmlToHtmlConverterSettings.ascx admin settings control

```
<%@ Control Language="C#" Inherits="WROX.ProMossWcm.Chapter18-
XmlToHtmlConverterSettings, Chapter18XmlToHtmlConverterFeature, Version=1.0.0.0,
Culture=neutral, PublicKeyToken=c591e70cfdf9ce4f" CompilationMode="Always" %>
<%@ Register TagPrefix="wssuc" TagName="InputFormSection"
Src="/_controltemplates/InputFormSection.ascx" %>
<%@ Register TagPrefix="wssuc" TagName="InputFormControl"
Src="/_controltemplates/InputFormControl.ascx" %>
<wssuc:InputFormSection runat="server"
                       Description="Select the predefined table formatting options
for the HTML table to be generated. The selection here will define what embedded
styles to add to the converted page.">
  <Template_InputFormControls>
    <wssuc:InputFormControl runat="server"
                           LabelText="Table formatting options:">
      <Template_Control>
```

```
        <asp:DropDownList ID="TableFormattingDropDownList"
                          runat="server">
          <asp:ListItem>Raw</asp:ListItem>
          <asp:ListItem>Gray</asp:ListItem>
          <asp:ListItem>Black</asp:ListItem>
        </asp:DropDownList>
      </Template_Control>
    </wssuc:InputFormControl>
  </Template_InputFormControls>
</wssuc:InputFormSection>
```

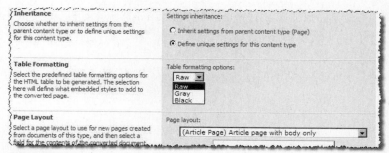

Figure 18-9

Next, create a new class to act as the code-behind for the user control and implement the
IDocumentConverterControl interface, as shown in Listing 18-11. Notice the highlighted property
ConverterSettings that handles the serialization and deserialization for the settings.

Listing 18-11: XmlToHtmlConverterSettings.cs settings control code-behind

```csharp
using System;
using System.Web.UI;
using System.Web.UI.WebControls;
using System.Xml;
using Microsoft.SharePoint;
using Microsoft.SharePoint.Publishing;
using Microsoft.SharePoint.WebControls;

namespace WROX.ProMossWcm.Chapter18 {
  public class XmlToHtmlConverterSettings : UserControl, IDocumentConverterControl
{
    private const string CONVERTER_NAME= "XmlToHtmlConverterSettings";
    private SPContentType _contentType;
    protected DropDownList TableFormattingDropDownList;

    SPContentType IDocumentConverterControl.ContentType {
      get { return _contentType; }
      set { _contentType = value; }
    }
```

(continued)

Listing 18-11 *(continued)*

```
      string IDocumentConverterControl.ConverterSettings {
        get {
          return "<tableFormatting>" +
  TableFormattingDropDownList.SelectedValue.ToString() + "</tableFormatting>";
        }
        set {
          if (!string.IsNullOrEmpty(value)) {
            XmlDocument xdoc = new XmlDocument();
            xdoc.LoadXml(value);
            XmlNode node = xdoc.SelectSingleNode("tableFormatting");
            TableFormattingDropDownList.SelectedValue = node.InnerText;
          }
        }
      }

      bool IDocumentConverterControl.RequiresConfiguration {
        get { return true; }
      }

      string IDocumentConverterControl.SectionDisplayTitle {
        get { return "Table Formatting"; }
      }
    }
  }
```

The highlighted code adds the `<tableFormatting />` element to the `<ConverterSettings />` node in the configuration XML file.

There is no need to create a custom administrator settings page because the OOTB one will do, so modify the Feature's element manifest file to point to the control, as shown in Listing 18-12. Because a custom control is being used, the settings page must be specified as well even if it is the OOTB one.

Listing 18-12: Document converter's Feature element manifest

```
<?xml version="1.0" encoding="utf-8" ?>
<Elements xmlns="http://schemas.microsoft.com/sharepoint/">
  <DocumentConverter Id="1937057B-51CC-4968-8D13-C1BC4DB67F39"
                     Name="XML Data to HTML (as HTML table)"
                     From="xml"
                     To="html"
                     App="Chapter18XmlDataToHtmlConverter.exe"
                     ConverterUIPage="CreatePage.aspx"
             ConverterSettingsForContentType="ConverterSettings.aspx"
             ConverterSpecificSettingsUI="XmlToHtmlConverterSettings.ascx" />
  </Elements>
```

At this point the Visual Studio project should now look similar to the one in Figure 18-10.

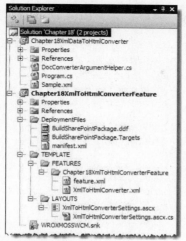

Figure 18-10

Next, modify the `WriteStyles()` method in the document converter to consume the configuration file and alter the generated output accordingly, as shown in Listing 18-13.

Listing 18-13: Document converter's WriteHtmlStyles() method, generating the styles

```
private static void WriteHtmlStyles (StreamReader reader, HtmlTextWriter writer,
string configFile) {
  // load the settings
  XmlDocument xDoc = new XmlDocument();
  xDoc.Load(configFile);
  XmlNode tableFormattingType =
xDoc.SelectSingleNode("/RcaTransformation/ConverterSettings/tableFormatting");

  // write <head> &<style> tags
  writer.RenderBeginTag(HtmlTextWriterTag.Head);
  writer.RenderBeginTag(HtmlTextWriterTag.Style);

  // write styles
  writer.WriteLine("TABLE {border-style:3px black solid;}");
  writer.WriteLine("TD {border-style:1px gray solid;}");

  switch (tableFormattingType.InnerText.ToLower()){
    case "raw":
      writer.Write("TH {font-weight:bold;}");
      break;
    case "gray":
      writer.Write("TH {font-weight:bold; color:black; background-color:gray;}");
      break;
```

(continued)

Listing 18-13 *(continued)*

```
    case "black":
      writer.Write("TH {font-weight:bold; color:white; background-color:black;}");
      break;
  }

  writer.RenderEndTag(); // </STYLE>
  writer.RenderEndTag(); // </HEAD>
}
```

Implementing User Settings

Developers are also free to specify custom settings pages that users who initiate the conversion process will be prompted with in order to provide any additional configuration information for the document converter. When any document converter creates HTML pages, this should be set to the OOTB `CreatePage.aspx` page.

Pre- and Post-Conversion Processing

After a file has been successfully processed by a document converter, the Launcher service runs some post-processing tasks, as covered previously in the chapter. However, developers may have a need to run some additional post-processing tasks or even some pre-processing logic before the document converter is initiated.

The only way to do either pre or post custom processing is to initiate the conversion process through the object model. Both use the same model — when initiating the conversion process, pass two arguments: the name of the class containing the logic and the strong name of the assembly containing the class.

In order to add pre- or post-processing logic to the conversion process, create a new class that inherits from the `Microsoft.SharePoint.ISPConversionProcessor` interface. This interface defines two self-explanatory methods: `PreProcess()` and `PostProcess()`. For the pre- and post-processing, the conversion must be initiated using the `SPFile.Convert()` method.

Working with Document Converters via the Object Model

The process of initiating document converters has been demonstrated in this chapter assuming a user-browser interface. However, just like everything else in SharePoint, if it can be done through the browser or `STSADM.EXE`, then it can be done with the SharePoint API. In fact, the conversion process must be initiated programmatically through the API if the document converter should run custom pre- or post-processing logic and the priority level of the conversion.

> *For a list of the most commonly used methods and properties when working with document converters via the object model, refer to the official documentation on MSDN: www.andrewconnell.com/go/266.*

While using document converters to create Publishing pages within a Publishing site, simply calling `SPFile.Convert()` will not do. This is because a page must be programmatically added to the site using the `Microsoft.SharePoint.Publishing` namespace. Specifically, to create a new page based on a document using a specific document converter, use one of the overloads provided on the `PublishingPageCollection.Add()` method. Two of the three overloads on this method enable the developer to specify the file (`SPFile`) to use as the original document, the GUID of the document converter (defined in the Feature's element manifest), the conversion priority, and optionally the configuration XML.

If a Publishing page has already been generated using a document converter, then the page can be programmatically refreshed with the updated document by obtaining a reference to the page and calling the `PublishingPage.UpdateContentFromSourceDocument()` method.

Summary

This chapter introduced an alternate way to create content within a Publishing site, or any MOSS site, using document converters. The document converter framework enables users to create new pages within a Publishing site by authoring the documents in Word 2007, InfoPath 2007, or a raw XML file. While only four document converters are included OOTB that are intended to be used in the context of Publishing sites, the document converter infrastructure is part of the MOSS Enterprise Content Management strategy and can therefore be used to take any type of document and convert it to another type.

Thankfully, the document converter framework is not sealed and can be leveraged by developers in creating custom document converters. Not only can custom document converters be created to satisfy any business requirements, but developers can also add custom settings pages and controls that site administrators and users alike can consume in order to personalize each execution of the custom document converter.

19

Performance Tips, Tricks, and Traps

Prior releases of SharePoint focused on team-based collaboration sites, corporate intranets or extranets that typically had a finite audience. Even though the total potential audience for a team site or corporate intranet is not as significant as an anonymous site, performance was still an issue with SharePoint sites. The same is true in the most recent release of SharePoint in both Windows SharePoint Services (WSS) 3.0 and Office SharePoint Server (MOSS) 2007. The added capability of hosting content-centric anonymous sites on the SharePoint platform makes performance even more of an issue today.

The significant architectural change in the SharePoint foundation, i.e., being built on top of ASP .NET 2.0 rather than in a side-by-side model as in WSS 2.0, provided the most significant performance benefit to the platform. This change facilitated the removal of the ISAPI filter from Internet Information Services (IIS) that glued SharePoint together with ASP.NET 1.1 and was the cause for a significant drag on the performance of any SharePoint 2.0 site.

MOSS 2007 provides additional performance optimization opportunities above and beyond what WSS 3.0 offers out of the box (OOTB). Site administrators and developers can take advantage of ASP.NET 2.0 caching techniques to reduce the burden on SharePoint Web Front End (WFE) servers as well as SQL Servers. This chapter covers the different caching techniques, as well as ways to extend and customize them for your specific needs.

Caching is not the only issue when it comes to performance. SharePoint 3.0 is a very powerful and flexible application. One of the downsides in providing this flexible and powerful environment is that SharePoint commonly generates rather large page sizes for low-bandwidth users. Thankfully, opportunities exist to control and reduce a page's size, or payload, for all requestors based on different conditions, such as whether they are anonymous or authenticated users. This chapter explores some of the different options available to assist in reducing the page's payload.

Finally, most performance issues that arise are caused by poorly written custom code that has been integrated into a SharePoint site. This chapter describes a few coding techniques that all SharePoint developers, especially Publishing site developers, should be aware of when creating SharePoint sites in order to avoid common pitfalls in custom solutions.

SharePoint Caching Options

SharePoint's architecture is set up such that most if not all site content lives inside the SharePoint content database. Not only is the content in the database, but so are a considerable amount of layout files such as master pages, page layouts, style sheets, and images. With so much content in the database, the SharePoint WFE servers are very chatty with the database server. This results in a considerable amount of traffic between the database(s) and WFE server(s). Aside from pulling data directly from the database(s), SharePoint also pulls data from across lists and sites for such things as navigation and cross-list and site queries for the Content Query Web Part (CWQP). All this data is then used on the SharePoint WFE servers to construct the pages, which are built and compiled by ASP.NET 2.0 to create the rendered HTML output that is returned back to the requestor.

WSS 3.0 leverages some of the caching techniques provided in ASP.NET 2.0 to optimize data retrieval and page processing. MOSS 2007 takes SharePoint's performance optimizations a step further in three areas: output caching, object caching, and disk-based BLOB caching. Each of these techniques is exclusive to MOSS 2007 and can be leveraged within Publishing sites to squeeze the most performance out of a site.

> *Each of the caching options has an extensive administrative interface associated with it. Instead of documenting the administration screens and options in a developer book, refer to the official documentation in the MOSS 2007 SDK on MSDN:* `www.andrewconnell.com/go/267`*. The topics covered in this chapter explain at a high level how these different caching options work and how they can be customized from a developer's perspective.*

Page Output Caching

Page output caching in MOSS 2007 is virtually identical to the same technology found in ASP.NET 2.0 — with two major differences. When implementing page output caching in an ASP.NET 2.0 site, developers add an `OutputCache` attribute to the `Page` or `Control` directive in an `*.ASPX` or `*.ASCX` file. This tells ASP.NET 2.0 to store the resulting HTML that is generated by the page life cycle in memory (RAM) for a period of time. Subsequent requests will receive the same rendered HTML output in memory, rather than cause the ASP.NET 2.0 page life cycle to start up and go through the process of compiling and executing the page to generate the rendered output.

How is SharePoint different? Generally speaking, the process and net result is identical. One of the major differences is that the `OutputCache` attribute is not used on the `Page` or `Control` directive. That's because pages created for a SharePoint site may be used in more than a single site; they may be used across multiple sites or site collections, all served up from the same template file on the file system. Instead, pages need to have the caching configured for certain circumstances (authenticated or anonymous requests), as well as specific sites.

Rather than manage the caching using the `OutputCache` attribute on pages and controls, MOSS 2007 Publishing sites have extra administrative screens added to the top-level site within a site collection. From the site collection's administration page, a site owner can create one or more profiles (Site Settings ⇨ Site Collection Cache Profiles). A profile consists of things such as how long the HTML in cache is retained, whether SharePoint should check whether the HTML in cache was generated using the same permissions as the current request, or whether SharePoint should check whether the underlying data has changed (and if so, purge the cached HTML and regenerate the page). While it may seem a bit excessive, these options are very helpful in certain cases:

❑ **Perform ACL Check** — For profiles used on an anonymous site, get a little extra performance boost by avoiding the check to see whether the requestor who caused the current HTML in cache had the same permissions as the current user requesting the page. On an anonymous site, everyone has the same permissions so this is not necessary. However, this is not the case on a non-anonymous site such as an intranet or extranet.

❑ **Check for Changes** — Is it more important to always show the most updated content or is it more important to have the greatest performing site possible? Good news: SharePoint enables the site owner to decide what is more important.

❑ **Allow writers to view cached content** — If a content owner is editing content on the same site where caching is utilized, does it make sense for that person to see potentially stale content even if it is just a few minutes old, or is it more important for them to see the latest version of the page? Again, SharePoint does not dictate this, leaving the decision in the hands of the site administrator.

Site administrators assign these profiles as either the anonymous profile or the authenticated profile on the site collection. Setting the profile at the site collection does not implicitly affect the entire site collection. Similar to master pages, site administrators can break the inheritance and configure a particular site's cache profile. This allows for more granular control than what is offered in out-of-the-box ASP.NET 2.0 sites.

What version of the page are the readers seeing? MOSS 2007 provides an easy way to see whether a page is pulled from cache or not, as well as to see how old the page is. When setting the cache profile on a site collection or site, site administrators can elect to include debug information. When this checkbox is selected, SharePoint adds an HTML comment just after the closing `<HTML>` tag that includes the name of the profile used as well as the timestamp indicating when it was added to cache:

```
<!-- Rendered using cache profile:Public Internet (Purely Anonymous) at: 2007-10-
15T16:53:40 -->
```

Object Caching

Object caching is another option available to Publishing site administrators when optimizing site performance. While output caching stores the rendered HTML in memory, object caching stores actual managed objects within memory that are later used by SharePoint. Object caching is most commonly used in behaviors such as cross-site and cross-list queries. Issuing queries for things such as navigation and CQWPs is an expensive process compared to other processes. To alleviate the burden, the resulting objects from these queries are stored in cache. Subsequent requests that require these same queries then retrieve the content directly from memory, rather than execute the exact same expensive query.

The object cache is configured on the Site Settings ⇨ Site Collection Object Cache page. From here, page administrators can configure how much RAM on the server to use when storing items in cache, as well as whether it is used. Site administrators can even force the invalidation (aka *flushing*) of the object cache on the current SharePoint WFE or on all WFEs in the SharePoint farm.

There is one setting on the Object Cache Settings page that warrants a bit more explanation than what is provided in the browser interface: Cross List Query Results Multiplier. When a query is executed, SharePoint retrieves extra results — that is, more than what is desired and used in the actual query. Sounds like a waste, so why is this even an option? Consider a non-anonymous site that contains a CQWP. The first time the page containing the Web Part is requested, the CQWP executes the query and stores the results in the database. If another user visits the same page a few seconds later but has different rights within the same target result set, SharePoint would need to rerun the query because the result set was generated using a different set of permission criteria. The multiplier enables SharePoint to widen the result set retrieved in the query and store it within the cache. Subsequent requests would be able to use the cached results and filter it, rather than rerun the expensive query. The greater the multiplier, the more data is retrieved in each query. Careful testing should be undertaken when manipulating the multiplier, as it can quickly result in adverse affects — consuming more memory much quicker on the WFE than desired. Note that security trimming of items from the search results is still applied to content in the cache.

Disk-Based Caching (BLOB Cache)

The final type of caching available to Publishing sites in MOSS 2007 is disk-based caching for very large *binary large objects (BLOBs)*. These are static media files stored in the database, such as sound, video, and image files. Pulling these files repeatedly from the SharePoint content database creates unnecessary overhead, as their content does not change. Instead, when disk-based caching is enabled, these files are stored on the SharePoint WFE server's hard disk upon the first request. Subsequent requests for the same file are then pulled from the WFE disk, rather than from the database, thereby reducing the network and database server load.

To enable disk-based caching, find the following line in the `web.config` file for the Web application containing the Publishing site:

```
<BlobCache location="C:\blobCache" path="\.(gif|jpg|png|css|js)$" maxSize="10"
enabled="false" />
```

This line dictates where the BLOB files are stored on the WFE, if disk-based caching is enabled; the maximum amount of space that can be occupied by the BLOB cache (measured in GB); and the filename pattern to use as the criteria if a file can be saved to the BLOB cache. This pattern, the `<BlobCache Path="" />` attribute, contains a regular expression that is matched against the names of the files pulled from the SharePoint content database. By default, all files in the BLOB cache are stored in cache for 24 hours. In addition, only items stored in SharePoint document libraries are cached using disk-based caching.

Limiting the Page Payload

One issue that always arises in regard to SharePoint 3.0 sites with respect to performance is the size of the complete payload for a requested page. The payload of a page is the combined size of all of the files needed for the page to be rendered and perform as desired. This includes not only the HTML of the page, but any referenced style sheets, images, media, and client-side script. Before looking at any of the options, understand that a Publishing site, or any SharePoint 3.0 site for that matter, can be completely customized to look like anything using master pages and CSS. Sure, SharePoint's OOTB layout is HTML table–based, rather than a more concise CSS-based design, but that does not mean a SharePoint site has to be table-based — that is just how it shipped. Developers and designers can create a completely customized SharePoint design and implementation with a small page size.

Regardless, there are some SharePoint infrastructure files that contribute quite a bit to the SharePoint page size. This section covers a few techniques developers can implement to reduce the payload of the page. For demonstration purposes, an OOTB site created using the Publishing Portal template is used. The only modification that has been made to the site is to configure it for anonymous access; no other content or branding changes have been made.

Developers Toolbox: Fiddler Tool

One of the most powerful tools available to Web developers is Fiddler (www.andrewconnell.com/go/268). Fiddler is an HTTP debugging proxy freeware utility that logs all HTTP traffic between the computer it is installed on and the network. Developers can use this tool to inspect all HTTP requests and responses. This tool is used to inspect the traffic, the files requested, and file size in this section.

A request for the home page of a Publishing site (created with the OOTB Publishing Portal template) generates a total of 22 requests for various files, as shown in Figure 19-1 — resulting in a combined file size of 204k. Most of these files (16) are used to provide the banding and rendering of the page, such as the ASPX page (containing the generated HTML), CSS, and image files. The content and branding files account for 91k (44.6%) of the request for the home page of a Publishing Portal site. This leaves six script files (shown as sessions 7–12 in Figure 19-1) to account for the remaining 111k (54.4%) of the request. While all script files are cached after the first request, this first request can add a considerable amount of time to the page load if the user is not on a broadband connection.

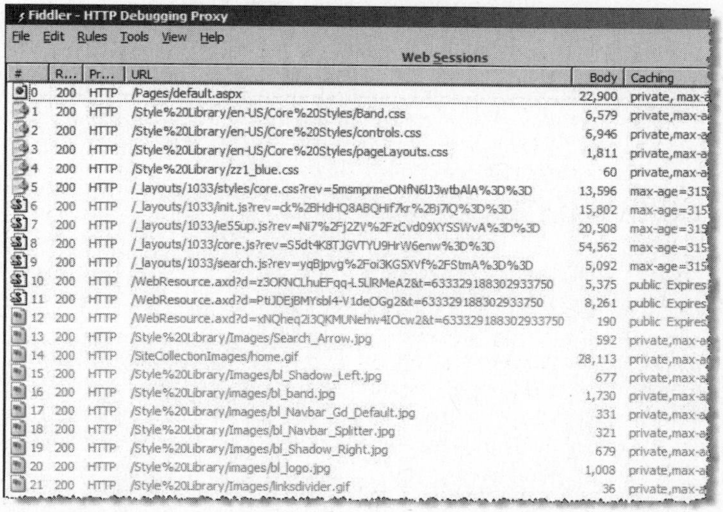

Figure 19-1

SharePoint's CORE.JS

The biggest of the script files is the one that provides the functionality in the Site Actions menu: core.js. This one file accounts for over 26% of the page payload, weighing in at 54k — and this is compressed (more on compression in the next section). Controlling when this file is loaded can yield a significant performance boost to the loading of the page (26%!). Because this file primarily contains the script that implements the SharePoint Site Actions menu, it is not always needed.

For instance, anonymous users who don't have access to the Site Actions menu do not need core.js at all. In these cases, core.js could be suppressed from being delivered to the page. What about authenticated users? While authenticated users will likely need access to the Site Actions menu, a technique referred to as delayed loading, or lazy loading, of the JavaScript file can be employed. Both of these techniques are explained in more detail in the following sections.

Note that these six JavaScript files that account for over 54% of the page payload are actually compressed before they are sent to the client. This is done using IIS compression.

IIS Compression

IIS compression, a capability of Internet Information Services (IIS), compresses static files before sending them to the requestor. These compressed file types, such as JavaScript and HTML files, are stored in a temporary directory when first requested. When creating a SharePoint Web application, IIS is configured to compress all files in the http://[..]/_layouts directory. Images are not included in IIS compression because they are already compressed.

As Figure 19-1 demonstrated, six JavaScript files are responsible for 111k, or 54.4%, of the payload when requesting the home page of the Publishing Portal site the first time. These files are actually much bigger because the 111k represents the *compressed* version of these files. Take a look in the [..]\12\TEMPLATE\ LAYOUTS\1033 folder to find four of the six files: core.js, ie55up.js (or ie50up.js), init.js, and search.js (the other two files are embedded resources in SharePoint assemblies, which are not easily accessible). These files in their uncompressed form total over 452k in size! Core.js alone is 258k! This means that IIS compression is already providing a 75% performance improvement; core.js alone is compressed down to only 20% of its original size.

While IIS compression plays a significant role in reducing the page payload, there is still 111k in JavaScript that needs to be sent down to the client. Of that amount, 54k is attributed to core.js. The next two sections demonstrate two techniques to mitigate the size issue of core.js.

Loading core.js Only When Necessary

As mentioned previously, core.js contains the JavaScript necessary to implement the Site Actions menu. When a page is requested, core.js is also requested, which slows down the page load on the first request (core.js is cached locally for subsequent requests). Because the core.js file includes the JavaScript to implement the Site Actions menu, on a site that supports anonymous access it can be suppressed from loading completely!

> *The approach of suppressing core.js completely is not supported by Microsoft and should be carefully considered. However, this technique is just one part of the technique described in the following section: delayed loading of core.js. Therefore, it is recommended that you implement the complete delayed loading solution. It still achieves a major goal in improving the page load time, while also loading core.js in the background.*

The first step is to either create a new master page or edit an existing one. This demonstration uses a copy of the `BlueBand.master` master page called `BlueBandSlimPayload.master`. In the `<HEAD>` section of the page, add the following server control, which tells SharePoint that unless another control on the page registers `core.js`, it should not be registered on the page:

```
<SharePoint:ScriptLink runat="server" />
```

Create a new server control that checks whether the current user is authenticated or not. If they are authenticated, then it should register `core.js`. The code in Listing 19-1 demonstrates how to create the server control.

Listing 19-1: Loading core.js for authenticated users only

```
using System;
using System.ComponentModel;
using System.Web;
using System.Web.UI.WebControls;
using Microsoft.SharePoint.WebControls;

namespace WROX.ProMossWcm.Chapter19 {
  [ToolboxItem("<{0}:RegisterCoreJsIfAuthenticated runat=\"server\" />")]
  public class RegisterCoreJsIfAuthenticated : WebControl {

    protected override void OnInit (EventArgs e) {
      // if the current user is authenticated...
      if (HttpContext.Current.Request.IsAuthenticated)
        // register the core.js script in delayed load
        ScriptLink.RegisterCore(this.Page, true);

      base.OnInit(e);
    }

  }
}
```

Compile and deploy the server control, adding the necessary safe control entry. This server control touches the SharePoint object model, so either the CAS trust level of the Web application needs to be running in `WSS_Medium` or a custom CAS policy needs to be created, granting this one assembly the necessary permissions. The associated code download for this book, available from www.wrox.com, demonstrates how to create a custom CAS policy for this server control.

After the server control is created, it needs to be registered and added to the `BlueBandSlimPayload` `.master` master page. Add the following register directive to the top of the master page:

```
<%@ Register TagPrefix="WROX" Namespace="WROX.ProMossWcm.Chapter19"
Assembly="Chapter19SlimPagePayload, Version=1.0.0.0, Culture=neutral,
PublicKeyToken=c591e70cfdf9ce4f" %>
```

Finally, add the server control to the `<HEAD>` portion of the page, as shown in Listing 19-2.

Listing 19-2: Implementing the RegisterCoreJsIfAuthenticated server control

```
<head runat="server">
  <meta name="GENERATOR" content="Microsoft SharePoint">
  <meta http-equiv="Content-Type" content="text/html; charset=utf-8">
  <meta http-equiv="Expires" content="0">
  <SharePoint:RobotsMetaTag runat="server"/>
  <title id="onetidTitle">
    <asp:ContentPlaceHolder id="PlaceHolderPageTitle" runat="server"/>
  </title>
  <Sharepoint:CssLink runat="server" />
  <!--Styles used for positioning, font and spacing definitions-->
  <SharePoint:CssRegistration name="<% $SPUrl:~SiteCollection/Style
Library/~language/Core Styles/Band.css%>" runat="server"/>
  <SharePoint:CssRegistration name="<% $SPUrl:~sitecollection/Style
Library/~language/Core Styles/controls.css %>" runat="server"/>
  <SharePoint:CssRegistration name="<% $SPUrl:~SiteCollection/Style
Library/zz1_blue.css%>" runat="server"/>
  <!--Placeholder for additional overrides-->
  <asp:ContentPlaceHolder id="PlaceHolderAdditionalPageHead" runat="server"/>
  <SharePoint:ScriptLink name="init.js" runat="server" />
  <WROX:RegisterCoreJsIfAuthenticated runat="server" />
  <SharePoint:ScriptLink runat="server" />
</head>
```

At this point, the core.js file will not be registered on the page when an anonymous user requests the Publishing Portal site's home page the first time, as shown by the following Fiddler capture in Figure 19-2.

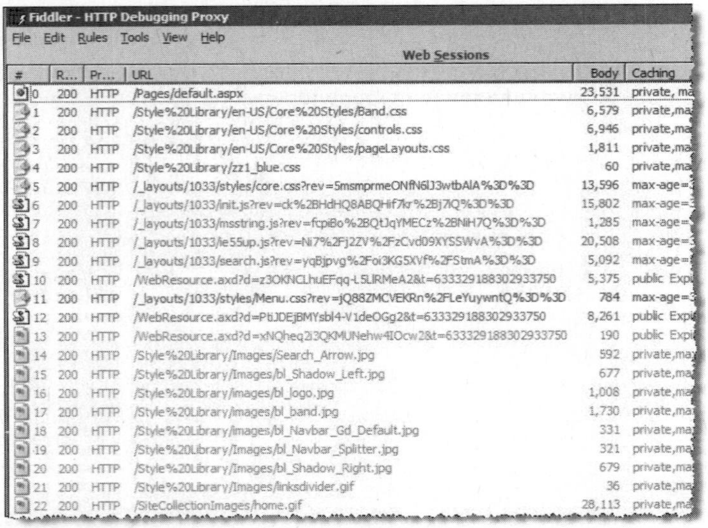

Figure 19-2

Delayed Loading core.js

Recall that `core.js` contains the JavaScript necessary to implement the Site Actions menu. When a page is requested, `core.js` is also requested, which slows down the page load on the first request (`core.js` is cached locally for subsequent requests). One option that can be employed in an effort to improve the page load time is to delay loading the `core.js` file until after the rest of the page content has been downloaded. While this does not eliminate the issue, it is a workaround that provides users of the site with a better experience, as the download of `core.js` is pushed to the back of the line so to speak.

Building off the `BlueBandSlimPayload.master` example in the previous section, create a new application page named `DelayLoadCoreJs.aspx` in the `[..]\12\TEMPLATE\LAYOUTS` folder and add the content in Listing 19-3 to the file.

Listing 19-3: DelayLoadCoreJs.aspx

```
<%@ Register Tagprefix="SharePoint" Namespace="Microsoft.SharePoint.WebControls"
Assembly="Microsoft.SharePoint, Version=12.0.0.0, Culture=neutral,
PublicKeyToken=71e9bce111e9429c" %>
<html>
<head>
<body>
   <SharePoint:ScriptLink name="core.js" runat="server" />
   <script language="javascript">
     // don't refresh the page when it gets focus
     DisableRefreshOnFocus();
   </script>
</body>
</head>
</html>
```

The only purpose of this page is to load `core.js` *in the background*. When this page is requested by the user, the user downloads `core.js` one time and uses the locally cached version for future requests. The next step is to get this page requested in the master page. To do this, add the code in Listing 19-4 to the bottom of the `BlueBandSlimPayload.master` master page.

Listing 19-4: Lazy Loading core.js

```
      <!-- omitted from the book for readability -->
    </form>
    <iframe src="/_layouts/DelayLoadCoreJs.aspx" style="display:none;" />
  </body>
</html>
```

Finally, test the solution by clearing the browser's cache and requesting the Publishing Portal site as an anonymous user. As the Fiddler trace shows in Figure 19-3, the `core.js` file is one of the last files requested.

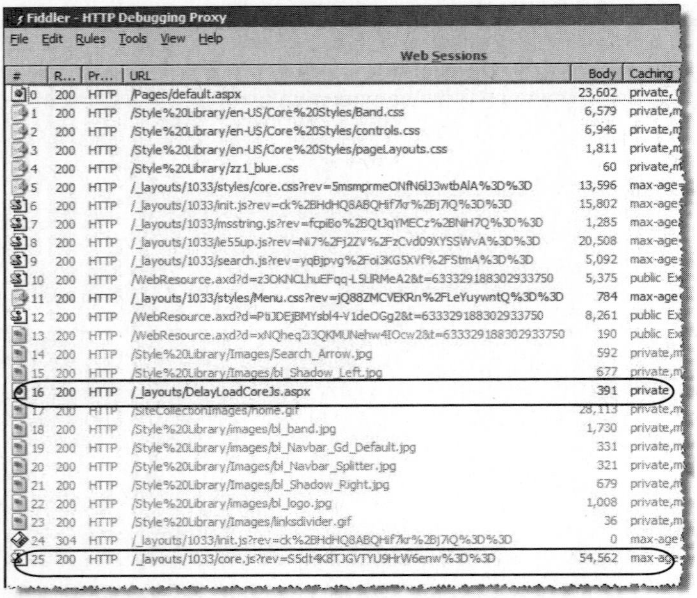

Figure 19-3

Browser Cache and Content Expiration

Another trick to managing page payload is by manipulating the browser caching settings on the client. This can be done by adding special <META> tags in the <HEAD> portion of the page. These tags control how long a page is cached or when it expires. For instance, the following tag tells the browser not to retrieve a new version of the page until after midnight on New Year's Eve 2007:

```
<meta name="expires" content="Mon, 31 Dec 2007 23:59:59 GMT" />
```

The *MetaTagsGenerator* project on CodePlex (www.andrewconnell.com/go/201) provides an easy way to manage the <META> tags in a Publishing site.

Performance Programming Techniques

Aside from the different caching options available in Publishing sites, and techniques to minimize the page size returned to the requester, custom code is likely to be the area where the biggest performance improvement can be realized. Custom code is typically where most of the performance issues arise in SharePoint applications because developers are not aware of the inner workings of the .NET Framework or some of the nuances in the SharePoint API.

This section explains some of the more common issues that arise from Publishing sites in the area of working with the SharePoint API. These concepts apply to any custom code written in SharePoint sites — not just Publishing sites or MOSS 2007 sites, but any WSS 3.0–based site. In fact, these concepts go all the way back to WSS 2.0!

.NET Framework Disposable Objects

Before explaining the specifics of disposable objects within the context of the SharePoint API, developers must first understand what it means in general .NET terms. One of the core capabilities the .NET Framework provides developers is managing system memory. This is what gives .NET applications the label "managed" applications — the applications typically do not manage their own memory; instead, the .NET Framework does it for them.

.NET applications create objects that consume memory. These include objects such as integers, strings, and classes, to name a few. After an object is created, developers do not have to explicitly destroy the object. Instead, the .NET Framework's garbage collector works behind the scenes to cleanup objects no longer in use and free up the consumed memory. The garbage collector is triggered under certain conditions such as when the CPU is idle for a given length of time or when a certain amount of memory has been consumed. As it goes through the managed memory looking for objects no longer used by an application, it keeps a record of all those objects that could be destroyed and have their consumed memory returned to the system. Because the creation and destruction of an object is by far one of the most expensive operations in the .NET Framework, the garbage collector uses the list of potential candidates to determine where it can get the best bang for the buck: It destroys only the largest objects to free up as much memory as possible, leaving the smaller objects alone until there are no more big objects to destroy.

Most developers are familiar with this aspect of the memory management infrastructure in the .NET Framework. What many are not aware of is that the unmanaged memory still comes into play. Some objects in the .NET Framework are actually small managed wrappers to much larger unmanaged blocks. For instance, a database connection or an open file each have a managed and unmanaged footprint. The challenge is that when the garbage collector runs, it can only see the managed portion. Therefore, it is not getting an accurate picture of how much memory some objects are actually consuming.

To address this issue, Microsoft created the `System.IDisposable` interface. This interface defines a single method: `Dispose()`. This interface is supposed to be used on objects that require an extra bit of cleanup before the garbage collector comes along. When an object implements the `IDisposable` interface, it is a signal to developers using that object that they should call the `Dispose()` method as soon as the object is no longer needed. The object's `Dispose()` method does any necessary cleanup such as releasing file references or closing database connections. Calling `Dispose()` ensures that the garbage collector sees an accurate representation of how much memory is being consumed by a particular object.

> *For more information on how the .NET Framework manages system memory, the garbage collector, and the disposable pattern, refer to the* Microsoft Patterns and Practices *guide* Improving .NET Application Performance and Scalability *on MSDN, specifically Chapter 5, "Improving .NET Application Performance and Scalability":* www.andrewconnell.com/go/269.

How High-Memory Usage Affects SharePoint Sites

While it is generally an accepted principal that high memory usage in an application is not a good thing, developers should understand the potential issues within the context of a SharePoint site.

Application pools are typically configured to recycle themselves once they cross a certain threshold of memory consumption. The recycling of an application pool is not the end of the world, as it does not cause the site to be unavailable and result in bad responses to the requestors. If a request is received when an application pool is recycling, the request is queued up until the application pool can serve it.

The downside of frequent application pool recycling is that it creates undue stress on the WFE, it loses everything in cache, and it forces a just-in-time (JIT) compilation of each ASPX page within the application on its next request. This results in a spike of the CPU, which is avoidable with good memory management coding techniques.

Another more drastic side-effect from high memory usage is the random OutOfMemory() exception. These are incredibly nerve-wracking because they can be quite challenging to reproduce and typically appear at random intervals in random spots throughout a SharePoint site.

The worst result of high memory consumption in a SharePoint site is unexplained application crashes. These are also challenging to debug because they may or may not occur at predictable times and with repeatable results.

Working with SharePoint Disposable Objects

Why is this information about the IDisposable() interface important to SharePoint development? It is critical because two commonly used objects in the SharePoint API are in fact small managed wrappers to a much larger unmanaged object: SPSite and SPWeb. These two objects, or at least one of them, are used in just about every single custom code component. When they are not properly managed they can result in excessive memory consumption, causing major headaches for developers trying to troubleshoot issues that arise in production but never appeared in development or load testing because the production load is much more significant than expected.

Generally speaking, just like .NET Framework objects, developers should dispose of SPSite and SPWeb objects as soon as the objects are no longer needed in order to free up the unmanaged portion of memory. SPSite has an extra little-known issue in that when a new SPSite object is created, the SPSite .RootWeb object is automatically hydrated with information about the site collection's top-level site. This is by design, as Microsoft anticipated that most calls to a site collection will also result in calls to the top-level site in the site collection.

When working with instances of a site collection (SPSite), developers should dispose of both the top-level site and the site collection as soon as possible:

```
SPSite siteCollection = new SPSite("http://wcm");
SPWeb topLevelSite = siteCollection.RootWeb;
// do some work
topLevelSite.Dispose();
siteCollection.Dispose();
```

The same is true when working with SharePoint sites (SPWeb):

```
SPWeb site = siteCollection.OpenWeb("/PressReleases");
// do some work
site.Dispose();
```

There are two generally accepted methods of coding when working with objects that implement the IDisposable interface. The first is using a try-catch-finally block, as shown in Listing 19-5. The Dispose() method is called within the finally portion when it's called — when either the try or catch portions complete.

Listing 19-5: Working with disposable objects with try-catch-finally

```
try {
  siteCollection = new SPSite("http://wcm");
  site = siteCollection.RootWeb;
}
catch {}
finally {
  site.Dispose();
  siteCollection.RootWeb.Dispose();
  siteCollection.Dispose();
}
```

The other, and recommended, way is to use the `using` statements, as shown in Listing 19-6. These require that the object provided in the `using` statement implement the `IDisposable()` interface, as it will automatically call the `Dispose()` method at the completion of the statement.

Listing 19-6: Working with disposable objects with using()

```
using (SPSite siteCollection = new SPSite("http://wcm")) {
  using (SPWeb site = siteCollection.RootWeb) {
    siteTitle = site.Title;
  }
}
```

Working with Collections

In addition to the `IDisposable` programming techniques that developers can use to avoid memory management issues, developers should also be cognizant of how the SharePoint API works under the hood when dealing with collections. Most SharePoint collections expose the members in the collection using indexes. These indexes offer an easy way to obtain references to particular objects. For instance, developers can get a reference to a specific list using any of the techniques shown in Listing 19-7.

Listing 19-7: Working with SharePoint collections

```
// get list by name
SPList taskList = SPWeb.Lists["Tasks"];

// get list by ID (integer)
SPList taskList = SPWeb.Lists[listID];

// get list by unique identifier
SPList taskList = SPWeb.Lists[listGUID];
```

Each of the commands in Listing 19-7 is functionally equivalent in that they return an instance of the same list. The objects returned, in this case an `SPList`, has properties such as `Title`, `Description`, and `Count`. Because each of the commands in Listing 19-7 returns an instance of a `SPList`, developers could skip a step and access the properties directly:

```
int itemsInTasksList = SPWeb.Lists["Tasks"].Count;
```

While there is nothing wrong with this code, developers should be aware of what is going on inside the SharePoint API. In the preceding code, SharePoint is creating an internal instance of a SPList object, hydrating it with the *Tasks* list, retrieving the value from the Count property, and then destroying the internal SPList object. Makes perfect sense, so why is this important? Consider the code in Listing 19-8.

Listing 19-8: Accessing properties directly on items in a collection

```
string listTitle = SPWeb.Lists["Tasks"].Title;
string listDescription = SPWeb.Lists["Tasks"].Description;
int itemsInTasksList = SPWeb.Lists["Tasks"].Count;
```

The code in Listing 19-8 results in SharePoint creating three instances of the Tasks list using an internal SPList object (one for each statement), retrieving the value from the property and then discarding the object. This means that the SharePoint API is making three round-trips to the database — not ideal, as developers should strive for only 2–3 round-trips to the database for core pages in a SharePoint site.

Instead, developers should get a local reference to the list and access each property using that, as Listing 19-9 shows.

Listing 19-9: Accessing properties using a local object

```
SPList tasksList = SPWeb.Lists["Tasks"];
string listTitle = tasksList.Title;
string listDescription = tasksList.Description;
int itemsInTasksList = tasksList.Count;
```

The code in Listing 19-9 is three times more performant than the code in Listing 19-8.

Querying/Aggregating Data via the API

Developers are often faced with the task of querying for data across multiple SharePoint sites. This task is made a bit easier in MOSS 2007, which ships with a new object that is optimized for cross-site queries: the PortalSiteMapProvider. The Microsoft.SharePoint.Publishing.Navigation .PortalSiteMapProvider is primarily used when there is a need to frequently rerun the same query on data that does not change very often. Microsoft uses this object extensively within MOSS 2007 sites, especially Publishing sites, because it is the fastest way to both generate navigation and retrieve the results for the CQWP. The best part is developers can use this same object in their own custom code!

This object contains three very useful methods:

❑   GetCachedListItemsByQuery() — This method retrieves items from a specific list, leveraging special caching techniques.

❑   GetChildNodes() — This powerful method retrieves SPWeb and SPListItem objects, including PublishingPage objects. It is very flexible in that developers can specify the types of objects to be returned using the NodeTypes enumeration. The result set does not include the configured *Welcome Page*, also known as the *home page* for a SPWeb.

❑ **GetCachedSiteDataQuery()** — This method enables developers to use a preconfigured `SPSiteDataQuery` object that returns a ADO.NET `DataTable` object. This method is useful when querying across multiple lists in the same `SPWeb`.

To use the `PortalSiteMapProvider`, first get an instance of an existing one such as the `PortalSiteMapProvider.CurrentNavSiteMapProvider`, as they are not designed to be created as new instances due to their high memory footprint. Next, get a reference to a specific node in the site collection hierarchy and create a CAML query using the `SPQuery` object. The code in Listing 19-10 demonstrates pulling all pages from the Press Releases subsite within the Division1 subsite that have been published in the last seven days.

Listing 19-10: Using the PortalSiteMapProvider

```
// get reference to provider for current navigation
PortalSiteMapProvider psmp = PortalSiteMapProvider.CurrentNavSiteMapProvider;

// get specific node in the navigation
PortalWebSiteMapNode node = psmp.FindSiteMapNode("/Division1/PressReleases") as
PortalWebSiteMapNode;

// get all pages created in the last seven days
SPQuery query = new SPQuery();
query.Query = "<Where><Geq><FieldRef Name=\"Created\" /><Value Type=\"DateTime\
">[Today-7]</Value></Geq></Where>";
SiteMapNodeCollection pages = psmp.GetCachedListItemsByQuery (node, "Pages", query,
SPContext.Current.Web);
```

While powerful and fast, the `PortalSiteMapProvider` should not be used without careful consideration. In order to achieve the high level of performance necessary for things such as navigation and the CQWP, it leverages sophisticated caching techniques. For this caching to be effective, the queries must be issued frequently or the cached object will expire. In addition, the underlying data should not be changing very frequently. Otherwise, all the overhead associated with creating and adding the object to the cache will be a wasted effort, negatively affecting the performance of the custom code rather than improving it.

Summary

This chapter has covered a few of the options available to site administrators and developers in getting the best performance out of their Publishing sites. In addition to the topics discussed here, other non-SharePoint-specific Web development techniques and guidelines should be followed when writing custom code for a Publishing site or any SharePoint site.

This chapter focused on improving performance in three ways: limiting the round-trips to the SharePoint content databases, minimizing the memory footprint on the SharePoint WFE servers, and minimizing the payload size of the page delivered to the end user. Other techniques not discussed here include leveraging AJAX callbacks, which avoids retransmitting the entire page across the wire.

20

Incorporating ASP.NET 2.0 Applications

As covered in this book and many others, Windows SharePoint Services 3.0 (WSS) can be used to host not only traditional collaboration sites, but also content-centric sites. However, many organizations may require some sort of functionality or custom application to be embedded within a SharePoint site. For instance, a SharePoint Publishing site may need to have a newsletter subscription and management application or an event registration system. In past versions of WSS 3.0 it was not very easy to incorporate custom applications into a site.

Thankfully, WSS 3.0 greatly expands on the number of options available to developers to build custom applications in SharePoint sites, both collaboration and Publishing sites. This chapter covers different techniques and options developers can utilize to incorporate custom ASP.NET 2.0 applications into SharePoint sites. In addition, many common questions that come up when building applications in SharePoint are covered in this chapter, such as when to store data in SharePoint lists compared to a custom database and how to customize the navigation.

While incorporating custom ASP.NET 2.0 applications into SharePoint sites is one option, another option is to use WSS 3.0 as the application development platform. In this case, the application is built on top of SharePoint, rather than being integrated into an existing collaboration or publishing site.

One thing not included in this chapter is a large number of code snippets and screenshots demonstrating the different techniques. That's because the techniques have been covered extensively throughout other chapters in the book and repetition does not add value. Therefore, this chapter contains references to other chapters throughout the book. Similarly, this chapter does not walk through the development of a custom application, as each application is very different and has unique business requirements. Think of this chapter as more of an overview of different options and possibilities when creating custom applications in SharePoint sites.

Before reading the rest of this chapter it would be helpful to adopt a particular mindset regarding the development of SharePoint sites (if it is not already apparent). SharePoint development is unlike traditional ASP.NET 2.0 development in the sense that instead of building large applications, developers build many smaller components and integrate them into a larger solution. For example, creating a custom list or content type with advanced custom workflows and event receivers involves building many little components, rather than a single large component. The sum of the components yields a much larger and valuable component than the individual pieces.

Each Component Adds More Value

Before jumping into custom application development it helps to take a closer look at all of the components that make up a SharePoint site and how they can be utilized in an application. This also helps when you are deciding whether or not SharePoint is the right platform for building applications on top of the WSS 3.0 platform. As explained in Chapter 2, "Windows SharePoint Services Development Primer," WSS 3.0 is built on top of ASP.NET 2.0, and Office SharePoint Server (MOSS) 2007 is built on top of WSS 3.0. Because the SharePoint architecture is additive to the underlying frameworks, every component's features and capabilities are available throughout the stack. This chapter covers the different major aspects of these components and why they are significant when building custom applications within SharePoint sites. The material provided in the following sections is by no means exhaustive, but covers many of the most significant components as they pertain to custom application development.

What ASP.NET 2.0 Brings to the Table

Chapter 2 details the primary components in ASP.NET 2.0 that are heavily leveraged within WSS 3.0. While all the components in ASP.NET 2.0 can be leveraged in SharePoint sites in the same manner, SharePoint provides some added value in certain areas, including the following:

❑ All pages within a section of the site can be configured to use the same master page, and site administrators are provided with a Web interface for selecting and changing the master page used for the site, rather than setting it on a page-by-page basis. For more information on master pages in SharePoint, refer to Chapter 7, "Master Pages and Page Layouts."

❑ The plumbing required by the Web Part framework, such as the `WebPartManager` control and various zones, is all provided OOTB in SharePoint. This is not the case in ASP.NET 2.0 sites, as developers need to ensure that all pages leveraging Web Parts have an instance of the `WebPartManager` control, and create the necessary Web Part zones to host Web Parts, a catalog zone to provide a list of Web Parts to add to the page, and an editor zone to enable users to modify the properties of the Web Parts on the page. For more information on Web Parts, refer to Chapter 11, "Web Parts."

❑ Although user and server controls can be used in SharePoint sites in the same way they are used in ASP.NET 2.0 sites, SharePoint takes it a step further. Using delegate controls, developers can create WSS 3.0 Features that enable site owners to dynamically inject and replace functionality and content very easily, complete with a built-in undo mechanism. For more information on delegate controls, refer to Chapter 7.

❑ The addition of Windows Workflow Foundation (WF) to the .NET 3.0 Framework enabled developers to create episodic and reactive programs such that while waiting for some event or state, the programs are serialized to a persisted state and are therefore not subject to server reboots or resource issues, as are traditional .NET applications. Applications utilizing WF must host the workflow runtime and provide the necessary services, such as the persistence service that handles serialization and deserialization of the workflow instance. SharePoint provides all the necessary plumbing to host the workflow runtime and persistence service, removing these burdens from developers. It also provides a human element by facilitating different types of forms and associating workflows with items, documents, and content types. For more information on WF in SharePoint, refer to Chapter 12, "Leveraging Workflow."

When it comes to building a custom application that either integrates into an existing SharePoint site or uses SharePoint as the foundation, developers can also take advantage of additional ASP.NET 2.0 components. The membership provider model enables developers to use any authentication store desired in a custom application. The abstraction of the particulars of each authentication mechanism at the ASP.NET 2.0 level dramatically simplifies the integration of custom applications at the SharePoint level.

All applications require some sort of navigation. The navigation provider model included in ASP.NET 2.0 enables developers to cleanly separate the data portion of the navigation from the rendering implementation, enabling teams to purchase full-featured third-party navigation components that easily snap into existing projects with very little, if any, custom code. SharePoint fully leverages the navigation provider model, covered in detail in Chapter 8, "Navigation," and even includes a few site map data sources that do most of the work in generating the navigation hierarchical structure.

While ASP.NET 2.0 provides a significant number of components that can be utilized by developers in custom applications, SharePoint provides much more. The next two sections provide an overview of the various components that both WSS 3.0 and MOSS 2007 add to the developer's proverbial toolbox.

What WSS 3.0 Brings to the Table

The previous section already mentioned a few of the additional WSS 3.0 benefits, such as how master pages are implemented and how the plumbing of the Web Part framework and Workflow Foundation are already provided out of the box (OOTB). However, the list does not stop there! Almost all custom applications store and retrieve data from tables in a database. Each of these tables usually requires some sort of administrative interface. This means that developers are left with the task of creating the CRUD (Create, Read, Update, and Delete) admin pages. Fortunately, when SharePoint lists are used to store such data, all these pages are included OOTB with each list.

Virtually all custom applications also require some sort of security model. Some users act as administrators to maintain and manage the application, while others fall into various buckets of roles such as general users, power users, managers, and so on. WSS 3.0 includes a robust and granular security model that leverages the ASP.NET 2.0 membership provider model. This model enables administrators to add and remove users and groups to a site using a familiar Web interface. Administrators can also configure sections of the site either to inherit the same permissions from its parent or to break inheritance and create a unique permission configuration at a site, list/library, or even list item level (including folders). In addition to the robust security model, WSS 3.0 also provides full auditing of all events, although this must be enabled and managed using custom code, as shown in Listing 20-1.

Listing 20-1: Enabling all auditing events on a site collection

```
SPSite siteCollection = new SPSite("http://foo");
siteCollection.Audit.AuditFlags = SPAuditMaskType.All;
siteCollection.Audit.Update();
```

Many content-centric applications demand some level of search. WSS 3.0 provides a simple built-in search capability. If more robust search functionality is required, developers can look to MOSS 2007 or Microsoft Search Server 2008 Express. In addition, many applications need to share their data with other applications or provide data feeds for some process. WSS 3.0 makes this task very easy, as it includes several Web services that enable users to manage SharePoint sites, as well as read and write data to SharePoint lists using the `lists.asmx` Web service.

Another powerful tool in application development that WSS 3.0 offers is WSS solution packages (WSPs). Covered in depth in Chapter 4, "SharePoint Features and the Solution Framework," WSPs make deployment of new or existing code and custom files a simple task, even in the largest load-balanced farm environment. Deployment of custom code and files in a traditional load-balanced ASP.NET 2.0 site requires the use of additional software packages or sophisticated scripts — or just traditional XCOPY deployment. WSPs dramatically simplify this task for SharePoint developers.

The navigation provider model mentioned in the previous section is a valuable component included in ASP.NET 2.0. WSS 3.0 fully leverages this model and includes two small additional pieces to the navigation puzzle. The included site map providers and data sources build the navigation hierarchical structure based on the structure of the site. When building the navigation structure, SharePoint factors in the current permissions of the objects to which the navigation nodes refer and compares them to the current user's permission rights, omitting anything to which the user does not have access. In addition, developers can add and remove items from the navigation programmatically.

Sometimes the requirements of a custom application demand some sort of plug-in support. Again, WSS 3.0 includes something to facilitate this requirement: the Feature framework! SharePoint Features can be used not only to deploy and add new functionality, but also to provide a plug-in style capability.

While WSS 3.0 offers quite a bit in the area custom application development, MOSS 2007 offers even more!

What MOSS 2007 Brings to the Table

Just like WSS 3.0, MOSS 2007 includes quite a few features that can be utilized in custom applications. Some of these may or may not make sense in custom applications, such as utilizing the Publishing Features or Excel Services (granted, the custom application may have some reporting capabilities that utilize Excel Services — this is just an example). However, other components included in MOSS 2007 can provide significant value in a custom application. This section takes a look at some of those components.

First, building off the previous section, MOSS includes a much more robust search capability than what WSS 3.0 provides. For example, the different components in SharePoint search (indexing and queries) can be isolated to specific application servers in MOSS, whereas in WSS 3.0 all servers contain all server roles. For more information on search in SharePoint refer to Chapter 13, "Search."

Another component of MOSS that can be very useful in custom application development is Forms Services. This addition to the latest release of the SharePoint platform enables developers and business users to author rich electronic forms using Office InfoPath 2007 and to consume those forms from the server. The forms are rendered either using the InfoPath 2007 client or as a typical Web form. Virtually all applications require some type of form for data collection or editing. Using InfoPath 2007, business users and/or developers can quickly build sophisticated forms that can be deployed to a MOSS 2007 server running Forms Services, and configure the forms to be rendered in the browser.

Many custom applications need to interface with existing applications deployed within an organization. These can be as big as CRM or ERP systems or as small as a homegrown time-keeping system. When one application needs to interface with another application, this is done either using direct calls to the database or by going through some middle business layer such as Web services. This can prove to be a maintenance nightmare because developers need to keep track of multiple database connection strings or Web service URLs, as well as the credentials needed to impersonate specific application accounts in order to access these resources.

In MOSS 2007, Microsoft introduced a new component called the *Business Data Catalog (BDC)* that helps with these challenges. Developers first create an application definition, which is an XML file containing the connection information and credentials used to connect to the source (a database or Web service); entities; and relationships. The application definition can be loosely thought of as an object relationship mapper (ORM). With the application definition created, SharePoint is then aware of the external application. This does not mean that data is copied and consumed in SharePoint; rather, SharePoint simply knows how to connect and retrieve data. Custom applications can utilize the BDC application definitions however they need to. The advantage to using the BDC to connect to another system is that all the connection information is maintained in one place by an administrator. In addition, the connection information can specify using a specific account, pass the current user's credentials through to the target system, or leverage SharePoint's single sign-on capability.

The list of features described in this section is by no means exhaustive — MOSS 2007 offers numerous capabilities, many of which were left off this list, such as the capability to create policies and manage auditing configuration via the browser. Only the capabilities that provide the biggest value for the majority of applications were included here. Even with all the components and added value that both WSS 3.0 and MOSS 2007 bring to the table when building custom applications, additional benefits should be considered when evaluating SharePoint as a potential application development platform.

Advantages to Using SharePoint As an Application Development Platform

The previous sections covered the many components that SharePoint adds to a developer's toolbox when creating custom applications that either integrate into existing SharePoint sites or utilize SharePoint as the foundation. However, it is not only the components that should be considered when evaluating SharePoint as an application development platform. Other factors should also weigh in to the decision process.

First, SharePoint development is much more along the lines of building many smaller components and integrating them. This is very different from traditional ASP.NET 2.0 development whereby the entire application is typically built from scratch (aside from some store-bought or reusable libraries). Typically, this results in less custom code, which in turn results in less chance for defects and bugs, as well as less code to write and maintain. Instead, more of the code is written and supported by Microsoft. This point cannot be discounted or overlooked, as it is quite significant.

Second, as discussed earlier, many of the things that all custom applications need are provided OOTB by SharePoint, including navigation, search, personalization and customization capabilities, self-service, a security model, and a plug-in framework.

As with any evaluation period when deciding on an application development platform, weighing the advantages against the disadvantages, as well as the capabilities, the next step is to determine the available options when it comes to implementation. The next section covers the various implementation options.

Incorporating Applications into SharePoint Sites

After evaluating the components provided by ASP.NET 2.0, WSS 3.0, and MOSS 2007, and understanding how they can assist in the development of a custom application, the next step is to devise an implementation plan. This is the stage in the process where most developers get confused and perplexed: How do you do it? Typically, three different techniques can be adopted, none of which are mutually exclusive. Many custom applications require a combination of two, if not all three, of the techniques depending on the application business requirements.

Implementing One or More Web Parts

The most obvious of the three options is to create one or more Web Parts for the application. In this case the developer would create a Web Part that housed the business logic and user interface of the application. Most commonly, the developer needs to account for the state of the application, including all postbacks.

When the application requires multiple Web Parts, deployment and configuration can start to get a little tricky. If the Web Parts reside on the same page, developers can utilize Web Part connections to pass data back and forth between them; but if the Web Parts live on different pages, then the deployment instructions need to include provisions ensuring that the application manager configures each Web Part to point to the other's page. How will the data be shared between the two Web Parts? Utilizing ASP.NET 2.0 session state in a SharePoint site can be quite challenging, so should data be passed around on the query string? These are the types of questions that should be raised in the implementation stage of the process when considering this approach.

For anything other than the simplest applications, those where everything resides on a single page, using Web Parts can prove problematic and a maintenance nightmare. For example, consider an entire application built within a single user or server control in an ASP.NET 2.0 site. For something on a par with a conference registration system, this can end up being a significantly challenging task. However, for something as simple as a newsletter registration and management applet, it would be quite easy.

Provisioning Site Pages

The second option is to create traditional ASP.NET 2.0 pages (`*.ASPX`) and provision them into SharePoint sites using a WSS 3.0 Feature. This approach is much more flexible than the Web Part approach because developers can provision multiple pages at once and control all the configuration settings in the deployment, or provisioning, process. This approach is not very obvious to most developers, yet interestingly enough it is the option that would be the most familiar. ASP.NET 2.0 developers are used to creating ASPX pages in a traditional ASP.NET 2.0 site, and the technique is very much the same. However, there are a few subtle differences.

First, the page directive should use one of the SharePoint-provided master page tokens (covered in Chapter 7) in the `MasterPageFile` attribute, although it is not required (developers can point to a specific master page if so desired). Second, the page directive should also contain `meta:progid="SharePoint.WebPartPages.Document"`. This attribute is needed if the provisioned page is opened through the site using SharePoint Designer 2007.

Developers often get tripped up when managed code is needed in the page. For example, many developers don't think SharePoint supports code-behind files, but in fact all pages in SharePoint sites can utilize code-behind files. Unfortunately, the developer experience in SharePoint is still a bit lacking in tools such as Visual Studio, so some manual work is needed.

When managed code is needed on a site page, the code should always be placed in a code-behind file, never as inline code within the ASPX file. The reason for this goes back to the safe mode parser discussed in Chapter 2. When a page instance is uncustomized, the request is not passed through the safe mode parser. However, when the page becomes customized using something such as SharePoint Designer 2007, the request is run through the safe mode parser.

One of the things the safe mode parser does is prohibit the execution of inline script on a page. This includes code surrounded by the `<script runat="server"></server>` tags, as well as any event handlers declared in the controls, such as `<asp:button OnClick="SomeHandler()" />`. To wire up event handlers for controls such as buttons, wire the events up in the code-behind file — specifically, by overriding the `OnInit()` method on the `System.Web.UI.Page` class. The use of inline script frequently trips up developers because a page runs just fine until it is customized, and then a cryptic error is returned. The safe approach is to avoid inline script at all costs.

In order to use code-behind files in site pages, create a new class that inherits from `System.Web.UI.Page`. The assembly containing this class should be signed, deployed to the host Web application's `\bin` directory or the global assembly cache, and registered as a safe control (`<SafeControl />`) in the Web application's `web.config` file. Next, the ASPX page needs to be made aware that it has an associated class. This is done by adding the fully qualified name of the class and the assembly (also known as the five-part name, i.e., [*namespace.type*], [*four-part assembly strong name*]) in the `Inherits` attribute in the page directive, as shown here:

```
<%@ Page Inherits="SitePage, WROX.ProMossWcm.Chapter20, Version=1.0.0.0,
Culture=neutral, PublicKeyToken=3be73eb52598ff2e" Language="C#"
MasterPageFile="~masterurl/default.master" %>
```

The process of provisioning site pages is almost identical to the technique of provisioning master pages and page layouts using Features, as demonstrated in Chapter 7 (refer to the code in Listing 7-3). The only difference is that the files are not provisioned into document libraries like master pages and page layouts; rather, they are provisioned into the site. This is done by setting the `Type` attribute on the `<File />` node to `Ghostable` instead of `GhostableInLibrary`:

```
<File Url="SomePage.aspx" Type="Ghostable" />
```

When does it make sense to use this technique in custom applications? One scenario might be when an application's pages need to support customization, such as utilizing Web Parts, or the application should be available only to a particular site or subsite. What about applications that need to be used across all site collections, such as creating an application for people within an organization to request a new SharePoint team site? The next section covers this scenario.

Application Pages

The previous section detailed the technique of provisioning pages into a SharePoint site. This is quite handy when an application needs to be deployed on a site-by-site basis, but what if the application should be available across the entire farm? This is where the last technique of leveraging application pages comes in. Application pages are those pages that reside within the `http://[site]/_layouts` URL. This is a virtual directory that all sites share. It points to a special folder located at `[..]\12\TEMPLATE\LAYOUTS`.

There are a few significant differences between application pages and site pages. First, because application pages are accessed via a virtual directory and pulled straight from the file system, they cannot be customized using something like SharePoint Designer 2007. Second, because they cannot be customized, these files are not subject to the safe mode parser and therefore they can contain inline script. Third, all applications use a single master page, `application.master`. This is covered in more detail in Chapter 7.

Application pages, just like site pages, can also utilize code- behind files. If a code-behind file is used in an application page, the class should not inherit from `System.Web.UI.Page` but from `Microsoft.SharePoint.WebControls.LayoutsPageBase`.

Data Storage Options

Almost every custom application needs to store data in some manner. In a traditional ASP.NET 2.0 application, data is usually stored in a relational database such as SQL Server. This is achieved in SharePoint using one of two options: SharePoint lists or an external database.

SharePoint Lists

The ASP.NET 2.0 developer's first instinct is to store data used by a custom application in a database. Before doing so, however, developers should consider using SharePoint's internal store constructs: lists! Utilizing lists has many advantages over using a database in a SharePoint application. SharePoint lists are similar in many ways to a database table. Both have columns and rows, although the terminology is used a bit differently. Database tables also have *triggers*, a way for developers to add business logic before and after an action is committed on the table. SharePoint lists have a similar concept called *event receivers*, which also support pre- and post-logic processing on actions.

All the CRUD pages are provided OOTB to perform inserts, updates, deletes, and selects on the contents. In addition, all the content in the lists can be indexed and searched using the OOTB search functionality provided in SharePoint.

Other common requirements in custom applications are included with SharePoint lists that would usually require custom development. The following list touches on some of the more popular ones:

- ❏ **Versioning and content approval** — Many applications require historical data to be retained or some sort of one-stage approval. This can be easily enabled on a list with a simple radio button toggle on the list's settings page.

- ❏ **Really Simple Syndication (RSS)** — All SharePoint lists can be configured to expose their contents via an RSS feed.

- ❏ **Exporting report views to Office applications** — Business users often need to work with the data provided in a report in an external application such as Office Excel or Access. Whereas this would require custom development within an ASP.NET 2.0 application, it is provided OOTB with SharePoint lists.

One thing SharePoint lists do not have or support OOTB that is easy to do in relational databases is implement referential integrity between two different tables (lists). While this can be achieved in SharePoint using event receivers and custom field types and controls, it does require some extra custom development.

Another advantage that lists have over database tables is that developers do not have to worry about connection information. All the connection information is provided by SharePoint as long as the list is in the same site collection. When working with a database, developers need to deal with the location and credentials necessary to connect to the database. Refer to Chapter 6, "Site Columns, Content Types, and Lists," for information on reading and writing to SharePoint lists.

A major difference between SharePoint lists and database tables is the capacity and storage of the data. Whereas database tables can scale to contain hundreds of thousands of records, if not millions, the performance of SharePoint lists starts to degrade at those levels. Specifically, the performance of a SharePoint container begins to degrade as the number of items in the container approaches 2,000. The primary reason for the performance degradation centers around the view architecture when rendering the contents of the list.

An easy workaround to this issue is to group the contents in a list into containers. For example, if a list contains 8,000 items, group the items into a handful of folders such that each container has fewer than 2,000 items. This does not mean that lists cannot contain more than 2,000 items. For one thing, this is not a hard limit. Second, there are other ways to retrieve the data from the list.

> *For more information on working with lists containing more than 2,000 items, refer to the TechNet white paper "Working with Large Lists in Office SharePoint Server 2007" (www.andrewconnell.com/go/270). This paper contains test results demonstrating the various methods of reading and writing data to SharePoint lists. It also provides good guidance on how and when to create indexes on fields in SharePoint lists to improve performance.*

While custom applications can certainly store their data within SharePoint lists, it does not always make sense to do so, in which case an external database should be used.

External Database

After reading the previous section, you are likely wondering when a developer should not use SharePoint lists, and instead use a database to store the data used in a custom application. The answer is quite simple: when using SharePoint lists does not make sense. For instance, does the application store vast amounts of data (tens of thousands of records or more) or must it absolutely contain a relational model? If so, then SharePoint lists may not be the way to go. Instead, consider using an external database for the application.

The database can reside on the same SQL Server that hosts the SharePoint farm and content databases. Just make sure that the custom application tables are not added to any of the SharePoint databases, as this is not supported.

Using an external database in SharePoint is almost no different from using one in an ASP.NET 2.0 application. All the same rules apply. First a connection must be established using ADO.NET and then queries are issued to either create, retrieve, update, or delete data in the database tables.

The only aspect that most ASP.NET 2.0 sites are not affected by in SharePoint deals with code access security. By default, SharePoint sites start out using a very restrictive policy called WSS_Minimal. This policy does not allow database connections to be made from third-party assemblies. In order to create a connection to a database, either the trust level must be bumped up to WSS_Medium or a custom policy must be created that grants the assembly and type the necessary permission: `System.Data.SqlClient.SqlClientPermission`.

Application Configuration Options

Virtually every custom application requires a place to store configuration information. Such configuration information may include Web service URLs, database connection data, as well as other application-specific configuration information. When building ASP.NET 2.0 applications, this configuration data can be stored in a custom database table or in configuration files, the most common being the `web.config` file. How should configuration data be handled in a custom application incorporated into or based on the SharePoint framework? Developers have a few options.

The configuration data can still remain in the `web.config` file, but this approach should be used with great care. Keep in mind that all sites (as well as site collections) in the Web application will have access to these settings, which might not be desirable for things such as database connection strings and login credentials. Another option is to store the configuration in a custom database or a special SharePoint list. The list can be secured quite easily to keep users from viewing the information, yet the application can use elevated privileges via the `SPSecurity.RunWithElevatedPrivledges()` method to retrieve values from the list. Refer to Chapter 15, "Authentication and Authorization," for more information on the `SPSecurity.RunWithElevatedPrivledges()` method.

There are two other options unique to SharePoint that ASP.NET 2.0 does not provide. One, many SharePoint objects contain a generic property bag that is exposed as a simple `StringDictionary` (via the `Microsoft.SharePoint.Utilities.SPPropertyBag` object). Two, you can use the hierarchical object store within a SharePoint farm. The latter approach involves creating a new object, adding it to the farm's store, and assigning it a unique identifier for easy retrieval later.

To use the hierarchical object store, developers first must create a class that inherits from `Microsoft.SharePoint.Administration.SPPersistedObject`. This class provides the necessary plumbing to create and remove an object from the store. It serializes or deserializes all the public fields decorated with the `Microsoft.SharePoint.Persisted` attribute to XML and stores it in the configuration database. This class must contain a default constructor (one with no parameters) in order to be serializable and override a constructor on the `SPPersistedObject` class to give the object a name, specify the object's parent, and optionally a unique identifier. The code in Listing 20-2 contains a sample object that could be used to store database connection information.

Listing 20-2: Database connection information stored in a farm's hierarchical store

```
using System;
using Microsoft.SharePoint.Administration;

namespace WROX.ProMossWcm.Chapter20 {
  public class Database : SPPersistedObject {
    [Microsoft.SharePoint.Administration.Persisted]
    public string _server = string.Empty;
    [Microsoft.SharePoint.Administration.Persisted]
    public string _database = string.Empty;
    [Microsoft.SharePoint.Administration.Persisted]
    public string _username = string.Empty;
    [Microsoft.SharePoint.Administration.Persisted]
    public string _password = string.Empty;

    public Database () { }
    public Database (string name, SPPersistedObject parent, Guid id) :
base(name, parent, id) { }
  }
}
```

With the object created, the next step is to create an instance of the object and store in the configuration database. This is demonstrated in Listing 20-3 using a Feature receiver to add and remove the object upon Feature activation and deactivation.

Listing 20-3: Adding and removing objects from the hierarchical store

```
using System;
using Microsoft.SharePoint;

namespace WROX.ProMossWcm.Chapter20 {
  public class HierarchicalDataStoreFeatureReceiver : SPFeatureReceiver {
    private const string LITWARE_DB_CONFIG_KEY = "08F7E568-3184-4D94-A559-
8E91DB39F858";

    public override void FeatureInstalled (SPFeatureReceiverProperties properties)
{}
    public override void FeatureUninstalling (SPFeatureReceiverProperties
properties) {}

    public override void FeatureActivated (SPFeatureReceiverProperties properties){
```

(continued)

Listing 20-3 *(continued)*

```
        Database db = new Database("LitwareDB",
                                   properties.Definition.Farm,
                                   new Guid(LITWARE_DB_CONFIG_KEY));
        db.Server = "LitwareServer01";
        db.DatabaseName = "Foo";
        db.Username = "Admin";
        db.Password = "pass@word1";
        db.Update();
    }

    public override void FeatureDeactivating (SPFeatureReceiverProperties
properties) {
        Database db = properties.Definition.Farm.GetObject(
                        new Guid(LITWARE_DB_CONFIG_KEY));
        db.Delete();
    }
  }
}
```

To retrieve the object from the store in the application, simply obtain a reference to it using the same method demonstrated in the FeatureDeactivating() method in Listing 20-3:

```
    Guid dbid = new Guid("08F7E568-3184-4D94-A559-8E91DB39F858");
    Database db = SPContext.Site.WebApplication.Farm.GetObject(dbid);
```

Thankfully, as demonstrated in this section, developers are provided with many different options when a custom application incorporated into or built on the SharePoint platform needs configuration information.

Utilizing SharePoint Components in Custom Applications

Aside from all the components provided in ASP.NET 2.0, when SharePoint is selected as the application development platform there are a few SharePoint components that warrant a bit more discussion. This section describes the customization options for SharePoint navigation, utilizing the grids that Microsoft uses throughout SharePoint (SPGridView), and leveraging permission levels.

SharePoint Navigation

SharePoint's navigation data sources and providers are already set up to build the navigation based on the structure of a site and site collection. Thus, if a custom application is based completely on SharePoint sites and lists, no custom code needs to be written. The only customization that might be required is to modify the navigation control to configure how many levels of dynamic flyouts are desired.

However, a custom application may provision custom pages with Features that need to be linked in the navigation, or there may be some other need to customize the navigation. In these cases, developers may want to customize navigation items. The first impulse is usually to create a custom navigation provider or data source that will achieve this, but it isn't necessary. Menus can be augmented using the Feature schema — specifically, `<CustomAction />`, `<CustomActionGroup />`, and `<HideCustomAction />`.

Another option is to add items to the navigation when the pages are provisioned or the application is installed using the SharePoint API. The API enables developers to interact with the top navigation area, `SPWeb.Navigation.TopNavigationBar`, or the left-hand navigation area, `SPWeb.Navigation.QuickLaunch`. The code in Listing 20-4 contains a Feature receiver that adds a new navigation item to the top navigation control in a SharePoint site.

Listing 20-4: Feature receiver adding a navigation node to the top navigation control

```
public override void FeatureActivated (SPFeatureReceiverProperties properties) {
   // get a reference to the current site's top navigation
   SPWeb site = properties.Feature.Parent as SPWeb;
   if (site == null)
      throw new SPException("Error obtaining reference to the parent SPWeb within
FeatureActivated event handler.");
   SPNavigationNodeCollection topNavigation = site.Navigation.TopNavigationBar;

   // create new drop down menu for our new pages
   SPNavigationNode newNode = new SPNavigationNode("Some Link", "SomeFolder/
SomePage.aspx", false);
   // add the new menu to the end of the top nav bar
   topNavigation[0].Children.AddAsLast(newNode);

   site.Update();
}
```

Leveraging SPGridView

Almost all applications need to display data. SharePoint lists display data in a special grid that is based on the ASP.NET 2.0 `GridView` control: `Microsoft.SharePoint.WebControls.SPGridView`. Although developers building custom applications can create their own grid controls, they should consider using the grid that SharePoint uses. The primary benefit is to inherit the same look and feel as the rest of a SharePoint site. When the SharePoint grid is used in a custom application, it uses the same CSS classes the other grids SharePoint uses.

One major difference exists when using SharePoint's `SPGridView` control over the ASP.NET 2.0 `GridView` control: Developers must set the `AutoGenerateColumns` property to `false` and explicitly bind the columns as shown in Listing 20-5. This listing retrieves data from a list containing sessions for a conference, adds them to an ADO.NET `DataTable`, creates the columns in the grid, and then binds the `DataTable` to the grid.

Listing 20-5: Utilizing SPGridView

```
private void BindConferenceDayToGrid
              (SPList sessionList, SPGridView gridView, string conferenceDay) {
  // run query for day 1 sessions
  SPQuery query = new SPQuery();
  query.Query = String.Format("<Where><Eq><FieldRef Name=\"StartTime\" /><Value
Type=\"DateTime\">{0}</Value></Eq></Where><OrderBy><FieldRef Name=\"StartTime\"
/></OrderBy>", conferenceDay);
  SPListItemCollection results = sessionList.GetItems(query);

  DataTable table;

  table = new DataTable();
  table.Columns.Add("TimeSlot", typeof(string));
  table.Columns.Add("AdminTrack", typeof(string));
  table.Columns.Add("CustomizationTrack", typeof(string));
  table.Columns.Add("DeveloperTrack", typeof(string));

  DataRow row;
  string presenter;
  foreach (SPListItem result in results) {
    row = table.Rows.Add();
    row["TimeSlot"] = string.Format("{0} - {1}",

Convert.ToDateTime(result["StartTime"].ToString()).ToString("h:mm tt"),

Convert.ToDateTime(result["EndTime"].ToString()).ToString("h:mm tt"));
    row["AdminTrack"] = string.Empty;
    presenter = result["Presenter"] == null ? "unknown" :
result["Presenter"].ToString();
    switch (result["Track"].ToString()) {
      case "Customization":
        row["CustomizationTrack"] = string.Format("{0} - by: {1}",
                                          result["Title"].ToString(),
                                          presenter);
        break;
      case "Developer":
        row["DeveloperTrack"] = string.Format("{0} - by: {1}",
                                          result["Title"].ToString(),
                                          presenter);
        break;
    }
  }

  // bind to the gridview
  SPBoundField boundField;

  boundField = new SPBoundField();
  boundField.HeaderText = "Sessions";
  boundField.DataField = "TimeSlot";
  boundField.ItemStyle.HorizontalAlign = HorizontalAlign.Center;
```

```
        boundField.ItemStyle.Wrap = false;
        gridView.Columns.Add(boundField);

        boundField = new SPBoundField();
        boundField.HeaderText = "Admin Track";
        boundField.DataField = "AdminTrack";
        gridView.Columns.Add(boundField);

        boundField = new SPBoundField();
        boundField.HeaderText = "Customiation Track";
        boundField.DataField = "CustomizationTrack";
        gridView.Columns.Add(boundField);

        boundField = new SPBoundField();
        boundField.HeaderText = "Developer Track";
        boundField.DataField = "DeveloperTrack";
        gridView.Columns.Add(boundField);

        gridView.AutoGenerateColumns = false;
        gridView.DataSource = table.DefaultView;
        gridView.DataBind();
    }
```

As Listing 20-5 demonstrates, working with the SPGridView control is very similar to working with the ASP.NET 2.0 GridView control. The primary differences are related to the source of the data and binding columns to the grid.

Creating and Managing Custom Security Roles

As previously covered, SharePoint includes a very robust and granular permission model that custom applications can take advantage of. Part of this architecture includes permission levels, which are groups of permission rights. Permission rights are granted to behaviors such as opening a page, adding items to a list, reading items in lists, and so forth. Permission levels are used to group one or more permission rights together. Then, administrators grant permissions to users and groups by assigning them permission levels, rather than permission rights. Administrators have the option to use the provided permission levels to create custom ones through the user browser interface. Unfortunately, custom permission rights cannot be created; administrators are limited to the ones provided by Microsoft.

Developers can still use permission levels within a custom application if the application has special security requirements. For example, consider a conference registration system as the custom application. People attending the conference should be provided a self-service registration system. Some users — registration agents, for instance — need the capability to modify registrations. One way to address this is to create a custom permission level through code (when a Feature is activated, for instance) and then create a custom event receiver that is attached to the registrations list. This event receiver would check whether the user is attempting to update or delete a registration record. If they have not been granted the special permission level created by the Feature, they should not be permitted to make the change.

The code in Listing 20-6 demonstrates creation of a permission level through code.

Listing 20-6: Creating permission levels in code

```
private void CreatePermissionLevel (SPWeb site) {
  SPRoleDefinition registrator = new SPRoleDefinition();
  registrator.Name = "Registration Agent";
  registrator.Description = "Users with this permission level can modify
registrations.";

  // assign no rights... used only by name
  registrator.BasePermissions = SPBasePermissions.EmptyMask;

  site.RoleDefinitions.Add(registrator);
}
```

The next step, shown in Listing 20-7, is to create the event receiver that will check whether the user has been assigned the permission level.

Listing 20-7: Event receiver checking for a custom permission level

```
using System;
using Microsoft.SharePoint;

namespace WROX.ProMossWcm.Chapter20 {
  public class RegistrationListItemReceiver : SPItemEventReceiver {
    private const string REGISTRATOR_PERMISSION_LEVEL = "Conference Registrator";

    public override void ItemUpdating (SPItemEventProperties properties) {
      this.DisableEventFiring();

      using (SPSite siteCollection = new SPSite(properties.WebUrl)) {
        using (SPWeb site = siteCollection.OpenWeb(properties.RelativeWebUrl)) {
          if (!IsUserAllowedToAddRegistrations(site)) {
            properties.Status = SPEventReceiverStatus.CancelWithError;
            properties.Cancel = true;
            properties.ErrorMessage = "Current user does not have permission to
manage registrations. Only users assigned the permission level <b>" +
REGISTRATOR_PERMISSION_LEVEL + "</b> can do this.";
          }
        }
      }

      EnableEventFiring();
    }

    public override void ItemDeleting (SPItemEventProperties properties) {
      this.DisableEventFiring();

      using (SPSite siteCollection = new SPSite(properties.WebUrl)) {
        using (SPWeb site = siteCollection.OpenWeb(properties.RelativeWebUrl)) {
          if (!IsUserAllowedToAddRegistrations(site)) {
```

```
            properties.Status = SPEventReceiverStatus.CancelWithError;
            properties.Cancel = true;
            properties.ErrorMessage = "Current user does not have permission to
manage registrations. Only users assigned the permission level <b> " +
REGISTRATOR_PERMISSION_LEVEL + "</b> can do this.";
            }
        }
    }

    EnableEventFiring();
}

private bool IsUserAllowedToAddRegistrations (SPWeb site) {
    SPRoleDefinition registratorRole =
site.RoleDefinitions[REGISTRATOR_PERMISSION_LEVEL];

    // if not found, there's an error with the setup
    if (registratorRole == null)
      throw new SPException("Permission level '" + REGISTRATOR_PERMISSION_LEVEL +
"' not found. This permission level is created by a Feature. Recreate a new
permission level using this same name.");

    return site.AllRolesForCurrentUser.Contains(registratorRole);
    }
  }
}
```

Note that when the permission level was created, no rights were specified:

```
registrator.BasePermissions = SPBasePermissions.EmptyMask;
```

That's because this permission level has a very specific use. This is a good technique to follow; otherwise, it could be inadvertently adding rights to users.

Summary

This chapter covered the various options available to developers in incorporating custom applications into SharePoint sites or building custom applications on top of the SharePoint platform. Developers should consider using SharePoint as an application development platform because it brings so much to the table that would normally have to be created from scratch. Things such as navigation, a granular security model, workflow integration, data storage and CRUD pages, a site provisioning engine, and personalization capabilities — all of this is provided OOTB with the free version of SharePoint: WSS 3.0. Adding MOSS 2007 simply adds additional components that can be utilized in a custom application such as electronic forms (Forms Services) or hooks into other applications (BDC).

Index

X

_x0020_, 90, 91–92, 107
XFN (XHTML Friends Network), 274, 275
   button, 275, 277, 278
   links, 275
   microformat, 274, 275
XHTML, 148, 151, 275
XHTML Friends Network (XFN). *See* XFN
XML configuration file, for document
      converter, 356–357
XML to HTML document converter, 353
XmlToHtmlConverterSettings.ascx admin
      settings control, 362–363
XmlToHtmlConverterSettings.cs settings
      control code-behind, 363–364

XPS file, 353
XSD.EXE tool, 229, 232
XSLT
   InfoPath and, 353
   search results and, 248, 251,
      256, 267
   style sheets, 6, 70, 73,
      195, 345
.xsn files, 345, 346, 353
XSN to HTML document converter, 353

Z

zero results, 16, 243, 256, 259
zones, Web Part. *See* Web Part zones